KINGDOM
. .
GRACE
. .
JUDGMENT

KINGDOM
GRACE
JUDGMENT

Paradox, Outrage, and Vindication
in the Parables of Jesus

ROBERT FARRAR CAPON

WILLIAM B. EERDMANS PUBLISHING COMPANY
GRAND RAPIDS, MICHIGAN

Originally published in three volumes under the titles
The Parables of the Kingdom
© 1985 the Zondervan Corporation, Grand Rapids, Michigan
The Parables of Grace
© 1988 Wm. B. Eerdmans Publishing Co.
The Parables of Judgment
© 1989 Wm. B. Eerdmans Publishing Co.
Combined edition © 2002 Wm. B. Eerdmans Publishing Co.
All rights reserved

Wm. B. Eerdmans Publishing Co.
2140 Oak Industrial Drive N.E., Grand Rapids, Michigan 49505
www.eerdmans.com

Published 2002
Printed in the United States of America

26 25 24 23 22 21   16 17 18 19 20

Library of Congress Cataloging-in-Publication Data

ISBN 978-0-8028-3949-7

Contents

THE PARABLES
OF GRACE

Contents

CONTENTS

THE PARABLES
OF JUDGMENT

Contents

A Word about Parables

A book about the parables of Jesus faces two obstacles at the outset. The first and more troublesome, oddly enough, is familiarity. Most people, on reading the Gospels' assertion that "Jesus spoke in parables," assume they know exactly what is meant. "Oh, yes," they say, "and a wonderful teaching device it was, too. All those unforgettable stories we're so fond of, like the Good Samaritan and the Prodigal Son." Yet their enthusiasm is narrowly based. Jesus' use of the parabolic method can hardly be limited to the mere handful of instances they remember as entertaining, agreeable, simple, and clear. Some of his parables are not stories; many are not agreeable; most are complex; and a good percentage of them produce more confusion than understanding.

Most of this book, therefore, will be devoted to the removal of the obstacle of a too-facile familiarity. Jesus spoke in strange, bizarre, disturbing ways. He balked at almost no comparison, however irreverent or unrefined. Apparently, he found nothing odd about holding up, as a mirror to God's ways, a mixed bag of questionable characters: an unjust judge, a savage king, a tipsy slave owner, an unfair employer, and even a man who gives help only to bona-fide pests. Furthermore, Jesus not only spoke in parables; he thought in parables, acted in parables, and regularly insisted that what he was proclaiming could not be set forth in any way other than in parables. He was practically an ambulatory parable in and of himself: he cursed fig trees, walked on water, planted

1

coins in fishes' mouths, and for his final act, sailed up into a cloud. In short, this book is not a routine, pious review of the parables; rather, it is a fresh, adventurous look at the parabolic words and acts of Jesus in the larger light of their entire gospel and biblical context.

Mentioning the Bible as a whole, however, brings me to the second of the obstacles: the doubt that exists in the minds of many people as to whether anything fresh or adventurous can ever be said about Scripture by one who, as I do, views it as inspired by God. Let me try to remove that difficulty by making my own position clear.

"I do believe the Holy Scriptures of the Old and New Testaments to be the Word of God and to contain all things necessary to salvation. . . ." So read the words of the ordination oath that I took many years ago and that I am still happy to keep. I suppose it may sound, to both believer and unbeliever, like one of those bell-book-and-candle pronouncements designed to end discussion, but as far as I am concerned, it was and still is the essential precondition of my biblical study. Precisely because it forbids the neglect of even the oddest bit of Scripture, I find it nothing less than the taproot of an endlessly refreshing openness to all the wonderful, perplexing, and intriguing words by which the Word himself has spoken.

Accepting the Bible as inspired is a bit like receiving an entire collection of one's grandfather's writings. Suppose, for example, that on opening such a treasure, I found it to contain everything my grandfather ever wrote: letters, poems, recipes, essays, short stories, diaries, family histories. And suppose further that I was fully convinced not only that they were authentically his but that he had sent them for the express purpose of providing me with everything he wanted me to know both about himself and about our relationship. Far from putting an end to my study of his words, those convictions would be the very thing that started me wrestling with them in earnest.

And not just to be able to spout his words or to confirm what I already thought. Indeed, I would be well advised to approach them with as open a mind as possible, always ready to sit loose to what *I* had decided about him and simply to listen to *him*. It should be only after long study and repeated readings that I would dare to conclude what any

2

particular passage meant, let alone what the entire thrust of his writing was. With such a wildly various collection, there would always be a temptation to let my own sense of what he was up to get in the way of what he himself really had in mind.

I might, for example, decide that, while his brief aphorisms lay close to the heart of the man, his longer stories had little to teach me about him. That would be a mistake; all that this conclusion would actually show was that I had a liking for agreeable bits of information served up on small plates but balked at the labor of trying to take his meaning when he expressed himself by putting on a feast of strange fictions. Or I might decide that only his serious metaphysical writings, and not his strictures on the proper way to make gravy, truly revealed the man. In the case of this particular grandfather, that would be an even bigger mistake: if there was ever a place where he disclosed himself as the lover of creation he really was, it was in the kitchen. Without a willingness to wade through his recipes, a reader would miss a good half of his charm.

So too with Scripture. Often when people try to say what the Bible is about, they let their own mindset ride roughshod over what actually lies on the pages. For examples: convinced in advance that the Bible is about God or Morals or Religion or Spirituality or Salvation or some other capital-letter Subject, they feel compelled to interpret everything in it in a commensurate way. To a degree, of course, that is a perfectly proper approach, but it has some catches to it. For one thing, it puts *their notion* of what God, or Morals, or Religion, or whatever is all about in the position of calling the tune as to what Scripture may possibly mean — or even of being the deciding factor as to whether they can listen to what it is saying at all. Jesus, for example, was rejected by his contemporaries not because he claimed to be the Messiah but because, in their view, he didn't make a suitably messianic claim. "Too bad for God," they seemed to say. "He may want a dying Christ, but we happen to know that Christs don't die."

For another thing, people's notions of the really big scriptural Subject can be quite beside the point. Suppose, by way of illustration, they were to decide that the Bible is a book about God. Harmless enough, you think? Look at how many difficulties even so apparently correct a statement can give them — and how many otherwise open scriptural doors it forces them to close. Such a position can easily lead them to expect that on every page they will find the subject of God addressed — or if it is not, that they will find there some other subject that is at least worthy of him (as they understand worthiness, of course). But that is a tricky proposition. In the Gospel of John, we read, "No man has seen God at any time; the only begotten Son [many texts read *God*], who is in the bosom of the Father, *he* has said the last word about him" (1:18). Only Jesus, apparently, is the full revelation of what God is and does; any notions we come up with are always partial, frequently misleading, and sometimes completely off the mark.

In the Bible, as a matter of fact, God does so many ungodly things — like not remembering our sins, erasing the quite correct handwriting against us, and becoming sin for us — that the only safe course is to come to Scripture with as few stipulations as possible. God used his own style manual, not ours, in the promulgation of his Word.

Openness, therefore, is the major requirement for approaching the Scriptures. And nowhere in the Bible is an un-made-up mind more called for than when reading the parables of Jesus. Indeed, if I were forced to give a short answer to the question "What is the Bible as a whole about?" I think I would ignore all the subjects mentioned so far and base my reply squarely on those parables. If they have a single subject at all, it is quite plainly the kingdom of God. Therefore, even though my answer would sound like no usual formulation at all, I would say that the Bible is about the mystery of the kingdom — a mystery that, by definition, is something well hidden and not at all likely to be grasped by plausibility-loving minds.

Jesus, when he was asked why he constantly used parables, why he so habitually resorted to roundabout, analogical devices in his teaching — why, in fact, he said almost nothing without a parable — answered that he taught the crowds that way precisely in order that "seeing they might not see and hearing they might not understand" (Mark 4:12). True enough, when he was alone with his disciples, he spoke more plainly — giving them, he claimed, nothing less than the mystery itself.

But it is hard to see that such directness had a different result. On three separate occasions, for instance, he spoke quite clearly about the certainly of his dying and rising at Jerusalem, but when he came to those mighty acts themselves, his disciples might as well never have heard a word he said. The mystery of the kingdom, it seems, is a *radical* mystery: even when you tell people about it in so many words, it remains permanently intractable to all their attempts to make sense of it.

In any case, a close examination of Jesus' parables may well be the best way we have of ensuring that we will be listening to what he himself has to say, instead of what we are prepared to hear — provided, that is, we are willing to take note of the almost perverse way in which he used parables.

Speaking in comparisons and teaching by means of stories are, of course, two of the oldest instructional techniques in the world. And in the hands of almost all instructors except Jesus, they are a relatively straightforward piece of business. Take an example: a professor is trying to give his students some idea of what goes on inside the atom. But because neither he nor they can actually see what he is talking about, he uses a comparison: the electrons, he tells them, are whirling around the nucleus as the planets whirl around the sun. The students suddenly see light where there was only darkness before, and the professor retires from the classroom to grateful applause.

With Jesus, however, the device of parabolic utterance is used not to explain things to people's satisfaction but to call attention to the unsatisfactoriness of all their previous explanations and understandings. Had he been the professor in the illustration, he would probably have pushed the comparison to its ultimate, mind-boggling conclusion, namely, that as the solar system is mostly great tracts of empty space, so too is matter. What they had previously thought of as solid stuff consists almost entirely of holes. He would, in other words, have done more to upset his students' understanding than to give it a helping hand.

Watch an actual instance of Jesus at his parabolic best. In the eighteenth chapter of the Gospel of Luke, we find him addressing a group of people who are smugly content in their confidence that they are upstanding citizens — and who are convinced that anyone not exactly like themselves has no chance of making it into God's guest register. So he tells them the parable of the Pharisee and the Publican. Note not only what an insulting story it is, but also how small the prospects are that his audience will ever be able to get past its details to its point. Far from being an illustration that shines an understanding they already have on something they haven't yet figured out, it is one that is guaranteed to pop every circuit breaker in their minds.

God, Jesus informs them, is not the least bit interested in their wonderful lists of moral and religious accomplishments. Imagine the scene for a moment. You can almost hear the reaction forming in their minds: "What do you mean, God's not interested? *We* have read the Scriptures — with particular attention to the commandments. *We* happen to know he is absolutely wild about fasting, tithing, and not committing adultery." But Jesus ignores them and presses the parable for all its worth. Not only is God going to take a dim view of all their high scores in the behaving and believing competition; he is, in fact, going to bestow the gold medal on an out-and-out crook who just waltzes into the temple, stares at his shoelaces, and does nothing more than admit as much.

But since that is not at all his audience's notion of how God should behave — since, suddenly, they now see only darkness where before they thought they had some light — since, in short, the professor has now explained something they have an utter dread of understanding, he retires from the classroom to nothing but hisses and boos.

On the way out, however, just to make sure they have not been incompletely confused, he unburdens himself of three more pieces of unwelcome instruction. First, he informs them that the kingdom of God will be given to babies sooner than to respectable religionists; second that a camel will go through a needle's eye sooner than a solid citizen will get into the kingdom; and third, that he himself, the messianic "Son of Man," is about to fulfill his messiahship by dying as a common criminal.

True enough, this last pronouncement was fairly unparabolic and was actually addressed to the disciples only. But once again, straight talk about the mystery of the kingdom produced not one bit more understanding. As Luke observed when he wrapped up the whole episode: "The disciples did not understand any of these things; the meaning of the words was hidden from them, and they did not know what Jesus was talking about" (Luke 18:34). So much for the utterances of Jesus as teaching aids.

G. K. Chesterton, who was a master of the apt illustration, once gave some sardonic advice about the limitations of parabolic discourse. He said that if you give people an analogy that they claim they do not understand, you should graciously offer them another. If they say they don't understand that either, you should oblige them with a third. But from there on, Chesterton said, if they still insist they do not understand, the only thing left is to praise them for the one truth they do have a grip on: "Yes," you tell them, "that is quite correct. You do not understand."

To put it simply, Jesus began where Chesterton left off. In resorting so often to parables, his main point was that any understanding of the kingdom his hearers could come up with would be a misunderstanding. Mention "messiah" to them, and they would picture a king on horseback, not a carpenter on a cross; mention "forgiveness" and they would start setting up rules about when it ran out. From Jesus' point of view, the sooner their misguided minds had the props knocked from under them, the better. After all their yammer about how God should or shouldn't run his own operation, getting them just to stand there with their eyes popped and their mouths shut would be a giant step forward.

We, of course, after two thousand years' exposure to Scripture in general and the Gospels in particular, might be tempted to think of ourselves as less likely to need such hard-nosed, parabolic tutelage. But Jesus still gives it to us. Despite our illusions of understanding him better than his first hearers did, we vindicate his chosen method by misnaming — and thus misunderstanding — even the most beloved and familiar parables. The Prodigal Son, for example, is not about a boy's vices; it is about a father's forgiveness. The Laborers in the Vineyard are by no means the central characters in the story; they are hardly more

7

than stick-figures used by Jesus to rub his hearers' noses in the out-rageous grace of a vineyard owner who gives equal pay for unequal work. And if there is a Christ-figure in the parable of the Good Samaritan, it is not the Samaritan but the battered, half-dead man on the ground. Our relationships are defined, the parable insists, by the one who walks through our history as victim, not as medicine man. All those Good Sam Medical Centers should really have been named Man Who Fell Among Thieves Hospitals; it is the patients in their sufferings and deaths, not the help in white coats, who look more like Jesus on the cross. Jesus drives the same point home in the parable of the Great Judgment: it is precisely in the hungry, the thirsty, the estranged, the naked, the sick, and the imprisoned that we find, or ignore, the Savior himself.

With a track record of misunderstandings like those, therefore, we should probably make as few claims as possible and be content to take up the parables from scratch, beginning with the word itself.

The Greek for parable is *parabolé*. As far as the Gospels are concerned, the word occurs only in Matthew, Mark, and Luke. John, infrequently, uses another word, *paroimía* ("adage," or "dark saying"). Although *paroimía* has occasionally been translated "parable," neither the Greek word *parabolé* nor any parables in the usual sense appear in the Fourth Gospel.

Etymologically, a *parabolé* is simply a comparison, a putting of one thing beside another to make a point. On its face, it refers to the simple teaching device that Jesus so often transformed into something that mystified more than it informed. But standing the parabolic method on its head was not the only peculiarity in his use of it. His "parables" comprise far more than the specific utterances that the Gospel writers refer to by that name, and they occur in a surprising variety of forms.

For example, some of the parables are little more than one-liners, brief comparisons stating that the kingdom of God is like things no one ever dreamed of comparing it to: yeast, mustard seed, buried treasure secured by craftiness, fabulous jewelry purchased by mortgaging everything. On many occasions, of course, Jesus lengthened and developed the parable form into the short but marvelously complete stories

8

to which we normally give the name. Yet for all their charm and simplicity, his story-parables are not one bit less baffling. Once again, they set forth comparisons that tend to make mincemeat of people's religious expectations. Bad people are rewarded (the Publican, the Prodigal, the Unjust Steward); good people are scolded (the Pharisee, the Elder Brother, the Diligent Workers); God's response to prayer is likened to a man getting rid of a nuisance (the Friend at Midnight); and in general, everybody's idea of who ought to be first or last is liberally doused with cold water (the Wedding Feast, the Great Judgment, Lazarus and Dives, the Narrow Door).

At other times, Jesus took his comparisons simply as he found them in the world around him. He was such an inveterate devotee of likening things to each other that these casual parables often seem to be little more than his natural habit of speaking. For example, he could mockingly contrast people's disinterest in the coming kingdom with their keen enthusiasm for weather-prediction. Or he could take some more or less current event, like the collapse of the Tower of Siloam, and use it to illustrate a point. Finally, he was not above the occasional dramatized parable in which he made his comparisons not by means of words but by acting them out — for instance, the Cursing of the Fig Tree and the Coin in the Fish's Mouth.

In any case, speaking in parables was second nature to Jesus, and it quickly became the hallmark of his teaching style. At the beginning of the Gospel of Mark in fact — after only a handful of statements actually called parables have been recorded — the author says that Jesus used many other parables, and that he would not speak to the people without using a parable (Mark 4:33-34). Clearly then, if we want to hear the actual ticking of Jesus' mind, we can hardly do better than to study his parabolic words and acts over and over — with our minds open not only to learning but to joy.

THE PARABLES
OF THE KINGDOM

PART ONE

Parables and the Paradox of Power

CHAPTER ONE

Right-handed and Left-handed Power

A few pages back, I grudgingly gave a short answer to the question of what the Bible is about. If Scripture has a single subject at all, I said, it is the mystery of the kingdom of God. Now I want to reformulate that answer in a way that will bring us not only to the parables of Jesus but also to the classification I propose to use in discussing them. If I may try your patience just a bit, let me do it by throwing you a long, slow curve.

Most authors tip their hand as to what they are really up to in their last chapters. The Holy Spirit, it seems to me, is no exception. The last book of the Bible is a gold mine of images for what God has had in mind all along. Therefore, I can think of no better way of reformulating my answer than to lean heavily on the imagery of the Revelation of St. John the Divine. Accordingly, my new version of what the Bible is about reads as follows: it is about the mystery by which the power of God works to form this world into the Holy City, the New Jerusalem that comes down out of heaven from God, prepared as a bride adorned for her husband.

Note, if you will, how much distance that puts between us and certain customary notions of the main subject of Scripture. It means that it is not about someplace else called heaven, nor about somebody at a distance called God. Rather, it is about *this place here,* in all its *this*ness and placiness, and about the intimate and immediate Holy One who, *at* *no distance from us at all,* moves mysteriously to make creation true both to itself and to him. That, I take it, is the force of phrases like "the city of God" and "the kingdom of God." They say to me that the Bible is concerned with the perfecting of what God made, not with the trashing of it — with the resurrection of its native harmonies and orders, not with the replacement of them by something alien. To be sure, "city" and "kingdom" are different images, with differing lights to shed on the mystery; but because they are both such marvelously earthy revelations of what God wants this world to become, I intend to use them interchangeably throughout this book.

In any case, whether in terms of city or kingdom, the question immediately arises, "How does God get the job done? What does the Bible have to say about the way he uses his power to achieve his ends?"

On theoretical presumptions, of course, God has all the power he needs to do anything he wants any time he chooses. But such theorizing is a very unscriptural way to approach the subject. It has exactly that let's-sit-the-Bible-down-and-read-it-a-theology-lecture attitude that does nothing but produce frustration with what is actually in the book. Come to Scripture with a nice, respectable notion of an omnipotent God and see what it gets you. Problems, that's what. Problems like: If God has the ability to turn the world into the city, why is he taking his own sweet time about it? Or: If the Bible is about an almighty, all-smart God, why is it so full of divine indirection and delay? Or to say it flat out: If God wants to turn this messed-up world into a city or a kingdom, why doesn't he just knock some heads together, put all the baddies under a large, flat rock, and get on with the job?

The Bible does, of course, have one recorded instance of God's having proposed just such harsh treatment: the narrative of the Flood in the Book of Genesis. But even that story — especially that story — has little comfort in it for theology buffs who like their omnipotence straight up. Notice how it goes.

God, having found all human attempts to build the city hopeless, decides simply to wash everybody but Noah down the drain. By the end of the story, however — when the final, scriptural point of the episode is made — it turns out to reveal a different notion of power entirely: God says he is never going to do anything like that again. He says that his answer to the evil that keeps the world from becoming the city of God will not, paradoxically, involve direct intervention on behalf of the city. Instead, he makes a covenant of nonintervention with the world: *he sets his bow in the cloud* — the symbolic development of which could be either that he hangs all his effective weapons against wickedness up on the wall or, more bizarrely still, that he points them skyward, at himself instead of us.

After that — to the consternation of generations of tub-thumpers for a hard-line God — the Bible becomes practically a rhapsody of indirection. God tells Abraham that he still intends to build the city but proposes an exceedingly strange way of going about it. He says he has infallible plans for the redeemed community but then proceeds to insist it be formed not at some reasonable site, but on the road — and among the future children of a man who hasn't a single descendant to his name. Furthermore, even when Abraham's childlessness is remedied and God does indeed have a people with whom to build the city, he makes them spend an inordinate amount of time in slavery, wandering, and warfare before he selects a suitable piece of real estate for the venture. Finally, when he does get around to providing them with an actual location, it remains theirs (rather tenuously at that) for only a few hundred years — hardly longer, it seems, than he felt necessary to engrave Jerusalem as an image on their corporate imagination. They certainly did not possess it long enough, or with sufficient success, for anyone to claim that the city definitively had been built.

As Christians believe, though, God did eventually show up on the property himself for the express purpose of completing the project. In the person of Jesus, the messianic King, he announced that he was bringing in the kingdom and, in general, accomplishing once and for all every last eternal purpose he ever had for the world. And, as Christians also believe, he did just that. But at the end of all the doing, he simply disappeared, leaving — as far as anybody has been able to see in the two thousand or so years since — no apparent city, no effective kingdom able to make the world straighten up and fly right. The whole operation began as a mystery, continued as a mystery, came to fruition as a mystery, and to this day continues to function as a mystery. Since Noah, God has evidently had almost no interest in using direct power to fix up the world.

Why? you ask. Well, the first answer is, I don't know, and neither does anyone else. God's reasons are even more hidden than his methods. But I have seen enough of the results of direct intervention to make me rather glad that he seems, for whatever reason, to have lost interest in it.

Direct, straight-line, intervening power does, of course, have many uses. With it, you can lift the spaghetti from the plate to your mouth, wipe the sauce off your slacks, carry them to the dry cleaners, and perhaps even make enough money to ransom them back. Indeed, straight-line power ("use the force you need to get the result you want") is responsible for almost everything that happens in the world. And the beauty of it is, it works. From removing the dust with a cloth to removing your enemy with a .45, it achieves its ends in sensible, effective, easily understood ways.

Unfortunately, it has a whopping limitation. If you take the view that one of the chief objects in life is to remain in loving relationships with other people, straight-line power becomes useless. Oh, admittedly, you can snatch your baby boy away from the edge of a cliff and not have a broken relationship on your hands. But just try interfering with his plans for the season when he is twenty, and see what happens, especially if his chosen plans play havoc with your own. Suppose he makes unauthorized use of your car, and you use a little straight-line verbal power to scare him out of doing it again. Well and good. But suppose further that he does it again anyway — and again and again and again. What do you do next if you are committed to straight-line power? You raise your voice a little more nastily each time till you can't shout any louder. And then you beat him (if you are stronger than he is) until you can't beat any harder. Then you chain him to a radiator till. . . . But you see the point. At some very early crux in that difficult, personal relationship, the whole thing will be destroyed unless you — who, on any reasonable view, should be allowed to use straight-line power — simply refuse to use it; unless, in other words, you decide that instead of dish-

ing out justifiable pain and punishment, you are willing, quite foolishly, to take a beating yourself.

But such a paradoxical exercise of power, please note, is a hundred
and eighty degrees away from the straight-line variety. It is, to introduce a phrase from Luther, left-handed power. Unlike the power of the
right hand (which, interestingly enough, is governed by the logical,
plausibility-loving left hemisphere of the brain), left-handed power is
guided by the more intuitive, open, and imaginative right side of the
brain. Left-handed power, in other words, is precisely paradoxical
power: power that looks for all the world like weakness, intervention
that seems indistinguishable from nonintervention. More than that, it
is guaranteed to stop no determined evildoers whatsoever. It might, of
course, touch and soften their hearts. But then again, it might not. It
certainly didn't for Jesus; and if you decide to use it, you should be
quite clear that it probably won't for you either. The only thing it does
insure is that you will not — even after your chin has been bashed in —
have made the mistake of closing any interpersonal doors from your
side.

Which may not, at first glance, seem like much of a thing to insure,
let alone like an exercise worthy of the name of power. But when you
come to think of it, it *is* power — so much power, in fact, that it is the
only thing in the world that evil can't touch. God in Christ died forgiving. With the dead body of Jesus, he wedged open the door between
himself and the world and said, "There! Just try and get me to take *that*
back!"

And here is where this long, slow curve starts to curl in over the
plate. Just as, in the whole of the Bible, it takes a while before God's
preference for paradoxical rather than straight-line power manifests itself — just as God seems to do a lot of right-handed pushing and shoving before he does the left-handed but ultimately saving thing on the
cross — so too it seems that, for quite some time, Jesus puts himself
forth in the Gospels as a plausible, intervening, advice-giving, miracle-
working Messiah before he finally reveals himself as a dying, rising, and
disappearing one. Indeed, it is one of the premises of this book that if
the parables are examined in the context of the development of Jesus'

thinking on the subjects of power and its use, light will be shed both on them and on him.

Accordingly, I divide the parables into three groups. The first group — the short, almost one-sentence *parables of the kingdom* that occur in the Gospels prior to the Feeding of the Five Thousand — is the subject of this book. In subsequent volumes, I shall deal with the longer, story-length *parables of grace* (as I shall call them) that occur between the Feeding and the Triumphal Entry into Jerusalem, and with the stern, strange *parables of judgment* that the Gospel writers set mostly between the Entry and the Crucifixion.

One question about this classification arises immediately: Why make the Feeding of the Five Thousand a pivotal point? Well, first of all, because it is the only miracle of Jesus that is reported in all four Gospels; better and closer-to-the-event minds than yours or mine have already singled it out for unique attention. But second, if it is examined closely, it turns out to be pivotal not only in people's attitudes toward Jesus but also in his own thinking about himself.

No one can prove anything about Jesus' innermost, unexpressed thoughts, of course, but just for a moment consider this. In the early part of his ministry Jesus put himself forth pretty much as the kind of messiah people could take a liking to: a wonder-working rabbi who, by a combination of miracles and good teaching, sounded like the answer to everybody's prayers. But even at the start he did not buy into that formula completely. His miracles were often followed by stern warnings not to make them (or him) known — hardly the sort of thing to delight the heart of a sensible press agent — and his teaching was largely given in parables nobody understood. From the very beginning, in other words, Jesus seems to have had second thoughts about the style in which he was exercising power, and especially about how that style might easily give people the impression he was engaged in little more than a patch job on the world.

But there is more. Unlike many miracle workers who actually make a point of offering to work miracles — or who at least give the impression that miracles are what it's all about and stake their claim to attention precisely on that basis — Jesus is curiously reluctant about doing his "signs." (An important note here: the Greek word usually translated "miracle" does not have miraculous overtones; it is simply the ordinary word for "sign," *sēmeíon*.) Not only does Jesus play down his signs; it almost seems that he doesn't do them unless they are practically wrung out of him by others. He looks for all the world like a kind of walking cafeteria table of power from which people serve themselves with hardly a by-your-leave. (The woman with the issue of blood who, unbeknownst to Jesus, touched the hem of his garment is perhaps the clearest case; but the "involuntariness," or at least the offhandedness of his miracles, is manifest time and again.)

And — to come to the point at last — I think it is in the Feeding of the Five Thousand that his reluctance about giving signs becomes decisively manifest. Consider: At the end of a long day in the middle of nowhere, Jesus' disciples come and nag him about the obvious facts that it is late and that he has a hungry crowd on his hands. Their suggestion is to send the people packing before it gets dark; but Jesus, seemingly exhausted by the day, tells them to handle matters themselves and go buy some food. They complain they don't have enough money. They even give him a caterer's estimate of the cost. Finally, as if he is more interested in solving their problem than the crowd's, he reluctantly involves himself in the project. "How much food have you actually got?" he asks them. They say, "Five loaves and two fishes."

The rest, of course, is history. But can anyone seriously conclude from such an account that the Feeding was part of his master plan for the day? Doesn't it read as if he simply dragged his feet as long as he could before doing anything — as if it was only when nothing else worked that he finally uncovered himself as the messianic cafeteria counter and let them take as much as they wanted? Indeed, it seems that even while the miracle was in progress he made as little of it as possible: no hocus-pocus, no long prayers, no holy exhortations — just break it up and pass it out. The whole thing was so underplayed that the bread probably reached the back row of the crowd before the first row figured out what was happening.

But — and here is where the Feeding manifests its pivotal nature — all the rows eventually did figure it out. And when they did, Jesus' reac-

21

tion was to become something very like unglued. Matthew and Mark depict him hurriedly ordering his disciples to get into the boat and go on ahead of him to Bethsaida. In John, the disciples seem to embark of their own accord, but the people in the crowd stay around with a vengeance. They get the brilliant idea that anybody who can produce food like that ought to be made king — by force, if necessary.

In any case, the next thing Jesus does is to send the crowd away and head for the hills himself. He prays. For a long time. Meanwhile, a storm comes up on the lake (Jesus could see the disciples having trouble rowing, so this had to be sometime before dark). So what does he do? He keeps on praying. In fact, he prays till between three and six in the morning; at which point, according to Mark, he walks out on the water to his disciples and acts as if he is going to pass them by. Needless to say, they do a little thinking about ghosts and then proceed straight to rather a lot of screaming. Jesus simply tells them to cheer up: "It's me," he says, "don't be afraid." Once again, the rest is history: not only the calming of the storm, but the disciples' sudden realization that they were more afraid of him than of any wind that ever blew.

But I think something else is also history: the galvanizing effect the whole day and night had on Jesus' thoughts about messiahship and power. It seems to me that from the Feeding of the Five Thousand on, he had a much firmer grip on the truth that the Messiah was not going to save the world by miraculous, Band-Aid interventions: a storm calmed here, a crowd fed there, a mother-in-law cured back down the road. Rather, it was going to be saved by means of a deeper, darker, left-handed mystery, at the center of which lay his own death.

In any case, it is only after the Feeding that his talk about dying actually begins. In Luke it starts a mere three verses later, at 9:21. In Matthew, the Feeding is in chapter 14 and the first prophecy of his death in chapter 16. In Mark, the chapters are 6 and 8 respectively. In all three, moreover, the death-talk is immediately followed by the Transfiguration — and that, of course, by the downhill slide of his once-upbeat career into the mystery of Good Friday and Easter.

Which brings us to a second question — perhaps difficulty is a better word — that Christians sometimes have when it is suggested that

Jesus' thinking about his life and work actually underwent development during the course of his ministry. Because they believe he is in fact God incarnate, they have problems with such an apparent limitation of the divine omniscience. Their belief leads them, unless they formulate their theology about it very carefully indeed, to think that development is somehow an unsuitable process for the Redeemer to undergo.

What they need to do, of course, is to make some distinctions. Jesus, as the Word made flesh, is both God and man and he possesses both of those natures "without confusion, without change, without division, and without separation" (to use the words of the Chalcedonian definition). That means, among other things, that while it is perfectly proper to use the attributes of either nature when you are talking about the Person who is both (for instance: *the carpenter of Nazareth made the world; God died on the cross*), you must be careful not to scramble the two natures when you are speaking of how each one operates in its own proper sphere (thus: *God, as God, does not die; Jesus, in his human mind, is not omniscient*).

The fact that Jesus is God in man means exactly that: he is true God, genuine Deity, in an equally genuine and therefore complete, even *mere* humanity. In his divine mind, for example, God the Son — the Second Person of the Trinity, the Incarnate Lord — knows absolutely everything; but in his human mind — in the only mind, we believe, through which that same Lord finally, authoritatively, and personally reveals himself in this world — Jesus cannot help but be absolutely ignorant of, say, first-century Chinese, modern French, Jeffersonian democracy, and nuclear physics. The inevitable condition of a historical incarnation — that he must have a particular human body and mind in an equally particular place and time — precludes his being either Superman or Mr. Know-It-All.

The upshot of this is that some Christians, failing to make such distinctions rigorously enough, fall into the trap of thinking that if Jesus is really God, it is somehow unfitting or even irreverent to posit any development at all, even in his human mind. They feel obliged to maintain that, right from the beginning, he had everything figured out com-

23

pletely and that any apparent developments in his awareness were simply due to the way he deferred to our slow-wittedness by doling out his revelations piece by piece. But to put it that way is to expose their fallacy. "From what beginning?" such theologians should be asked. Presumably, they are thinking of the beginning of his public ministry or perhaps of those first words of his at age twelve when he told his parents he had to be "about his Father's business." But those are plainly not beginnings enough.

Back at the real beginning of his earthly ministry — at the annunciation, say, or in the stable at Bethlehem — how much did he know about anything? Not only was he ignorant, in the only human mind he had, of Chinese and French; he didn't even know Aramaic. *That* knowledge, since he was truly human, would come only in the way it came to all the other truly human little boys born at the same time: by the natural processes of human development.

More to the point, as a baby he was equally ignorant not only of the implausible, left-handed style of exercising power, but even of the simpler, more logical, right-handed one. Truly orthodox, classical Christian theology does not require us to posit for Jesus a human mind that works by freakish stunts. We may posit all the influences of the Holy Spirit upon him that we care to, but it is simply against the rules to turn that mind into a third something-or-other that is neither divine nor human. Jesus has two unconfused, unchanged, undivided, unseparated natures in one Person. He is not a metaphysical scrambled egg.

This chapter, however, is running the danger of becoming nothing but a series of long, slow curves, so let me end it with one pitch right to the strike zone. The last four paragraphs have been about theology — an enterprise that, despite the oftentimes homicidal urgency Christians attach to it, has yet to save anybody. What saves us is Jesus, and the way we lay hold of that salvation is by *faith*. And faith is something that, throughout this book, I shall resolutely refuse to let mean anything other than *trusting Jesus*. It is simply saying yes to him rather than no. It is, at its root, a mere "uh-huh" to him personally. It does not necessarily involve any particular theological structure or formulation; it does not entail any particular degree of emotional fervor; and above all, it does not depend on any specific repertoire of good works — physical, mental, or moral. It's just "Yes, Jesus," till we die — just letting the power of his resurrection do, in our deaths, what it has already done in his.

My purpose in saying this so strongly, however, is not simply to alert you to some little band of intellectuals called theologians who may try to talk you into thinking otherwise. Such types exist, of course, but they are usually such bores that all they do is talk you out of wanting even to breathe. No, the reason for my vehemence is that *all* of us are theologians. Every one of us would rather choose the right-handed logicalities of theology over the left-handed mystery of faith. Any day of the week — and twice on Sundays, often enough — we will labor with might and main to take the only thing that can save anyone and reduce it to a set of theological club rules designed to exclude almost everyone.

Christian theology, however, never is and never can be anything more than the thoughts that Christians have (alone or with others) *after* they have said yes to Jesus. Sure, it can be a thrilling subject. Of course, it is something you can do well or badly — or even get right or wrong. And naturally, it is one of the great fun things to do on weekends when your kidney stones aren't acting up. Actually, it is almost exactly like another important human subject that meets all the same criteria: wind-surfing. Everybody admires it, and plenty of people try it. But the number of people who can do it well is even smaller than the number who can do it without making fools of themselves.

Trust Jesus, then. After that, theologize all you want. Just don't lose your sense of humor if your theological surfboard deposits you unceremoniously in the drink.

CHAPTER TWO

The Frame of the Gospel Picture

B efore moving on to the parables of the kingdom, I think it is important to spend a little more time driving home the idea that the ministry of Jesus, taken in its entirety, is the manifestation of God's deep preference for a left-handed, mysterious exercise of power as opposed to a right-handed, plausible one. And I think that's so because while it is obvious from the Gospels that Jesus' real program — his ultimate saving action on behalf of the world — is his death and resurrection, too many Christians seem excessively fond of preaching a different message. They talk as if his miraculous cures and assorted other right-handed interventions were the heart of his program. What they do not say, but what the New Testament clearly maintains, is that his displays of straight-line power were not his program at all, but only the *signs* of it.

Consider therefore the two "parabolic events" — as I shall call them here — with which the Gospel writers actually frame the whole of Jesus' active ministry: the Temptation in the Wilderness and the Ascent into Heaven. Both deal specifically with the messianic use of power. In the former, the devil pleads (rather convincingly, too) for Jesus to do three altogether sensible things: to use his might to turn stones into bread (and by extension, to do something useful about human hunger); to display his power over death in a well-staged spectacle that would get people's attention; and last and most important, to use the devil's own eminently practical, right-handed methods for getting the world to shape up. Moreover, at the Ascension, the disciples — who even as late as forty days after the Resurrection still seem not to have grasped what Jesus spent three years telling them — ask him if he will now at last put aside the mystery and openly restore the kingdom to Israel. To which Jesus gives two answers. The first is a rebuke: such matters, he tells them, are not theirs to know. The second is an action: to underscore the fact that what he is doing will not be done in any such recognizable fashion, he simply ascends and disappears.

Two sets of questions arise out of the last paragraph. You may well wonder whether I haven't perhaps overstated myself about the "framing" function of these two episodes, and you may have your doubts as to the propriety of my calling them "parabolic events." Let me deal with each problem in order.

I am aware that the Temptation story appears only in Matthew, Mark (briefly), and Luke. Its absence from John, however, does not detract from my thesis. John omits a number of important events in Jesus' life, but he deals with their import or ramifications in other ways and contexts. He does not, for example, include a narration of the institution of the Eucharist; yet he devotes more space (chapters 13 through 17) to the Last Supper than the other three writers put together.

Not only that, but in chapter 6, after the Feeding of the Five Thousand, John includes the very cornerstone of eucharistic doctrine: Jesus' proclamation of himself as the Bread of Life. Accordingly, my own disposition when I find something "missing" from John is to look for the place (or places) where he works it in under another guise. The Transfiguration, for instance, seems to be adumbrated by John in Jesus' great high-priestly prayer in chapter 17. No other place in the Gospels better manifests in discourse what the Transfiguration account in the synoptics portrays in narrative, namely, that Jesus' divine unity with the Father is the very foundation of his relationship with both the disciples and the world.

In the case of the Temptation narrative, therefore, we need to ask where its equivalent occurs in John. Is there any place where the same debate over power occurs — where tempting voices urge Jesus to use plausible, right-handed power and where he responds by dragging his feet with mysterious left-handed responses?

When you put the question that way, the answer becomes obvious: the Johannine Temptation is contained, like the Johannine eucharistic passages, in chapter 6 of the Gospel. Consider: The crowd that witnessed the Feeding of the Five Thousand catches up with Jesus the next day in Capernaum and starts feeding him all sorts of straight-lines in the hope that he will respond with a public commitment to using his now-obvious power in an intelligible, right-handed way. Their whole performance is worthy of the devil himself: with condescending pieties fronting for their firm belief that they, and not Jesus, know best how to run a tight messianic ship, they press him harder and harder to make some plausible demonstration.

"Our ancestors ate manna in the desert," they remind him. "What will you do to match that?" Jesus, though, retreats deeper and deeper into mystery: "What Moses gave you," he tells them, "was not the bread from heaven; I am the bread of life." And he continues in that vein until he loses not only his audience but many of his disciples as well.

At the end only the twelve are left — and with only dumb, blind faith keeping them there at that. When Jesus asks them if they, too, want to go away, Peter answers, "Lord, to whom can we go? You have the words of eternal life." But Peter, unable as usual to keep quiet, goes on to blow his commitment with some gratuitous babble: " . . . and we have believed and known that you are the Holy One of God." Had he stopped at "believe," it might have been all right, but the claim to *know* simply gave Jesus the willies. It made him jump straight to thinking that even among his chosen twelve there was a devil — a worshiper of intelligible, right-handed power who would sooner or later betray him. John, therefore, no less than Matthew, Mark, and Luke, does full justice to the devilish trial of the Messiah.

But if that much can be said for a four-Gospel, full-court press as regards the Temptation, what about the Ascension? In particular, what about the fact that only Luke seems to record it?

Once again it strikes me that the omission of the Ascension from Matthew and Mark and especially from John is more apparent than real. As a matter of fact, I make my same argument: in one form or another, all four Gospels have the equivalent of the Ascension. For example, although the literal business of Jesus' going up in the air is not mentioned in Matthew 28:16-20, the passage describes an otherwise identical hilltop departure scene. And as I have said, it seems to me that it is precisely *departure* that lies at the root of Jesus' parabolic last act.

In Mark, on the other hand, although the Ascension does not appear in some of the oldest and best manuscript sources of the Gospels (some of these manuscripts have Mark end at chapter 16, verse 8, even before the resurrection appearances have occurred), it does appear at 16:19 in many other sources. At the very least, whatever the explanation may have been for its omission from certain fourth-century manuscripts, there was a strong feeling on the part of the early church — the group that, please note, had included "ascended into heaven" in its baptismal creed much earlier — that the Ascension scene simply had to be included in Mark.

Since the Lucan record of Jesus' being "taken up into heaven" is perfectly clear (Luke 24:51 and Acts 1:9), that leaves only the Gospel of John to reckon with. As before, I invoke my principle of looking for important missing material in the Fourth Gospel by trying to discover where John dealt with the subject thematically rather than narratively. And when I do that, far from finding John to have the least space of all devoted to the Ascension, I find him, hands-down once again, to have the most. All through the discourse at the Last Supper (John 13–17), Jesus returns over and over to the theme of his departure. True, the genius of John for dealing with several things at once is such that a good deal of what Jesus says applies as much to his crucifixion and death as it does to his ascension. But an equally great deal of it is pure departure talk: "Yet a little while and the world will see me no more" (14:19); "I am leaving, but I will come back to you" (14:28); "It is better for you that I go away" (16:7); "Father, now I am coming to you" (17:13).

Accordingly, I find the Ascension just as essential a piece of Gospel framework as the Temptation: both, it seems to me, are acted parables of power aimed at driving home — one at the end of Jesus' ministry and one at the beginning — a clear lesson about how his power is *not* going to be used. Taken seriously, they can go a long way toward keeping our otherwise easily derailed theological locomotives securely on the Gospel track.

That leaves only the question of whether calling them "parabolic events" is suitable to their importance. True enough, such a phrase, in the hands of certain biblical critics, could be a bit off-putting; some of them use the word "parabolic" to excuse themselves from the unpleasant prospect of having to deal with miraculous episodes as actual events. That, however, is not my intention. Let me make my own position clear by examining first the Ascension, then the Temptation.

The critics I refer to usually say something like this: In Jesus' time, people thought heaven was literally *up;* we, however, having abandoned the flat-earth theory, know that it is not a "place" at all — at least not one you can reach by traveling from here to there. Thus, they argue, the story of the Ascension was probably made up by Luke, or somebody, to provide a suitably parabolic interpretation of the obvious fact that Jesus wasn't around any more after the great forty days.

I have a number of objections to that kind of fast-and-loose shuffle. The first is: If the critics are willing to give Luke credit for being bright enough to *think up* the parable of the Ascension, why are they unwilling to give Jesus credit for having the cleverness and the ability to *act it out?* The answer, of course, is that they have a prejudice against miracles and will do almost anything to avoid having to posit one as a legitimate, historical event. They are entitled to that prejudice; but they are not, for my money, entitled to put it forth as a piece of biblical criticism. The Ascension just sits there on the pages of Luke, obstinately refusing to get out of the text. They don't have to like it, but they should do everyone the favor of acknowledging that their dislike is based on an a priori philosophical judgment and not on Scripture itself.

My second objection proceeds from that. The veneer of scientific respectability they put on their argument ("Heaven can't possibly be just *up*") is another dodge. Of course heaven isn't up. But if you are going to act out a cosmically significant departure, you have — even in the twentieth-first century — a choice of only three directions: up, down, or sideways. Of those only *up* has the parabolic significance you are after.

Down implies the exact opposite of what you want to symbolize, and *sideways* might make people think only that you had moved to Grand Rapids.

Finally, it seems silly for these debaters to mention the flat-earth–round-earth controversy. Their whole argument attacks only a straw man. Whatever your view of terrestrial and celestial mechanics, neither Scripture nor sound theology requires you to get Jesus any further spatially than the first cloud. After that, the Ascension as an event in this world is over, and the cosmic significance of it becomes — as it was meant to be all along — the main thing.

So I am perfectly happy to take the Ascension as an event, and I am equally comfortable trying to plumb its parabolic significances to my heart's content. The two activities do not conflict in any way. Indeed, they absolutely require each other. If you insist on the Ascension as a mere happening, you miss its meaning; if you harp only on its meaning, you cut it off from history — which is the only arena in which God has revealed to us, parabolically or otherwise, his purpose.

The Temptation, on the other hand, presents fewer problems. Once again, it just sits there on the pages, refusing to apologize for its presence. To be sure, critics who have a priori objections to the devil will try, as always, to claim that the episode was the product of a fertile imagination rather than an actual happening. But that is an instance of letting your prejudices carry you into a totally pointless enterprise.

First of all, unless you are absolutely bent on doubting the obvious, the most likely candidate to have had that fertile imagination and to have disclosed the Temptation story was Jesus himself. (The devil is a possibility too, of course, but since neither the critics nor myself wants to be caught dead advocating that one, let it pass.) Presumably, therefore, it was Jesus who was the original source of the Temptation narrative.

Second, unless you are unwilling to give Jesus' parabolic abilities as much credit here as elsewhere, it is altogether reasonable to expect that in recounting the whole experience of being tempted by the devil, he would cast it in suitable narrative form. It might even be, of course, that the three temptations enumerated were in fact the very ones that occurred. Indeed, it may well have been that every detail in the episode literally took place in some specific "there" and "then." But none of those problems is either capable of solution or important to solve. The significance of the whole narration is Jesus' disclosure of the great debate over messianic power, *as he experienced it.* Whether it took place at 3:00 P.M. or in Jerusalem or on a mountaintop or simply in his mind is quite secondary to the fact that it occurred in his person at the instigation of somebody or something that had a deep interest in turning the mystery of saving, left-handed power into just another right-handed, strong-arm job that would leave the world still on the skids.

Finally, there is the question of *when* Jesus informed the disciples about the Temptation. No one can prove anything. The Gospel writers simply thread in the account of it right at the beginning of his ministry, and there is no reason to doubt that that is when it happened. But it seems to me quite likely that that is not when he told them about it. They had enough trouble grasping relatively simple parabolic material like the Sower, the Yeast, and the rest. Even when he informed them later, in so many words, about his impending and utterly left-handed plan to die and rise, they still failed to comprehend. So my own choice for the point at which Jesus filled them in about the Temptation is the great forty days between the Resurrection and the Ascension. It was precisely then, when his renunciation of right-handed power was almost as clearly revealed as it ever would be, that they would have the best chance of finally seeing what he was talking about.

In any case, both the Temptation and the Ascension seem to bear up fairly well as parabolic events that frame an equally parable-filled history. Both are about the subject of power, and if I am even warm in my hunch about when Jesus revealed them, each may well have a good bit of the other mixed up in it. Time now to examine them in detail.

CHAPTER THREE

The Temptation and the Ascension

The first thing to note about the Temptation of Jesus is that it happened under the guidance of the Spirit. Mark, who mentions it by little more than title (Mark 1:12-13), nevertheless manages to include a vivid reference: the Spirit, he says, *drives out* (RSV) — or even *throws out: ekbállei* — Jesus into the desert. Matthew and Luke, who spell out the specific temptations, say that Jesus was led *(anéchthē, ēgeto)* by the Spirit (Matt. 4:1; Luke 4:1). All of them agree, though, that Jesus did not just wander into his confrontation with the devil. The meeting is clearly portrayed as part of a larger plan — a plan, please note, that Jesus' *human mind* may very well not have been privy to before the event.

Which raises once again a theological consideration that needs constant emphasis. Jesus, we believe, is indeed truly divine and truly human. But those two natures, while inseparably joined in God the Son, the Second Person of the Trinity, are distinct and unconfused. The Incarnate Lord is not a mishmash of divinity and humanity. There is not a scrap of human nature in his Godhead, and most important here, there is not a smitch of deity in his manhood, any more than there is in yours or mine. He came to save *us*, in *our* nature, not to put on some flashy, theandric, superhuman performance that would be fundamentally irrelevant to our condition.

Accordingly, when the deity of Jesus acts or impinges upon his humanity, it does so not in the order of nature — not by souping up his humanity into something more than human — but in the order of *grace:* that is, by divine influences that empower human nature but do not tamper with it. In Scripture it is precisely the Holy Spirit, the Third Person of the Trinity, who is given credit for enabling and guiding the humanity of Jesus. For example, Jesus casts out demons not by means of some more-than-human power that he has in and of himself, but by the Spirit — by, as he puts it, the Finger of God.

Therefore, when we talk about the development of Jesus' messianic consciousness, we should stay light-years away from any suggestion that he had a kind of trap door between his divine and human minds. We should avoid, in other words, the humanity-destroying trick of positing leaks from his deity into his humanity. The influence of the Spirit alone — acting upon his human nature in no fundamentally different way than it does on ours — is quite sufficient: it covers all the biblical bases; it provides for all the divine "informing" we ever need to speak of; and it does so without turning Jesus into Superman.

Indeed, the Superman analogy is a perfect illustration of what Jesus is not. He is not from another planet but from this one. He does not have, in his human nature, powers beyond those of mortal men; instead, he is just as mortal as we are. Neither is he immune to any of our other debilities and limitations: not hunger, not thirst, not exhaustion, not exasperation, certainly not speeding locomotives, and probably not even the common cold. Above all, he is born among us as Clark Kent; he lives among us as Clark Kent; he dies as Clark Kent; and he comes forth from the tomb as Clark Kent — not as some alien hotshot in blue tights who, at the crucial moment, junks his Clark Kentness in favor of a snappier, nonhuman style of being.

Furthermore, the Superman myth provides us with an equally perfect bridge to, and handle on, the subject of the Temptation. For what is the dialogue in the wilderness if not the devil's attempt to sell Jesus a set of messianic blue tights? "If you really are the Son of God," Satan wheedles, "put a little moxie in your act. Don't just stand there (or even, unthinkably, *hang* there); *do* something. The world is going to hell in a handbasket. People are starving for food; they're wandering in mental darkness because God never gives them any straight-line demonstrations of power to latch onto; and they're suffering from the chaos of a world that could turn into a gorgeous place if only someone with enough power would smack it into line. Get into the phone booth, then, and come out swinging. With my brains and your brawn, we could really get this show on the road."

To all of this Jesus simply replies from chapters 6 and 8 of Deuteronomy, the sections recapitulating the ten commandments in chapter 5. Do you see what that means? It means that when the devil talks messiah, Jesus answers with passages that are not messianic at all, but simply addressed to humanity as such. He says, in effect, "*You* can't conceive of a messiah unless he's dedicated to a lot of superhuman, right-handed punching and interfering; but as far as I'm concerned, just plain human obedience to God's prescriptions for plain old humanity will do the messianic trick. Thank you very much, but peddle your phone booth somewhere else."

The dialogue between Jesus and the devil, you see, is a conversation between two people who simply cannot understand what each other is saying. Satan talks right-handed power; Jesus talks left. They might as well be in different universes. As a matter of fact, they *are* in different universes: Jesus, in the only one there really is; and the devil, in the distorted, secondhand version of it that he, as the father of lies, has managed to fake out.

Still, to our discredit (we abandon our devotion to the methods of the Prince of this world very slowly indeed), the devil does strike us as having all the best lines. What he says makes sense to our inveterately right-handed souls. But what Jesus says in reply — not to mention what he ends up doing over the full course of his ministry — seems not only nonsense, but heartless nonsense at that.

Take the temptations in the order they occur in Matthew (Luke transposes the second and the third, but that makes little difference here). For the first, the devil suggests to Jesus — who after forty days of fasting has got to be hungry — that he use his messianic, Son of God power to make himself a stone sandwich right on the spot. "Do something, for earth's sake," he seems to be saying. "You have the power to wipe out not only your own hunger but the whole world's. What's wrong with using it?"

"Man shall not live by bread alone," Jesus answers, quoting Deuteronomy 8:3, "but by every word that comes out of the mouth of God."

"Now hold on a minute," Satan says (if we may give him, like members of Congress, the privilege of extending his remarks). "Not so fast. Who said anything against God? You mean you can't eat bread *and* live by God's words at the same time? If that's true, it looks like pretty bad divine planning. Look, you're going to eat something soon, aren't you?"

Jesus nods.

"Maybe you'll even have an early supper today, right? You certainly deserve it."

Jesus nods again.

"You might even stop at a delicatessen on the way home and pick up a little something, no?"

Jesus shrugs.

"Well, then. If you're going to eat soon — and if there's no necessary conflict between, say, a chopped liver on rye and obeying God — why not eat now?"

Jesus shakes his head no.

The devil thinks for a moment and then tries a different tack. "Tell me," he says, "would you turn these stones into bread, not for yourself but for some really hungry people?"

Jesus turns his hands over and back in a little gesture that says, possibly.

"Aha!" the devil says. "Then I've got you. In Leviticus 19:18, it says, 'love your neighbor as yourself.' If it's not all right to feed yourself, how can you feed others?"

Jesus yawns. The devil shifts gears.

He takes Jesus up on a pinnacle of the temple in Jerusalem. "Look," he says, "forget the bread business. I'm talking now about people's really deep spiritual needs. As I see it, the trouble with God's operation is that it's entirely too vague. I mean, if he wants people to obey him, not to mention to love him, how come he's so reluctant to give them a clear shot at seeing him in action? Everything he does is so . . . covert. And people suffer because of that. They can't help it if he made them dependent on what they see with their own eyes or experience in their own bodies. It's the old story of the donkey and the two-by-four. They're not really bad; all you have to do is give them a good whack to get their attention. How about a nice, miraculous two-by-four then? Jump down from here. Psalm 91:11-12 even guarantees God will approve: angels will catch you before you hit the sidewalk, and you'll have done the world the favor of concentrating its mind a whole lot."

Jesus says, "You shall not tempt the Lord your God."

"For crying out loud," the devil complains, "this is your idea of tempting? I can't believe what I'm listening to. I hand you a first-rate messianic prophecy, and you refuse to fulfill it. Did it ever occur to you that maybe you're not the Messiah? What are you going to do, spend your entire career studiously avoiding anything that people could recognize as divine action?"

Jesus purses his lips.

"Listen," Satan says, "I can see this is getting us nowhere. Let me give you a real mountaintop experience. I want you to picture yourself on a high, high hill — so high that from the peak you can see all the kingdoms of the world. And I would also like it if we could both please drop the polite pussyfooting and just speak plainly. I admit it. I was putting you on with all that 'if you're the Son of God' stuff. I have absolutely no question about who you are. But on the other hand, neither do you have any question about who I am — and especially about the rights and privileges you gave me over this shooting match you call a world. Not that it was exactly a terrific gift: you recognized my talents by making me Prince here, but you were a bit stingy when it came to giving me the power I needed to run it.

"What I'm suggesting is that, since we both have a major investment in this operation, we stop all the bickering and, for the world's sake, make common cause. You have the power and I have the smarts. All you have to do is help me get my plans operative, and between the two of us we'll have this place turned back into Eden in six months. What do you say? Not only would it work, but it would get you one hell of a lot better press than you've had for centuries."

Jesus smiles at him, shaking his head up and down as if to say, "That's exactly what I'm afraid of." Then he turns grim. "Look," he says, "just get out of here, huh? I take my orders from one source only, and you, Charley, are definitely not it."

But enough of the Temptation itself. Paradoxically, Jesus eventually does all the things the devil suggests. But he does them in his own time and in his own way. He turns five loaves and two fish into an all-time eatout for five thousand. This, while it is essentially the same trick as making himself a miraculous snack, is not only more of a sign but also one that serves to intensify rather than vitiate his commitment to left-handed power.

Furthermore, instead of merely circumventing death by having angels catch him (a sign, please note, that would promise nothing to the rest of us who are not messiahs), he dies as dead as anyone and then rises to become the first fruits of them that slept (a phrase that means — since no child of Adam and Eve is exempt from that sleep — absolutely everybody). Finally, he does indeed take up the rulership of this world, but instead of doing so by the devil's device of moving in and applying strong-arm methods, he ascends and sits as King of Kings and Lord of Lords at his Father's right hand. He continues to govern, in other words, as the Wisdom of God he always was, reaching from one end of the universe to the other, and mightily and sweetly — *fortiter suaviterque* — ordering all things.

A question. Does the phrase "his Father's right hand" undo my whole case for Jesus' abiding commitment to left-handed power? Does it suggest that when all is said and done, the divine Wisdom is going to get the sweetness out of his act and revert to rockem-sockem tactics? Not to my mind, it doesn't. First of all, God as God does not have a literal right hand; the phrase is clearly a metaphor for the highest and holiest station of all. But second, the Greek simply doesn't mention "hand." It says (cf. Mark 16:19) that he enthroned himself *ek dexión toú theoú* — literally, "out of the right-sidednesses [the idiom is oddly plural] of God." Therefore, if I choose to argue that, in ascending, he declares his eternal intention to act out of the *right hemisphere of God's brain* — and thus forever to commit himself to left-handed power — who is to say me nay? "Brain" is as legitimate (and as illegitimate) an image as "hand" to apply to God; the real point is that we should feel free to *play* with the images of Scripture, letting their light fall on as many facets of experience as possible. Still, if that sort of argument strikes you as over the foul line, let it pass. Go directly to the Ascension.

The first thing to be said about Jesus' last earthly act is that it was utterly consistent with the rest of his ministry. It was, from the point of view of exercising power, a bizarre and paradoxical conclusion to a bizarre and paradoxical career. It was not, however, and it never will be our idea of what he ought to have done.

Suppose that you or I had been appointed the producers of a messianic final act. Is there any doubt about how we, as the promoters and press agents of a resurrected Savior, would have acted? Of course there isn't. We would have played every card we had to get him on Carson, Donahue, and the cover of *Time*. Or failing that, we would have blitzed local TV and radio with him until the last, least talk-show host lost interest — and then we would have carted him around to county fairs, revival meetings, and supermarket openings till the end of time.

In short, we would have turned the cosmic, risen Jesus — the one who is the Resurrection and the Life of the whole world; the one who, as the creating and redeeming Word of God, is intimately and immediately present to everything that exists; the one who, when he is lifted up, draws *all* to himself; and the one who, at his coming again (his *parousia*), is everywhere at once like lightning that shines from east to west — we would have turned the universal Lord into just another side-show freak. We would have succeeded, to put it succinctly, in convincing the world of our belief that his power lay chiefly in our publicity of him and that his promises — since we gave people no reason to expect anything but right-handed and therefore illusory fulfillments — were just so much hot air.

I realize that the last paragraph was neither "short" nor particularly succinct, but bear with me. The New Testament proclaims an unlikely Savior. The work of Jesus in his incarnation, life, passion, death, resurrection, and ascension makes no worldly sense at all. The portrait the Gospels paint is that of a lifeguard who leaps into the surf, swims to the

39

drowning girl, and then, instead of doing a cross-chest carry, drowns with her, revives three days later, and walks off the beach with assurances that everything, including the apparently still-dead girl, is hunky-dory. You do not like that? Neither do I. But I submit that it is — unless we are prepared to ignore both the Gospels and the ensuing two thousand years' worth of tombstones with bodies still under them — very much like what the Man actually said and did. And — to come to the main point at last — it is the Ascension of Jesus, and the Ascension alone, that keeps us from missing the reason for his doing it that way.

For by ascending, by making a *departure* from this world the capstone of all his earthly acts, he underscores once and for all what he said with ever-increasing clarity through his whole ministry. The kingdom of God, the Ascension insists, does not come about because of what the world does to itself — nor even, in any obvious sense, because of what God does to the world. Rather, the kingdom already exists in the King himself, and when he ascends, the whole world goes with him (John 12:32).

It is not that someday Jesus will do this, that, and the other thing, and then the Kingdom will come. It is not, for example, that *at some future date* the dead will rise or that *in some distant consummation* we will reign with him. Rather, it is that we have already been buried with him in baptism, and that we are already risen with him through faith in the operation of God who raised him from the dead, and that we are now — in this and every moment — enthroned together in heavenly places in Christ Jesus.

But there is more. It is not that, after some further series of transactions, the city — so long mired in sin and failure — will finally be built. Rather, it is that the city, like the kingdom, is already an accomplished fact in Jesus himself. We are invited not to make it happen, but to believe that it *is* and to let it come. It exists, in other words, because in Jesus the world is already the Bride adorned for her husband, because we now sit as his wife at the marriage supper of the Lamb — because, once and for all, *now* and not *then*, he has taken the drowned girl home in the mystery of his death, resurrection, and ascension, and presented her to his Father as the Holy City, the New Jerusalem.

I am aware that many Christians, when they read the passages and images I have just referred to, give them an exclusively future interpretation. But in light of the Ascension, it seems to me, that simply will not wash. Jesus says he *is*, not *will be*, the Way, the Truth, and the Life. He insists to Martha — who quite plausibly figured that her brother Lazarus would rise again at the last day — that he, the Christ himself, is the Resurrection and the Life right now. And he raises Lazarus then and there to drive the point home.

Throughout his ministry, Jesus points relentlessly to himself ("believe in *me*") as the mysterious center from which and in which the Father reconciles the world to himself. Therefore, when he ascends — when he goes away, promising an imminent return — what can that mean but that he has the city fully in hand and ready to be delivered? He always had the whole world in his arms; what the Ascension uniquely proclaims is that he's got the kingdom in his pocket.

To be sure, at the point of his departure, he has it in a highly mysterious pocket: as far as we're concerned we will not see it openly until the delivery is actually made. But that is not because sometime between his Ascension and his Second Coming he will have gotten down to brass tacks and made real what was only virtual. It is only because we can't see mysteries. On the last day, Jesus will not do anything new; he will simply make manifest what he has been doing all along — what, in fact, he has long since done by preparing for us a kingdom from the foundation of the world. It will be in seeing him, as *he* is, that it will finally dawn on us what, in him, we have always been.

In any case, what clinches the argument that the Ascension is the proclamation of a mysterious, left-handed kingdom (already actual in the King himself) is the fact that Jesus discourages any speculation about why he is going or what plans he might have for coming back. The apostles are specifically told that times, seasons, and schedules of events are none of their business. Their relationship to the mystery of the kingdom is to be based not on their knowledge or performance, and certainly not on their guesswork about God's plans; it is to be rooted only in trust in his promise. They are to believe only in the King. Everything else is out of their hands, beyond their ken, and both literally and parabolically, over their heads.

Indeed, it seems to me that the precise reason the early church did not fall apart when Jesus failed to return with any reasonable promptness was that they saw both the Ascension and the Second Coming chiefly as matters of promise. True enough, a certain amount of eschatological explicitness shows up here and there in the records we have (e.g., 1 Thess. 4:13–5:11); but the contexts are often pastoral, and the details vouchsafed are quite plainly put second (as in the passage cited) to that trust in Jesus that is the one foundation of the church's hope. It was not right-handed, intelligible timetables that kept the first Christians strong in the Lord and armed to resist the methods of the devil — such straight-line plausibilities are just the devil's cup of tea, spoons not long enough by half for anyone to risk supping with him. No, their faithfulness to the kingdom that comes rested solely on the left-handed promise of the King himself. No questions asked; no answers given; just "Amen, come, Lord Jesus."

And what a comfort that is to us, both theologically and pastorally. Not a single specific prediction over the past two millennia has ever come true, but that makes no difference at all. A promise is a promise: whether its fulfillment takes ten seconds or ten billion years, the simple act of trusting it puts us fully, if mysteriously, in the very center of its power.

There is only one thing to add. When Jesus ascended, he not only said he would return; he also promised to endue his church with power from on high (Luke 24:49) — to send them, as he said in John, the Comforter, the Holy Spirit. Interestingly and happily enough, that promise was fulfilled with considerable promptness. The delivery date on it was Pentecost, less than two weeks later. Equally interestingly, but not nearly so happily, the church has made almost as many mistakes about the role of the Spirit in its life as it has about the Second Coming. In spite of the fact that Jesus insisted that the Comforter would not speak of himself but would simply take what was Christ's and show it to us, Christians have all too often decided that there was indeed one thing of Christ's that the Spirit would not bother to show us — one whole set of things, in fact, that Jesus stressed but that the Comforter would not bring to our remembrance — namely, Christ's insistence on using left-handed power.

The idea quickly got around in the early church — and has stayed with us to this day — that when the Spirit came to act, he would do so in plausible, right-handed ways. Whether those acts were conceived of as involving a program of miraculous, healing interventions in the world, or as displaying various straight-line "spiritual" phenomena such as speaking in tongues or guaranteeing the Papacy's infallibility in matters of faith and morals, the church all too often gave the impression that the Spirit could be counted on to deliver in a way that Jesus never did. And thus the mischief was done. The mystery of a kingdom fully accomplished in the risen and ascended King was replaced by a vision of a kingdom to be accomplished by a series of intelligible, selective patch jobs. The Good News of a city founded on grace for everybody became the bad news of a suburb for spiritual millionaires. Jesus said, loud and clear, "I, if I be lifted up, will draw *all* to myself"; the church, louder and clearer, insisted he only meant *some*.

The sad part of it all is that if the world could have been saved by that kind of relatively minor meddling, it would have been — long before Jesus and a hundred times since. But spiritual works no more bring in the kingdom than moral or intellectual ones. The death, resurrection, and ascension of Jesus — especially the Ascension, since it is the final affirmation of the hands-off policy implicit in the other two — proclaim that *no* meddling, divine or human, spiritual or material, can save the world. Its only salvation is in the mystery of the King who dies, rises, and disappears, and who asks us simply to trust his promise that, in him, we have the kingdom already.

PART TWO

The Parables of the Kingdom

CHAPTER FOUR

The Ministry before the Parables

S o far we have dealt with the scriptural framework surrounding the parables and with some of the theological concepts, apt and less apt, by which Christians attempt to grasp it. But if I assess your mood correctly, you have had your fill of talk about the frame and would dearly like to look at the picture. Fair enough. On with the first of the three groupings I originally proposed: Jesus' parables of the kingdom.

By way of a graphic reminder of the general shape of the Gospels, I have included a chart giving the chapter numbers of some of the events of Jesus' ministry that seem to me to bear on the interpretation of the parables (see p. 48). Perhaps the only thing that needs to be said here is that the *parables of the kingdom,* as I see them, occur between columns II and IV of the chart; the *parables of grace,* between columns IV and X; and the *parables of judgment,* between columns X and XI. That much noted, we're ready to proceed.

Since context is crucial, however, we need to begin our consideration of the parables of the kingdom a bit before their appearance in the narration. And since the Gospel according to Mark presents the early events of Jesus' ministry more succinctly than either Matthew or Luke, I propose to limit my examination of those events to the Marcan account.

What do we find in Mark between chapters 1 and 4? Predictably enough, we find Jesus at the very beginning of his public ministry. But

Gospel	Total No. of Chaps.	I Jesus' Baptism	II Jesus' Temptation	III The Parable of the Sower	IV The Feeding of the 5,000	V Peter's Confession	VI Jesus' First Prophecy of His Death	VII The Transfiguration	VIII Jesus' Second Prophecy of His Death	IX Jesus' Third Prophecy of His Death	X Palm Sunday	XI Jesus' Death	XII Jesus' Resurrection	XIII Jesus' Ascension
Matt	28	3	4	13	14	16	16	17	17	20	21	27	28	(28)
Mark	16	1	1	4	6	8	8	9	9	10	11	15	16	(16)
Luke	24	3	4	8	9	9	9	9	9	18	19	23	24	24 (+ Acts 1)
John	21	–	–	–	6	–	–	–	–	–	12	19	20	–

Chapter Numbers of Some Pivotal Events in the Gospels

what kind of ministry did he seem to be offering to those who heard and saw him? My own answer is that for all concerned, enthusiasts and critics alike, it was an odd and troubling one. And even though its peculiarities, as Mark presents them, succeed one another with such speed and apparent randomness that they are easy to miss, I think that they can be made at least a bit more evident by classifying them under the headings of four tendencies.

First and foremost, Jesus seems quite clearly to be claiming a messianic role for himself. Yet his claim seems also to involve a certain unmessianic flouting of the very Law that his Jewish hearers expected the Messiah to fulfill to perfection. Second — and quite perversely for someone engaged in self-proclamation — Jesus insists that the exorcisms and healings that manifest his messianic identity be kept as much of a secret as possible. Third, both the style and the substance of what he is proclaiming seem to border on something very like irreligion — or at least on something quite beyond his hearers' concept of religion. And fourth, right from the start he manifests a penchant for bent rather than straight discourse: in the first three chapters of Mark, we find not only that Jesus tells parables (3:23), but that he resorts to parabolic sayings no fewer than seven times. Consider, therefore, these four tendencies in order.

As far as the first is concerned, Jesus begins almost immediately to encourage the messianic expectations of the people. As early as Mark 1:15 — a mere two verses after the Temptation — words about the kingdom are already on his lips. "The *time* is here," he says (the Greek word is *kairós*, "due season" — a word with definitely messianic overtones), "and the kingdom of God has drawn close; repent and believe the Good News." But then two verses later, when he sees Simon and Andrew fishing, he says to them, "Come with *me* and *I* will make you fishers of men." Unlike John the Baptist — indeed, unlike most other religious figures — he points toward, not away, from himself when he proclaims his message. And later on, in 2:10 and 2:28, he refers to himself in presumably messianic terms as the Son of Man.

There is more in the same vein. People are amazed at the way he speaks (1:22): unlike the scribes, he teaches with "authority" (*exousía*, power), as if what he says is validated only by his saying it and not by external criteria. Again, he casts out an unclean spirit (1:25) by the same *exousía*. The people are so amazed at his personal authority, in fact, that they wonder whether he is putting forth some totally new teaching. And he continues, doing obviously messianic signs (the healing of Simon's mother-in-law [1:30]; the healing of many sick people and the driving out of many demons [1:34, 39]; the cleansing of a leper [1:40]; the healing of a paralytic [2:3]).

But he then proceeds to associate with sleazy types that no proper Messiah would have any truck with. In 2:14, he calls Levi, a tax-farmer, to follow him (in his audience's mind, a good tax collector was simply a contradiction in terms — rather like a poverty-stricken dermatologist in our day and age). He follows that up by eating dinner with a whole crowd of tax collectors and low-lifes (2:15), and when some Pharisees question the appropriateness of the company he keeps (2:16), he justifies himself by saying that it is precisely sinners, and not the righteous, that he has come to call. It's worth noting, too, that neither in this last passage nor in the parallel account in Matthew 9:13 does Jesus say anything more than that he has "come to *call* sinners." He does not add "to repentance" as he does in Luke 5:32; he just insists that his call is to the disreputable rather than to the upright — an insistence that, to the Pharisees who were its target, could only mean that Jesus, for all his messianic pretensions, had a strange lack of interest in looking like a respectable Messiah.

Finally (to complete this first heading), Jesus flies still further in the face of messianic expectations. He justifies the apparent irreligiousness of his disciples' failure to fast by asking, "Who can avoid being at a party when I'm around?" (2:19). He says that old notions about the Messiah are totally inappropriate to his new and definitive messiahship (2:21). And he violates the Sabbath not once, but twice: by picking grain (2:23) and by healing a man with a withered hand (3:1). After the first of those violations, he justifies himself by saying that he, the Son of Man, is in charge of the Sabbath, not the other way around. And after the second, the Pharisees have heard all they need to convince them that Jesus is unqualified bad news: as early as Mark 3:6, plans to kill Jesus are already afoot.

In other words, by the time Mark reaches chapter 4 and introduces the parable of the Sower (the first of the explicit parables of the messianic kingdom), he has already established Jesus not only as a wonder-working, demon-exorcising claimant to the messianic title but also as a Sabbath-breaking upstart with a dangerously arrogant sense of his own authority — as somebody, in other words, who is neither interested in, nor palatable to, the religious sensibilities of expert Messiah-watchers. To sum it up, therefore: by the end of chapter 3, his family thinks he is crazy (v. 21); the scribes are sure he is possessed by Beelzebub (v. 22); and Jesus' patience is already beginning to wear thin. The Satan-talk, he insists, is sheer nonsense (vv. 23-29); his real family consists of anybody who does the will of God (v. 35); and those who say he has an evil spirit are themselves guilty of blaspheming against the Holy Spirit (vv. 29-30).

My second heading — the matter of the "messianic secret" — can be dealt with more briefly. Let it simply be read into the record here that in at least three places (Mark 1:34, 44; and 3:12) Jesus, who is obviously in the process of putting himself forth as a messianic figure, paradoxically charges those who have the most proof of his messiahship not to utter a word about it. On the first occasion he will not let the demons he has driven out speak; on the second, he tells a cleansed leper not to say anything to anybody; and on the third, he extensively warns the unclean spirits not to blow his cover. Why? Mark does not say. Perhaps it was because Jesus saw clearly, right from the start (he certainly said as much soon after this in 4:12), that any Messiah his hearers would recognize would not be the kind of Messiah he was. Or perhaps it was just because he felt he did not want to give hostile critics more ammunition than they already had.

In any case, the facts stand: Jesus not only revealed himself, he hid himself at the same time. It was a pattern, it seems to me, that eventually became a passion with him. Whatever we make of it, there is no question but that right up to his seemingly inconsequential death, his elusive resurrection, and his uncommunicative ascension — indeed, with ever-increasing clarity through all three of those climactic events — he went right on doing the same thing: reconciling the world by a kind of divine double-talk, proclaiming approach-avoidance as the paradigm of salvation.

The third heading — the apparent "irreligiousness" of Jesus' early words and acts — needs even less space, since some instances of it have already been mentioned. I add here only that, to judge from the responses Jesus provoked from the religious experts of his day, it is quite plain that what he said and did didn't look much like religion to them. Respectable religionists can spot an absence of conventional piety a mile away; and the scribes and Pharisees did just that. In Mark 2:6, 16, 18, 24, and 3:2, they're increasingly sure there is something about Jesus' message that they want no part of. By 3:6 their certainty has been extended to not wanting any part of Jesus himself either, and to actually making plans to kill him. And by 3:22 they have their case complete. Not only is he an irreligious and therefore bogus messiah who should be killed as soon as possible; he is also the exact opposite of the Messiah: he is, they are convinced, the devil incarnate.

On then to the last of the four tendencies in the early chapters of Mark: the fact that Jesus speaks parabolically even before he begins uttering the parables we recognize as such. I shall do no more than list the instances. If they are not quite up to the standards of some of his later performances, neither were all of his later performances. The acted parables of the Cursing of the Fig Tree, for instance, or of the Coin in the Fish's Mouth, do not seem of as great a stature as, say, the Prodigal Son or the Unforgiving Servant. Jesus had better and worse days, I suppose, just like everyone else. In any case, they show quite clearly that from the outset, he habitually thought in terms of comparisons and that, whenever he spotted an opening for it, he liked nothing better than to speak about two subjects at the same time.

Here, then, are the "parables before the parables" as they appear in Mark: "I will make you fishers of men" (1:17). "Those who are well do not need a doctor, only those who are sick" (2:17). "Are the wedding guests able to fast while the bridegroom is still with them?" (2:19). "Nobody puts new wine into old wineskins" (2:22). "If a kingdom be divided against itself, it is not possible for that kingdom to stand" (3:24). "If a house be divided against itself, that house will not be able to stand" (3:25). "He looked over the people who were sitting around him and said, 'Look, here are my mother and my brothers'" (3:34).

As I said — and as the chart at the beginning of this chapter makes clear — Matthew and Luke take longer to cover the preliminary ground that Mark traverses in three chapters. They also, of course, include additional material — most notably, perhaps, the "Sermon on the Mount" (or "in the Plain"). But since they omit very little of the Marcan account, the summary given here of the early events of Jesus' ministry is reasonably adequate for them as well. True enough, the other two synoptic Gospels may seem to take some of the "edge" off the story. Many of the passages they add display a Jesus who seems to be a shade less at odds with the authorities than the one portrayed by Mark; events in Matthew and Luke move at a more leisurely pace.

Still, it is fair to say that when all three of the synoptic Gospels arrive at the point where the parables of the kingdom begin (Matt. 13; Mark 4; Luke 8), they are in substantial agreement: they show us Jesus as a Messiah who already fits no known messianic mold, and they set the stage for the utter breaking of the mold that is about to begin.

CHAPTER FIVE

The Sower: The Watershed of the Parables

B y far the largest concentration of the parables of the kingdom occurs in the Gospel of Matthew. Using chapter 13 of Matthew as the principal source, therefore — and simply noting where duplications, omissions, or additions occur in Mark and Luke — we come up with the following list:

Matthew	Name of Parable or Passage	Mark	Luke
13:1-9	The Sower	4:1-9	8:4-8
13:10-17	The purpose of parables	4:10-12	8:9-10
13:18-23	Interpretation of the Sower	4:13-20	8:11-15
5:15	The Lamp	4:21-25	8:16-18
(missing)	The Growing Seed	4:26-29	(missing)
13:24-30	The Weeds	(missing)	(missing)
13:31-32	The Mustard Seed	4:30-32	13:18-19
13:33	The Leaven	(missing)	13:20-21
13:34-35	Jesus says nothing without a parable	4:33-34	(missing)
13:36-43	Interpretation of the Weeds	(missing)	(missing)
13:44	The Treasure Hidden in a Field	(missing)	(missing)
13:45-46	The Pearl of Great Price	(missing)	(missing)
13:47-50	The Net	(missing)	(missing)
13:51-52	The Householder	(missing)	(missing)

The first thing to note about this list is the star billing that the synoptic Gospels give to the parable of the Sower. Not only do all three of them make it the introduction to the first deliberate collection of Jesus' parables; they also devote a disproportionate amount of space to it and to the comments Jesus made in connection with it. For the record, Matthew gives this material twenty-three verses; Mark, twenty-five; and Luke, fifteen. It is well known that a number of biblical critics have found fault with the Sower, and particularly with Jesus' allegorized interpretation of it. It is, they claim, less than a parable in the true sense of the word. The synoptic Gospel writers themselves, however, apparently found nothing deficient about it; and their unanimity in using it as a preface to Jesus' parables strikes me as far more significant than any critical nit-picking. Indeed, I think that in the minds of careful Bible readers, a flag should go up every time the Gospels give such across-the-board treatment to anything.

To take but two other instances (leaving aside such major items as the Triumphal Entry, the Cleansing of the Temple, the Last Supper, the Crucifixion, and the Resurrection), consider the Feeding of the Five Thousand and the Transfiguration. It seems to me that in each case the writers have a clear sense that they are dealing with a major turning point in Jesus' history. Something that heretofore was only (or barely) hinted at is about to be made manifest. Pressures that were scarcely felt are shortly to be given another turn of the developmental screw.

The Feeding of the Five Thousand, as I already noted, is the preface to a fairly explicit shift in Jesus' mind toward left-handed rather than right-handed uses of power. And the Transfiguration (along with Peter's confession, which serves as a prologue to it) is even more clearly presented as a turning point. Prior to it, the synoptics show us a fairly upbeat Jesus who, for all his mysteriousness, can still be taken as a standard-issue, wonder-working Messiah. But after the Transfiguration the story becomes dark and brooding. Jesus says in so many words that his messiahship will inevitably involve death and resurrection; the certainty of that terrible "exodus" of his (as Luke calls it) colors all his subsequent sayings and actions.

The parable of the Sower, therefore, seems to be yet another of the

Gospel "flags." Take, for example, the matter of the "messianic secret." Prior to the Sower, Jesus' reluctance to come right out and declare his messiahship in plain terms was mostly a matter of occasional warnings — both to demons and to the beneficiaries of his signs — not to reveal who he really was. Subsequently, though, it becomes a kind of intentional mystification that he incorporates into his teaching as a deliberate principle. To see that, all you have to do is note the words of Isaiah that Jesus interposes between the Sower and its interpretation: He says that he speaks to the people in parables in order that "seeing they might not see and hearing they might not understand." Till now, in other words, he has been aware in a general way that his kind of messiahship is not what people have been expecting; but from here on he takes this preliminary, mostly negative perception and turns it into a positive developmental principle of his thinking. "Well," he seems to say, "since they've pretty well misunderstood me so far, maybe I should capitalize on that. Maybe I should start thinking up examples of how profoundly the true messianic kingdom differs from their expectations. They think the kingdom will be a parochial, visible proposition — a militarily established theocratic state that will simply be handed to them at some future date. Hm. What if I were to stand every one of those ideas on its head? What if I were to come up with some parables that said the kingdom was catholic, mysterious, already present in their midst, and aggressively demanding their response? Let me see. . . ."

Whatever his thoughts, their outcome was what we have in Matthew 13 and its parallels: the proclamation of exactly such a paradoxical kingdom. Furthermore, these passages show Jesus giving not only a new substance but also a new style to his proclamation — a style that will turn out to be the most important single development in his teaching technique. For the first time (in the Sower and the Weeds), he goes beyond mere comparisons and produces parables that are actually stories.

Admittedly, by comparison with his later refinements of the technique, these early narrative parables may seem a bit thin. But then, early Mozart and early Beethoven are open to the same criticism. What needs to be said for Jesus — and for all other great artists — is that such comparisons are largely irrelevant. The early productions of the masters are marvels in and of themselves; whatever else might be said about them, they are, in retrospect, exactly what seems to have been called for at the point where they appeared. The rest of the *oeuvre* occurred not only after them but also, in some important sense, because of them. Therefore, the parable of the Sower stands quite easily as what the synoptics make it: the great watershed of all Jesus' parables.

Turning to the parable itself, then, the first thing to note is its three-step presentation by the synoptics. Each of them begins with the parable itself, unadorned by any commentary. Then comes a section in which the disciples ask Jesus a question. In Matthew and Mark, they inquire in a general sort of way why he uses parables when he speaks to the people; in Luke, the question is specifically about the meaning of the parable of the Sower. Finally, all three Gospel writers conclude their accounts with Jesus' own allegorical interpretation of the parable.

This three-step sequence, I think, is crucial to an understanding of the Sower. Not only should we take it seriously as the order in which Jesus put forth this material; we should also make a special effort to avoid a common Christian presumption about it. As a result of two thousand years of familiarity, we find it oddly redundant. We assume all too easily that the disciples must have been particularly dense to have had so much trouble understanding such a simple story. To us, the parable seems obvious quite on its own; the interpretation sounds like nothing so much as a belaboring of the obvious. In particular, we are at a loss to explain the insertion, between the two, of the passage about Jesus' reason for speaking in parables. The truth of the matter, however, is that if we had been the original hearers, we would probably have understood it no better than the disciples did. As proof, consider the fact that we quite regularly miss its meaning even now.

Despite what we may think, the parable as Jesus first gives it is not at all obvious to people hearing it for the first time. For one thing, he does not say what it is that he's talking about; he simply launches into a seemingly straightforward story about a farmer whose scattered seed falls into four different situations: some on the road, some on rocky ground, some among thorns, and some on good ground. Obviously, he is talking about something besides agriculture; but as to what that other subject might be, he gives not a single clue. It seems to me that if we are honest with ourselves, we would have come up with exactly the same questions as the disciples. We, right along with them, would have asked either, "Why are you talking in riddles like that?" or, "What on earth is the meaning of what you just said?"

Obligingly, Jesus tells them what the other subject is: the kingdom. (In Matthew, he calls it "the kingdom of the heavens"; in Mark and Luke, "the kingdom of God" — but the phrases are otherwise equivalent.) "To you," he tells the disciples, "it has been given to know the secrets [*tá mystéria* — the hidden things, the unobservable workings] of the kingdom, but for those outside, it is given only in parables."

Then follow two startling statements. The first is "for to him who has, more will be given; and from him who has not, even what he has will be taken away." This seems to me to be one of those hard sayings of Jesus that cries out, not for a prescriptive interpretation, but for a descriptive one. Jesus, though he could be taken as issuing a statement about what God will do to reward or punish those who hear the parables, seems to be more reasonably understood as giving a simple description of the way things are. "If you grasp the fact that the kingdom works in a mystery," he seems to say, "then that very grip will give you more and more understanding; but if you don't grasp that, then everything that happens will make it look as if your plausibility-loving understanding is being deliberately taken from you."

Jesus made such descriptive comments at other times: for example, in Mark 10:23, his "How hard it is for those who have possessions to enter into the kingdom of God" seems more a lament at the way riches get in people's way than a statement that God is going to put obstacles in front of them just because they are rich. At any rate, in this case the descriptive interpretation is the one borne out by the Gospel history: those who had a grip, by faith, on the fact that the mystery was ultimately *Jesus himself* were able to find the Crucifixion/Resurrection the source of ever greater understanding; those who didn't, on the other hand, found it nothing but a colossal unintelligibility.

The second startling statement is another hard saying that likewise makes little sense if given a simplistic, prescriptive interpretation. Jesus justifies his use of parables by quoting Isaiah: "So that they may look and look, yet not see, and listen and listen, yet not understand . . . lest they should turn again and be forgiven." Once again, this is not the announcement of a divine double-cross by which God is going to trick people into a situation where he can finally zap them with condemnation instead of forgiveness (a notion, incidentally, that goes clean against the heart of the Gospel). Rather, it is another one of those sad, head-shaking reflections on the way things are. Jesus thinks about the obtuseness he sees all around him — about the unlikelihood of anybody's getting even a glimmer of the mystery, let alone a grip on it — and the passage from Scripture pops into his mind as the perfect summary: "Isaiah really had it right," he thinks, and then he simply recites the verses out loud.

"But," you wonder, "what about the fact that Jesus then proceeds to interpret the parable of the Sower? Doesn't spelling it out for them like that indicate he really does want them to understand after all?"

There are two ways of answering that. The first is to make a distinction: Jesus gave the *disciples* the interpretation, but left those outside in the dark. On that basis, the proper interpretation seems to be that he was giving the disciples, who already had at least a clue, a bit of the "more" he had spoken of a minute earlier; and by not explaining it to the masses, he was taking away even what they had. But that seems to me a poor answer. For one thing, the disciples don't seem — at least until after the Crucifixion/Resurrection — to have had noticeably more understanding than anybody else. For another, while the masses may not have been given the interpretation the first time around, the fact that the Gospel writers included it in the account guaranteed that they would have it forever after. Therefore, the crux of the interpretation should not be made to lie in the matter of who was given an explanation and who wasn't; rather, it should rest on what Jesus was up to in giving the explanation at all.

That brings us to the second and better way of looking at the passage. To be sure, the usual view of the parable of the Sower is that Jesus, when he allegorizes it for the disciples (Matt. 13:18-23 and parallels), is

59

taking the dark, unintelligible parable he first told and somehow making it simpler and more accessible to their minds (in spite of the fact, please note, that he has just gotten through saying that that is not at all what he intends, at least not for those outside). But such a view has one whopping flaw: the "explanation" of the parable does not in fact make it easier to understand; instead, coming as it does after the flat statement (Matt. 13:11 and parallels) that Jesus is talking about the kingdom, it presents even the disciples' minds with a whole raft of ideas that are harder still to digest.

Jesus' explanation of the Sower, if it is looked at with an open mind, does not reduce what was a complex story to a simple meaning; rather, it takes a merely puzzling fable and drives it for all it's worth in the direction of supremely difficult interpretations. By insisting as it does on what I have referred to as the kingdom's notes of *catholicity, mystery,* and *present actuality* — and by presenting the kingdom as calling for a *response* in the midst of a largely *hostile* world — it causes the lights in the minds of all Jesus' hearers to go out, not on.

Even in ours. For example, take only the very beginning of the explanation. In Mark and Luke (though not in Matthew) Jesus says (if I may conflate the texts) that the sower sows the Word of God. What do we make of that? Do we "get" it? Do we act as a church in a way that takes such an assertion seriously? I submit that we do not.

Whom do we usually identify as the sower? We think it's Jesus, don't we? And we have in our minds an image of him — and then of ourselves as the church — going around sprinkling something called the Word of God on places that haven't yet received it. But that, on any fair reading of Jesus' words, makes no sense at all. The primary meaning of the phrase the *Word of God* in the New Testament, and in Christian theology as well, has got to be one that is consistent with the Johannine teaching that the Word is the one who was in the beginning with God and who is, in fact, God himself. More than that, it has to include the notions that the Word is the one by whom all things were made, that he is the one who, coming into the world, lightens every person, and that he is the one, finally, who became flesh and dwelt among us in Jesus. In short, and above everything else, *the Word* has to mean the eternal Son — God of God, Light of Light, True God of True God — the Second Person of the Holy and Undivided Trinity.

Do you see what that says? It says, first of all, that the Sower is God the Father, not Jesus. What Jesus turns out to be — since he is the Word — is the seed sown. But note what that in turn means. It means that on the plain terms of the parable, Jesus has already, and literally, been sown everywhere in the world — and quite without a single bit of earthly cooperation or even consent. But can you tell me that Christians in general have ever for long acted as if that were the case? Have we not acted instead as if the Word wasn't anywhere until we got there with him? Haven't we conducted far too many missions on the assumption that we were "bringing Jesus" to the heathen, when in fact all we had to bring was the Good News of what the Word — who was already there — had done for them? Haven't we, in short, ended up just as he said we would as a result of his explanation of the Sower? We see and hear and still don't catch on. For twenty centuries we have read that the Word of God is what is sown; yet to judge from the way the church does business most of the time, Jesus might just as well have said that the Word is precisely what is *not* sown.

Therefore, the apparent simplification involved in Jesus' allegorization of the parable of the Sower is nothing of the kind; in fact, his interpretation makes the parable profoundly complex. And we bear witness to that complexity: in these passages, Jesus has kicked the whole mystery of the kingdom so far upstairs that many Christians, for most of the church's history, have missed his point completely and chosen instead to busy themselves with downright contradictions of it. It is time, therefore, to examine the parable in detail — and to note, as we go, how many examples of our inveterate noncomprehension there are in addition to the one just cited.

CHAPTER SIX

The Sower, Continued

O ne concession. You may feel I have given you a fast shuffle by introducing into the parable of the Sower not only the theology of the Word from John 1 but also the full-blown christology of the Nicene Creed. I grant you that, but with a distinction: if it was a shuffle, it was not an illegitimately fast one.

I do not think, of course, that when Jesus told the parable for the first time he necessarily had any of those later theological formulations in his human mind. For all I know, he may even have thought of himself as the sower, and conceived of the Word sown as little more than the Good News of the kingdom. It probably did not occur to him that he was, in fact, that very Word, and I think it quite certain that the Johannine concepts of the Word as God and the Word as made flesh never entered his head.

And yet. There is no way of completely separating the parable of the Sower from the subsequent developments of its themes in other parables. Indeed, if we believe in the inspiration of Scripture, there is nothing finally desirable about divorcing it from the later contributions of, say, John or Paul or any other New Testament writer. For example, on the presumption that the author of the Fourth Gospel was familiar with the parable of the Sower, it is likely that he was not unaware that his development of the doctrine of the Word as divine would bear directly on the interpretation of the Word as sown. At the very least, the

Holy Spirit was definitely aware of it, and as the ultimate genius presiding over the formation of the whole canon of Scripture, the Spirit had no more difficulty working backward than forward. Concepts that he had not fit in by means of an earlier passage, he easily retrofitted, as it were, by means of a later one.

Even if we do no more than confine ourselves to chapter 13 of Matthew, its string of shortish parables of the kingdom develops mightily the mysterious themes sketched in the Sower. If we toss in the parables of grace as well, we find the mystery of the kingdom more and more closely identified with Jesus himself (the parable of the Watchful Servants in Luke 12:35-48). If we include the parables of judgment, we find him saying that the final constitution of the kingdom rests entirely on relationship with him — and on that relationship as operative in the mystery of his catholic presence in all human beings (the parable of the Great Judgment, Matt. 25:31-46). And finally, if we take in the rest of his words and deeds, we find him claiming at the Last Supper that the cup is the New Covenant in his blood (Luke 22:20). In short, we find him asserting that in himself — in his death, resurrection, and ascenion — whatever is necessary for the fullness of the kingdom has been accomplished purely and simply by what he has done.

It seems to me, therefore, that the right way to express both the continuity and the development of Jesus' thoughts about the connection between the kingdom and himself is to say that, from the parable of the Sower to the end of the New Testament, we are watching the opening of a bud into full flower. The early stages of the process may not look much like the final result, but if we examine the entire development carefully, we will find that everything in the end is, one way or another, totally consonant with what was there from the beginning. With that interpretive principle in mind, I return to the parable of the Sower itself — and to the headings of *catholicity, mystery, actuality, hostility,* and *response* under which I have proposed to treat it.

CATHOLICITY

The idea of the catholicity of the kingdom — the insistence that it is at work everywhere, always, and for all, rather than in some places, at some times, and for some people — is an integral part of Jesus' teaching from start to finish. True, at the outset of his ministry it is expressed by little more than his irksome tendency to sit loose to the highly parochial messianic notions of his hearers — by, for example, his breaking of the Sabbath, his consorting with undesirable types, and his constant challenging of the narrow views of the scribes and Pharisees. But it becomes practically the hallmark of his teaching once he begins his use of the parabolic method in earnest.

Not only does he resort, as in the parable of the Leaven (Matt. 13:33), to the occasional illustration that quite literally uses the word "whole" (the *hólon* in *cath*olic); far more often, he sets up his parables in such a way that by their very terms they cover nothing less than the whole world. The device he uses may not be obvious to the casual reader, but once it has been spotted, it can be seen again and again. When Jesus sketches his parabolic characters or circumstances, he often drafts them so inclusively that no one, at any time or in any place, is left out of the scope of his teaching.

Consider some instances. In the Sower, the four kinds of ground listed are clearly meant to cover all sorts and conditions of human beings; there are no cracks between them into which odd cases might fall, and there is no ground beyond them to which his words do not apply. In the parable of the Weeds he simply says that "the field is the world" (Matt. 13:38). In the Net (Matt. 13:47) he says the kingdom catches *all* kinds. And in his later parables, he develops this technique of including everybody into something close to an art form. Let me give you a handful of random examples. In the parable of the Forgiving Father (Luke 15:11-32), the whole human race's relationship to grace is neatly divided between the prodigal and the elder brother. Likewise, in the story of the Pharisee and the Publican (Luke 18:9-14) there is no one in the world who can't be comprehended under one or the other character. And in the parable of the Feast for the King's Son's Wedding (Matt.

22:1-14), there is not a single kind of response to grace that is left out: the characters in the parable — whether they are graciously invited or compelled to attend, whether they accept or reject the King's party — are plainly intended as stand-ins for the great, gray-green, greasy catholic mass of humanity with which God insists on doing business.

In the case of the parable of the Sower, however, there is still another, if more subtle, indication of the note of catholicity. Jesus' parables, even when they were not spoken to anyone outside the small group of the disciples, were set forth, as I have said, in a context of highly parochial ideas about God's relationship with the world. If you have any feeling for the way narrow minds work, you will realize that the Sower, as told, would immediately strike such minds as reeking of the catholicity they had spent their entire religious lives deploring. People who are that narrow do not really listen to what someone says; rather, they sniff at his words — they check them over to spot the squishy, rotten spots through which ideas they hate might seep in.

In the case of the Sower, they would have had a field day. First, by making no specific reference to Israel, Jesus feeds their suspicions about his lack of proper parochialism. Of course, the parable could perfectly well be about God's relationship with the Jews alone, but for suspicious minds, *could be* is never an acceptable substitute for *has got to be*. They want an airtight case, not a leaky one; what Jesus gave them has enough holes in it to let in all the Gentiles in the world.

Second, their nervous-Nelly fear of a truly catholic kingdom leads them to an even deeper reason for distrust. Not only has Jesus told a story on whose terms the Gentiles might be brought in; worse yet, he has told one that just as plainly gives no guarantee that the chosen people might not be left out. By skirting the whole Jew-Gentile issue, you see, Jesus has, in fact, raised it more strongly than ever in his hearers' minds. What he *says*, they can't very well argue with, but what it *smells like* — ah, *that* they are not about to take sitting down.

Am I putting too much weight on this? I don't think so. At the end of his interpretation of the Sower, Jesus adds a few remarks (Mark 4:21-25 and parallels). All of them, it strikes me, are rather edgy. He does not sound like a cool rabbi who has delivered an unexceptionably pious lesson; instead, he sounds like someone who has just said something he knows is offensive but who is bound and determined to make it stick.

The first remark — "Does anyone ever bring in a lamp and put it under the bed?" — seems to me roughly equivalent to "What am I supposed to do, hide the truth just because people don't like it?" His second — "There is nothing hid, except to be made manifest" — has to have been offensive to those who believed that God had already disclosed, *to them*, everything that really mattered. His third — "He who has ears to hear, let him hear" — sounds like nothing so much as "I dare you to think about all these implications that are terrifying you." His fourth — "Watch how you hear: the way you measure out judgment will be the way it's measured out to you, and even more severely" — practically makes my case all by itself. And his final remark, in which he repeats his preface to the interpretation of the Sower — "To him who has, more will more be given; and from him who has not, even what he has will be taken away" — is entirely too vague about the identity of the several "whos" to be of much comfort to anybody.

But the real clincher of the case for the catholicity of the Sower is the collection of parables following in Matthew 13:24-52 (and parallels) that so clearly develops the catholicity of the kingdom. The synoptic writers plainly feel that all this material is of a piece: even if one or the other of the notes I have listed is merely adumbrated in the parable of the Sower, each of them, as the succeeding parables unfold, is given its turn at a full-dress exposition. Therefore, leaving the rest of the subject of catholicity to be treated when we look at those parables individually, I proceed to the next of the notes as it is manifested in the Sower.

MYSTERY

I have made it clear that I consider Jesus' ever-increasing preference for left-handed rather than right-handed uses of power to be the most significant development of his thinking over the course of his ministry. But it is in the parable of the Sower that he takes the first quiet but major step in the direction that will eventually lead him into the heart of

66

the paradox of power. And not only him. If we pay close attention to the Sower, we, too, will be led the same way: we, too, will come to see the apparent inaction of the Cross, the only minimally noticeable fact of the Resurrection, and the totally disappointing episode of the Ascension as the final flowering of the Good News he proclaimed from the very beginning.

I refer, of course, to his use of the imagery of *seed* and *sowing* as the principal analogue in the parable. To be sure, this is not the only place he refers to them; his use of *spóros* (seed), of *speírein* (to sow), and of *kókkos* (seed, grain) occurs in other passages (Matt. 13:24-27; Matt. 13:31 and parallels; Matt. 17:20 and parallels; and John 12:24). But this is the first and thus the most significant reference from the point of view of development.

Consider the imagery of seed. First of all, seeds are disproportionately small compared with what they eventually produce. In the case of herbs — which, for some reason, Jesus took special delight in — they are in fact almost ridiculously small. Anyone who has planted thyme or savory knows the strange sensation of practically losing sight of the seed after it has been dropped into the furrow: you might as well have sown nothing, for all you can observe. And what does that say about the Word of God that the Sower sows? Well, it certainly does not say what we would have said. Left to our own devices we would probably have likened the Word's advent to a thunderclap, or to a fireworks display, or to something else we judged sufficiently unmistakable to stand in for our notion of a pushy, totally right-handed God. Instead, this parable says that the true coming of the Word of God, even if you see it, doesn't look like very much — and that when it does finally get around to doing its real work, it is so mysterious that it can't even be found at all.

That is the second thing about seeds: they disappear. In the obvious sense, they do so because of their need to be covered over with earth in order to function. (Think of the light that *that* sheds on the "messianic secret": Jesus is taking what may have been only an instinctive dislike for publicity and turning it into a theological principle.) But in the profound sense, they disappear because once they are thus covered, they eventually become not only unrecognizable but undiscoverable as well: as far as their own being is concerned, they simply die and disappear.

Think of what that says about Jesus and how it reechoes through his whole ministry. He, as the Word, comes to his own and his own receive him not. He is despised. He is the stone the builders rejected. He is ministered to, not in his own recognizable form but in the sick, the imprisoned, and the generally down-and-out. And to cap his whole career as the Word sown in the field of the world, he dies, rises, and vanishes. His entire work proceeds as does the work of a seed: it takes place in a mystery, in secret — in a way that, as Luther said, can neither be known nor felt, but only *believed, trusted.*

Once again, that is not our idea of how a respectable divine operation ought to be run. We would rather have causalities and agencies that were a bit more proportionate to their results. Given our druthers, our pet illustration of the kingdom would probably be a giant nail — driven into the world, appropriately enough, by a giant hammer in the hand of a giant God. Something noisy and noticeable. But a seed? Oh, come now.

ACTUALITY

If we have difficulty adjusting to a Word of God who works as minimally and mysteriously as a seed, we will have even more difficulty with the next point to be made about seeds, namely, that they actually do work. The sower in the parable is depicted in the act of sowing. He is not sitting in his armchair reading seed catalogs in February; he is not tilling and fertilizing the soil in March; and above all, he is not standing in the garden in May, simply thinking about taking the seeds out of their packages. If he were shown doing any of those things, we might fairly conclude that the power of the Word — like the power of seeds under similar circumstances — was only *virtually* present in the world. We might assume, in other words, that it would not achieve *actual* effectiveness until some further steps were taken.

In the terms of the parable as told, however, there is no room for such virtualism. The seed, and therefore the Word, is fully in action in and of itself at every step of the story. Everything necessary for its perfect work is *in the works* from the start. Even the apparent contradictions of its effectiveness that appear in the course of the parable turn out not to deny that effectiveness at all.

First, consider the seed that falls on the road and is eaten by birds. That is no denial of its properties as seed. Seeds, from an ecological point of view, have purposes other than the reproduction of species: they are attractive to birds; they are nourishing to almost all animals; and they are quite literally the spice of human life. To be sure, Jesus equates the birds with the devil. But the comparison, while perhaps hard on the birds, is by no means unflattering either way. The demons knew who Jesus was even when people didn't. Therefore, just as the birds recognize seed for what it is even if the pavement doesn't, so the devil recognizes the power of the Word even when human beings don't. Furthermore, just as the effective power of seeds to reproduce themselves is in no way seriously inhibited by the depredations of the birds (in fact, animal ingestion and excretion of seeds is one of nature's ways of insuring their distribution), so too the effective power of the Word is not lessened even though the devil may try to digest it for his own purposes and turn it into offal. The Word, like the seed, still works on its own terms.

Next, however, consider the seed that falls into the other three situations. In all of them — whether on the rocky ground, in the thorny underbrush, or in the well-prepared soil — the seed actually does its proper, reproductive work: it springs up. True, there are differences in the outcome of that work, and I shall have something to say about them by and by. But what needs to be emphasized here is that the differences can never be interpreted as meaning that the operative power of the seed — or the operative power of the Word — is in any way dependent on circumstantial cooperation.

Perversely, though, we seem to prefer that interpretation. The history of Christian thought is riddled with virtualism. "Sure," we have said, "the Lamb of God has taken away all the sins of the world." But then we have proceeded to give the impression that unless people did something special to activate it, his forgiveness would remain only virtually, not actually, theirs. Think of some of the things we have said to people. We have told them that unless they confessed to a priest, or had the sacrifice of the mass applied specifically to their case, or accepted Jesus in the correct denominational terms — or hit the sawdust trail, did penance, cried their eyes out, or straightened up and flew right — the seed, who is the Word present everywhere in all his forgiving power, might just as well not really have been sown.

Once again, this note of power *actually present* — this flat precluding of even a hint of virtualism in the proclamation of the Gospel — comes through even more clearly in the rest of the parables of the kingdom, especially when they involve, as they do here, the imagery of seeds. Before coming to those, however, let me end this consideration of the Sower by dealing with my last two headings at the same time.

HOSTILITY AND RESPONSE

The idea that the Good News of the kingdom is proclaimed in a hostile environment is written all over the New Testament. Whether we look at the demons who recognize Jesus or at the religious establishment that refuses to, it is quite plain that antagonism is every bit as much the soil of the Word as is acceptance. The point is, literally, crucial: the supreme act by which the Word declares the kingdom in all its power is not an act at all but a death on the cross inflicted on him by his enemies. Therefore, whatever else needs to be said about hostility to the Word — about its power and function in the Gospels or about the presumed menace it poses in our own day — the first thing to be insisted on is that all the antagonism in the world has already been aced out by Jesus. Not overcome by force as we would have done — not bludgeoned into submission or out of existence — but precisely *aced out:* finessed, tricked into doing God's thing when all the while it thought it was doing its own thing.

Consider the devil first. Christians have spent too much time in one or the other of two pointless pursuits. Either they have denied the reality of praeter-human evil, or they have given the Old Deceiver far more time and attention than he deserves. This is no place to settle the question of the existence of Satan and his henchmen, so, along with Scripture, I shall simply assume it. But this is also no place to get upset about it, to act as if the hosts of evil were not already, in the mystery of his death and resurrection, beaten by Jesus. Like the birds that nibble on the seeds and then pass them out of their bodies unimpaired, the devil has no power against the Word. Whatever warfare might have been necessary against him has already been undertaken and won. "My sheep hear my voice," Jesus says, "and I give them eternal life, . . . they shall never perish, and no one shall pluck them out of my hand" (John 10:27-28).

Nobody, in other words — not the devil, not the world, not the flesh, not even ourselves — can take us away from the Love that will not let us go. We can, of course, squirm in his grip and despise his holding of us, and we can no doubt get ourselves into one hell of a mess by doing so. But if he is God the Word who both makes and reconciles us, there is no way — no way, literally, even in hell — that we will ever find ourselves anywhere else than in the very thick of both our creation and our reconciliation. All the evil in the universe, whether from the devil or from us, is now and ever shall be just part of the divine ecology.

And the Sower says that. The seed eaten by birds is as much seed as the seed that produced a hundredfold. The snatching of the Word by the devil — and the rejection of it by the shallow and the choking of it by the worldly — all take place *within* the working of the kingdom, not prior to it or outside of it. It is the Word alone, and not the interference with it, that finally counts. True enough, and fittingly enough, the most obvious point in the whole parable is that the fullest enjoyment of the fruitfulness of the Word is available only to those who interfere with it least. But even in making that point, Jesus still hammers away at the sovereignty and sole effectiveness of the Word. Those on the good ground, he says, are those who simply hear the Word, accept it, and bear fruit: some thirty-, some sixty-, and some a hundredfold. It's not that they *do* anything, you see; rather, it's that they *don't* do things that get in the Word's way. It's the Word, and the Word alone, that does all the rest.

71

One note in passing: In our day and age, we have come to understand that seeds don't do all the work — that the environment, materially speaking, contributes almost one hundred percent of what is contained in the full-grown, fructifying plant. But in Jesus' day, and for a very long time after it, that was not the common supposition. However much we might be tempted to drag human contributions into our interpretation of the parable, therefore, the story *as told* rests squarely on the sole agency of both the seed and the Word.

Nevertheless, it remains true that *response* to the sowing of the Word is made the final thrust of the parable (though even at that, the thirty-, sixty-, one hundredfold yield — based on no apparent differences in the good ground — is tossed in as a further indication of both the Word's power and its mysterious sovereignty over the whole process). In speaking about response, however, we need to take note of a peculiarity in Jesus' explanation of the parable. He clearly says that the seed sown is the Word of God. But when he comes to the results of the sowing, he is a bit more vague: he refers to those who respond as "the ones along the road," or as "what was sown among thorns," or as "those sown upon the good ground," and so on (Mark 4:15-20).

At first blush, these phrases seem to refer to the seed; but unless we want to welsh on the identity of the seed as the Word, we should probably read them as referring not to the seed but to either the situation into which it was sown (as in the case of those along the path) or to the plants that grew from it (as in the cases of the rest).

Obviously, the several responses listed in the parable and in its interpretation are meant to represent, in terms of either soil conditions or resultant plants, the various kinds of human behavior that can be offered in response to the proclamation of the kingdom. The Word, of course, takes care of itself, infallibly doing what it should in every case; it is no skin off its nose if only the last response listed produces fruitful results. But it is definitely skin off our noses if we respond in ways analogous to one or another of the first three.

The whole purpose of the coming of the Word into the world is to produce people in whom the power of the kingdom will bear fruit. But since the kingdom is fully, albeit mysteriously, present in the Word (since, in other words, the Word's fruitfulness is not in question but is already an accomplished fact), it is chiefly for our sakes that the parable enjoins the necessity of response. The biggest difference made by responses to the Word is the difference they make to us, for us, and in us. They decide not whether the Word will achieve his purposes but whether we will enjoy his achievement — or find ourselves in opposition to it.

Admittedly, I am leaning once again in the direction of a descriptive rather than a prescriptive interpretation of Jesus' words. What he is saying in this parable seems to me to be of a piece with all his other loving, if often sad, commentaries on our condition. He is not threatening some kind of retaliation by the Word against people who fail to make the best response; rather, he is almost wistfully portraying what we miss when we fall short and fail to bear fruit.

And there is the Word. In the case of even the most promising of the deficient responses to the sowing of the Word (namely, in the verse about the seed that fell among thorns — Matt. 13:22; Mark 4:18), the result specified is that it becomes *ákarpos,* without fruit, unfruitful. For a plant, the failure to bear fruit is not a punishment visited on it by the seed, but an unhappy declination on the plant's part from what the seed had in mind for it. It is a missing of its own fullness, its own maturity — even, in some deep sense, of its own life. So too with us. If we make deficient responses to the Word, we do not simply get ourselves in dutch; rather, we fail to become ourselves at all.

A look at the word *karpós* (fruit) as Jesus and the New Testament writers use it provides insight. The concordance citations are too numerous to list here, but two in particular stand out. The first is the discourse in which Jesus calls himself the true vine and characterizes his disciples as branches (John 15). The point he makes is complementary to the parable of the Sower: as the branch is not able to bear fruit unless it remains in the vine, so they cannot bear fruit unless they remain in him. In other words, the response most needed is that of simply abiding in the power of the Word himself — which means, in terms of the Sower, neither putting obstacles in the way of the seed nor involving ourselves in the search for other, more plausible responses to it.

The other passage that reinforces the lesson about response in the parable of the Sower is the famous one of Galatians 5:16-26 in which Paul distinguishes between the works of the flesh and the fruits of the Spirit. The *works* are a list of disastrous character traits that the apostle says result from our trying to achieve the fullness of life in our own way: that is, *according to the flesh* (not just the body, please note, but the entire range of human responses — be they physical, mental, or even spiritual — that proceed from our inveterately right-handed wrong-headedness). They are a grim shelf-ful of products, hazardous not only to our health but also to our education and welfare: among other things, they include fornication, witchcraft, strife, envy, and murder. The *fruits* of the Spirit, however — those results that are not manufactured by our plausible and deliberate efforts but simply allowed to grow unimpeded under the guidance of the Spirit who takes what is the Word's and shows it to us — are, every one of them, truly human traits: love, joy, peace, longsuffering, gentleness, goodness, faith, meekness, temperance. They are not results of, or rewards for, our frantic efforts to make ourselves right; rather, they are the very rightness for which our nature was made, bestowed upon us as a free gift.

It is in the light of such passages as these that the parable of the Sower needs to be seen. It does indeed call for a response from us; but that response is to be one that is appropriate not to the accomplishing of a *work* but to the bearing of *fruit*. The goal it sets for us is not the amassing of deeds, good or bad, but simply the unimpeded experiencing of our own life as the Word abundantly bestows it upon us. And that, as I said, is entirely fitting; because the parable is told to us by none other than the Word himself, whose final concern is nothing less than the reconciled you and me that he longs to offer his heavenly Father. He did not become flesh to display his own virtuosity; he did so to bring us home to his Father's house and sit us down as his bride at the supper of the Lamb. He wills us whole and happy, you see; and the parable of the Sower says he will unfailingly have us so, if only we don't get in the way.

CHAPTER SEVEN

The Lamp and the Growing Seed

B efore proceeding to the rest of the parables of the kingdom, I think it is important to take note of the peculiar discontinuity with which they are presented in the Gospels. The writers, instead of running through them one after another, interrupt the natural sequence of these parables in a way that seems illogical — and with a frequency that is surprising.

For one thing, Jesus' interpretations of both the Sower and the Weeds are not given, as we might expect, right at the end of the original parables. Rather, they come only after other material has intervened. I shall have more to say about this when we look at the Weeds (which is separated from its explanation not by an answer to a lone question but by two additional parables plus a reiteration of the observation that Jesus said nothing without a parable). All I want to say here is that my own preferred way of dealing with these insertions is to take them quite seriously — to assume that either Jesus or the Gospel writers felt they were necessary to the argument these parables make for the kingdom and to try to fathom just what that necessity was.

But there is another and even more pervasive pattern of interruption. Short comments on Jesus' use of the parabolic method, or on its effects, are thrust into the accounts remarkably often. In Matthew, they are inserted at 13:10-17 (between the Sower and its interpretation); at

13:34-35 (just before the interpretation of the Weeds); and at 13:51-52 (where Jesus asks the disciples if they have understood him).

In Mark, the interruptions are at 4:10-12 (parallel to Matt. 13:10-17); and at 4:21-25 (right after the interpretation of the Sower and before the Growing Seed and the Mustard Seed). In Luke, we find them at 8:9-10 (again, parallel to Matt. 13:10-17); at 8:16-18 (parallel to Mark 4:21-25); and at 8:19-21 (where Jesus' relatives are unable to reach him on account of the crowd).

Once again, my disposition is to try to make something of these insertions rather than simply shrug them off as evidence of a not too successful scissors-and-paste job. In any case, the germane passage here is Jesus' parabolic remark about not putting a lamp under a bushel or a bed but on a lampstand — Mark 4:21-22, Luke 8:16-17, and the parallels in Matthew 5:15 and 10:26 — and it seems to me to repay that kind of serious attention. Coming as it does immediately after his explanation of the Sower, I feel it is best expounded by tying it as closely as possible to the notes of catholicity, mystery, actuality, and so on, that he has already begun to attribute to the kingdom.

What do I come up with, then, on the subject of the Lamp? I find that it refers quite nicely to the difficult, scarcely obvious exposition of the parable of the Sower he has just given. The Lamp is the Good News of the sowing of the Word who is the all-sufficient cause of the kingdom; but unless that Lamp is set squarely on the lampstand of a relentlessly paradoxical interpretation of the kingdom, its light simply will not be seen. All the easier, more plausible interpretations — those that try to expound the kingdom as parochial, or nonmysterious, or merely virtual — are just so many bushel baskets or beds that can only hide the Lamp's light. And if I add to that my habitual ringing in of John whenever possible, an even fuller meaning of the passage becomes clear: Jesus himself is the Lamp. The incarnate Word — the Light that, coming into the world, lightens every human being — cannot be recognized as the Light he is except on the lampstand of a properly paradoxical, left-handed interpretation of his person and work. Stand him on anything else, and you see not just one more dim bulb like the rest of us; you see no saving Light at all.

Finally, though — as if to reassure us that the paradox by which the hard, almost hidden interpretation is worth the patience it takes to grasp it — he rounds out this particular interruption of himself with an insistence that his apparent hiding of the truth in parables is not an end but a means. "Nothing is hid," he says, "except in order to be made manifest; nor is anything made secret but that it might become plain" (Mark 4:22). The kingdom, like the sown Word, is in the works, and it will settle for nothing less than full manifestation. We are not waiting for its power to come; we believe that it is already here — and that it will inevitably have its perfect and utterly triumphant work.

Fascinatingly enough, this last note convinces me of something else: Jesus' interruptions of himself, far from being mere insertions of stray material, turn out in fact to be artfully constructed bridges to the next development. For as his remarks about the Lamp appear in Mark, they not only wrap up the material on the Sower; they also form the prologue to the first of the explicit parables of the kingdom, namely, the parable of the Growing Seed. Without missing even a beat, Jesus proceeds to give a stunning illustration of the very points he has just been developing.

Consider the Growing Seed. The parable appears only in Mark (4:26-29); and while it once again uses the images of seed and sowing, it contains some remarkable differences from the Sower. First and foremost, it ties the imagery expressly, within the parable itself, to the kingdom: "The kingdom of God," Jesus says, "is as if a man should cast seed upon the ground." Note the strength, even the extravagance, of the comparison: the kingdom is presented as the very thing sown. The kingdom is not the result of the sowing of something quite different from itself (in which it would be contained only virtually, as a plant is contained in a seed); rather, the kingdom as such is present, in all its power, right from the start. Moreover, by the very force of the imagery of sowing, the seed is clearly to be understood as having been sown *in this world,* squarely in the midst of every human and even every earthly condition. This emphasis on the kingdom as a worldly, not just an otherworldly piece of business was already clear in the Sower; but Jesus' repetition of it here as well as later makes me want to underscore it.

Christians have often been lamentably slow to grasp the profound secularity of the kingdom as it is proclaimed in the Gospels. Because Matthew (though not Mark or Luke) uses the phrase "the kingdom of *heaven*" — and perhaps because the greatest number of parables of the kingdom do indeed occur in Matthew — we have frequently succumbed to the temptation to place unwarranted importance on the word "heaven." In any case, we have too often given in to the temptation to picture the kingdom of heaven as if it were something that belonged more properly elsewhere than here. Worse yet, we have conceived of that elsewhere almost entirely in "heavenly" rather than in earthly terms. And all of that, mind you, directly in the face of Scripture's insistences to the contrary.

In the Old Testament, for example, the principal difference between the gods of the heathen and the God who, as Yahweh, manifested himself to Israel was that, while the pagan gods occupied themselves chiefly "up there" in the "council of the gods," Yahweh showed his power principally "down here" on the stage of history. The pagan deities may have had their several fiefdoms on earth — pint-size plots of tribal real estate, outside which they had no interest or dominion, and even inside which they behaved mostly like absentee landlords; but their real turf was in the sky, not on earth. Yahweh, however, claimed two distinctions. Even on their heavenly turf, he insisted, it was he and not they who were in charge. And when he came down to earth, he acted as if the whole place was his own backyard. In fact, it was precisely by his overcoming them on utterly earthly ground, in and through his chosen people, that he claimed to have beaten them even on their heavenly home court. What he did on earth was done in heaven, and vice versa, because he alone, as the One Yahweh, was the sole proprietor of both.

In the New Testament, that inseparability of heavenly concerns from earthly ones is, if anything, even more strenuously maintained. The kingdom Jesus proclaims is *at hand, planted here, at work in this world.* The Word sown is none other than *God himself incarnate.* By his death and resurrection at Jerusalem in A.D. 29, he reconciles everything, everywhere, to himself — whether they be things on earth or things in heaven. And at the end, when he makes all things new, he makes not just a new heaven but a new earth — a glorified re-creation of nothing less than his old stamping ground. The Bible's last chapters proclaim a heaven and earth more inextricably intertwined than ever. Whatever else the "New Jerusalem" may signify, it says plainly that the final "heaven" will be as earthy as the eschatological earth will be heavenly — and that that's the way it is going to be forever.

Indeed, it is worth noting that most uses of the words "heaven" or "heavenly" in the New Testament bear little relation to the meanings we have so unscripturally attached to them. For us, heaven is an un-earthly, humanly irrelevant condition in which bed-sheeted, paper-winged spirits sit on clouds and play tinkly music until their pipe-cleaner halos drop off from boredom. As we envision it, it contains not one baby's bottom, not one woman's breast, not even one man's bare chest — much less a risen basketball game between glorified "shirts" and "skins." But in Scripture, it is a city with boys and girls playing in the streets; it is buildings put up by a Department of Public Works that uses amethysts for cinder blocks and pearls as big as the Ritz for gates; and indoors, it is a dinner party to end all dinner parties at the marriage supper of the Lamb. It is, in short, earth wedded, not earth jilted. It is the world as the irremovable apple of God's eye.

And that (to come to the end of a not unearthly digression) is what Jesus is proclaiming in the parable of the Growing Seed. The kingdom itself, he insists, is the very thing that is sown. And in the rest of the parable, he drives home, with a clarity matched almost nowhere else, the absolute sovereignty of that kingdom over the earth it wills to make its home. There are no references at all here to the dangers that hostility might pose for it; nor are there even any references to the detrimental or beneficial effects of the various responses that human beings might make to it. Instead, Jesus ignores these matters entirely. As Jesus depicts it, once the man in the parable has sown the seed, he does nothing more than mind his own and not the seed's business. He goes to bed at night and gets up in the morning — and then he shops at the supermarket, unclogs the sink, whips up a gourmet supper, plays chamber music with his friends, watches the eleven o'clock news, and goes to bed again.

And he does that and nothing but that, day after day after day — while all along, the seed that is the kingdom sprouts and grows in a way that he himself simply *knows nothing about.*

But then comes one of the most startling statements in all of Scripture: *Automátē hē gḗ karpophoreí,* Jesus says; the earth (and all of it, mind you: good, bad, or indifferent) bears fruit *of itself,* automatically. Just put the kingdom into the world, he says in effect; put it into any kind of world — not only into a world of hotshot responders or spiritual pros, but into a world of sinners, deadbeats, and assorted other poor excuses for humanity (which, interestingly enough, is the only world available anyway) — and it will come up a perfect kingdom all by itself: "first the blade, then the ear, then the full grain in the ear." It takes its time about it, to be sure; but the time it takes is entirely its own, not anyone else's. There is not a breath about crop failure, any more than there is about the depredations of the devil or the knuckleheadedness of humanity. There is only the proclamation of a catholic sowing that, mysteriously but effectively, results in a catholic growth toward a catholic harvest.

At this point, though, I detect in your mind a premature readiness to utter a sigh of relief: "Finally!" you think. "The harvest! And about time! Enough of this dangerously indiscriminate catholicity. Too much of this silence about all the criminal types who will obviously take this omnium-gatherum gospel as permission to go right on committing their felonies, even in the New Jerusalem. At last, Jesus is about to threaten the world with the eschatological comeuppance we know and love so well."

In this parable, however, your mind's desire is doomed to disappointment. To be sure, there are other passages (notably the parable of the Weeds) where Jesus does indeed use the word *therismós,* "harvest," to introduce the notion of millennial police work. But not here. Here he simply contents himself with a last line not one bit more discriminating than the rest of the parable: "But when the fruit is ripe, at once he puts in the sickle, because the harvest has come." Not a word, you see, about separating the wheat from the weeds. Not a syllable about getting the baddies out of the kingdom and burning them up in fire unquenchable. Why?

You could argue, of course, that the omission is a space- and time-saving one — that because Jesus supplies those details elsewhere, they should simply be understood as applying here too. But I don't like that. Jesus, it seems to me, achieved his status as a world-class teacher not only by what he put into his utterances but by what he left out of them as well. Whenever he felt himself in the presence of minds that were itching to jump to their favorite conclusions about how God should run the universe, he deliberately refused to give them a platform to jump from. As I tried to show earlier, he did that in the parable of the Sower when he paradoxically raised the Jew-Gentile question by not raising it at all, thus depriving his hearers of the assurances they felt a proper Messiah should give. And he does it even more clearly in John 6 where the whole dialogue between him and the Judean Jews is one long exercise in messianic foot-dragging — with Jesus insisting right to the end on giving them naught for their comfort.

And that, it strikes me, is just what he is doing here. Every last man Jack (or Jill) of us — and every bit as much back then as right now — is an eschatology junkie. We are so consumed with the idea that wrongs must be set right and that evildoers must be run out of the New Jerusalem on a chiliastic rail that we convince ourselves the Holy City can actually be brought into being by means of cops-and-robbers games. Our favorite solutions to the world's deep and humanly intractable problems with sin are punching people in the nose, locking them up in the slammer, and — failing all else — buying them a one-way ride out of town in the electric chair. Worse yet, when we come to the point (as we always do) of giving God advice about how to deal eternally with the same problems, we simply concoct eternal variations of the same procedures.

I am aware, of course, that Scripture quite plainly speaks of just those sorts of activities on the part of God. And even though you might not expect me to say so after that last tirade, I am perfectly willing to take such right-handed strong-arm stuff seriously: that is, as just as inspired as — but not, please note, as more inspired than — the Bible's other, more left-handed ways of talking about the ultimate triumph of divine justice. But. But, but, but: *that is not what we are talking about here.*

And for even more of a *but:* that is the very subject that Jesus is scrupulously avoiding at the end of the parable of the Growing Seed. His subject is the utterly fundamental one of *how* the kingdom grows, of *the means by which* the city is built. It is not the relatively minor one of how the Divine Police Department keeps muggers off the streets of the New Jerusalem.

The kingdom grows, he says, because the kingdom is already planted. It grows of itself and in its own good time. Above all, it grows *we know not how.* Any bright ideas we might have about the subject will always and everywhere be the wrong ideas. Indeed, their wrongness will be proved simply by our having them; because if the kingdom could have been made to grow in this world by bright ideas, it would have sprouted up all over the place six times a day ever since Adam. But it never did and it never will, except in a mystery that remains resolutely beyond our moralizing, score-evening comprehension.

In my view, it is for just that reason that the Growing Seed has nothing in it about God's ultimate cleanup operation. Jesus withholds from his hearers at this point anything that might distract them from the saving mystery and bog them down once again in hopeless plausibilities. Admittedly, in the next group of kingdom passages (the Weeds, the Mustard Seed, the Leaven, the comment about Jesus' saying nothing without a parable, and the interpretation of the Weeds), he does indeed give his hearers grist for their eschatological morality mills. But — and I think this will be borne out as we proceed — he does it with at least some reluctance. In Mark and Luke, of course, he does it not at all at this juncture. On balance, therefore, the synoptics make out a fair case for looking a lot longer and harder at the constitution of the kingdom before we engross ourselves in its prison statistics.

CHAPTER EIGHT

The Weeds

Perhaps the best way to deal with the portion of the Gospel that runs from Jesus' parable of the Weeds through his eventual interpretation of it (Matt. 13:24-43) is simply to proceed through the material in order, noting as we go both the points that corroborate the general approach I have been taking and those that call it into question.

Jesus' first version of the parable of the Weeds, like his first version of the Sower, is a straight story about farming: he resists yet again the temptation to say what it means until after he has unburdened himself of other, and seemingly unconnected remarks. Farmers and gardeners, of course, may raise an eyebrow at the story's strictly agricultural aspects. The practice of not pulling out weeds until harvest time is no way to run a farm. All that such neglect insures is two undesirable results. First, it contributes to the choking out of the good plants that Jesus deplored in the Sower; second, it guarantees a bumper crop of unwanted weed seeds to plague the next season's planting. Nevertheless, the parable as told simply flouts these truths of agronomy in order to make its theological point. Maybe Jesus was just not as good a gardener as he was a carpenter (his comments about building houses on proper foundations [Matt. 7:24-27] sound a lot more like the words of an expert). In any case, his real trade was Messiah-ing, about which, fittingly enough, he wrote the book. Back, then, to the way he actually begins the parable of the Weeds.

"Another parable he put before them," the Gospel says (Matthew, as if to underscore the cohesiveness of the whole string of kingdom parables, starts three of them with the word *állē*, "another," and two more with *pálin*, "again"); "the kingdom of heaven may be likened to a man sowing good seed in his field."

At first blush, Jesus seems to be shifting away here from his insistence (for instance, in the Growing Seed) that the kingdom as such is what is sown. Even more, he seems to be setting up the story in such a way that, when he does come to interpret it, he will be forced to represent himself not as the Word or the seed sown but simply as the one who does the sowing. However, the phrase he uses here for "good seed" is a bit of a departure from the references he has so far made to the subject. In the Greek, it is *kalón spérma,* and a brief look at the concordance turns up some fascinating information.

In the New Testament, there are some forty occurrences of the word *spérma.* In the old days, it was common practice to English all of them with the word "seed"; but *spérma* only rarely refers to the actual thing planted. Indeed, by my reckoning, there are only four such airtight references: two in the first telling of the parable of the Weeds (Matt. 13:24 and 27) and two in the immediately following parable of the Mustard Seed (Matt. 13:32 and Mark 4:31) where Jesus says that when the seed is sown, it is *mikróteron . . . pántōn tṓn spermátōn,* "smaller than all the seeds." By contrast, in most of its occurrences (over thirty of them), it is used to refer not strictly to seed as seed but to *the progeny that comes from seed. Spérma Abraám,* "seed of Abraham," is the commonest citation; it refers obviously not to Abraham's sperm cells but to his descendants — that is, to what grows from the seed rather than to the seed itself.

It seems to me that it is ultimately this force that the word *spérma* takes on in the parable of the Weeds — and for that matter, in the remaining handful of places where it does not refer to the descendants of human beings. True enough, when Jesus initially tells the parable in its unexplained form, *planted seed* is the fairest interpretation of the word; but just as plainly, when he comes to identify the "good seed" in his allegorization of the parable (Matt. 13:38), he makes it refer more to what has grown up as a result than to what was planted to begin with. "The good seed," he says, "are the *sons of the kingdom*," that is, the off-spring of the kingdom, those whose lives are the flowering and fructify-ing of what was sown by the Son of Man. Interestingly, too, it is just this usage of "good seed" (and "bad seed") that eventually made its way into English: "he's bad seed," for example, refers not simply to a man's origin but to his subsequent character and actions.

At any rate, whatever sense we assign to *spérma* at this point, there is no question about the force of the word "sow": Jesus is referring to the broadcast planting of an entire field. Once again, he presents the action of his parable in a way that necessitates a sounding of the note of cath-olicity in its interpretation. By speaking only of one man's field, and by avoiding any hint of a partial sowing of that field, he clearly indicates that there are no places — and by extension, no times and no people — in which the kingdom is not already at work.

But then Jesus continues with a whole string of fascinating details: "While everyone was sleeping," he says, "the man's enemy came and sowed *zizánia*, weeds, among the wheat and went away." Note first the "sleeping." What is referred to is not culpable napping on the job but, as in the Growing Seed, the normal nocturnal habits of even the most dedicated farmers. They have no duties to the sown crop that need to be done at night; every positive measure called for has already been done by day. Other things being equal, the seed in the ground will do the rest of the job entirely on its own. The mystery, in other words — the mystery of both the sowing of seed and the sowing of the kingdom — can, will, and does fend nicely for itself, thank you very much. Further-more, while Jesus develops the imagery of the parable of the Sower in such a way that the mystery itself seems in danger (from the birds, from the rocky ground, from the thorns), the parable of the Weeds gives no hint of such perils. From start to finish, the working of the seed is not seriously threatened at all.

Something does go wrong, of course, but it is important to be clear about how the parable presents it: the man's *enemy* comes and sows weeds. But since the weeds in no way seem to interfere with the growing of the wheat, it is the word "enemy" that should become the crux of the interpretation. It is not danger to the crop's growth but inconvenience to the farmer and his servants that lies at the heart of the agricultural-theological dilemma in the parable. The servants, naturally enough, have the most intense feelings about the inconvenience, and it is they who have the bright idea of taking immediate and direct action against the weeds. The farmer, though, seems to have in mind some grander strategy — one that involves not fighting a minor battle against transitory inconveniences but winning an entire war, once and for all, against his enemy.

In other words, the parable says that *doing nothing* is, for the time being, the preferred response to evil. It insists that the mysterious, paradoxical tactic of noninterference is the only one that can be effective in the time frame within which the servants are working. No matter that they may have plausible proposals for dealing with the menace as they see it; their very proposals, the farmer tells them, are more of a menace than anything else. To be sure, he goes on to assure them that at some later, riper time, he will indeed interfere to a fare-thee-well with his enemy's plans. But the principal thrust of the parable, especially as Jesus first tells it, is that until the harvest, the "evil" is to be suffered, not resisted. The parable's main point, in short, is not eschatological redress of wrongs, but *present forbearance of them*. And even though Jesus' subsequent interpretation of the story tilts it mightily in the direction of eschatology, his insistence on nonresistance to the enemy's trouble-making still comes through clearly enough.

But that is to get ahead of the story. Note next what it is that Jesus says the enemy sows among the wheat: *zizánia*, weeds, tares — specifically darnel, *Lolium temulentum*, an annual grass that, with its long, slender awns, or bristles, looks very much like wheat indeed. And what does *that* say about the present relationship between the kingdom and the evil in the world?

Well, it seems to me to say that programs and, a fortiori, pogroms designed to get rid of evil are, by the muddleheadedness of the world and the craft and subtlety of the enemy, doomed to do exactly what the farmer suggests they will do. Since the only troops available to fight the battle are either too confused or too busy to recognize the real difference between good and evil, all they will accomplish by their frantic pulling out of the weeds is the tearing up of the wheat right along with them. Worse yet, since good and evil in this world commonly inhabit not only the same field but even the same individual human beings — since, that is, there are no unqualified good guys any more than there are any unqualified bad guys — the only result of a truly dedicated campaign to get rid of evil will be the abolition of literally everybody.

Indeed, that puts the finger on the whole purpose of the enemy's sowing of the weeds. He has no power against goodness in and of itself: the wheat is in the field, the kingdom is in the world, and there is not a thing he can do about any of it. Evil, like darnel, is a counterfeit of reality, not reality itself. It is a parasite on being, not being itself.

As the parable develops its point, though, the enemy turns out not to need anything more than negative power. He has to act only minimally on his own to wreak havoc in the world; mostly, he depends on the forces of goodness, *insofar as he can sucker them into taking up arms against the confusion he has introduced,* to do his work. That is precisely why the enemy *goes away* after sowing the weeds: he has no need whatsoever to hang around. Unable to take positive action anyway — having no real power to muck up the operation — he simply sprinkles around a generous helping of darkness and waits for the children of light to get flustered enough to do the job for him. Goodness itself, in other words, if it is sufficiently committed to plausible, right-handed, strong-arm methods, will in the very name of goodness do all and more than all that evil ever had in mind.

One word in passing. If you are worrying that this exposition might form the basis of a case for pacifism, you should continue to worry. But you should also make a distinction. The parable, it seems to me, does not say that resistance to evil is morally wrong, only that it is salvifically ineffective. You may, therefore, make out as many cases as you like for just wars, capital punishment, or any other sensible, right-handed solution to the presence of malefactors on earth; but you must not assume that such solutions will necessarily make the world a better place. You may, in short, take the sword, but you should also remember that those who do so inevitably perish by the sword — descriptively, not prescriptively. God does not punish people for being nonpacifists; war alone is punishment enough. But even though pacifism seems not to be enjoined by Scripture, we should note for the record that the parable of the Weeds suggests that — *pro tem* at least — God himself is a pacifist. You don't have to be one, therefore; but *pro* the only *tem* you have, you might find the company quite good.

Back to the parable. "So when the plants came up and bore fruit [*karpón*]," Jesus continues, "then the weeds also appeared." The mystery of goodness is going swimmingly: the kingdom is coming along *automátē*, quite of its own accord, and its growth and fructifying are actual, catholic facts. But the mystery of iniquity seems unfortunately to be doing just as well. True to its nature as a counterfeit of reality, it too pretends to catholicity and actuality. The weeds may not be real wheat, but they look just like it; if the servants can be inveigled into taking up arms against them, a truly catholic and actual disaster can be brewed.

And one almost is. Coming to the farmer, the servants are totally preoccupied with the problem of evil. "You sowed good seed in your field, didn't you, Sir?" they ask him. "Where then did the weeds come from?" Just like two thousand years' worth of Christian theologians — though more excusably, perhaps, since the workers were ignorant of the crucifixion — their first intellectual efforts are directed, not to finding out how they should act in the presence of evil, but to looking for an explanation of it that they can understand. "If God is good, why is the world bad?" they ask in effect; "why does he allow all these terrible things to happen?"

Fascinating though such a question may be, there is a distinct note of pointlessness about it. It's not that it is unanswerable; it's just that there are so many contradictory answers to it that they produce only confusion. Consider just three possible replies to the question just raised: (1) God is *not* good; so why should the world be any better? (2) God *is* good, but he is also not very powerful (or smart or caring or whatever), so things are just beyond his competence. (3) God is good — and brilliant, clever, loving, and anything else you would like to mention — but for some reason he also has enemies who make a lot of trouble.

Pause here for a moment and note two things. First, not a single one of these answers — nor any other answer that could imaginably be given — is the least help to you when it comes to actually dealing with evil. All that any of them addresses is the distinctly armchair problem your intellectual bookkeeping department is having with a divine operation over which it has no control. The only possible action that can come out of your concern is the bestowal or withholding of your personal approbation — something that, in either case, makes no difference whatsoever. If a mugger is stabbing you with impunity, your biggest problem is hardly whether you can manage to approve or disapprove of a cosmic Somebody who, by design or default, makes such unpleasant behavior possible.

Second, note that all the answers to theological posers about God and evil serve only to raise more questions. Particularly the third answer listed above, which is, obviously, the one closest to the reply the farmer gave his servants. "Disgraceful!" the indignant question-maven snorts when he learns that God, like the farmer, has enemies. "What kind of God would put up with such nonsense? Why doesn't he just swat them? Do you mean to tell me he's not powerful enough? Do you expect me to believe in a Supreme Being like that?"

But enough. To the credit of the servants in the parable, they do not go down that theological blind alley. Instead of trying to find a way of holding somebody responsible for the enemy's inconveniencing of them, they content themselves with inquiring about possible steps they might take. "Do you want us," they ask the farmer, "to go out and pull up the weeds?" Ultimately, of course, that reaction was not much more germane than an abstract worrying of the bone of theodicy; but at least it displayed a cooperative rather than a contentious spirit — and it should stand as a warning to all theologizers.

The Bible's only real answer to the problem of evil is, like it or not, the same as the farmer's answer to the question posed by the presence of the weeds: *"An enemy hath done this"* (KJV). That may play hob with your notion of God, but it's all the answer you are going to get from Scripture. And after it, there are only two other important questions left. The first is, "Whose side are you on?" — a question, please note, that the servants got an "A" on. And the second is, "Whose methods do you propose to use in dealing with the problem?" On that one, alas, they got an "F." But if we can manage to learn from their mistake, we have a good chance of passing the whole test.

"No!" the farmer says to them. "Pull up evil, and you'll pull up goodness right along with it." But then comes the most remarkable word in the whole parable: "*Áphete* [let, permit, suffer] both to grow together until the harvest." Simply to pause over this statement, however, is not enough; it calls for a full-scale application of the brakes — a complete parking of the theological car in order to take in an incredibly rich landscape.

The verb *aphíēmi* (infinitive: *aphiénai* or *aphíein*), from which *áphete* is conjugated, has two major meanings in the New Testament. The first is the one represented by its use in this parable: send away, let go, leave, permit — not to mention about ten other similar senses that flow quite directly from the formulation of the word: *apó (aph')* is a prepositional prefix meaning "from"; and *híēmi* is a verb meaning "send, let go, dismiss." As translated into Latin, *aphiénai* came out as, among other things, *dimittere, omittere, emittere, admittere, permittere,* and *remittere;* and due to the influence of Latin upon English, almost all of those senses — expressed by either Anglo-Saxon or Latin roots — were simply imported into the English versions of the Scriptures.

But the second meaning of the word is the fascinating one here: *aphiénai,* when applied (via the Latin *dimittere* or *remittere*) to debts, trespasses, sins, and so on, comes out in English as "forgive." A glance at a concordance shows how important this use is: in the King James Version, for example, forty-seven of the hundred-fifty-six occurrences of *aphiénai* are translated by "forgive" (the rest are Englished in various ways — with "leave," in fifty-two places, as the commonest rendering).

Time out for a commercial on the concordance as the best of all possible aids to Bible study. If we take seriously our belief that the Holy Spirit presided over the entire process by which the Bible was formed, then clearly there can be no better commentary on Scripture than Scripture itself. And a concordance is the preeminent device by which that biblical self-commentary can be grasped — especially if the concordance is so arranged as to allow the readers (whether they know Greek or not) to search out all the occurrences of a word not only in English but in the original Greek.

This is crucial because, after all, it was upon authors writing in Greek — and upon a Christian community responding to their work in Greek — that the Spirit sent the guidance of his inspiration. Consider the present case of the *áphete* in the parable of the Weeds. A modern reader with access to nothing but English would see it translated as "Let both grow . . ." and simply read on. But when that *áphete* was read in the early Christian church — say, during the liturgy on the Lord's day — it would have rung a very large bell in the congregation's mind. They had just prayed (or shortly would pray) the Lord's Prayer: "*Áphes*," they would have said, "*Forgive* us our debts, as we also *aphíemen*, forgive, our debtors." On hearing, therefore, that the farmer's answer to the malice of the enemy was yet another *áphete*, they might well have grasped the Holy Spirit's exalted pun immediately: the malice, the evil, the badness that is manifest in the real world and in the lives of real people is not to be dealt with by attacking or abolishing the things or persons in whom it dwells; rather, it is to be dealt with only by an *áphesis*, by a *letting be* that is a *forgiveness*, that is a *suffering* — that is even a *permission* — all rolled into one.

Notice I said only that they *might* have grasped that. A good many Christian theologians, even among those who know Greek, have managed to miss the point completely. Indeed, the first objection usually raised to letting evil be — let alone to forgiving it — takes the form of agitated moralistic hand-wringing: "But if you simply tell people in advance that they're going to be forgiven, won't they just go straight out and take that as *permission* to sin? Don't we have to keep them scared out of their wits by continually harping on the big difference between forgiveness and permission?"

I have a number of replies to all that. The first is, "*What* big difference? In Greek, the same word is used for both." The second is, "There's no difference between them at all. If you're an utterly serious forgiver, and if you make your forgiving disposition known to a solid brass snake-in-the-grass, he will obviously play you for the sucker you are as often as he feels like it: what do you think the world, the flesh, and the devil thought about a Jesus who died on the cross instead of nuking his enemies?" The third is, "What on earth are you talking about? God, in the act of creating you, gave you permission to do any damned fool thing you could manage to bring off. Forgiveness neither increases nor decreases the level of God's permissiveness; instead, it just fishes us out of the otherwise inescapable quicksand we so stupidly got ourselves into and says, 'There! Isn't that better?'" My fourth and final reply, though, is, "Of course there's a difference; and it's a whopping one. But since even that makes no difference at all to either the farmer in the parable or to Jesus on the cross — or, for that matter, to any Christian committed to forgiving his skunk of a brother seventy times seven times — why harp on it?"

Follow that up. On the basis of the parable as told, the farmer has announced, publicly and in advance (do you seriously think the servants told nobody about his crazy plan to leave the weeds alone?), that his enemy is quite free to come back any night he chooses and sow any weeds he likes. Not just more *zizánia*, but purslane, dock, bindweed, pigweed, or even — when he finally runs out of seriously mischievous ideas — New Zealand spinach.

There is more. On the basis of Jesus' ministry as lived and died, God has announced the very same thing. No enemy — not the devil, not you, not me, and not anybody else — is going to get it in the neck, in this life, for any evil he has done. The Old Testament to the contrary notwithstanding — and despite all the subsequent tub-thumping by "God is not mocked" Christians who seem unaware that a New Testament was given because there was no way in which the Old one could break the entail of sin — Jesus on the cross doesn't threaten his enemies, he forgives them: *"áphes,"* he says, one last time.

And then there's the clincher. On the basis of Jesus' ministry as risen, there is no change in that policy. He comes forth from the tomb and ascends into heaven with nail prints in his hands and feet and a spear wound in his risen side — with eternal, glorious scars to remind God, angels, and us that he is not about to go back on his word from the cross.

Oh, of course. I know that by now you are mighty tired of all this emphasis on the Divine Sweetness. You are just itching to remind me that at the harvest, the weeds are going to be bound up in bundles and burned in an appropriately eschatological fire. And so they are. And to finish off the text, so is the wheat going to be gathered into the barn. But if I may try your patience just one minute more, let me ask you to consider the *proportions* of this parable as Jesus first tells it. The words that you have all along been holding your breath to hear constitute only two thirds of its final verse. The rest of the parable — Matthew 13:24-30a — is entirely about the *áphesis* of evil, not about the avenging of it.

To be sure, Jesus does indeed end on the note of the ultimate triumph of justice. Why? Well, presumably because it stresses a truth: God is in charge, and he will, under eschatological circumstances, get his own way. But the great bulk of the parable is told to stress another, and equally central truth: namely, that in the present circumstances of the world (the only circumstances, please note, in which we now find ourselves), the *mystery of the kingdom* is likewise quite in charge and thoroughly capable of getting its own way. It is sown, sprouted, and bearing fruit: all the *zizánia* in the world haven't got a finger they can effectually lift against it.

But I think there is also another reason why Jesus gives the ultimate vindication such short shrift at this point. As I said, the human race is hooked on eschatology: give us one drag on it, and we proceed to party away our whole forgiven life in fantasies about a final score-settling session that none of us, except for forgiveness, could possibly survive. Jesus, it seems to me, senses that about us as he reaches the end of this parable. "Well," he thinks to himself, "I gave them the fire and brimstone stuff they were dying to hear; and I'm glad, I guess, because after all, it *is* the truth. But oh, how I hate to think of what they're going to do with it: throw them just one eschatological dog biscuit like that, and they'll never stop yapping. Let me see. What to tell them next? Hm. Probably I should get off the end-of-the-world business completely. One thing's for sure though: I'm definitely not going to say another word about these damned weeds until I'm good and ready."

CHAPTER NINE

The Mustard Seed and the Leaven

B efore we proceed, let me give a roundup of the box scores that the parable of the Weeds has so far chalked up under the five headings I have been using for the parables of the kingdom.

On *catholicity* it gets high marks. Not only does it portray the kingdom as having been sown everywhere in the world but, for the first time, it introduces into the narrative a parallel insistence on what we might call the catholicity of evil. Indeed, it is just this grappling with the radical intermixture of goodness and badness in the world — with the "problem of evil" the parable so succinctly raises — that sets it off as a remarkable step forward in Jesus' teaching about the kingdom.

The note of *mystery* is likewise expanded to apply to evil as well as good: both the weeds and the wheat grow from hidden beginnings as seed. But the most notable heightening of the element of mystery lies in Jesus' attempt, again for the first time, to assign a reason for the presence of evil. By attributing it to an enemy who works surreptitiously, at night, he makes the mystery of evil yet another parallel to the mystery of the kingdom. It is a counterfeit, of course; but precisely because of that, hasty and overenthusiastic attempts to get it out of circulation are flatly discouraged.

As far as the *actual, present working* of the kingdom is concerned, the parable of the Weeds scores just as well as any so far. In fact, there is even less room left for virtualism in its interpretation than there was, say, in the Sower. The wheat, from start to finish, successfully does its proper work. The enemy may be a gigantic nuisance; but he is never a serious, ultimate threat.

But it is under the headings of *hostility* and *response* that the parable of the Weeds tops all previous scores. As I pointed out in connection with *mystery,* the enemy's machinations are presented in images that are supremely suitable to the father of lies. There is no openness here, none of the simplicity that characterizes the straightforward hostility of the birds or the rocky ground or the thorns. Rather, there is the full-blown paradox of the appearance of evil in a situation where there is absolutely no reason to expect it ("You sowed *good* seed, didn't you? How come, then . . . ?"). Finally, though, in its development of the note of response to the kingdom, the parable of the Weeds really breaks the record.

When we think of the subject of response, especially with regard to sacred subjects, our inveterate Pelagianism — our tendency to think that our own moral efforts are necessary to the plan of salvation — leads us to set up scenarios in which the work of the kingdom simply will not go forward without our cooperation. And that in turn — since we are much better at antagonistic responses than at positive ones — leads us to imagine that the best way for us to give the kingdom a helping hand is to take up arms as promptly as possible against the enemies of the Lord. But the parable of the Weeds stands in direct contrast to any such moral muscle-flexing.

Only God, it says, only the Farmer in charge of the universal operation, knows how to deal successfully with evil. And note well that his sole competence applies both here and hereafter — both now, during the growing season, and then, at the harvest. Here and now, while the mystery of evil is intermingled with the mystery of the kingdom, he wills to deal with it only by *áphesis:* by forgiveness, by permission, by letting it be. But there and then, in the eschatological fullness of the kingdom — as that fullness is portrayed in the rest of the New Testament — he still deals with it in terms of something that is a mystery to us now, namely, the mystery of the Resurrection.

When we dwell too simplistically on the Final Judgment, we almost always picture it as the day when God finally takes off the gloves of mystery with which he has so far handled the world and gives his enemies a decisive taste of eschatological bare knuckles. That image, however, leaves one important truth out of account: the judgment occurs only *after* the general resurrection of the dead. And since the resurrection of the dead (of the just and the unjust alike) is something that happens to them solely by virtue of Jesus' resurrection — about which we have very little unparadoxical information — we should be very slow to imagine scenarios for it that are based on simplistic extrapolations of our present experience. Everything that happens after the second coming of Jesus — judgment, heaven, and even hell — happens within the triumphantly reconciling power of his death and resurrection. We simply don't know how or to what degree that power affects the eschatological situation.

Take, for example, the question of whether *we* are in a position to discuss the meaning or even the possibility of ultimate human rejection of the reconciliation. To be sure, Scripture says clearly enough that the sovereign, healing power of Jesus can and will be refused by some. I have no problem with that. What I do object to, however, are the hell-enthusiasts who act as if God's whole New Testament method of dealing with evil will, in the last day, simply go back to some Old Testament "square one" — as if Jesus hadn't done a blessed or merciful thing in between, and as if we could, therefore, skip all the paradoxes of mercy when we talk about the Last Day and simply concentrate on plain old gun-barrel justice.

Admittedly, the Bible talks about all sorts of creatures going to hell. But my point is that if they do go, they go even there in the power of a resurrection by which God in Christ has reconciled all things to himself, hell included. There is no one anywhere in the final scheme of things who is floating around in his own old unrisen state. Resurrection is not a reward for the chosen few; it is the only game there is in the whole eschatological town. And that resurrection, I submit, while it will presumably not be a mystery to anybody, good or bad, *then*, remains very much of a mystery to us *now*. We don't know beans about what the actual, ultimate dynamics of people's situations will be in that day; so we should be a bit more reluctant than we are to rattle on so blithely about it in our own day — especially in ways that practically ignore the mystery that governs all days, first, middle, or last.

In any case, even Jesus himself seems to exhibit a touch of just that reluctance. Having broached the problem of evil to his hearers — and having waved under their noses the tempting bone of millennial grievance-settling — he suddenly drops both subjects completely. In my view, he does so because he senses that his hearers are doing a lot of premillennial salivating over postmillennial justice. And because he judges that sort of thing hazardous to their grip not only on the mystery of the kingdom but especially on the mystery of the divine *áphesis* of evil, he simply puts off giving it to them. If you don't like that view, however, feel free to sit loose to it: nobody really knows what Jesus *thought* anyway. The important thing is what he *said* next, namely, the parables of the Mustard Seed and of the Leaven.

All three of the synoptic Gospels contain the Mustard Seed (see the chart in chapter 5), so a look at the similarities and differences of the accounts suggests itself as a way of approaching it. Matthew, as I have noted, stresses continuity by beginning with the words "another [*állēn*] parable," and he sets forth the parable itself with his by now usual introduction: "The kingdom of heaven is like. . . ." But Mark and Luke begin by having Jesus pose a question. In Mark, Jesus asks, "How shall we compare the kingdom of God, or by what parable shall we set it forth?" In Luke, he eschews the editorial or majestic plural and simply asks, "What is the kingdom of God like, and to what shall I compare it?"

Obviously, it is entirely possible to take these utterances simply as rhetorical questions, mere throat-clearing introductions to the point he is about to make. For all I know, that may even be the best thing to do with them. But they do suggest another line of interpretation — one that takes into account Jesus' sudden shift away from the eschatological problems posed by evil. While the juxtaposition of the Weeds and the Mustard Seed occurs only in Matthew, in both Mark and Luke the Mustard Seed can still be seen as an attempt on Jesus' part to distance himself from eschatology. His beginning with a question, therefore, can be taken simply as his wondering out loud just how to do so. In

Mark, the Mustard Seed follows the Growing Seed — which, albeit glancingly, does refer to both *sickle* and *harvest*. In Luke, however, both it and the parable of the Leaven occur in the midst of a welter of eschatological passages. In short, no matter where the Mustard Seed appears, it stands in some contrast to its immediate setting. I do not find it preposterous, therefore, to imagine that it came out the way it did precisely because Jesus — in response to his own question — decided that such contrast was more than called for.

At any rate, what he says the kingdom is like is *kókkọ sinápeōs,* a mustard seed. Note once again that the kingdom is the very thing sown, not something that results from the sowing of a seed other than itself. Note, too, some minor differences in the accounts: In Matthew and Luke, it is compared to a seed that a man took and sowed in his field (Luke, for some reason — perhaps because he was a physician with a bit of a *Better Homes and Gardens* approach to agriculture — has the man put the seed into his *garden*). Mark, however, goes straight to the point that Matthew takes his time getting to (and that Luke never gets to at all), namely, that the kingdom is like a mustard seed "which, when it is sown upon the ground, is smaller than all the seeds on the earth." Score another point, therefore, in both the *catholicity* and the *mystery* columns. The *whole* field is sown (Mark uses the word *gẽ,* meaning both the "ground" and the "earth" — with the pun, I like to think, intended). And it is sown in a way that is hidden: mustard seeds, while by no means the all-time smallness champions that Jesus makes them, are at any rate a lot smaller than peach pits.

But it is on the score of the *actual working* of the kingdom — and in particular, of its successful working — that the parable of the Mustard Seed scores the most points: the seed grows up (to put all three accounts into one basket) into something bigger than all vegetables (Matthew, Mark); it puts forth big branches (Mark); and it becomes a tree, a *déndron* (Matthew, Luke), under whose shade (Mark) the birds of the heaven make their nests (Matthew, Mark, Luke). "Tree," of course, may strike those of us who are gardeners as a touch of excessive vividness, but the comparison still stands: even the common garden mustard plant is taller than brussels sprouts or untrellised cucumbers. And while bird's nests are not what we would expect to find in one, we'd be a lot more surprised to discover them in bush beans. Field corn would be something else, admittedly . . . but it would also be an illustration of pointless exegesis, so skip it.

The real point of the parable is the marvelous discrepancy between the hiddenness of the kingdom at its sowing and the lush, manifest exuberance of it in its final, totally successful fruition. "So you want me to tell you about the end of the story, do you?" Jesus seems to be saying. "Well, here it is; but without a word about evil to throw you into your usual eschatological tailspin. All you get here is the peaceable kingdom: the sun shining in the sky, birds flying in and out of the shade, and all the little ones twittering away forever and ever. No elements of *hostility* to tempt you to think the kingdom won't arrive unless you ride shotgun for it. And no elements of *response* to suggest it might need your co-operation in order to come out right — unless, of course, you consider larking around in the trees a proper response; in which case, *that* I'll let you have."

And then, as if to continue driving home the same point, Jesus segues straight into the parable of the Leaven. I shall not even try to restrain my natural enthusiasm for this parable. Not only does its reference to yeast delight my deepest roots (I have for decades made my own bread, without even once losing my fascination with the process); even more, it corroborates, with what has to be a divine economy of words, everything I have been trying to say. Let me comment on it then — with not the slightest attempt to imitate the divine brevity.

The parable appears in Matthew and Luke; and with the exception of the fact that Luke begins it with a question ("To what shall I liken the kingdom of God?" instead of the Matthean "Another parable he spoke to them"), the two accounts can be dealt with as one. The kingdom, Jesus tells his hearers, is like "leaven [*zýmē*], which a woman took and hid [*(en)ékrypsen*] in three measures of flour [*aleúrou sáta tría*], until the whole [*hólon*] was leavened."

Let it simply be noted in passing that the surrogate for God in this parable is a woman. Set that down, along with Jesus' calling himself a mother hen, as evidence not only to paternalistic traditionalists but also to inclusive-language genderphobes that things have never been quite as good as the former, nor as bad as the latter seem to think. Indeed, the woman presented here by Jesus seems to possess, in the fullest possible measure, both masculinity and femininity. It may be stereotypically female work she's pictured as doing, but she does it with more than stereotypically male energy. This is no slip of a girl making two tiny loaves for her husband's pleasure. This is a *baker*, folks. Three measures *(sáta)* is a bushel of flour, for crying out loud! That's 128 cups! That's 16 five-pound bags! And when you get done putting in the 42 or so cups of water you need to make it come together, you've got a little over 101 pounds of dough on your hands.

Which leads me, as long as we are at the end of the parable anyway, to exegete it backwards. Take the "whole" *(hólon)* first. When Jesus says the *whole* is leavened, he's not kidding. The lump stands for the whole world. It's not some elite ball of brioche dough made out of fancy flour by special handling. And it's not some hyper-good-for-you chunk of spiritual fad bread full of soy flour, wheat germ, and pure thoughts. It's just plain, unbaked bread dough, and Jesus postulates enough of it to make it even handle like the plain old world it represents: that is, *not easily*. Indigestible in its present form, incapable of going anywhere, either to heaven or hell, except in a handbasket — and absolutely certain to wear out anybody, God included, who tries to deal with it — it is, if we dare rate such things, one of Jesus' parabolic triumphs: a perfect 100+, if there ever was one.

The note of the *catholicity* of the kingdom, therefore, stands as the major emphasis of this parable, and I will not wave it in front of you any more than I already have. But when you go back to the word *ékrypsen*, "hid," and spend some time on the obvious element of *mystery* it introduces, additional light begins to shine on both notes.

The hiding of yeast in a batch of dough is both more mysterious and more pervasive than any of the hidings Jesus has so far used to illustrate the kingdom. Seeds may disappear into the ground; but if you are willing to take the trouble to hunt and peck for them, you can conceivably get every last one of them back up and out of the field. Furthermore, even when they are thickly broadcast, there is still more of the field unsown than sown. But yeast? No way, on either count. Just as yeast enters into the dough by being dissolved in the very liquid that makes the dough become dough at all — just as there is not a moment of the dough's existence, from start to finish, in which it is unleavened dough — so this parable insists that the kingdom enters the world at its creation and that there is not, and never has been, any unkingdomed humanity anywhere in the world.

For by, with, and in the very fluids that make and restore creation — by the waters on whose face the Spirit moved, by the mist that watered Eden, by the paschal blood on the doorposts, by the blood of the covenant on Sinai, by the waters of Jordan in Jesus' baptism, by the blood and water from his side on the cross, and by the river of life in the New Jerusalem — the Word, who is the yeast that leaves not one scrap of this lump of a world unleavened, has *always* been hidden in his creation. He did not start being hidden in 4 B.C.; all he did in his time on earth was show us his face and tell us his name — and send us out to share that Good News with everybody.

And just as the yeast, once it is in the dough (unlike the seed, once it is in the ground), is so intimate a part of the lump as to be indistinguishable from it, undiscoverable in it, and irretrievable out of it, so is the kingdom in this world. Indeed, this image of the perpetual intimacy of yeast to dough leads to a refinement of the notion of the kingdom in these parables. I have been saying that the kingdom is the *very thing sown*, not something that results from the sowing of a different thing. But now I can take it further. If the kingdom is like *yeast hidden in dough,* then we should stay well away from even the apparently harmless assertion that the kingdom is the yeast and the world is the dough. If the world *alone* (the world without the kingdom) is represented by anything in the parable, it is by the flour, not the dough. But in the action of the parable, the flour is never portrayed as alone. Rather, it is portrayed as dough with the yeast already hidden in it. Consequently, what the kingdom is actually represented by is the yeast-in-the-dough, the dough-cum-leaven — just as, when you come to think of it, the kingdom in the "seed" parables is most fully represented by the seed-in-the-ground, not simply by the seed alone.

101

Finally (under this same heading of the hiding of the yeast), I find that I can put my case even more strongly than I have so far for both the pervasiveness and the actuality of the kingdom's working in the world. It is all too tempting, after hearing the "seed" parables, to envision a time (namely, before the sowing) when the world was a world without the kingdom in it. (That tends to make hash of a serious view of the Old Testament, of course, and it makes no sense at all of the Word's intimate presence to the world as the one by whom all things were, and are, made; nevertheless, it's still a temptation.) But after hearing the parable of the Leaven, there is no choice: for every second of the time the dough is dough, the yeast is inseparable from it. Therefore, for every second of the time the world has been a world, it has also been the kingdom. Its progress through history is not a transition from nonkingdom to kingdom; rather, it is a progress from kingdom-in-a-mystery to kingdom-made-manifest. (I know. You want to tell me it's at least possible to make a dough first and after that work the leaven into it. Don't bother. I'm a baker. Sure it's possible: I've done it. But it's also dumb: nobody in his right mind would choose to make bread that way unless he'd made a mistake to start with. And since this parable isn't about mistakes, I'm not about to allow them into my interpretation.)

Catholicity, mystery, and *actuality,* therefore, are in this parable in spades. But what about *hostility?* Obviously it is not here as such in any way; but there is one thing that heightens Jesus' admonition (in the parable of the Weeds) against taking up arms against it. Here, it is not simply that it is unadvisable or inconvenient or dangerous for us to interfere while the kingdom is doing its thing: it is plain, unvarnished impossible. So intimate is the yeast to the entire lump — so immediate is the working of the kingdom to every scrap of the world — that there is no way on earth of getting at it, or even to it, at all. Not for the enemy. Not even for the divine Woman Baker herself, apparently. And certainly not for any odd little bits of the lump like you and me.

And so we come at last to the note of *response* — and, fittingly enough, to the first image in the parable, that of the yeast. What are the only responses you need to offer to yeast-in-the-dough? Well, patience, for one thing. And possibly discernment — to be able to recognize when it (not you, please note) has done the job. And maybe a little vigilance to make sure impatient types don't talk you into despairing of the lump before its time comes. But no matter what you do, the yeast works anyway. At the most, your responses advance your satisfaction, not its success.

And even your negative responses — even your pointless resistances to the kingdom — interfere only with your own convenience, not with its working. Indeed, by the imagery of bread making, they may even help the kingdom. Unless the dough is kneaded thoroughly — unless it resists and fights the baker enough to develop gluten and form effective barriers to the yeast's working — then the gases produced by the yeast will not be entrapped in cells that can lighten the lump into a loaf. Who knows, therefore? Maybe even our foot-dragging and our backsliding — maybe even the gummy, intractable mass of our sins — is just all in a day's leavening to the Word who is the Yeast who lightens our lumpishness.

One last, first point about the *zýmē*, the leaven itself. How does yeast lighten dough? By filling it with thousands of tiny pockets of carbon dioxide. And how do those pockets of gas cause bread to rise? By expanding when heated. Behold, therefore, the way the imagery of the Leaven reflects and refracts Scripture's other references to warm carbon dioxide: that is, to *breath*, both human and divine.

The whole kingdom of God — the catholic, actual mystery that, come fair response or foul, is irremovably mixed into creation — operates by *warm breath*. It takes its origin from a Father's breathed-forth *Word* who, spoken once for all eternity, brings the world out of nothing into being. It marches through its history under the guidance of a *Spirit* — a *ruach*, a *pneúma*, a wind, a breath — who, proceeding from the Father's speaking of the Word, confirms that Word with signs following. And the imagery grows more and more complex. Jesus breathes out the Spirit upon his disciples after his resurrection. After he has ascended, he sends that same Spirit upon the church as a rushing mighty wind. And finally, when the church goes forth to announce the leavening of the world by all this trinitarian heavy breathing, it is by yet more warm breath — even by hot air — that the proclamation is made: "For after . . .

the world by wisdom knew not God, it pleased God *by the foolishness of preaching* to save them that believe" (KJV, emphasis mine).

And do not try to cast a chill on the warmth of that Good News by telling me my last quotation means that the kingdom is at work only in "them that believe." To make belief the touchstone of the kingdom's operation is simply to turn faith into just one more cold work. Of course we must believe; but only because there is nothing left for us to do *but* believe.

All we need to do, and all we can do, is simply trust that the leaven is, was, and always will be entirely mixed into the lump of our existence — and that it will infallibly lighten every last one of us. The job is already, if mysteriously, done: by the power of the Word who breathed out his life for us on the cross — by the might of him who, in the glory of his resurrection, forever whispers our reconciled names into his Father's ear — we are as good as baked to perfection right now. We have been accepted in the Beloved; the only real development left for us to experience is the final accolade to be spoken over us by the divine Woman Baker: "Now *that's* what I call a real loaf of bread!"

CHAPTER TEN

The Interpretation of the Weeds

E ven after the parables of the Mustard Seed and the Leaven, though, Matthew still seems unwilling to let Jesus proceed directly to an interpretation of the parable of the Weeds. At verses 34 and 35 of chapter 13, he inserts an editorial comment about Jesus' use of parables in general. The parallel passage in Mark occurs at 4:33-34, but since Mark omits the parable of the Weeds entirely, the function of these verses in his account is different than it is in Matthew. Coming as they do at the end of the Marcan collection of the parables of the kingdom, they serve principally as a coda on the parabolic method: "And with many such parables he spoke the word to them as they were able to hear it, but without a parable, he did not speak to them; privately, though, to his own disciples, he explained everything." Perhaps all that needs to be added here to what I said earlier about this text is a note of wonder: however marvelous the parables we possess may be, we simply don't have all of Jesus' parables.

Not that there is any point in speculating about why some (or many) were omitted: what might have been, wasn't — and that's all you can say about that. But the comment does suggest an explanation for Jesus' popularity with the crowds. To us the Gospels display a Jesus who is, as often as not, a feisty character. This playing up of his contentious side has, no doubt, a simple explanation: Jesus was eventually done in by the hostility that surrounded him; therefore, the Gospel writers were at pains to explain its origin and development. The result, however, is that we easily forget the enthusiasm with which the crowds listened to him. He spoke colorfully, with surprising illustrations practically tripping over each other in his discourse. In a word, he was an entertainer as well as a teacher; by contrast, the scribes and Pharisees must have seemed like stuffed shirts.

But it is in the Matthean account that this editorial comment is given a positively fascinating twist. Matthew begins the passage more simply than Mark: "All these things," he says, "Jesus spoke to the crowds in parables; indeed, without a parable he said nothing to them." But then his Gospel-writer's mental concordance pops open at Psalm 78:2, and he cannot resist ringing the changes on the quotable passage he finds there. Jesus' whole use of the parabolic method, Matthew writes, has a scriptural precedent: he taught that way "in order to fulfill what was spoken by the prophet: 'I will open my mouth in parables [*en parabolaís*], I will utter things that have been hidden [*kekrymména*] from the foundation of the world [*apó katabolḗs kósmou*].'"

One note. I am about to comment here only on Matthew's mental concordance and on some other New Testament uses of the Greek words it flushed for him. Neither the meaning of the original Hebrew in the Psalm (probably something like, "I will utter dark sayings from of old"), nor the adequacy of the Greek version Matthew quoted from (for example, *kekrymména* is not in the Septuagint; rather, *problḗmata* is), nor the state of the Greek text of the Gospel (*kósmou*, "of the world," is omitted from a few of the best and oldest manuscripts) — none of these things, interesting or even important though they might be, enters into my case at all. My argument goes simply to the reasons why Matthew included the passage at this point, and to what we can conclude, in the light of those reasons, about the parables of the kingdom in particular.

Fair enough then. Why Matthew's mind went to Psalm 78:2 in the first place is quite obvious: he had already written the phrase *en parabolaís*, "in parables," at verse 34; its occurrence in a psalm he probably knew from memory no doubt made it leap right out at him. Having gotten that far, however, he naturally proceeded to recite a bit more of the psalm; and that, finally, was what decided him on quoting the passage. For right there — right after he had just finished writing the parable of the Leaven and using the word *enékrypsen,* "hid," to describe what God does with the kingdom — there, plain as day, is the same root *kryp* hidden away in *kekrymména.* The psalmist, Matthew thinks, really was a prophet who anticipated Jesus' emphasis on hiding and even extended it backwards in time: the kingdom is not something that God will send at some future date to a world that is presently without it; rather, it is a real and operative mystery that God has *long since* encrypted in the world.

But it is as he recites the verse to its end that the reason for quoting it becomes overwhelming. These *kekrymména,* these hidden things, have been around a lot longer than just *since;* they have been here *apó katabolés kósmou,* from the foundation of the world. The mystery of the kingdom, therefore (if I may take over from Matthew at this point), has never *not* been in the world — just as the yeast that the woman dissolves in the water to make the dough has never not been in the lump. Because the creative Word is the eternal contemporary of every moment of the world's existence, the kingdom is catholic in time as well as space. The Word who restores humanity to its status as a kingdom of priests is the same Word who made Adam a priestly king to begin with. To be sure, since those first days in Eden, the kingdom has indeed been hidden and only the *signs* of the mystery (the people of Israel, the humanity of Jesus, the holy catholic Church) have been visible. But it has only been hidden, not absent; it has never once been something merely *yet to come.*

And therefore (to hand the wheel back to Matthew), it is finally safe, the Gospel writer thinks, to set down Jesus' interpretation of the parable of the Weeds. Having at last gotten the point across that, whatever things there may be still to come, the kingdom itself isn't one of them — having characterized it, once and for all, as *here* — he decides that maybe now a little eschatology wouldn't do too much damage.

Which brings us, naturally, to Matthew 13:36-43. The interpretation that Jesus gives of the parable of the Weeds in these verses is a flatfooted allegorization. Point by point, he ticks off a list of almost

completely obvious correspondences between the details of the agricultural tale he has told and the details of the kingdom's contest with evil.
Ordinary readers, of course, have found it not only acceptable, but grat-
ifying: it's always nice when the teacher's explanations jibe neatly with
the pupil's guesses at his meaning. But biblical critics have almost always been driven up the wall by it.

Many of them have felt that the interpretation is simply
inauthentic — an ecclesiastical gloss poked into the text by some third-
rate mind whose forte was beating people over the head with the self-
evident. Others, though — more firmly committed to the notion that
the canon of Scripture is, after all, the canon of *Scripture* — have soft-
pedaled it in a different way: Jesus, they claim, was either having an off
day when he unburdened himself of it, or else he gave it so early in his
teaching career that his subsequent top-drawer parabolic style never
had a chance to inform it. Whichever way they argue, though, they
agree on one thing: the interpretation of the Weeds doesn't fit their
specifications for an important piece of parabolic discourse.

Everybody, I think, can sympathize to a certain extent with their
reservations. This allegorization of the parable is, after all, a bit trite;
and it is even more than a bit premature. Follow up that last point. Jesus, in this passage, takes a parable that was only tangentially about the
eschatological solution to the problem of evil and turns it into a full-
fledged parable of judgment. Most of Jesus' parables of judgment, however, come much later in the Gospels than this; in fact, many of the
most significant ones occur, as I noted in chapter 4, during Holy Week
— that is, when Jesus' forthcoming passion and death were uppermost
in his mind. In other words, his judgment parables tend to be more
"hot" than "cool." They are not abstract treatises on the theology of the
last things; rather, they are vivid stories told by a totally committed dying Messiah who is also wrestling with the obvious fact of the rejection
of his sacrifice by nearly everyone around him.

Still, understandable though all those reservations may be, I don't
like what the critics usually do with them. Enter here, therefore, my
"dog biscuit" theory of Jesus' interpretation of the Weeds.

On a number of occasions, Jesus does and says things that I think are best understood not as his own considered opinion of what is called for in the circumstances but as sops for those he is dealing with. Consider the following. The healing of the demoniac boy (Matt. 17:14-23): Jesus' disciples can't cast out the demon; the boy's father pesters Jesus to cure him; Jesus answers, "O faithless and perverse generation, how long do I have to put up with you?" — and then he heals the boy anyway. Or consider the wedding at Cana (John 2): Jesus' mother tells him they have no wine; he says, "What have I got to do with you, woman? This isn't my time" — and then he turns water into wine. And there are plenty of other instances: the coin in the fish's mouth (Matt. 17:24) is best understood as a half-serious, throwaway miracle to shut up the yapping of the tax authorities; the raising of Lazarus (John 11) has the same "bone tossed to the dogs" element in it (Jesus is irked, *enebrimésato,* and upset, *etáraxen heautón,* at the prospect of having to do it just "on account of the crowd hanging around"); and finally, in Mark 7:27, Jesus actually refers to throwing things to the dogs. His calling the Syrophoenician woman a dog is part of an "in" joke between himself and her; the real dogs — to whom the bone of the healing of her daughter is thrown to spite them — are those whose superorthodox theology said the Messiah would never have any truck with Greeks.

But enough. To me, Jesus' allegorization of the Weeds — his terse tossing off of a straight "judgment" interpretation of a fundamentally nonjudgmental parable — is just one more dominical dog biscuit. His hearers have been itching to hear eschatology, so — mostly, I think, to get them off his back — he gives them eschatology. And eschatology that insults whatever intelligence they may have had. "O . . . kay," he says to them. "You're dying to mess up my point, so I'll mess it up for you. That way you get two parables for the price of one: the first is mine; but this second one is all yours. Chew on it all you like. Maybe some day it'll dawn on you it's not exactly the world's best bone."

To come to the text itself, then, note first that as Matthew sets up the passage, this last putative crack of Jesus' is aimed at the disciples themselves. Leaving the crowd, Jesus comes to the house and the disciples approach him. "Explain to us the parable of the Weeds of the field," they say. Ah, how fearful and wonderful it must have been to be the teacher of such a brilliant collection of point missers. Behold how, even in their first framing of the question, they have managed to turn the parable into something else. Jesus told it as a story of a kingdom that was like a man who sowed good seed in his field and then had weeds sown in it by his enemy; but they heard it as a story about weeds, period. What he gave them was a judiciously balanced analogy of the complex relationship between good and evil; but what they received was an out-of-whack fable about the problem of evil alone.

To give them credit, they did at least have a suspicion they hadn't quite understood his meaning. But to give Jesus even more credit, he probably realized that if they didn't get his first comparison, they wouldn't get any subsequent ones either. Therefore, anticipating Chesterton by 1900 years, he simply said, "Yes, you don't understand," and told them only what they were prepared to hear. In short, he backed away from the difficult concepts of the catholicity, mystery, and present actuality of the kingdom and gave them the "take up the sword against the sword" theology he would spend his whole life negating.

Quite possibly, you find that too fast a shuffle. And quite possibly it is. But on the other hand, I have no compunction about offering it to you. My commitment to Scripture as the inspired Word of God — as a sacred deck of cards, not one of which may be discarded and not one of whose spots may be altered or ignored — in no way inhibits me from *playing* with Scripture. Better minds than mine have done it before. For example, *Crux muscipulum diaboli*, said St. Augustine: the cross is a mousetrap for the devil; and then he proceeded to work out the whole scenario of the Crucifixion in pure mickey-mouse, complete with the devil salivating over the prospect of Christ's demise, and then being caught in the trap of the Redeemer's death, and finally realizing, in the Resurrection, that he had been tricked by fake bait. So enjoy. Or don't enjoy. There'll be another hand of cards along in a moment.

I have commented already on most of the identifications Jesus makes in allegorizing the parable of the Weeds: the sower of the good seed is the Son of Man; the field is the world; the good seed are the sons of the kingdom; the *zizánia*, the "bad seed," are the sons of the evil one; the enemy who sows them is the devil; the harvest is the end of the world. In no more space than I have taken to write them down here, he skips blithely over the heart of his original parable and heads for the eschatological barn; what got a mere two-thirds of a verse in the first version is about to get fully half the total space in this one.

The angels, he says, are the harvesters. I am sorry: it may be one of the drawbacks of the way my mind works, but I cannot resist imagining that Jesus is simply on a roll here. Who cares who the harvesters are? Their identity is completely irrelevant to his parable. But having set himself to "explain" everything to this bunch of dummies, he cannot resist laying it on thick. Indeed, I am a little surprised, given his flair for irony, he didn't lay it on even thicker: the angels are the harvesters; the pitchforks they use to gather up the weeds are the seven cardinal virtues; the strings they use to bind them into bundles are the moral attributes of Deity; the wagon they use to cart them off is the chariot of the wrath of God; and the team that pulls the loathsome load is the four horsemen of the Apocalypse.

I take back my apology. Putting it that way convinces me of something: Jesus didn't need biblical critics to tell him he shouldn't allegorize parables; he knew instinctively not to do it. And when he did actually indulge in it, he did so with such a heavy hand that the results were almost as good as the famous spoofing allegorization some critic made up for the parable of the Good Samaritan: the man who fell among thieves is the human race; the Samaritan is Christ; the oil and wine are the two Testaments; the inn is the holy catholic church; the innkeeper is the Pope; and the two pence are the two major sacraments, baptism and communion. And when the critic was told he had omitted the beast on which the Samaritan transported the wounded man, he replied, "Oh right, the ass: the ass is the fellow who made up this interpretation of the parable."

Again, though, enough. The rest of Jesus' allegorizations make the point all by themselves. "Just as the weeds are gathered and burned with fire," he says, "so will it be at the end of the age. The Son of Man will send his angels, and they will gather out of his kingdom all causes of sin [*skándala*] and doers of iniquity [*poioúntas tēn anomían*]."

Yes. That is indeed, in all seriousness, what God will do: it would be a pretty poor New Jerusalem that couldn't manage to get such menaces off the streets. But yes, again: Jesus' extensive dwelling on it here is still a dog biscuit thrown to the disciples to get himself shed of their simplistic eschatology. For between the ultimate cleanup of evil and his disciples' plausible but misguided eagerness to get their version of it going in high gear right now, he has yet to interpose the dark, mysterious, incomprehensible, unsatisfactory *áphesis* of his death, resurrection and ascension — the *letting be* of his redeeming, reconciling work that is both forgiveness and permission at once. Evil will be dealt with, but in no way as unparadoxically as they think: even hell — in the light of the general resurrection — is a kind of *áphesis,* an eternal *suffering* of evil. "So go ahead and think all you want about the scandals and the bad guys for the time being," he seems to say to them; "but you'd better hold onto your hats when you finally see what I'm going to do about them between now and the time to come."

All of that goes unmentioned, though: Jesus simply continues to heap up mocking reinforcements of his disciples' eschatological naïveté. "And they will throw them into the furnace of fire, *eis tén káminon toú pyrós* [straight out of Nebuchadnezzar; by Daniel; Shadrach, Meshach, and Abednego], where there will be weeping and gnashing of teeth." Loud cheers from the apostolic band; the enemies of the Lord are getting it in the neck. God's in his heaven and all's as wrong as it possibly can be in hell. The saints look down and laugh themselves silly over the agonies of the damned. "Hurrah for justice! We knew God would finally see it our way — we who will be the righteous shining like the sun in the kingdom of our Father. What a wonderful way to end such a satisfying interpretation! Oh, thank you, Jesus; thank you very, very . . ."

But Jesus doesn't end there. He adds one final, devastatingly ironic note: *He who has ears, let him hear.* "You like all that eschatological vengeance, huh?" he says to them. "Well, keep listening, kiddies, because while it's true enough in its plausible little way, there are going to be so many other implausible truths before you get to it, you may not even recognize it when you see it. You've still got a lot more to take in."

112

CHAPTER ELEVEN

The Treasure and the Pearl

The next two parables of the kingdom — the Treasure Hidden in the Field and the Pearl of Great Price (Matt. 13:44-46) — are simply dropped without ceremony into the account. With no preface at all, Matthew writes: "The kingdom of heaven is like a treasure hidden [*kekryménǭ*] in a field [*agrǭ̂*], which a man found and hid [*ékrypsen*]; then in his joy [*apó tês charás autoú*], he goes and sells [*pōleî*] whatever things he has and buys [*agorázei*] that field. Again, the kingdom of heaven is like a merchant in search of fine pearls, who, on finding one pearl of great value [*polýtimon*], went and sold [*pépraken*] all that he had and bought [*ēgórasen*] it." I propose to exegete these two parables in one breath, as it were, and to do so by commenting on the Greek words I have flagged in the text.

First take the word *kekryménǭ*, "hidden." It is a participle of the verb *krýptein*, which, in addition to its already noted appearances in the parable of the Leaven and in the quotation from Psalm 78 in Matthew 13:35, turns up in a number of other places where it underscores the note of the mysteriousness of the kingdom. In Matthew 11:25, Jesus says — referring to the unrepentant cities that paid no attention to the mighty works by which he was proclaiming the kingdom — "I thank you, Father, Lord of heaven and earth, that you have hidden [*ékrypsas*] these things from the wise and learned and revealed [*apekálypsas*] them to babies." Not even brilliant specialists in plausibilities, he insists, can discern the kingdom at work in their midst; only the mystery-loving simplicity of children can recognize its hidden reality.

Again, in Luke 18:31-34 — when Jesus foretells his death and resurrection for the third time — the Gospel writer notes that even at this point the twelve "did not understand any of these things, and this word was hidden [*kekrymménon*] from them, and they did not know what he was talking about." The mystery, in other words, even when its literal details are spelled out in so many words, remains inaccessible to anyone's understanding. Finally, in two other non-Gospel citations, the root *kryp* is used in direct reference to the mystery of redemption. In Revelation 2:17, he who stands in the midst of the seven lampstands says to the church in Pergamum, "To him who overcomes, I will give some of the hidden [*kekrymménou*] manna"; and in the most pregnant reference in all of Scripture, Paul tells the still-living Colossian Christians, "You have died, and your life is hidden [*kékryptai*] with Christ in God. When Christ, your real life, appears, then you too will appear with him in glory" (Col. 3:3-4).

Taken together, therefore, these passages give the full force of the hiding of the mystery. It is by no means some merely invisible proposition that won't bother you if you don't bother it; rather, it is the chief constitutive principle of the whole creative-redemptive order — and it is present in all its reconciling power whether you pay attention to it or not. The mystery, in short, is exactly what the parable of the Treasure hidden in the field says it is: something worth selling anything you must to enjoy possessing.

Consider next the word *agrṓ*, "field." We have already come across it many times in the seed parables, where it functioned as a surrogate for the whole world. In this parable, though, the note of catholicity is stood on its head, so to speak. Obviously, the treasure is not broadcast throughout the field; it is hidden in only one spot (or to be completely accurate, two spots: first, in the place where the man found it; and second, in the place where he himself hid it so he would have time to convert his nonliquid assets into purchase money). But the field Jesus speaks of here still has a fascinatingly catholic aspect: the smart businessman of the parable buys the *whole* field. Jesus' reference, therefore, is not to the catholicity of the mystery but to the catholic, you've-got-to-go-for-the-whole-deal kind of behavior that the mystery demands of those who choose to respond to it. The man in the parable, accordingly, is a surrogate not only for individual responses to the kingdom hidden in the world but also, and especially, for the church's response.

Every now and then at ecumenical gatherings, the Apostles' Creed is recited; and too often someone gets the kindly meant but misguided idea of substituting the words "holy Christian church" for "holy catholic church." In terms of the Gospel, that is a disastrous switch. The church is not, in any proper sense, Christian. Its members are indeed called Christians (though it is worth noting that the name was first applied to them, in Acts 11:26 and 26:28, by outsiders); but it is not some sectarian society whose members have a monopoly on the mystery. It is not a club of insiders who, because of their theology, race, color, or sex — or their good behavior, intelligence, or income bracket — are the only channels through which the Word conveys himself to the world. Rather, it is a sign to the world of the mystery by which the Light has already lightened the whole shooting match, by which the divine Leaven has already leavened the whole lump of creation.

Therefore, the church is precisely *catholic,* not Christian. It is not a sacrament to the few of a salvation that they have but the world does not. Rather, it is the chosen sign of the salvation of the entire world. And (to return to the purchase of the entire field by the man in the parable) the church has not only to "buy," to "deal with," the whole world; it must also, if it is to be any decent kind of sign at all, look as much like the world — and be as little different from the world — as possible.

Yes, I know. The church is indeed to be the salt of an otherwise bland earth. But that doesn't mean that the church itself is supposed to be *all* salt or that it is supposed to turn the world into *nothing but* salt. Therefore, when it represents itself to the world, it probably should not first of all be seen as salt. That's misleading advertising. You don't put doughnuts in the window of a shoe store: that only confuses the public about your real business. Likewise you don't turn the church into a sodality that consists only of bright, white Anglo-Saxons who are happily married, have 1.8 children, and never get drunk. Instead, you just let it be what it in fact already is: a random sampling of the broken, sinful, half-cocked world that God in Christ loves — dampened by the waters of baptism but in no way necessarily turned into perfect peaches by them.

The church, like the purchaser of the field, can never afford to leave "unbought" any part of the earthly field in which God has hidden the treasure of the mystery. It does not dare to risk its own sure knowledge of where the mystery of the Word is — to risk its certainty that it has the right name of the Word (Jesus) and that it knows the precise location (the Incarnation) of the treasure that makes the whole world precious — by failing to purchase to itself every last bit of the field. The man who discovered the treasure did not simply buy the cubic yard or so of nice clean dirt in which he cleverly buried it. He bought the whole property: sinkholes, dungheaps, poison ivy, and sticker bushes, plus all the rats, mice, flies, and beetles that came with it. So too the church: if it can't bring itself to buy all sorts and conditions of human beings — white and nonwhite, male and female, smart and stupid, good and bad, spiritual and nonspiritual — it can't even begin to pretend it's catholic. Instead of being a sign of what the Word is up to in the world, it will become a sign of the very thing the Word is *not* up to, namely, the lightening of only some people, the sowing of less than the whole field, the leavening of two buns and a pretzel stick — and the discarding of all the rest.

But there is still more that can be said about the image of the field as this parable presents it. The treasure, clearly enough, is the mystery of the kingdom. The field in which it was buried, however, can be interpreted not only as the world but as the place in which, more than in all other places, the mystery's power lies hidden. It can be read, that is, as standing for *death*. Watch.

When we read this parable we automatically envision the treasure as buried underground in an otherwise wild or unused plot of land. Let me change the picture a bit, though. Since the parable mentions only a *hiding* of the treasure and says not a word about any burying of it, let me make the "field" an abandoned farm with a ramshackle farmhouse and an assortment of dilapidated barns and outbuildings. And let me further suppose that the prospective buyer, in checking over this not-too-promising addition to his holdings, first finds the treasure in a barn and then craftily moves it to the old henhouse for safe-keeping until the day when, having finally *bought the farm*, he can announce his phenomenal good luck at striking it rich.

Do you see? The phrase "bought the farm" (a euphemism for death, coined presumably by airline pilots whose demise would provide their wives with mortgage insurance to purchase outright their homesteads in Vermont) triggers a whole new set of meanings for this parable and gives us yet another insight into the catholicity of the mystery. *We all buy the farm:* death, along with birth, is an utterly catholic experience. Some of us get rich; some of us get sick; some of us get funny in the head; some of us write books; some of us behave ourselves; and some of us live in Grand Rapids. But every last one of us dies. Willy-nilly, every single person in the world, Christian or non-Christian, will someday come into full and secure possession of the field of death in which Jesus has hidden the treasure of his redeeming work. And therefore, since no one, anywhere, at any time, will ever finally be without death, no one — on earth, in heaven, or in hell — will ever be without Jesus' reconciliation.

Oh, dear. I hear two objections. Let me interrupt myself to deal with them. The first is: "But hold on. Doesn't Scripture say that there will be some (or even many) who will reject the reconciliation?" Of course it does. But the very hell of hell lies precisely in the fact that its inhabitants will be insisting on a perpetual rejection of an equally perpetual gift. It will be an eternal struggle to escape from the grip of a love that will never let them go. And for that everlasting stand-off, I think, there is not a word in Scripture that is too strong: not the "fire that is not quenched," not the "worm that dieth not," not the "outer darkness," not the "bottomless pit," not the "weeping and gnashing of teeth" — and certainly not the utterly fruitless "second death."

The second objection is more trivial, but it leads to something far more profound. "First Thessalonians 4:15-17!" the objectors howl: "We which are alive and remain unto the coming of the Lord shall not prevent them which are asleep. For the Lord himself shall descend from heaven with a shout, with the voice of the archangel, and with the trump of God: and the dead in Christ shall rise first: Then we which are alive and remain shall be caught up together with them in the clouds, to meet the Lord in the air: and so shall we ever be with the Lord" (KJV).

Pass over nearly everything about this text. Skip the question of whether it is enough of a foundation for all the pre-, post-, and amillennial theological architecture that has been piled on top of it. Forget about numbering the raptures. If you like, I'll sign my name to any eschatological scenario you want to write out. But in return, I want you to do me one favor: think just a little bit about the most likely historical circumstances under which your scenario will be played out. Unless the Lord mercifully cuts short the time — and cuts it very, very short indeed (like, say, down to tomorrow or the next day) — we will, by Murphy's law if nothing else, stage the end of the world for him with a nuclear holocaust. And while I'm sure God will have no theological problems with that (*any* end can serve as his end, just as *any* death, even the judicial murder of a common prisoner, can serve as his death), I'm equally sure that we who are alive and remain will have some serious practical problems.

In that day — when we are radiation-sick, ulcerated, bone-chilled, stupefied, and starving — whatever life we have left will make the dead look lucky. And whatever air there is to meet the Lord in will be death itself to breathe. Do you see? The glib and almost unpardonable effrontery of most eschatological hairsplitting fairly leaps out at you. To speak of two-bit theological distinctions in the face of a day like that is almost obscene — like making cool, theological small talk in the face of Jesus on the cross. For the fact is that the last day of this world — in the most likely script from which we will be allowed to act it out — is almost certainly going to be nothing less than the passion of literally everybody and the death of the whole earth.

So I hope you see why I have a certain profound impatience with quoters of 1 Thessalonians 4. This entire world is very nearly ready to buy the farm. Whether we meet the Lord in the air or not, there isn't one of us who will be saved by any other means than meeting the Lord in his death. *That* is the saving mystery; and one way or another, nobody is going to be excused from having the full force of it applied personally. Trouble me not, therefore: we are all going to be troubled to a fare-thee-well, and by experts.

But back to the parable. The next word, *ékrypsen,* brings up the second hiding of the treasure, this time by the very man who found it. I have said that the discoverer of the treasure stands for the church; does this rather shifty maneuver of his imply that the church may, under certain circumstances, hide the mystery? Well, not easily, I admit. It is hard to take an outfit supposedly operating under a charter to be a city set on a hill, a lamp not stuck under a bed, and make out a scriptural case that tells it to hide its message completely. But this parable suggests that a less radical hiding just might be a possibility. The man who found the treasure hid it so he could buy the field before anyone knew what he was really up to. He did not parade around beating people over the head with the news of his correct information about the treasure. He needed the whole field, so he acted in a way that would not jeopardize his eventual acquisition of it. So also the holy catholic church: its mission is to every single person in the world; therefore, it should not cut itself off from being heard by running around telling people where to head in before it even bothers to find out where they are coming from.

How many opportunities to proclaim the mystery has the church missed because it never took the time to learn the "language," cultural or historical, spiritual or practical, of the people it addressed? How often have the "unchurched" — the great catholic mass of unevangelized humanity who are, mind you, the very field in which the treasure of Jesus is already hidden, and who, but for their unbelief, would be enjoying him as mightily as believers do — how often have the unchurched put up a "not for sale" sign on their farm because they simply couldn't stand the arrogance of Christians?

And how much has the church itself missed? What treasures of understanding has it failed to buy? The Word that lightens everybody, everywhere, has been in business a long time. Not everything that "heathen" thoughts and deeds have produced came out of ungodly darkness. The wisdom of the East, for example, is not *all* foolishness, any more than the follies of Christians are all wise. But when the church approaches people as if God's whole, age-long, mysterious indwelling of the world had brought forth only two kinds of people — the utterly right and the totally wrong — then it deserves to have its money thrown back in its face. Whoever owned the field in the parable certainly wouldn't have sold it if the purchaser had shot his mouth off the way the church so frequently does.

But that is a very large subject indeed, so I simply leave it and return to the passage at hand. Consider next the word *pōleí,* "he sells," in verse 44, and the parallel word *pépraken,* "he sold," which occurs in the immediately succeeding parable of the Pearl. *Pōleín and pipráskein* (to use the infinitive forms) are very nearly synonymous: both are used to refer to perfectly ordinary selling, and both have (as in the phrase "selling someone down the river") acquired the secondary sense of *betraying.* But *pipráskein* is also used for *selling into slavery* (e.g., Matt. 18:25 and Rom. 7:14), so it may have a bit more of an all-or-nothing flavor to it. At any rate, in the parable of the Treasure, the man simply sells *(pōleí)* "what things" *(hósa)* he has; but in the Pearl, the merchant sold *(pépraken)* "all things whatsoever" *(pánta hósa)* he had.

In "Little Gidding," the last of his *Four Quartets,* T. S. Eliot says that the only possible response to "the drawing of this Love and the voice of this Calling" is "A condition of complete simplicity/(Costing not less than everything)." The pearl is *polýtimon,* of great value, to the merchant, just as the treasure in the field was to the man who found it hidden; but both spent whatever they needed to make their purchases. The merchant of course, unlike the real-estate operator, was actually looking for fine pearls *(kaloús margarítas).* His discovery was not a lucky accident but the logical result of his being already and utterly committed to the pearl business. And what does that say about the catholicity of the mystery of the kingdom? Well, I think it makes yet another interpretive twist possible — one in which the world becomes the buyer, rather than the seller of the mystery.

All the children of Adam — all human beings, at all times, and in all places — are in the kingdom business, shopping night and day for the mystery of the city of God. Oh, true enough, like any random group of shoppers, they have their share of gullibility, questionable taste, and proneness to buy what's in the store rather than wait for what they're really looking for. But they *are* shopping. And they *are*, as often as not, quite willing to put their money where their heart's desire is. They are *not* simply a bunch of cheapskates; and they do *not*, given half a chance to see some first-rate goods, simply fob off the storekeeper with an "Oh, we're just looking."

Score yet another point, therefore, for the insistence that the church cannot safely afford to deal — indeed, that it dare not refuse to deal — with anything less than the whole world. It is catholic not only because the mystery it proclaims is already hidden everywhere but because the market for the mystery is a catholic market. The philosophies, religions, and mysticisms of the world — however bright or dim, kindly or cruel, lofty or loony they may be — are, as Paul intimated in the first chapter of Romans, evidence of a taste (albeit a sometimes perverted taste) for the truth. Show them the one pearl of great price, and they just might finally recognize it as the very thing they have been hunting for all along.

But the comparison says even more about the church's missionary enterprise. Not only should mission be entered into with full confidence that the world, wittingly or unwittingly, actually wants what we have to sell — and not only should we put the news of its high price as winningly as possible — we should also not be too quick to insult their taste in pearls before they get to our shop. And we should be equally slow to scare them out of the store with a lot of negative talk either about high prices or about the awesome, burdensome responsibilities incurred by those who acquire top-of-the-line merchandise. Of course there are responsibilities. Buying the world's finest pearl means guarding it and worrying about it and paying monstrous insurance premiums on it. But first and above all, it means actually owning the world's finest pearl — which, if you have even a smitch of a taste for pearls, has got to be a real "up."

How sad it is, then, to reflect on what the world actually hears from the church in so many instances. We offer to sell them the mystery of the love of God in Jesus; but the way we talk about God and Jesus only makes it sound as if we are trying to peddle a live rattlesnake. People converted by fear-mongering are people converted *from* evil, not *to* the truth. And if they ever work up enough nerve to make friends with the evil, woe to the missionary enterprise: the truth will be as if they had never bought it. If the merchant had bought the pearl only because he was afraid his friends would despise him if he hadn't, then the minute he got strong enough to tell his friends to fly a kite, he would have sold the pearl and bought something else.

All of which, I suppose, makes the Pearl a parable about a lot of the conversions in the history of the church. The mystery has been sold at spearpoint, at gunpoint, and at economic pressure-point; and such hard sells have even been justified on the basis of the mystery's catholicity: "It's good for everybody in the world," the church has said in effect, "so who cares how we get them to buy it?" But the mystery is a mystery of love and wants nothing less than a free offering of complete simplicity. If it waited for aeons even to show its face, it can certainly wait a few more days, months, or years for people to decide they actually like its name.

Which brings us to the last of the flagged words in the text, the verb *agorázein,* "to buy." Purchasing — and purchasing gladly, at whatever cost — is the point of both of these parables. Indeed, in the case of the treasure, it is precisely *apó tēs charás autoú,* out of his joy at the prospect of its possession, that the man sells the things he owns. For if the treasure and the pearl can be said to stand for the mystery — and if (to return to my original identifications) their unnamed owners can be said to stand for the church, and if the man in the first and the merchant in the second can be said to stand for the unevangelized world — then the buying of both the field and the pearl must be made to stand for nothing less than the ecstatic enjoyment of a *polýtima,* an utterly precious mystery that would have been cheap at twice the price.

The woman who walks out of Bendel's with a $15,000 mink and the man who pulls into the driveway with a brand-new, cream-and-gold Rolls Royce Corniche are not, in that moment at least, gloomy characters. And to bring the parable full circle, neither are the salespeople who closed the deals on such fabulous purchases. There is *joy* in heaven over one sinner that repents, not a lot of handwringing and brow-furrowing, and certainly not a boring "watch your step now" lecture from the divine counterparts of Bendel, Rolls, and Royce.

Therefore, there should be at least smiles in the church over the same happy turn of events. Not because we have made a buck, and not, God forbid, because we have compassed sea and land to make a proselyte; but only because the customers are satisfied — because they have put on the mink of righteousness, sat down in the Rolls Royce of salvation, and are now just laughing themselves silly over the incongruous wonderfulness of it all.

CHAPTER TWELVE

The Net

The parable of the Net, like Jesus' interpretation of the parable of the Weeds, is a story about judgment. But because it is also the last of the parables of the kingdom, I propose to reverse field and expound it in a way that postulates no irony whatsoever in Jesus' mind. Its very ultimacy suggests to me that my "dog biscuit" theory should be kept in the box this time around: Jesus himself, I think, quite seriously meant the Net to be a parable of judgment.

Authors commonly try to end their sections or chapters with items that provide a fitting climax to what went before. Accordingly, I am going to assume that either Jesus or Matthew (neither of them slouched when it came to authoring) did just that by ending the sequence of kingdom parables with the Net. For two reasons. The first is that its reference to the *synteleía toú aiónos,* the completion, the end, the wrap-up of the age, makes it a natural as a finale. The same phrase, of course, occurs in the interpretation of the Weeds; but since that passage was placed more or less in the middle of the kingdom section, I felt freer to deal with it obliquely. But its occurrence here makes me want to give its eschatological points as much weight as they will bear.

The second reason follows from that. Whether this parable occurs last because Jesus habitually wound up his early, "kingdom-story" sessions with it, or because Matthew, as his editor, felt that logic called for it to be put at the end — whichever was the case, my commitment to the inspiration of Scripture leads me to believe that the Holy Spirit had his finger firmly in the pie. *All* of this parable's salient points, therefore — whether about judgment or anything else — should be examined with an eye to the way they sum up the picture of the kingdom so far. The Net is the final parabolic pass at the notes of catholicity, mystery, and so on, under which I have organized my exposition. I am curious to see if I can detect what the Spirit may have meant by this last move.

To begin: the net is a *sagénē*, a dragnet, a seine. ("Seine," by the way, is actually derived, via Latin and French, from *sagénē*. Even more interestingly, *sagénē* is what textual critics call a *hapax legomenon*, i.e., a word that occurs only once in the New Testament.) There are also two other words for "net" in the Greek text: *amphíblēstron*, "throw net," which occurs twice; and *díktyon*, the general word for "net" and "net-work," which occurs twelve times. But *sagénē*, appearing as it does only in this passage, is a particular kind of net, namely, one that is dragged through the water, indiscriminately taking in everything in its path. Accordingly, the kingdom of heaven (and by extension, the church as the sacrament of that kingdom) manifests the same indiscriminateness.

First reflection, therefore: As the net gathers up everything in its path — not only fish but also seaweed, flotsam, jetsam, and general marine debris — so too the kingdom gathers up everything in its path. Our usual mental image, of course, depicts the net as containing nothing but fish. Moreover, since the most obvious referent of the fish is people, we commonly suppose that the kingdom deals only with human beings. But in fact, the net of the kingdom touches everything in the world: not just souls, but bodies, and not just people, but all things, animal, vegetable, and mineral. In the context of the kingdom, for example, *Nero* is not just a dead Roman emperor; he is also a pet dog named to insult the memory of a persecutor of the kingdom. And hot cross buns are not just bread; they are the fruit of the plains marked with the sign of the mystery of the kingdom. And to come to a final, weightier illustration, gothic cathedrals are not just rock piles or shelters from the weather; they are stone parables of the splendor of the kingdom.

Accordingly, the note of catholicity is once again present in this parable, but with its range of meaning still further extended. Not only is the whole human race gathered into the kingdom; the entire physical order of the world is also drawn into it by the mystery of the Word. "I, if I be lifted up," says Jesus in John 12:32, "will draw *all* to myself." One note: Some texts read *pántas,* "all people"; others read *pánta,* "all things." The textual evidence leans in the direction of the former; but the latter remains at least a possibility. And that possibility, please note, is mightily enhanced by the imagery of the Book of Revelation: animal, vegetable, and mineral creatures throng the new earth as well as the old. There is a veritable bestiary of remarkable beasts; there is the tree of life in the New Jerusalem; and there is, at the center of it all, the city that lieth foursquare, the poetry of whose stonework makes even medieval cathedrals look like sand castles. In any case, just as the net fetches out everything it meets in the sea, so the kingdom fetches home to God everything in the world. The new heavens and the new earth are not replacements for the old ones; they are transfigurations of them. The redeemed order is not the created order forsaken; it is the created order — all of it — raised and glorified.

But that is to get ahead of the story: this seine, this *sagénē,* Jesus says, gathers "of every kind" *(ek pantós génous).* It is fascinating that nowhere in this parable does the word "fish" actually occur. Naturally enough, we (along with most translators) automatically supply it as we read, and perhaps that is just what Jesus had in mind. But since it is not there, it occurs to me to make something of its absence. In line with that, I have already enlarged the contents of the net to include other things besides fish; let me simply ask you to bear that inclusion in mind as we go along. It will, I think, cast considerable light on the whole parable.

Right now, though, I want to concentrate on the phrase "of every kind." Obviously, it is a reference to the catholicity of both the net and the kingdom, but it is a reference that is a bit different from any made so far. In the parables of the Seed and of the Leaven, the emphasis was on the presence of the mystery of the kingdom to the whole world. But in this parable the emphasis is narrower: it is on the presence of *all the variety in the world* to the mystery of the kingdom. The parts of the sea through which the net was not dragged do not enter into the case in this parable; we are simply assured that, whatever kinds of things there may have been in the sea — good, bad, or indifferent — every kind is represented in the net.

Far more important, though, the parable does not rush into the business of judging between the various kinds. Consider: In the sea, all kinds of fish and all kinds of junk simply coexist. Before the net goes through it, there isn't even a hint of judging between good and bad, useful and useless. Indeed, the undragged sea, if it represented anything, would represent an unkingdomed world; but in the light of the other parables so far, there is just no such thing. In this parable, therefore, only the net-with-its-contents can fairly be said to represent the kingdom-in-the-world that the parables of the kingdom are at pains to portray.

But even that representation still does not introduce the note of judgment: neither the net as it makes its way through the sea, nor the kingdom as it makes its way through the world, can be said to reject anything. True enough, a sorting, a day of judgment, is clearly on the way in both cases, and once the eschatological shore has been reached, it will begin in earnest. But it does not take place before then. Therefore, neither the purse seine while still in the sea, nor the kingdom while still in this world has any business setting itself up in the judging business. And neither, a fortiori, does the church.

Which leads to a second reflection: if the kingdom works like a dragnet, gathering every kind, the church, as the sacrament of the kingdom, should avoid the temptation to act like a sport fisherman who is interested only in speckled trout and hand-tied flies. In particular, it should not get itself into the habit of rejecting as junk the flotsam and jetsam of the world — the human counterparts of the old boots, bottles, and beer cans that a truly catholic fishing operation will inevitably dredge up. Because while the kingdom itself will indeed make it onto the eschatological beach, the church, as now operative, will not. The church is only the sacrament of the kingdom — a visible sign of a presently invisible mystery. But in the Last Day, the church as such will not be necessary at all; the mystery of the kingdom will stand revealed in and of itself and will need no sacraments or signs whatsoever.

The church, in short, has a role to play *only here and now*; so if it wants a role model for its operations, it should imitate the kingdom's present, nonjudgmental way of doing business, not its final one. It definitely should not attempt, in this world, to do the kind of sorting out that the kingdom so plainly refuses to do until the next.

But alas, beginning right in apostolic times — indeed, beginning even in Scripture itself — excommunication has been one of the church's favorite indoor sports. Second in popularity only to jumping to conclusions about who should be given the heave-ho first, the practice of tossing out rotten types while the net is still in the water has been almost everybody's idea of a terrific way to further the kingdom. Everybody's, that is, except Jesus' — the one who put the church in the business of being fishers of men to begin with. The net result, to use an apt phrase for such ineptness, has been an operation that looks as if it is being run more by his competitors than by his partners.

Jesus didn't shy away from sinners, so why should the church? And don't tell me the church welcomes sinners. I know better. It welcomes only sinners who repent and then never seriously need forgiveness again. It can reclasp to its bosom members who gossip or lose their tempers (*little-bitty* sins, apparently — though where that qualification came from is not clear); but God help those who fornicate or lose their will to stay married. And it has the gall to make such invidious distinctions in the name of a Lord who unqualifiedly told Peter, the Chief Fisherman, to forgive his sinful brother (Andrew, perhaps? — maybe he wasn't the good old boy he was cracked up to be) seventy times seven times.

"Ah, but," you object. "What about *reform?* Are we to give the world the impression it doesn't need to straighten up and fly right? Are we simply to imply that it can get away with murder if it likes?"

Well, for openers, the world has already gotten away with — no, that's too weak; it has already been absolutely saved by — its murder of God himself incarnate. But for closers, neither the world nor the church has ever had much more than the glide angle of a coke bottle. Sure, there is the power of the Holy Spirit to make people better. But note carefully that that's not what you were talking about when you broke in with your objection. You were talking about what *we* should or shouldn't do to improve the human race's aeronautics. And about that, I have only one thing to say: "If there had been a law given that could have given life, verily righteousness should have been by the law. But the scripture hath concluded all [*tá pánta*, fascinatingly, 'all *things*'] under sin, that the promise by faith of Jesus Christ might be given to them that believe" (Gal. 3:21-22, KJV).

Do you see? If even the divine jawboning on Mount Sinai couldn't reform the world, why should we think that our two-bit tirades against sin will do any better? So once again: sure there's reform; and it is even an important subject. But like everything else about the kingdom, it works in a mystery: it comes not when we decide to enforce it but only when God, by his paradoxical power, brings it about in his own implausibly good time. If he is willing to wait for it, why should the church be in such a rush? After all, it is *his* fish business we are supposed to be in.

Eventually, though (to return to the parable), Jesus does indeed get around to the subject of judgment. The fishermen did three things when the net was finally full: they hauled it up on the beach; they sat down; and they gathered *(synélexan)* the good *(tá kalá)* into a bucket and threw the bad *(tá saprá)* away. Time for a full-scale halt: I have deliberately given faulty translations for all of those Greek words.

First, *synélexan*, "they gathered." The verb *syllégein* is used seven times in the New Testament. Four of those uses occur in the parable of the Weeds and its interpretation (Matt. 13:29, 30, 40, 41) in connection with the gathering up of the *zizánia* (weeds), the *skándala* (things that offend), and so on; the other two uses occur in Matthew 7:16 and its parallel, Luke 6:44 ("Do men *gather* grapes of thorns or figs of thistles?"). Translators have been divided over how to render the word: their versions have ranged from the quite clearly judgmental "sort out" to the almost neutral "collect." On balance, though, "sort" has perhaps the best claim — especially when it comes to translating a parable of judgment.

The words "the good" and "the bad," however, are much more dubious translations. *Kalós* in Greek does indeed mean "good," but with overtones of "beautiful," "fine," or "fair"; it is not as narrowly moralistic as the other common Greek word for "good" *(agathós)*. Jesus, for example, calls himself "the good shepherd" *(ho poimén ho kalós)*, implying, presumably, that he is something more than just an ethical shepherd — that he is, in fact, an admirable one, even an extravagantly beneficent one. Still, *kalós* and *agathós* are often used more or less interchangeably for both moral and aesthetic (or utilitarian) goodness, so I want to put only a blunt, rather than a fine point on the distinction.

Saprós, though, is another matter. Like most languages, Greek bears witness to the wretched state of human nature by having more words for badness than for goodness. *Kakós* is perhaps the most common word for "bad." But there are plenty of others: there is *ponērós,* "evil"; *ánomos,* "lawless"; *áthesmos,* "unsettled"; *phaúlos,* "worthless"; and there is, of course, *saprós:* "rotten, putrid, corrupt, worthless, useless." *Saprós* appears in five passages, four of which show its obvious suitability for use as the ugly opposite of *kalós.* Consider, for example, Matthew 7:17 (which displays, along with the opposition of *kalós* and *saprós,* some other twists and turns of the Greek "good/evil" vocabulary): "So every good [*agathón*] tree bringeth forth good [*kaloús*] fruit; but a corrupt [*saprón*] tree bringeth forth evil [*ponēroús*] fruit" (KJV). Or for an even clearer illustration of the opposition of *kalós* and *saprós,* consider Matthew 12:33: "Either make the tree good [*kalón*] and his fruit good [*kalón*]; or else make the tree corrupt [*saprón*] and his fruit corrupt [*saprón*]" (KJV). (The remaining passages, by the way, are Luke 6:43, parallel to Matt. 12:33, and Eph. 4:29, where *saprós* is contrasted with *agathós.*)

What can be said, therefore, about the sorting of the contents of the net into *kalá* and *saprá?* Well, let's talk first as if the net contained only fish. If that were the case, the sorting might be based on a variety of considerations. Quite likely, it could involve a separation of desirable food species from unacceptable "trash" species. Just as likely, it could involve a separation of marketable big fish from unmarketable small ones. Less likely, it could involve a dividing of sickly, unacceptable specimens from healthy, desirable ones. Least likely of all, it could involve the separation of dead, putrid fish from live, sound ones. In any case, though, the criterion is not the innate goodness or badness of the fish themselves, but *their acceptability to the fishermen*. It is their utility or their beauty, in short — their being found *kalá* in the eye of the beholder — that lands them in the "save" bucket. And it is the judgment of *saprá* (rotten! ugly! icky! crummy! yech!) that gets them thrown away on the beach.

And the same thing is true if we postulate general marine garbage as well as fish in the net. Whatever serves the fishermen's purposes is kept; whatever does not is tossed out. But notice an important element here: there is always the possibility that some of the damnedest things might be saved: old rusty anchors, bald tires, and broken lobster pots might just make the cut if somebody took a shine to them. In short, the net contains many things, but there is nothing, however decrepit in and of itself, that absolutely has to be gotten rid of. Whatever sorting is done depends entirely on the disposition of the sorters. If they don't say "yech!" to something, then it's not *saprón*.

Admittedly, when Jesus comes to apply the imagery of this parable to the end of the world, he introduces another word for badness, namely, *toús ponēroús,* "the wicked," those who are willfully evil. But at the present point in the parable, that notion is simply not here. Reserving willful wickedness for later comment, therefore, I propose to press a little on this matter of the eye of the beholder being the key to the difference between *tá kalá* and *tá saprá*.

I have said that it is the fishermen, not the fish, who set the standards for the day of judgment on the beach. Therefore, it is the kingdom — and a fortiori, the King — who sets the standards for the Last Day of the world. But notice something peculiar about that day. It occurs, as I have already said, *after* the general resurrection: every last person who arrives at it arrives in the power of Jesus' reconciliation. The judgment, therefore, is first of all the announcement not of vindictiveness but of vindication. Everyone who comes before the Judge has already been reconciled by the dying and rising of the Judge. The only sentence to be pronounced, *as far as the Judge himself is concerned,* is a sentence to life, and life abundant.

Someone once said, "The world God loves is the world he sees in his only-begotten Son." If that is true, it means that at the last day, the

131

whole world — the *all* that Jesus, in his being lifted up, has drawn to himself — is accepted in the Beloved. No one has to accept that acceptance, of course. It is entirely possible, both humanly and scripturally speaking, for anyone to thumb his nose at the reconciliation and try to go it on his own forever. And it is totally certain that if anyone wants to indulge in that kind of behavior, there is no possibility of keeping such a party pooper at the marriage supper of the Lamb. Hell is the only option for the finally recalcitrant.

But note well that nobody goes to hell because he had a rotten track record in the world — any more than anyone goes to heaven because he had a good one. Everyone, of every kind, who lands on the millennial beach has been fished up there by the net-work of the death and resurrection of Jesus. No one is judged by what he was like before that net caught him; the standards for the judgment are the divine Fisherman's standards, not those that were used to approve or disapprove of the fish as they formerly existed in the sea. And since those standards are one and the same as the divine Judge's, they are vindicative, not vengeful standards. We are not judged by our previous performances (on that basis, nobody would go anywhere but to hell); rather, we are judged by what Jesus did for us on the cross. He pronounces an authoritative *kalá* over the whole world that he has caught in the net of his reconciliation. It is only those who want to argue with that gracious word who are then pronounced *saprá*. Both heaven and hell are populated entirely and only by forgiven sinners. Hell is just a courtesy for those who insist they want no part of forgiveness.

And if the King wills finally to favor every last sinner with his reconciling *kalá*, how much more should the church — which is a sign to the world of his kingdom of forgiveness — pronounce the same *kalá* over the sinners with which it has to deal? Everybody, even the worst stinker on earth, is somebody for whom Christ died. What a colossal misrepresentation it is, then, when the church gathers up its skirts and chases questionable types out of its midst with a broom. For the church to act as if it dare not have any dealings with sinners is as much a betrayal of its mission as it would be for a hospital to turn away sick people or for a carpenter to refuse to touch rough-cut wood.

Sinners are the church's *business,* for God's sake. Literally. Let the scribes and the Pharisees — the phony-baloney, super-righteous, unforgiving scorekeepers who delight in getting everybody's number — take care of any judging that they want to: *judgment now* is their cup of tea, and they can poison themselves all they want with it. But let the church — which works for somebody who delights in getting everybody's *name* — stay a million miles away from it. We are supposed to represent a Lord who came not to judge the world but to save it. Our business should be simply to keep everybody *in* the net of his kingdom until we reach the farther shore. Sorting is strictly his department, not ours.

But on with the parable. After Jesus has set up the earthly imagery of his story, he turns to the task of applying it to the eschatological reality it stands for: "So will it be at the end of the age [*en tę synteleíą toú aiónos*]. The angels [*ángeloi*] will come and separate [*aphorioúsin*] the evil [*toús ponēroús*] out of the midst of the righteous [*ek mésou tōn dikaíōn*]."

Note first the word *syntéleia,* the end, completion, consummation, wrap-up. It stands not just for a denouement, a last unwinding, but for an arrival at something that has been in the works all along. *Télos,* the Greek root of the word, means "end, goal, purpose"; *syn* is a prepositional prefix meaning "with" or "together." *Tetélestai,* "it has been accomplished," was one of Jesus' last words on the cross; *tele*ology is the branch of philosophy that deals with the concept of *purpose.* This *syntéleia,* this wrap-up, then, is the final fruition of Jesus' work; and as such, it should be understood as of a piece with all the gracious rest of that work. It should not be propounded as a last-minute switcheroo that turns his entire redemptive ministry into nothing but a temporary — and deceptive — come-on.

Next, note what this *syntéleia* is the consummation of: it is the completion of *toú aiónos,* "of the age," that is, of the whole history of the world. In older English versions, *tou aiónos* is commonly translated simply as "of the world" (*aión* in Greek became *saeculum* in Latin, which in turn gave us "secular" in English: hence, "world" as a possible translation). But *aión* means far more than just the world as world or even the world as fallen creation: it means the entire historical process — good in some respects but fatally flawed in others — by which the world marches and/or stumbles toward its destiny. Once again, then, the note of *completion* creeps in. The world may have done its damnedest to reach what it considers its proper conclusion, but God in Christ has done his blessedest to take away the curse it put on itself in the process; now, at the *synteleíą toú aiṓnos,* at the final meeting of the blessing and the curse, he is about to make the blessing stick once and for all.

And how does he do that? Well, by George, he does it by *ángeloi,* by angels. In my comments on the interpretation of the Weeds, I dismissed the angels in that context with a "who cares who they are?" Let me take that back now. The angels stand for something of major significance here: fascinatingly, there is no strict counterpart to them in the first half of the parable of the Net as Jesus told it. It was the *fishermen* who did the sorting on the beach. The implication, therefore, was that the very same crew who dragged the net ashore would be the ones doing the job of separation. But when Jesus comes to the second half of the parable, he brings in a whole new crew, totally and irreversibly committed to doing only and always what *he* wants done. Do you see? "The Father . . . has committed all judgment to the Son" (John 5:22): nobody else — not the Father, not the Spirit, and certainly not the church — gets into the act. The job is strictly in the hands of Jesus and his utterly subservient heavenly bailiffs — which means, when all is said and done, just in Jesus' hands, period.

And what is it that these minions of his do? They "separate" *(aphorioúsin).* They make no decisions; they implement no policies of their own; they simply move resurrected bodies around as directed by him who is the Resurrection and the Life. And on what basis, finally, does he direct them to make that separation? On the basis of his decision to get *toús ponēroús,* the evil ones, out of the midst of *tṓn dikaíōn,* the righteous ones.

Time for another large-size halt. *Question:* How did those righteous ones get to be righteous? *Answer:* By the free gift of Jesus' righteousness. *Question:* To whom was that free gift offered? *Answer* (unless you believe in double predestination): to every human being who ever lived. *Question:* Do you actually mean that there's nobody at the Last Judgment who hasn't been given the righteousness of Christ? *Answer:* Yes, that's exactly what I mean. *Question:* Then how come some of them are judged *ponēroús? Answer:* Because even though they've got his righteousness, they've decided they don't like it; they can't stand the thought of not being accepted on their very own personal merit (which is one of the world's great nonexistent quantities, of course — but then, they seem to miss that point). *Question:* Wherever did you dig up ideas like this? *Answer:* Matthew 22:1-14. Any more questions?

This parable, you see, I take to be an honest-to-God parable of judgment, not just a dog biscuit. And therefore I am disposed to read it in the light of all the weightier parables of judgment that Jesus eventually told. Hence, Matthew 22:1-14. The fellow without the wedding garment in the parable of the King's Son's Wedding was precisely *ponērós:* he willfully balked at the one easily met condition of his attendance at the party. *Nobody* who was actually at the reception had a *right* to be there. Earlier in the story, of course, there were indeed people who deserved to be invited, but they had all refused the invitation — one going to his farm, another to his merchandise, and the rest of them murdering the king's servants. The ones who finally did get into the party were those who, despite their unfitness and their undeserving, were simply dragooned into attending. The indiscriminate dragooning, in fact, was the very thing that made them acceptable even in their unacceptableness; just as the catholic netting action of the kingdom is what proclaims the whole human race to be accepted in the Beloved. All the inhabitants of the world, in other words, are being drawn toward the final *kalá* that the Word wants to pronounce over them. Jesus does say, quite obviously, that if anyone doesn't like that ending of the story, he can lump it in outer darkness; but still, anyone who wanted to could have enjoyed it free-for-nothing.

There, then, is the force of *ponērós:* not just moral or aesthetic badness, but willful evil. The *ponēroús* whom the angels finally separate out of the midst of the righteous are not just *kakoús* (i.e., un-*agathoús* or un-good in a narrowly moral sense), and they are not just *saproús* (i.e., un-*kaloús* or un-good in the aesthetic or beautiful sense); they are positively and cussedly determined to reject Jesus' offer to ignore both their badness and their rottenness and to welcome them to the party anyway as *dikaíous,* that is, as clothed with his very own righteousness. They are, in short, ill-willed troublemakers. Like *ho ponērós* himself — like the evil one from whom we pray to be delivered in the Lord's Prayer — like the father of lies who hates the truth simply because he didn't invent it — they refuse to accept any gift, however gracious, unless they themselves are convinced they have an inalienable personal right to it.

And what, therefore, do the angelic bouncers do with such malefi- cent, belly-aching types? They separate these *ponēroús* out of the midst of the righteous *(ek mésou tón dikaíon).* In short, they pitch them out on their ear so they won't ruin the party. Even the eternal banishment of the wicked, you see, is a celebrative, vindicative judgment. There is to be *joy* in heaven not just over one sinner who repents but over the ninety and nine as well — over a whole New Jerusalem populated by nothing but sinners whose citizenship is based on nothing but their acceptance of forgiveness. If anybody doesn't want to be there on that basis, he can, quite literally, just get the hell out.

But then comes the end of the parable: "And they will throw them into the furnace of fire [*eis tén káminon toú pyrós*]; out there [*ekeí*], there will be wailing and gnashing of teeth [*ho klauthmós kaí ho brygmós tón odónton*]."

The "furnace of fire," as I have noted, occurs at the end of Jesus' in- terpretation of the Weeds; it also turns up in another eschatological context, Revelation 9:2. But the "wailing and gnashing of teeth" occurs in a whole raft of such contexts: Matthew 8:12; 13:42, 50; 22:13; 24:51; 25:30; and Luke 13:28. In any case, each phrase has its unique force: the furnace suggests discomfort applied from the outside; the wailing and gnashing of teeth suggest anguish that springs from within. Not that there is much to choose between them; either would seem quite suffi- cient punishment for those who insist on being eschatological wet blankets. But taken together, the phrases bear witness to a double truth about the redeemed order: the furnace testifies to God's absolute insis- tence that nothing and nobody is going to rain on his final parade; and the wailing, to the equally absolute certainty that his parade is the only show in town that's going to be any fun. All that there is out there — in outer darkness — is an eternal, stinking pile of self-pity, festering its way to an equally eternal production of angry gas. The damned are not a crowd of wistful types, pining away for a wonderful deal that some mean scorekeeper of a God did them out of. They are a bunch of unreconstructed haters who threw away the best deal they were ever offered and now can't find anybody but themselves to be furious with.

It's not a pretty picture. But then, the *ponēroí* are not very pretty themselves. Still, except for their willful refusal of the reconciliation, they could have gone, just as easily as the righteous, from the net into the bucket. There was no compelling reason for them to spend eternity gasping on the beach.

Epilogue

M atthew's compendium of the parables of the kingdom — as well as my own treatment of them — ends with a passage (13:51-52) that, while parabolic enough, is not exactly a parable in the sense we have so far come to expect. Instead, it is a parabolic utterance of the sort we came across in the quotation from Psalm 78:2, that is, a "dark saying." And though it could easily be expanded into a narrative parable by any preacher who was willing to supply his own details, it is, as we have it, more a one-line comparison than a story.

Furthermore, it begins without any introduction. This has happened before (in the parables of the Treasure Hidden in the Field and in the Pearl of Great Price) but not quite as abruptly as here. Indeed, so absent is any clear pause for breath that this passage might logically be taken as a mere coda to the parable of the Net. Nevertheless, I find it makes even better sense as the capstone of the whole collection, so that is how I propose to read it.

"Jesus saith unto them," Matthew writes, "have ye understood [*synékate*] all these things [*taúta pánta*]?" (KJV). Note first of all that these words are not addressed to the crowds. Matthew, if you recall, has had Jesus in the house with his disciples ever since the beginning of the interpretation of the Weeds; it is the disciples, therefore, who respond to the question. "They say unto him, Yea, Lord [*nai, kyrie*]" (KJV).

And in response to that answer Jesus gives the parabolic summation of everything he has been saying about the mystery of the kingdom. "Then said he unto them, Therefore every scribe [*grammateús*] which is instructed [*mathēteutheís*] unto the kingdom of heaven [*tę̃ basileíą tõn ouranõn*] is like unto a man that is an householder [*oikodespótę̃*], which bringeth forth [*ekbállei*] out of his treasure [*thēsauroú*] things new and old [*kainá kai palaiá*]." (This preliminary translation of the passage is taken verbatim from the KJV: since there are so many comments to be made about the flagged words, I want to start out on at least familiar, if not exactly unimpeachable, ground.)

To begin with, only the Byzantine manuscript tradition, plus a handful of other sources, has the words "Jesus says to them" at the beginning of the passage. They are omitted in the older manuscripts that make up the so-called Hesychian or Egyptian tradition, so most modern editors simply leave them out of the text and have Jesus begin directly with his question, "Have you understood all these things [*synēkate taúta pánta*]?"

Synēkate is from *syniénai:* to send, bring, set together. By extension, it also means to take notice of, know, understand. Accordingly Jesus is asking his disciples, "Do you grasp what I've been trying to tell you? Do you think you're able to put all this stuff together?" In spite of the disciples' track record for being slow on the uptake, he still seems to have his hopes: the crowds outside may have heard only odd, entertaining stories, but maybe this hand-picked, advanced class of insiders will do better.

If you have ever done any teaching, you know that it takes no small amount of courage for an instructor to ask such a question. Jesus has been at pains to expound a very different kingdom from the one his hearers, outsiders or insiders, were expecting. It is *catholic,* not limited just to the chosen people; it is paradoxically and vexingly *hidden,* not plausibly and gratifyingly manifest; it is *at work now,* not simply waiting for some future date; it operates in the midst of *hostility,* not welcome; and the *responses* it calls for are, hands down, the most mystifying propositions yet: not warfare, not haste, not a helping hand, not a quick, easy purchase, but rather nonviolence, patience, noninterference, and an investment the size of the national debt. It's a brave teacher who has the nerve to hope his pupils will have grasped even a tenth of such mind-boggling information.

Once again, if you have ever done any teaching you will understand that the answer Jesus gets to his question is not exactly encouraging. "They say to him, 'yes' [*nai*]." The Greek word, like the English one, can mean anything from a "Yes indeed, we've taken in every last item, and we're ready to explain it at length to anybody who comes along," all the way down to an "Uh-huh," muttered chiefly in the hope that it will hoodwink the teacher into not asking them to recite. I am relatively certain that Jesus — who besides being a practiced pedagogue also "knew what was in man" — was quite clear in his own mind that it was the latter, rather than the former sense of *nai* that his disciples had in mind. In any case, it is a fact that they hardly understood him at all — and that they continued to misunderstand almost all of his deeds and words, parabolic or not, until well after his Resurrection.

The Byzantine manuscript tradition, incidentally — with its sometimes "churchy" overtones — corroborates this impression. In those manuscripts, the disciples say *nai, kyrie,* yes, Lord; they add a deferential "Herr Professor" to their affirmation as a further smokescreen for their incomprehension. Still, the older and better tradition leaves it at the almost-dumb *nai,* and so, accordingly, do most editors. The unvarnished "Uh-huh," has quite enough punch all by itself — a punch, in fact, that would hit any veteran teacher right in the solar plexus.

Jesus, however — pro that he is — doesn't even miss a breath. Plunging right ahead, treating his question as purely rhetorical so they won't have a chance to gum up the lesson with their own tacky explanations, he simply delivers his prepared last line anyway. "And he said to them, 'Therefore [*diá toúto*], every scribe [*pás grammateús*]. . . .'"

But stop there for a moment. *Diá toúto* means literally "on account of this"; but the disciples' "yes," as I have interpreted it, scarcely seems to provide much of an antecedent for the "this." Accordingly, it's hard to see how what he says next follows from their reply with any great logic. "On account of" seems entirely too strong; but even such translations as "therefore," or "this means, then," or "you can see, then," or even "well, then" (all of them used in various modern versions) seem overly consequential. What is needed, therefore, is a rendering that makes his next words a kind of two-way response — one that is a consequence of both their professed comprehension and their actual incomprehension at the same time. My own suggestion (admittedly just a tad colloquial, but expressing both gratification and skepticism) is this: "And he said to them, 'O–kay; then just listen: every scribe. . . .'"

Which brings us to *grammateús*, "scribe." *Grámma* in Greek means "letter," as in a letter of the alphabet. A *grammateús*, therefore, is a "lettered," that is, a "learned," person. The scribes (of the well-known team, scribes and Pharisees) were lay Jewish scholars of the four or five pre-Christian centuries, and they are referred to (as *hoi grammateís*) some sixty or so times in the New Testament. In most of the references they are represented almost as a sect or a political party; but in a few places — this one in particular — that just may not be the case. In Matthew 23:34, for example, Jesus says, "Behold, I send to you prophets and wise men and scribes [*grammateís*]" — implying simply "learned men." In 1 Corinthians 1:20, Paul asks, "Where is the wise man, where is the scribe [*grammateús*], where is the debate-enthusiast of this world?" — *grammateús*, once again, apparently referring more to just plain scholarship than to membership in a faction.

In this passage, therefore, it is quite possible that Jesus was using the words *pás grammateús* to mean "every one who has been instructed" in the kingdom of God — or even more narrowly, "every one who has received *my* instruction." Nevertheless, since the precise thing in which the scribes themselves were scholars was the Old Testament Law, the Torah — and since Jesus later refers to "things old" as well as "things new" — it is probably neither wise nor perhaps even possible to eliminate the notion of scribal Torah-learning from the word *grammateús* here. Hence the rather confusing field day that modern translators have had with this passage. Check out any number of them, and you will see that they are caught over several barrels at once: they want to get away from the usual, derogatory sense of "scribe," but they don't want to go so far in the direction of general scholarship that they lose the reference to the Torah altogether.

Probably, there is no satisfactory, simple solution to the problem:

no single English word has all the shadings of *grammateús*. Perhaps the only workable approach is to abandon literal translation completely, as J. B. Phillips does, for example, and just toss in as many extra words as you may need to get the general idea across.

To an almost equal degree, the same difficulty plagues the translator of the phrase "instructed unto the kingdom of heaven" *(mathē-teutheís tḗ basileíą tṓn ouranṓn)*. *Mathēteutheís* means simply "taught," as in, "she has been taught how to cook." And *tḗ basileíą* is simply the dative singular of *hē basileía,* the kingdom. It is used here, possibly, as a dative of relation ("taught the things *related* to the kingdom"), or possibly as a dative of interest ("taught *for* the kingdom"), or less possibly, perhaps, even a dative of agent ("taught *by* the kingdom").

At any rate, in the Greek, "kingdom" is simply a word in the dative case. The specific hairsplittings of the grammarians are not commonly uppermost in the minds of people who understand the language. Rather, when any particular grammatical usage is presented to them, they tend to hear not only its most natural sense but also as many of its additional shadings as the passage in question will bear. Therefore the following translations are all possibilities: "taught *for,*" "taught *unto,*" "taught *in relation to,*" "taught *about*" — or even such periphrases as "has become a learner *in*" or "becomes a disciple *of*" the kingdom of heaven. Hence, once again, the bewildering variety of modern translations.

Nevertheless, Jesus' fundamental meaning seems fairly clear: "Okay," he says, "you say you understand; so now I'll tell you something: every careful listener to what I've been teaching you about the kingdom of heaven is like a man who is an *oikodespótēs* [a householder]." The translation "householder," however, is a bit weak for *oikodespótēs* — and "homeowner," a more modern choice, is even worse. The Greek word (which comes from the roots *oik-,* house, and *despot-,* lord, master, slaveowner) means "house manager," or even "majordomo." Therefore, what Jesus is saying to them seems closer to: "Once you've been taught about the kingdom of heaven by me, you're going to be like someone who's been given full authority over an incredibly rich castle. There will be nothing you lack and nothing you'll ever exhaust the wonder of — and, of course, nothing over which you won't have utterly satisfactory control. And like the lord of the castle who brings out [*ekbállei*] all kinds of things from his treasure [*thēsauroú*] — not only things that were stored up a long time ago but things that were acquired only this morning — you, too, will bring forth things new and old [*kainá kai palaiá*]."

Ekbállei first. The word commonly means "throws out," "casts out," or even "drives out." (Jesus, people said, casts out — *ekbállei* — demons by Beelzebul: Luke 11:15; the Spirit drives — *ekbállei* — Jesus out into the desert: Mark 1:12.) But in addition, it often means "brings out," or "brings forth." ("A good man, out of the good treasure of his heart, brings forth [*ekbállei*] good things," Matt. 12:35.) Therefore, the bringing forth referred to here by Jesus is no rummage-sale unloading of junk; rather, it is a displaying of rare treasures for the fascination of the castle's guests.

And there is a lesson in that for preachers. So often, whether because of thickheadedness, lack of study, scanty preparation, or just plain boredom, they unceremoniously heave the treasures of Scripture out of the pulpit as if they were flopping out so many dead fish. There is no fascination in their monologues, no intrigue, no sense whatsoever that the ministry they have been given is precisely that of being major-domo over a house to end all houses. The most they ever achieve is a kind of monomaniacal enthusiasm for the one or two items that happen to suit their own odd tastes: hellfire, perhaps; or their sawed-off, humanistic version of love; or their short-order recipe for spirituality; or the hopelessly moralistic lessons in good behavior that they long since decided were more palatable than the paradoxes of the Gospel. There is nothing that resonates with anything like the enthusiasm of, "Hey, look at this fantastic footstool I just discovered!" or, "You've simply got to taste this incredible old Port!" But alas, only that kind of enthusiasm is contagious and joy-producing. We should all pray for them. May God hasten the day on which they will stay in the castle storeroom long enough to get stark staring bonkers about the Word and hilariously drunk on Scripture.

Which brings us to the storeroom itself, the *thēsaurós*, the treasure. We have been shown this treasure once before, hidden in a field. Here, however, it is a treasure finally bought, owned, and manifest. The word

143

thēsaurós, incidentally, can denote anything from the stuff you value to the repository you keep it in — and, like the English word "treasure," it can be applied, literally or metaphorically, to almost anything you want. But it is its English derivative "thesaurus," I think, that casts the most light on the way Jesus uses it here.

A thesaurus (as in *Roget's Thesaurus of English Words and Phrases*) is a dictionary of synonyms in which the light of various words and phrases is allowed to shine on practically the whole array of human ideas and concepts. Fascinatingly enough, the entire revelation of God is also just such a thesaurus. The Bible, from start to finish, is a matter of *words;* and even when those words are about *actions* (in particular, when they are about major actions like the Creation, for example, or the choosing of Israel, or the Exodus, or the giving of the Law, or the sacrificial system of the Old Testament — not to mention the Incarnation, or the earthly ministry of Jesus, or his death, resurrection, ascension, or second coming), these actions are presented to us as the work of nothing less than the divine *Word* himself.

It is just that *thēsaurós,* just that treasury of the words of the Word, over which those who have received Jesus' instruction in the mystery of the kingdom have been made *oikodéspotai,* lords and masters. And from it, as from an inexhaustible storeroom, they bring forth an endlessly fascinating display of things new and old. How? By the very same method that owners of a literary thesaurus use: by comparing and contrasting what occurs in one place with what the Word says and does in other places. The Bible is not a collection of discrete passages, each of which has only the single meaning it possesses in its isolated spot; rather, it is the vast and unified work of a genius of an author who is constantly cross-referencing himself. Like a first-rate novelist, the Holy Spirit "buries bones" all over the place. Early on, for example, he sneaks in a slain animal that protects the Israelites from the death of the first-born in Egypt; later, when he is heading for the grand finale, he digs up that bone and turns it, as the Paschal Lamb, into the very crux of his story.

And that is only one illustration out of thousands. There is the tree of life in Eden which surfaces later as both the tree of the cross and the tree for the healing of the nations in the New Jerusalem. There is the virgin conception which, at its first appearance in Isaiah, looks like little more than a political metaphor but which, at the great turning point of the story, reappears as the grand entrance of the Word himself. And there is, to come to one of the most momentous words in Scripture, *blood,* whose imagery grows richer and more complex with each succeeding appearance. From the blood of Abel to the blood on Joseph's coat — to the blood on the doorposts, to the blood of the Old Covenant, to the blood from the Messiah's wounds, to the eucharistic blood of the New Covenant, to the blood of the Lamb in which the saints dip their robes and make them white — there is not a single reference that does not incorporate and enlarge all the meanings that have gone before.

Do you see? The entire revelation is a *thēsaurós* of things new and old that the Spirit is constantly comparing, contrasting, and ringing the changes on. That's why a foolish literalism is such a blind alley. You can't read a great author phrase by phrase as if each word were meant to mean only what it says in the place in which it occurs. Early uses of a word illuminate later ones; and even more important, later uses illuminate earlier ones. Indeed, the Spirit has *all* uses in mind everywhere: he has full and deliberate control over his story throughout the book. Therefore, unless you wait him out — unless you store up in your own mind a *thēsaurós* of all the bones he has buried — you will make no sense of either the story or its parts. To be sure, many things in the Bible can be taken literally — and just as many can not; but even the literal passages can have nonliteral meanings — and even the nonliteral ones can be utterly crucial to the story.

Therefore, I come back once again to my insistence that, in high seriousness and with equally high glee, we should *play* with Scripture. The *thēsaurós* of the kingdom is not something to be kept in the attic and dragged out only on Sundays for loan exhibitions in museums; nor is it something that people should stare at only when wearing solemn faces and three-piece suits. We may be the *oikodéspotai* of the treasure of God, but we were meant first of all to spend huge amounts of time in the attic just poring over it and trying all of it on for size. And we were meant, above all, to invite the world up into the attic to play dress-up with us. We are supposed to be *kids,* you see: "I thank you, Father, Lord of heaven and earth, that you have hidden these things from the wise and prudent, and revealed them to babes." You can't get more encouragement than that for holy horsing around.

And so we come to the end of the passage: what all this playing with the mystery brings forth is *kainá kaí palaiá,* things new and old. The treasure of the kingdom does not consist of certain things that are old and certain other things that are new; rather, it consists of old things that are perpetually springing up and new things that turn out to have been around since before the foundation of the world. Pick up any item in it and it will, always and without fail, turn out to be both an antique and a novelty at the same time. And that, when you think of it, is no surprise: the Word who lays up this whole *thēsaurós* for us lays it up first and foremost in the Land of the Trinity where everything is, all at once, older than eternity and as fresh as the breath of the Word who speaks it into being. "Behold, *kainá poiō pánta,* I make all things new," says he who sits, from beginning to end, on the throne of the kingdom. As scribes instructed unto the kingdom of heaven — and as children turned loose in the treasure room of the castle — we've got more than enough to keep us fascinated forever.

THE PARABLES
OF GRACE

CHAPTER ONE

Introduction

A PARABLE OF THEOLOGY AND FAITH

I know it is a risky thing to begin a book on Jesus' parables of grace with a parable of my own on the perils of theologizing; nevertheless . . .

A certain couple once built a house. They set it on solid foundations and made it proof against all weathers. But in their haste to take up occupancy, they made no provision for access to the front door. To enter, they simply leaped up onto the doorsill and yanked themselves in. As they began to feel more at home, however, they decided to make their comings and goings more convenient. First, they built a short flight of steps. These served well for a while, but eventually they replaced them with a small, plainish porch on which they could sit and contemplate the excellences of their house. In good weather, they even entertained friends there with wine, cheese, and conversation.

Soon enough, though, they tore down this first porch and built a much larger one. They gave it a roof supported by carpenter gothic columns; they surrounded it with intricate railings; they provided it with a wide, low-pitched staircase; and they decorated it everywhere with gingerbread ornamentation.

Many years passed, during which they enjoyed both the porch and the house. But then, on a cold and stormy night, the woman came to the man as he sat by the fire and shook a sheaf of bills in front of him. "Have you ever considered," she said annoyedly, "how much we spend on the upkeep of our porch? For something that's usable only four months of the year — and not even then, if one of us is sick — the cost-benefit ratio is appalling. Between the dry rot and the peeling paint, not to mention the lawsuit your friend Arthur brought against us when he caught his ankle in the gap left by those missing boards, it's more trouble than it's worth. Tear it down and let's go back to the way we started: no porch, no steps, no nothing; just up into the house by one leap."

My parable, obviously, is about the relationship between faith and theologizing. Equally obviously, it is more an allegory than a parable; but since even Jesus allowed himself a number of such simple, this-stands-for-that stories, let it pass. My point in starting with it is to put what I am up to in this book into perspective. The house in which the couple lived represents faith — the simple act of deciding to trust Jesus (and, consequently, Jesus' words as we have them), no matter what we, on any given day or in any given intellectual weather, may happen to think about them. On the other hand, the various accesses, plain steps or fancy porches, that they added to their house stand for our attempts at theologizing — that is, for any and all of the explanations we come up with when we try to render our house of faith more intelligible, more attractive, or more acceptable to the intellectual tastes of our neighbors or friends.

Inevitably, any author who tries to interpret Jesus' parables will spend most of his time on the porch. He will, of course, take it for granted that there is a house of faith to which the porch should remain firmly attached, and he will, if he is wise, make it clear that only the house can provide a completely safe place in which to live. Nevertheless, since the woman in my parable came to such a dim view of porches, a few comments on her objections would seem to be in order.

It is tempting simply to agree with her. So much of what both the world and the church consider to be the essential message of the Gospel is simply interpretation. It is generally assumed that Christianity teaches that people cannot be saved unless they accept some correct, or at least some Official Boy Scout, understanding of what Jesus did or said. Take the atonement, for example — the scriptural insistence that

150

our sins are forgiven by trusting a Jesus who died on the cross and rose from the dead. The usual view is that this trust inevitably involves accepting some intellectual formulation of *how* Jesus' death and resurrection could possibly have achieved such a happy issue out of all our afflictions. You know: he was able to bring it off because he was both God and man and so could bridge the gulf that sin had put between the two; or, his death was effective because it was a ransom paid to the devil; or, it did the job because the power of his sacrificial example softened even hard hearts and moved people to better behavior; or, his resurrection solved the problem of sin because it brought about a new creation in which sin had no place. The point is not whether any of those interpretations is true, or even adequate (some are more so, some less); it is that none of them is strictly necessary for laying hold of the atonement Jesus offers. All you need for that is to believe in *him* — to say "Yes, Jesus, I trust you," as opposed to "No, Jesus, get lost." Your subsequent understanding of how such a simple yes can do so vast a work may make you glad, sad, scared, or mad; but in no case can it be what saves you — or, for that matter, condemns you.

This distinction needs to be applied just as much to the words of Jesus as it does to his works. People tend to think that unless they can arrive at some satisfying interpretation of this parable or that, the parable in question may safely be left out of account. But just as the work of Jesus (say, in his death and resurrection) has whatever effect it has quite independently of the theologies we happen to hammer onto it, so Jesus' words — simply because they are Jesus himself speaking — have whatever power he has, no matter what we may think about them. His parables are not so much word-pictures about assorted external subjects as they are *icons* of himself. Like good poems, they not only *mean,* but *be:* they have a *sacramental* effectiveness. Whether we "get" them or not, therefore, they remain first and foremost his way of *getting to us.* They are lights shining out of the house of faith itself, inviting us home. What we do with them as we sit out on the porch of interpretation may make us appreciate them more or less, but it cannot damage the lights, and it certainly doesn't turn them off.

As an instance of how all this applies in practice, consider how it corrects a misconception of what we commonly call the teaching of the faith. Christian education is not the communication of correct views about what the various works and words of Jesus might *mean;* rather it is the stocking of the imagination with the icons of those works and words themselves. It is most successfully accomplished, therefore, not by catechisms that purport to produce understanding but by stories that hang the icons, understood or not, on the walls of the mind. We do not include the parable of the Prodigal Son, for example, because we understand it, nor do we omit the parable of the Unjust Steward because we can't make head or tail of it. Rather, we commit both to the Christian memory because that's the way Jesus seems to want the inside of his believers' heads decorated. Indeed, the only really mischievous thing anyone can do with the Gospel is insist on hanging only the pictures he happens to like. That's what heresy really is: picking and choosing, on the basis of *my* interpretations, between the icons provided to me. Orthodoxy, if it's understood correctly, is simply the constant displaying of the entire collection.

Still, interpretation, like porch-building, is practically inevitable. We are, after all, *thinking* beings, and we think about everything we do, up to and including the act of faith: almost no one lives out an entire lifetime simply by leaping into the ungarnished doorway of the house of faith. Accordingly, the woman in my parable was advocating a rather more austere lifestyle than most of us are in fact willing to put up with. Let's see, then — assuming that her husband took exception to her comprehensive demolition plans — what might be said for his more tolerant view of the situation.

No doubt he would begin by conceding her valid points: first, that a porch is no place to live; second, that porch-builders often betray a taste for the rococo; and last, that porches rot faster than houses. The work of theological interpretation has the same drawbacks. To begin with, it is mostly just a fun thing to do in good company on a warm afternoon when your kidney stones are not acting up. If it is taken much more seriously than that — if it is seen as the center from which life derives its meaning — it will fail us in precise proportion to our need to make it succeed. In all of us, there are doubts and despairs (to paraphrase Auden) smoldering at the base of the brain; everyone who rests his life on his ability to hold his world together by an intellectual synthesis runs the risk that someday, years hence perhaps, the doubts will suddenly "blow it up with one appalling laugh."

Likewise, theological thought has a penchant for elaborating itself beyond not only sense but good taste. Once someone devises a system or theme for building the porch to his faith, the temptation is to continue the work of construction whether it serves the purposes of the house or not. Hence all the theologies that manage to take the Gospel of grace — of forgiveness freely offered to everyone on the basis of no works at all — and convert it into the bad news of a religion that offers salvation only to the well-behaved. Hence, too, all the moralistic interpretations of the parables: sermons on the duty of contentment from the Laborers in the Vineyard, and little lessons in loveliness from the parable of the Good Samaritan.

Finally, all systems of theological interpretation, plain or fancy, rot out at an alarming rate. Unlike the house of faith, they are exposed to the wind and weather of prevailing opinion. Even if a theologian never once doubts anything about his system, it remains endlessly vulnerable to scorn, ridicule, or just plain disinterest from the outside. The sheer labor of keeping up with the repairs necessitated by such forces has kept more theologians than one from ever spending as much as a single night under a snug roof.

Still, having made those concessions, the man in my parable would insist that porch-building, whether it is inevitable, worthwhile, tasteful, expensive, or not, is a fact. Most people who have faith have some intellectual structure tacked in front of it. But precisely because that is true, those who invite others to visit or to stay in their house of faith are faced with a difficulty: *the only way to get guests to the door is to walk them across the porch.* Theologizing may not be a saving proposition, but it lies between almost everybody and the Saving Proposition Himself.

Accordingly, he would point out that there is something to be said, no matter how much or how little porch you have on your faith, for keeping that structure as attractive and sound as you can. Its uprights should be set solidly on concrete Gospel footings. Its stringers — the principal interpretative devices by which the flooring is held up — should be made of something scripturally sound, not of humanistic balsa wood or used timbers from someone's old, collapsed theological building. Above all, its floorboards must be all in place and all nailed down tight. It will not do for anyone to leave spaces in the decking — to install only the scriptural boards he likes and to omit those he doesn't. A theological porch must include every side of every scriptural paradox. A system, for example, that is all love and no wrath is no better than one that is all wrath and no love. In either case, the unsuspecting guest is liable to break an ankle because of what was left out.

But enough. My parable was as much, or more, for me as for you. If you will try not to insist that my porch be exactly like yours, I shall resist the temptation to force mine on you. All I really care about is that both our structures have no missing boards. So for now, come up on my porch and have a seat. Here begins the work of interpreting the parables.

CHAPTER TWO

Death and Resurrection

THE TOUCHSTONE OF THE PARABLES OF GRACE

O n the principle that the simplest plan is the best, I propose to deal with the parables of Jesus in the order in which they occur in the Gospels of Matthew, Mark, and Luke. Naturally, this requires that the discrepancies in these accounts — their sometimes differing sequences of events and materials — be harmonized into a single order; but rather than invent a harmony of my own, I shall take the liberty of adopting the numbering system for Gospel passages devised by Kurt Aland in the Greek-English edition of the *Synopsis Quattuor Evangeliorum* (United Bible Societies).* Beyond that, there are only a few other housekeeping details to be noted. I shall be working from the original Greek, principally from the text employed by Aland in the *Synopsis* but also from the second edition of the Aland, Black, Martini, Metzger, Wikgren text, from the twenty-second edition of the Nestle text, and from the Schmoller Concordance. The translations offered will be largely my own, but they will take into account the versions I habitually consult, namely, the King James Version (KJV), the Revised Standard Version (RSV), Today's English Version (TEV), the New International Version (NIV), and, to a lesser degree, the Clementine Vulgate (VgCL),

*An English edition of *Synopsis of the Four Gospels* is available from the American Bible Society. It is the ideal companion to this book for study purposes.

the Jerusalem Bible (JB), the New English Bible (NEB), and the New Testament in Modern English by J. B. Phillips (JBP).

Looking at Jesus' parables as a whole, I find that they can be divided into three consecutive groups. The first group consists of what I call the parables of the kingdom, namely, the parables that occur in the Gospels prior to the feeding of the five thousand (that is, before Matt. 14, Mark 6, and Luke 9). I have already dealt with these in *The Parables of the Kingdom*. The second group, which I shall call the parables of grace, includes all the parables, acted as well as spoken, that the Gospel writers place between the feeding of the five thousand and the triumphal entry into Jerusalem (the latter occurring at Matt. 21, Mark 11, and Luke 19). The final group, the parables of judgment, consists of the remaining parables, almost all of which the Gospel writers place between the triumphal entry and the beginning of the passion narrative (at Matt. 26, Mark 14, and Luke 22).

While all such divisions are to some degree arbitrary, it seems to me that this one has the merit of relating Jesus' parables to the development of his thought about the nature of his messianic mission. Consider, for example, my choice of the feeding of the five thousand as the point of transition from the parables of the kingdom to the parables of grace.

At the beginning of his ministry, Jesus presents himself as a fairly standard-issue messianic claimant. He exorcises demons, he gives sight to the blind, he makes the lame walk, he heals lepers, he restores hearing to the deaf, he raises the dead, and he proclaims good news to the poor. Not only that, but he teaches as one having authority in himself, and not as the scribes and Pharisees. In short, he appears as the kind of wonder-working rabbi to whom at least the common people flock enthusiastically. Even at this early stage, however, he also indulges in certain unmessianic actions that inevitably upset the religious authorities of the day. He breaks the sabbath, he associates with tax collectors and prostitutes, and, in general, he sits conspicuously loose to the law-abiding expectations that the Jewish establishment had for any proper Messiah. Indeed, even before he presents his parables of the kingdom, the Pharisees and the Herodians have already begun to think about killing him (Matt. 12, Mark 3, Luke 6).

156

Still, there is an element in his thinking — namely, the centrality to his mission of his own death and resurrection — that has not yet been clearly formulated. True enough, the early kingdom parables (especially those that employ the imagery of seed being put into the ground) are not incapable of being given a death-resurrection interpretation; but in telling them, Jesus does not yet seem to be talking about his own dying and rising. These early parables focus chiefly on the paradoxical *characteristics* of the kingdom; they portray it as catholic rather than parochial, actually present rather than coming at some future date, hidden and mysterious rather than visible and plausible; and they set forth the bizarre notion that the responses the kingdom calls for in the midst of a hostile world can vary from total involvement to doing nothing at all. But these first parables do not, in any developed way, enunciate the paradoxical *program* by which the kingdom is in fact accomplished, that is, by death and resurrection.

The development of that theme comes, as I see it, only in the parables of grace — and it comes after a series of events and utterances (Aland nos. 144-164) that show Jesus more and more preoccupied with death. Beginning with the death of John the Baptist (Matt. 14, Mark 6; cf. Luke 3), and continuing through the feeding of the five thousand (Matt. 14, Mark 6, Luke 9, John 6), the first prediction of his death and resurrection (Matt. 16, Mark 8, Luke 9), the transfiguration (Matt. 17, Mark 9, Luke 9), and the second prediction of his death and resurrection (Matt. 17, Mark 9, Luke 9), he gradually reaches a clear realization that the working of the kingdom is mysteriously but inseparably bound up with what Luke (9:31) calls his "exodus" — in other words, with the passion and exaltation that he is shortly to accomplish in Jerusalem.

Accordingly, I plan to argue that just as this line of thinking was bound to become manifest in Jesus' actions from those events onward, so too it informed his mind as he developed his parables of grace. True enough, some of those parables do not seem immediately susceptible of a death-resurrection reading. Still, since many of them have such an interpretation written plainly on their face — and since even some of the more obscure of them are remarkably patient of it — I propose to interpret as many of them as possible under that rubric. I am aware of the dangers of trying to turn a single notion into the master key to an admittedly diverse collection of materials; but since death-resurrection becomes, from this juncture in the Gospels onward, the overmastering notion in Jesus' mind, I propose at least to try it in every possible parabolic lock. Where it does not fit, I shall cheerfully give up on it; in all honesty, though, I do not anticipate having to exercise such stoic cheer too often.

One slight digression to meet an objection sometimes voiced by biblical critics. It is often said that Jesus himself (Jesus as he actually lived and thought as opposed to the Jesus presented to us by the writers of the Gospels) could not possibly have seen his ministry in death-resurrection terms — that such categories were the handiwork of the community of faith that succeeded him and that they are far too "churchy" for attribution to anyone in Jesus' circumstances. I do not know about that, nor do I think the critics know either. As far as I am concerned, the Jesus of the Gospels is the only available Jesus there is and it is idle to postulate any other, no matter how likely such a Jesus may seem on the grounds of form criticism or historical surmise. For my money, it was over the literary presentation of this Jesus of the Gospels that the Holy Spirit brooded when inspiring the Scriptures; the same cannot be said for subsequent literary efforts on Jesus' behalf. If the presentation we accept by trusting biblical inspiration is in error, then not only are we stuck with it; we will never even (on any basis, "inspired" or "factual") be able to say exactly what it is in error about.

I go, therefore, directly to the record as we have it. In Matthew, the account of the death of John the Baptist (Matt. 14:3-12; Aland no. 144) is put into narrative almost immediately after the completion of the parables of the kingdom. In Mark (at 6:17-29), it comes after only a handful of other events (Jesus stills a storm, exorcizes the Gerasene demoniac, raises Jairus's daughter, and commissions the Twelve — Aland nos. 136-142). Moreover, both Gospel writers introduce the death of John with the statement that Herod the tetrarch, on hearing about Jesus' reputation, took the view that Jesus was John the Baptist risen from the dead (Matt. 14:1-2; Mark 6:14-16; Aland no. 143; cf. Luke 9:7-9).

It strikes me that we do not make enough of the occurrence of John's death in this early stage of Jesus' ministry. To begin with, the identification of Jesus as the risen Baptizer (not only by Herod, but by a good many others) could easily have had the effect of making Jesus wonder about the relationship of his mission to that of John. He could well have asked himself whether his messiahship would continue to stress the plausible, interventionist kind of program that John proclaimed, or whether it would turn out to be something far more mysterious, indirect, and paradoxical — all of which notions, it should be observed, he had already developed to a considerable extent in his parables of the kingdom.

Fascinatingly, even before John was killed, Jesus had begun to make distinctions between himself and his cousin. When John heard in prison about the works of the Christ (Matt. 11:2), he sent his disciples to ask Jesus if he was "the coming one." Jesus initially replies almost as if John is a superior who deserves a full report. He gives the messengers a reassuring list of his actions: the blind receive their sight, the lame walk, lepers are cleansed, the deaf hear, the dead are raised, and the poor have the good news preached to them. But then he adds, perhaps sensing that John may nevertheless find his style too bizarre, "happy is he who is not scandalized by me" (Matt. 11:5-6). In any case, the messengers leave and Jesus addresses himself to the crowds. John, he tells them, is not just a prophet; he is much more than a prophet. In fact, he is the forerunner of Jesus himself and thus is greater than anyone who ever lived. Still, Jesus goes on, anyone who is even the least in the kingdom of heaven is greater than John (Matt. 11:7-11).

Then, however, Jesus delivers a comment in which he begins to develop the distinction between himself and John. Admittedly, the passage in question (Matt. 11:12-15) can be taken simply as an extension of what he has already said about John; but I am disposed to make something more of it. "From the days of John the Baptist until now," Jesus says, "the kingdom of heaven suffers violence and the violent seize it by force. All the prophets and the law up to John prophesied; and if you want to accept it, John is Elijah whose coming was predicted. If you have ears, listen." It seems to me that even at this early juncture (the passage precedes even the parables of the kingdom in Matt. 13), Jesus is groping to differentiate his ministry from John's. John and the prophets, he says, proclaimed a kingdom that would be brought about by plausible exercises of force — by what might be called direct, or straight-line, or right-handed power. Jesus does not say here, in so many words, that his own style of exercising power will be indirect, paradoxical, and left-handed; but in the parables of the kingdom he is about to unfold, he will depict a kingdom that works in a veritable snowstorm of mystery, indirection, and implausibility. Not only that, but just before beginning those parables (on the occasion of the scribes' and Pharisees' asking him for a sign: Matt. 12:38-42), he says that no sign will be given to this evil and adulterous generation except the sign of Jonah — which he then goes on to identify as a reference to the death and resurrection of the Son of man. It is at least possible, therefore, to hold that even before the account of the death of John the Baptist in Matt. 14, Jesus is portrayed as putting some intellectual distance between his mission and John's. It also seems fairly likely that, in Jesus' mind, the defining principle of that distance will ultimately have some important connection with death.

We can only surmise, of course, how much intellectual contact Jesus had with John through his formative years. Even though they were cousins, it is probably unwise to make merely putative closeness the basis for either agreement or disagreement between them. From the Gospel records we have, however, it seems clear that Jesus, while he may have started out in a vein like John's, gradually came to see his cousin as the proclaimer of a less paradoxical kingdom than the mysterious one he found himself delineating. In any case, by the time Jesus finally arrived at the point of his own death, his distancing of himself from John's approach was profound and absolute. I feel free, therefore, to hold that from John's death onward, Jesus found himself progressively more liberated from whatever ties he may still have had to the non-paradoxical style of kingdom proclamation. His last link to the old order was gone; he could now get on with the new.

The way is open, accordingly, to see the events that come next in the sequence (the feeding of the five thousand, the predictions of his death and resurrection, the transfiguration) as perhaps the greatest single crux in Jesus' human thinking about his mission. To take generalities first, consider the obvious fact that the tone of Jesus' ministry changes radically after the transfiguration. From that point on, the messianic claimant who began his career as a wonder-working rabbi does fewer and fewer "miracles" and indulges in far less purely "ethical" discourse. More than that, the largely "upbeat" style of his earlier ministry is replaced by a "setting of his face toward Jerusalem" — that is, toward his coming death and resurrection.

But there is harder evidence. Consider the feeding of the five thousand. After a long day in a deserted spot — a day in which Jesus preoccupied himself with the old-style work of healing and teaching that had marked his ministry so far — the disciples come to him and suggest dismissing the crowd so the people can go and get something to eat. At first, Jesus seems hardly to have heard them: "You feed them," he says. It is only after they have nattered on about the cost of such a project that Jesus even begins to concern himself with the problem. With an air of grudging involvement (John's Gospel, admittedly, does not support this), he says, "Go see how much bread you have." Even then, though, his concern manifests itself in an almost minimal way. He simply takes the five loaves and two fish, gives thanks, and proceeds to have the disciples pass them out. The "miracle" is about as understated as it can possibly be: Jesus, from start to finish, seems largely "out of it." Not only that, but when the miracle is over and everyone has finally caught on to what has happened, it looks for all the world as if he cannot get away from the scene soon enough.

He dismisses both the disciples and the crowd (the four accounts differ slightly about the details at this point) and goes up on the mountain all by himself. John's Gospel actually gives the reason for this retreat: Jesus knew they were going to come and seize him *in order to make him king* (John 6:15). Even without that assertion, however, the other accounts are susceptible of the same interpretation: Jesus seems to be having second thoughts about the style of his ministry so far and he goes off by himself to wrestle with these doubts in prayer. And pray he does — for most of the night, in fact. Then, in a scene that has a dreamlike quality, he comes walking to his disciples on the water. The usual interpretation of this scene is that he was coming to their aid in a storm; but Mark (6:48) says that "he was going to pass them by" — suggesting once again that Jesus was less involved in their problems than in his own. In any event, the disciples end up more afraid of Jesus (despite his airy "Cheer up, it's me; don't be afraid") than they were of the storm. The impression given by the account is that something darkly mysterious was preoccupying not just his mind but his entire being. The disciples seem to have been responding more to that mystery than to the sudden calming of the storm: they were, as Mark says (6:51-52), "completely amazed and utterly confused, because they did not understand about the loaves, and their hearts were hardened."

Obviously, it is possible to interpret this last comment as meaning that, having failed to grasp the first "miracle," they likewise missed the second. Possible, but hardly likely. They had already seen Jesus do enough signs and wonders to keep them, presumably, from that kind of egregious point-missing. No, their incomprehension was caused not by their inability to know a miracle when they saw one but by an unfathomable scariness emanating straight from Jesus himself. He was being *weird*. He was, for all his visibility, off their mental radar screens.

In a fascinating way this weirdness is underscored in the Fourth Gospel by the discourse (John 6:22-71) that follows the feeding and the walking on the water. The next day, as John has it, the crowd finally catches up with Jesus at Capernaum on the other side of the lake. They, too, are puzzled — specifically by the fact that Jesus seems to have made the crossing without using the only available boat. "Rabbi," they ask, "when did you get here?" Jesus' response simply adds to their confusion: he first launches into a petulant comment on the unworthiness of their motives in seeking him; then, in reply to their plausible, even sincere, questions, he indulges himself in a series of progressively more obscure answers.

What they really want, as John has already noted, is to make him king; but they also hope that he will claim for himself the kind of kingship they have in mind. Accordingly, having just witnessed the "sign" he has done in feeding the five thousand, they begin asking him "bread from heaven" questions designed to elicit the desired response from him. "Our fathers ate manna in the desert," they say (6:31), obviously expecting that he will pick up on the lead and come out with a punch line characterizing his messiahship as an updated version of the kind of plausible, interventionist salvation they know and love.

But Jesus gives them naught for their comfort. He tells them not only that Moses didn't give them bread from heaven but that the true bread from heaven is the one who comes down from heaven and gives life to the world. The rest of the dialogue proceeds in the same way: they ask sensible, leading questions and Jesus gives weird, non-responsive answers. He promises resurrection at the last day (6:39, 40, 54); he reaffirms that *he* is the living bread from heaven and then adds that the bread he will give is his flesh (6:51); and he ends with the assertion that unless they eat his flesh and drink his blood, they cannot have life in themselves (6:53). Finally, not only the crowd but also many of Jesus' disciples simply go away and no longer walk with him (6:66). In short, by his references to flesh and blood, he has broached the subject of the death of the Messiah — and the weirdness of it all has simply put them off. Even the twelve, who do in fact remain with him, stay on only in a dumb and desperate, "to whom can we go?" kind of way.

I am aware that many critics are unwilling to admit the testimony of John's Gospel into the kind of argument I am making. I have no such reluctance. It seems to me that however this material came to be included in the Fourth Gospel, it is still very much of a piece with the weirdness already present in Matthew, Mark, and Luke up to this point, as well as with the weirdness yet to come in their accounts of the remaining events prior to the parables of grace. For if the synoptic Gospels have not yet plainly set death at the center of Jesus' strangeness at this time, they have nevertheless carefully laid the foundation for proclaiming its centrality. Not only that, but they will shortly, in their accounts of Peter's confession and of the transfiguration, set it forth in just so many words. Accordingly, I find that what John's Gospel presents in chapter 6 agrees nicely with what the other three give in the parallel passages, and I make no apologies for arguing from it.

But to continue. Look next at Peter's confession (Matt. 16, Mark 8,

Luke 9) and note how it brings together all the elements I have been expounding so far: Jesus' relationship to John the Baptist; his unique messiahship; and his bizarre linking of that messiahship to his own death and resurrection. The passage begins with Jesus' asking his disciples who people say he is. They answer, John the Baptist — or Elijah, or one of the prophets. In other words, they tell Jesus that he is being taken for someone who is part of the old, plausible, non-paradoxical order of things. Jesus then asks them who *they* say he is, and Peter answers, the Christ. But Jesus rebukes them (I am following Mark at this point, 8:30), telling them not to talk to anyone about him. Presumably, he does this to preclude their broadcasting their own old-style, non-paradoxical notions of messiahship; and he follows it up by predicting, in plain words, his coming death and resurrection. Peter, in turn (proving that Jesus was right not to trust his disciples' understanding of messiahship), rebukes Jesus (as Matthew has it, Peter simply cannot stand hearing such "down" talk from someone he's just proclaimed Messiah). Finally, Jesus once again rebukes Peter ("Get behind me, Satan . . ."), telling him he's out of step with God's way of doing the messianic business at hand. The whole exchange, as far as I am concerned, produces exactly the same reading on the "weirdness scale" as did the dialogue in John 6. It shows Jesus as a paradoxical dying-and-rising Messiah who fits no previous mold, and it continues to stress the off-putting strangeness he has been manifesting all through this sequence.

Which brings us to the capstone of the entire series of events, the transfiguration of Jesus (Matt. 17, Mark 9, Luke 9). Except for the resurrection itself, it is the single strangest event in his ministry; and it sets together once again the theme of old-order-versus-new and the theme of death as the key to Jesus' messiahship. The first of these is evidenced by three details: it is Moses and Elijah (old-order figures) who speak with Jesus; Peter suggests building three tents — indicating that he could think of no way to commemorate the event other than with a ritual from the old religion; and God, apparently out of sheer impatience with the disciples' failure to grasp the new order in Jesus, simply drops a cloud on the lot of them and tells them to pay attention to his beloved Son. The theme of death is manifested not only by Luke's already-mentioned reference (9:31) to the topic of the conversation among Jesus, Moses, and Elijah (namely, his "exodus"), but by Mark's report (9:9) that Jesus ordered the disciples to tell no one what they had seen until the Son of man had been *raised from the dead.*

The transfiguration, accordingly, brings us to the end of my argument for placing the paradox of Jesus' death at the center of his thinking as he approaches the first of his parables of grace, that is, the parable of the Lost Sheep. Before moving on, though, it is worth noting the precise passages that intervene here. The transfiguration (Matt. 17, Mark 9, Luke 9) stands at Aland no. 161, and the Lost Sheep (Matt. 18, Luke 15) at no. 169. Let me simply list the materials that nos. 162-168 comprise. They are: the disciples' question about the "second coming" of Elijah (Matt. 17:10-13; Mark 9:11-13; no. 162); the healing of a boy with an unclean spirit (Matt. 17:14-21; Mark 9:14-29; Luke 9:37-43a; no. 163); Jesus' second prediction of his death and resurrection (Matt. 17:22-23; Mark 9:30-32; Luke 9:43b-45; no. 164); the miracle of the coin in the fish's mouth (Matt. 17:24-27; no. 165); the disciples' argument about who is the greatest (Matt. 18:1-5; Mark 9:33-37; Luke 9:46-48; no. 166); the comments about the freelance exorcist (Matt. 10:42; Mark 9:38-41; Luke 9:49-50; no. 167); and the warnings against giving scandal by failing to appreciate the bizarre demands of Jesus' paradoxical ministry (Matt. 18:6-9; Mark 9:42-50; Luke 17:1-2 and 14:34-35; no. 168). Of these, only three need comment here. (A fourth, the coin in the fish's mouth, is actually an acted parable and thus deserves separate treatment as a prologue to the parables of grace.)

Jesus' second prediction of his death and resurrection (Aland no. 164) stands, obviously, as yet another nail hammered into the already solid structure of mysterious messiahship that he has been building before the disciples' eyes. But it is not the only such nail driven home here. When the disciples argue about who is greatest (no. 166), Jesus tells them that anyone who wants to be first must be last of all and servant of all. He then stands a little child in their midst and puts his arms around him, saying, "Whoever receives one such little child in my name receives me."

We twentieth-century Christians — with our basically nineteenth-century view of childhood as a wonderful and desirable state — miss the point of this passage. In Jesus' time, and for most of the centuries since, childhood was almost always seen as a less than human condition that was to be beaten out of children as soon as possible. Therefore when Jesus sets up a little child as an example, he is setting up not a winsome specimen of all that is simple and charming but rather *one of life's losers.* He is telling his disciples that if they follow him in his mysterious messiahship, they will — like him — have to become something no one has any real use or respect for. He is exalting not the plausible greatness that is the only thing the world understands but the implausible greatness that he himself intends to pursue. He is, in short, proclaiming his own version of what Paul in 1 Cor. 1 later set forth as the "foolishness of the preaching," namely, that God works not in the great, the wise, and the powerful but in the weak and the foolish: "for the foolishness of God is wiser than men and the weakness of God is stronger than men" (1 Cor. 1:25).

Accordingly, even though Jesus' holding up of the little child contains no reference to death as such, I find that his emphasis here on life's "little deaths" — his exaltation of a panoply of unsuccesses which, before he is done, he will round out to include lastness, leastness, and lostness, as well as littleness and death itself — is part and parcel of his ever-deepening awareness of himself as a Messiah who will do his work not at the top of the heap, as everyone expects, but in the very depths of the human condition. Likewise, I find that Jesus' warnings (no. 168) against scandalizing "one of these little ones" have the same force. His disciples are to be extreme in their pursuit of lastness, lostness, and littleness: "If your hand scandalizes you, cut it off . . ." (Mark 9:43ff.). They are to become, in other words, what he will become: despised and rejected. Only at that extremity, Jesus insists, can anything saving be done about the world.

With that much as stage-setting, therefore — and with a paradoxical Messiah now standing in the wings fully cognizant of death and rcsurrection as the modus operandi of his saving work — we are finally ready to hear, perhaps with newly opened ears, his parables of grace.

CHAPTER THREE

The First Parable of Grace

THE COIN IN THE FISH'S MOUTH

I find it intriguing that the first of the parables of grace — the coin in the fish's mouth — is acted out rather than told as a story. While this is not an uncommon technique for Jesus to use (into the category of acted parables I put not only this episode but also his temptation in the wilderness, his walking on the water, his casting of the money-changers out of the temple, his cursing of the fig tree, and above all, his resurrection and ascension), it is a method that has given many biblical critics acute discomfort. Since actions like the ones cited have in them a generous helping of the frankly mysterious or the gratuitously spectacular, critical minds are sometimes tempted to dismiss them as inauthentic — as fabrications by later and lesser writers bent chiefly on miracle-mongering.

The coin in the fish's mouth, for example, strikes such critics as far too close in tone to the miracles attributed to Jesus in the so-called apocryphal Gospels. Confronted with the spectacle of Jesus' telling Peter he will find money for a tax payment in the first fish he pulls up out of the sea, they can only take it as an instance of theological larking around. They find it more akin to the spurious stones in which the boy Jesus makes clay animals and birds come to life than to what they consider his more "serious" or "worthy" miracles of compassionate healing. And even if they do not dismiss the story completely, their consternation at it leads them to view it as a mere "floating fragment," a piece

167

of scriptural jetsam that a canonical Gospel writer (Matthew alone, in this case) has moored at 17:24-27 for lack of any better notion of where to put it.

There are two things wrong with that approach. First, the apocryphal Gospels are not *mere* fabrications: on any fair view, they are extrapolations of authentic traditions made by writers who felt that extra doses of the miraculous were just the thing to bring the picture of Jesus more into line with their particular theological predilections. In other words, they took genuine, if minor, elements in the orthodox tradition and created additional and more bizarre instances of them. Jesus, in the canonical Scriptures, does in fact do a number of things that cannot easily be fitted into anyone's theological system. It is questionable procedure, however, to dismiss such peculiarities simply because they do not come up to some critic's idea of scratch.

Take, for example, the parables in general. While it is fair to say that almost all of them are light-years away from being mere allegories — and while it is equally just to issue warnings to preachers that they should avoid allegorical interpretations of major parables like the Prodigal Son or the Laborers in the Vineyard — it is definitely not cricket to hold that when we find Jesus making an allegory out of one of his own parables (as in his interpretations of the Sower and of the Wheat and the Weeds) we must conclude that such allegorizing is not the work of Jesus but of some later hand. Likewise, it is just as much of a mistake to dismiss the apparently frivolous miracle of the coin in the fish's mouth. At the very least, we should make every attempt to give it an interpretation — even if it turns out to be a wildly unusual one — that takes seriously and *in context* the admitted unusualness of the act itself.

Indeed, it is precisely this failure to take difficult passages in context that is the second thing wrong with the dismissive approach. To decide in advance that the coin in the fish's mouth has been parked where it is just because Matthew, or somebody, felt obliged to preserve something he did not understand is to fly in the face of both common sense and biblical inspiration. It violates common sense because Matthew (I have no interest in arguing whether the evangelist was a he, a

168

she, or a they) was obviously closer to the event itself, or at least to witnesses of the event, than were any subsequent commentators. Not only that, but he was clearly no slouch at putting together Gospel materials (his work did, after all, beat out the apocryphal competition). At the very least, we should begin our efforts at commentary by assuming he had sound reasons for every particular placement of his pericopes, and we should be slow to decide he didn't.

In addition, the dismissive approach runs counter to a serious attempt to do justice to biblical inspiration. For even if Matthew did in fact end up inserting the episode of the coin in the fish's mouth at 17:24 out of sheer desperation, there was still (as far as Christians are concerned) Somebody Else brooding over Matthew's work — a sovereign Somebody, if you please, who could use even mindless insertion to get the material where he wanted it. I have in mind, of course, the Holy Spirit, the ultimate presiding genius of Scripture — for whom indirection is as good as direction, which in turn is as good as verbal dictation — and who was not above using any or all of those devices when, where, and as he saw fit. Once you believe *that* — once you hold that by the inspiration of the Spirit, "the Holy Scriptures of the Old and New Testaments are the Word of God and contain all things necessary to salvation," it seems fairly reasonable to assume that the Spirit got not only the words but their placements right. Accordingly, it is also appropriate to bend over backward if necessary in your efforts to figure out just what he might have had in mind. Context, therefore — whether of Matthew's devising or of the Spirit's — will govern my consideration of the coin in the fish's mouth from start to finish.

To begin, though, let me simply set down the story itself, noting some problems of translation as I go. Matthew 17 contains the following materials: the transfiguration (17:1-13), the healing of a boy with a demon (17:14-21), Jesus' second prediction of his death and resurrection (17:22-23), and the coin in the fish's mouth (17:24-27). Throughout the chapter, Jesus and his disciples are in Galilee (where they have been, in fact, since chapter 13, when Jesus told his parables of the kingdom). Matthew begins the account of the coin in the fish's mouth by recording that they were now at Capernaum and that the collectors of the *dídrachma* (the annual two-drachma temple tax, equal to about two days' pay, required of each Jew) came to Peter with a question. "Doesn't your teacher pay the *dídrachma?*" they ask. Peter answers with a simple yes, but his meaning, presumably, is something like a "sure" or an "of course he does" — a quick reply, in other words, based more on Peter's own desire to make his master look respectable in the eyes of the authorities than on his actual knowledge of Jesus' intentions. When Peter comes into the house, however, Jesus (who seems not to have been present at the interrogation) begins to speak about the temple tax before Peter says even a word. "What do you think, Simon?" he asks. "From whom do the kings of the earth take tax or tribute? *From their sons [huión] or from others [allotríon]?*"

The italicized words arc difficult to translate. What I have given is a literal, but not strictly accurate, rendering. "Sons" is a Hebraism meaning not the literal children of the kings but the citizens of their dominions — much as the "sons of Israel" or "children of Israel" most often means simply "the people of Israel" or "the Israelites." What the text actually says, therefore, would be better represented by *"from their own citizens or from foreigners?"* — which is, with certain variations, the way most recent translators have Englished it. The difficulty with such a rendering, however, is that it makes precious little sense to a modern American reader. Ever since the invention of the income tax (not to mention the sales tax, the excise tax, and the Triborough Bridge and Tunnel Authority), those who have paid toll and tribute to the governing authorities of America have been not foreigners but the American citizenry themselves. Consequently, if "sons" is translated "citizens" and "others" is translated "foreigners," then when Peter says that kings take tribute from foreigners — and Jesus responds with the punch line of the whole parable, namely, "then the citizens are free" — all you will get from an American audience (or almost any other) is a cynical "Fat chance!" I propose, therefore, to put up with whatever strain may be involved in using the gnat-sized inaccuracy "sons" or "children" rather than swallow the correct but point-destroying camel of "citizens." After all, ninety-nine Americans out of a hundred are probably convinced that the Prince of Wales has no income-tax liability. Whether they are right or wrong as to the fact of that matter, only "sons" or "children" has any chance of communicating to them the note of freedom from religious liability that is, to me at least, the point of the whole parable.

Let me interrupt myself with a slight digression on the subject of literal versus periphrastic translation. Admittedly, one cannot always translate word for word from one language to another (try putting "knucklehead" into French literally). Nevertheless, there is something to be said, especially when dealing with complex and skillful authors, for trying as often as possible to give literal translations to at least their more important words.

In the case of the text we are dealing with, the choice of the Greek word *huión* ("sons") by Jesus (or Matthew, or the Spirit, or all three) involves a deliberate and complex play on the uses of the word "son" *(huiós)* in the preceding episodes. Let me list them. In Peter's confession (e.g., Matt. 16:13) Jesus asks his disciples, "Who do men say that the Son of man is?" — and when Peter replies (16:16), he says, "You are the Christ, the Son of the living God." In the first prediction of his death (e.g., Luke 9:22), Jesus refers to himself as the "Son of man." In the transfiguration (e.g., Matt. 17:5), God speaks out of the cloud and says, "This is my beloved Son." In the question about the coming of Elijah (17:12), Jesus again refers to the "Son of man" — and he does it once more (e.g., 17:22) in the second prediction of his death. In the light of all those passages, therefore, when Jesus refers to kings' tax-exempt citizens as "sons" — and then proceeds to tell Peter that "the sons are therefore free" — he is incorporating into his remark all the freight of the previous usages of the word "son." He means, of course, that the citizens of the messianic kingdom are free. But unless a translator indulges in extensive periphrasis to make that point clear, the use of any word other than "sons" — e.g., "citizens" (TEV), "family" (JBP), "own people" (NEB), or even "children" (KJV) — simply deprives the reader of the association with the sonship of Jesus himself on which the assertion of freedom is actually based. (For the record, the VgCL, the RSV, and the JB — which actually points out the play on words in a footnote — all opt for the literal rendering "sons.")

I raise this issue for several reasons. The first is based on what I have just said about not unnecessarily depriving the reader of associations present in the original text. Good authors expect their readers to build a mental concordance of every major word in their writings so that when a new twist is given to a word already used, the readers will be able to enter into and be enriched by the pun intended. But when translators make a habit of always rendering a word as what it *means* at a given point rather than as what it *is*, they derail authors from their purposes. In my view, therefore, the job of saying in detail what a text means should be left to expositors, exegetes, and preachers. Translators should content themselves with being as literal as they can be, short of setting down nonsense.

The second reason follows from that. The abundance of modern versions of the Scriptures has not been an unmixed blessing — as anyone who knows the Greek text will attest. It is a cautionary experience, for a teacher working from the Greek, to hand a Bible class half a dozen different English versions of, say, Matt. 17:24-27 and invite them to debate the meaning of the passage. More often than not, their natural inclination to take the English words in front of them as what the original really says tricks them into all kinds of fanciful, even false, starts as to what the passage might actually mean. And that happens most frequently, mind you, precisely when the versions used are ones whose guiding purpose was to translate what the Greek meant rather than what it said.

For ordinary study purposes, therefore, I direct students who do not know Greek to the more committedly literal versions (KJV and RSV), and to the TEV as a backup in case they want to check a little further as to meaning. But for major investigations of meaning, I urge them to use a concordance (such as *Young's* to the KJV) that has an index-lexicon to the original Hebrew and Greek. The advantage of this feature is tremendous: it enables the student to look up *every* use of a given Hebrew or Greek word, no matter how it was translated. Admittedly, in addition to those positive suggestions, I do have some unkind words to say about versions that strike me as unduly periphrastic, or as having been devised to advance the cause of particular religious movements or theological orthodoxies. Rather than name names here, how-

172

ever, I shall content myself with one all-encompassing observation: the work of dealing with the text itself is demanding enough; it is not made any easier when it has to be done through a programmatic overlay, or while wearing doctrinal mittens.

But back to the text at hand before this digression slips into mere pique. Jesus now (Matt. 17:27) shifts gears. Having told Peter that "the sons are therefore free" — that is, having established by the spoken part of his parable that neither he himself nor his brethren in the new order of his sonship are under any obligation to the old order represented by the authorities and their temple tax — he proceeds to the *acted* part of the parable. "In order that we don't scandalize them, though," he says, "go to the sea, cast in a hook, and take the first fish that comes up. When you open its mouth you will find a *statḗr* [a coin worth four drachmas]; take that and give it to them for me and you."

Let me get one useless question out of the way immediately. To those who ask, "Do you think this really happened?" I will answer yes and take whatever critical lumps I have to just to get off the subject. I can't prove I'm right, of course; but then neither can anyone else prove I'm wrong. Furthermore, there is no a priori system of biblical interpretation (except for the obviously wrong-headed one that says everything in the Bible must, ipso facto, be literally true) that can decide the issue one way or the other. The episode just sits there in the text, waiting to be commented on, not argued with. If it so happens that you find it impossible to swallow (as the fish, perhaps, found the *statḗr*), I respect that. Let's just agree to disagree about the moot point and get on with the more enjoyable business of playing, scripturally, with what's on the page.

My interpretation of the whole passage can be put briefly: Jesus, having arrived at the recognition that his own death will lie at the heart of his messiahship, finally feels free enough of the old political, religious, and ethical messianic expectations to make a joke about them. Not that he hadn't always sat loose to them to some degree (from the start, he broke the sabbath and consorted with morally unacceptable types); rather, he now finds himself totally beyond all the plausible, right-handed programs of salvation and therefore "free among the dead" — as well as among the last, the least, the lost, and the little, all of whom will loom large in the parables of grace he is about to unfold. The coin in the fish's mouth, therefore, is Jesus' first drawing in of the breath of utterly fresh air that he himself will ultimately be for the whole world.

Those, of course, are my words; Jesus probably never thought or felt about the matter in such terms. But the episode *is* a lark: he seems to be, for whatever reason, more at ease, more relaxed than before. He uses a kind of rabbinical whimsy to set Peter up; when Peter gives the obvious, right response, Jesus delivers a blithely sweeping declaration of independence; and to cap the climax, he concocts a hilarious mixture of consideration for others ("let's not scandalize them"), frivolous wonder-working ("take the first fish"), and financial precision ("you'll find a *statér*" — four drachmas, right on the nose). At the very least, therefore, he intimates what Paul would eventually express in so many words, namely, "the glorious liberty of the children of God" (Rom. 8:21).

On then with the scriptural playing around. I shall focus on only two elements in the story: the tax in question was the *temple* tax; and Jesus declares his (and our) freedom from it on the basis of *sonship*. Let me weave you a tissue of biblical quotations.

There are two words for temple in the New Testament: *hierón* (sacred place), referring either to the temple itself or to the temple precincts, and *naós* (from the verb *naíein*, to dwell), referring sometimes to the temple and sometimes to its inner sanctuary. Neither word actually occurs in the passage at hand; but since the word *dídrachma* had come to stand not only for a coin but for the temple tax that was paid with it, that word is quite sufficient to bring with it the freight of *religion* that Jesus, in my view, ultimately makes light of.

Consider the general picture. In a good many of the Gospel passages about the temple, Jesus is portrayed as putting a certain distance between himself and what the temple stood for in the religion of his day. He declines Satan's invitation (e.g., Matt. 4:5-6) to jump off a pinnacle of the temple *(hierón)* and be miraculously caught by angels. When his disciples pluck grain on the Sabbath (Matt. 12:1-8), he justifies them by saying that the priests in the temple *(hierón)* profane the sabbath guiltlessly when they eat the bread of the presence and that, in any case, someone greater than the temple (namely, himself) is here. After his triumphal entry into Jerusalem, he goes into the temple *(hierón:* Matt. 21, Mark 11, Luke 19, John 2) and casts out the money-changers. (John, interestingly, puts this event early in Jesus' ministry rather than in Holy Week, thus giving it a "tone-setting" function similar to the one I am attributing to the coin in the fish's mouth in Matthew.) During the cleansing of the temple in John, Jesus says (at 2:19) "destroy this temple [*naós*] and I will raise it up in three days." (John says that Jesus meant the temple of his body — as no doubt he did; but nearly everyone took him to mean [see Matt. 26:61 and 27:40; Mark 14:58 and 15:29] the temple itself.) Finally, at his death (Matt. 27:51; Mark 15:38; Luke 23:45) the veil of the temple *(naós)* was torn in two — signifying, presumably, the end of the old religion of the temple by virtue of its fulfilment in the new mystery of Jesus' death.

One last reference to the temple *(hierón)* provides a bridge to the word "sons" or "children" as it appears in the episode of the coin in the fish's mouth. As a result of the healings Jesus did immediately after the cleansing of the temple, the high priests and the scribes became angry. They were upset, Matthew says (21:15), when they saw "the wonderful things he was doing, and the children [*paídas*] crying out in the temple, 'Hosanna to the Son [*huió*] of David.'" So they said to him, "Do you hear what they are saying?" And Jesus said to them, "Yes. Haven't you ever read that 'Out of the mouths of babies [*nēpíon*] and nursing children [*thēlazóntōn*] you have brought perfect praise'?"

Let me simply set down a list of the words in the New Testament that can be translated "son" or "child." There are *huiós* (son, descendant, offspring); *téknon* (child, descendant); *país* (child, boy, servant); *paidíon* (little boy, lad); and there are *nēpios* (baby) and *thēlázōn* (suckling child), as cited above. Perhaps you see now why I am so strongly against "citizens" as a translation for "sons" *(huioi)*. And perhaps you also see why, despite what I said earlier, I now find myself hard put to decide between "sons" and "children" in translating Jesus' punch line in the parable of the coin in the fish's mouth. The RSV rendering ("Then the sons are free") does indeed catch the associations of the freedom with Jesus' own Sonship and thus with the mystery of death and resurrection that reigns in his (and our) filial relationship with his Father. But the KJV ("Then are the children free") seems to me not only less limiting as to gender but in particular more evocative of the rest of the "child" imagery in the New Testament.

Consider a few of the more salient examples. On a number of occasions, Jesus holds up a child *(paidíon)* as an example of the "littleness," etc., in which the mystery of his death and resurrection preeminently works. Again, he himself is referred to in the Book of Acts (3:13, 26; 4:27, 30) as God's holy *país* (translated by the KJV as "son" or "child" and by the RSV and TEV as "servant"). Not only that, but this appellation occurs, remarkably enough, in connection with references to his crucifixion, thus making it evocative, once again, of lastness, leastness, lostness, littleness, and death. Finally, the remaining major word for "child" *(téknon)* brings into the picture the scriptural references to our share in the sonship (and thus in the passion) that is the root of the freedom of which Jesus is speaking. See, for example, John 1:12: "to them gave he the power to become the children [*tékna*] of God"; and Rom. 8:16-17: "the Spirit himself bears witness with our spirit that we are children [*tékna*] of God, and if children [*tékna*], then heirs as well — heirs of God and fellow heirs with Christ, provided we suffer with him in order that we might also be glorified with him."

But enough of this hammering home of specific scriptural words. The general thrust of my treatment of the coin in the fish's mouth — and especially of Jesus' words, "then the children are free" — is to interpret the whole passage as a proclamation of the end of religion. To me, the episode says that whatever it was that religion was trying to do (the religion of the temple in particular and, by extension, all religions everywhere) will not be accomplished by religious acts at all but in the mystery of Jesus' death and resurrection. As I said, that perception seems to have been so liberating to Jesus that he allowed himself the frivolity of this very odd miracle indeed. But beyond that, it is also (or at least it should be) radically liberating to everyone.

The entire human race is profoundly and desperately religious.

From the dim beginnings of our history right up to the present day, there is not a man, woman, or child of us who has ever been immune to the temptation to think that the relationship between God and humanity can be repaired from our side, by our efforts. Whether those efforts involve creedal correctness, cultic performances, or ethical achievements — or whether they amount to little more than crassly superstitious behavior — we are all, at some deep level, committed to them. If we are not convinced that God can be conned into being favorable to us by dint of our doctrinal orthodoxy, or chicken sacrifices, or the gritting of our moral teeth, we still have a hard time shaking the belief that stepping over sidewalk cracks, or hanging up the bath towel so the label won't show, will somehow render the Ruler of the Universe kindhearted, softheaded, or both.

But as the Epistle to the Hebrews pointed out long ago, all such behavior is bunk. The blood of bulls and goats cannot take away sins, nor can any other religious act do what it sets out to do. Either it is ineffective for its purpose, or the supposedly effective intellectual, spiritual, or moral uprightness it counts on to do the job is simply unavailable. The point is, we haven't got a card in our hand that can take even a single trick against God. Religion, therefore — despite the correctness of its insistence that something needs to be done about our relationship with God — remains unqualified bad news: it traps us in a game we will always and everywhere lose.

But the Gospel of our Lord and Savior Jesus Christ is precisely Good News. It is the announcement, in the death and resurrection of Jesus, that God has simply called off the game — that he has taken all the disasters religion was trying to remedy and, without any recourse to religion at all, set them to rights by himself. How sad, then, when the church acts as if it is in the religion business rather than in the Gospel-proclaiming business. What a disservice, not only to itself but to a world perpetually sinking in the quagmire of religiosity, when it harps on creed, cult, and conduct as the touchstones of salvation. What a perversion of the truth that sets us free (John 8:32) when it takes the news that while we were yet sinners, Christ died for us (Rom. 5:8), and turns it into a proclamation of God as just one more insufferable bookkeeper.

I realize this is a long fetch from the parable of the coin in the fish's mouth, but I make no apologies. In fact, I end with something even farther fetched. The Messiah whom Jesus' contemporaries expected — and likewise any and all of the messiahs the world has looked to ever since (even, alas, the church's all-too-often graceless, punishing version of Jesus' own messiahship) — are like nothing so much as religious versions of "Santa Claus is coming to town." The words of that dreadful Christmas song sum up perfectly the only kind of messianic behavior the human race, in its self-destructive folly, is prepared to accept: "He's making a list; he's checking it twice; he's going to find out who's naughty, or nice" — and so on into the dark night of all the tests this naughty world can never pass. For my money, what Jesus senses clearly and for the first time in the coin in the fish's mouth is that he is not, thank God, Santa Claus. He will come to the world's sins with no lists to check, no tests to grade, no debts to collect, no scores to settle. He will wipe away the handwriting that was against us and nail it to his cross (Col. 2:14). He will save, not some minuscule coterie of good little boys and girls with religious money in their piggy banks, but all the stonebroke, deadbeat, overextended children of this world whom he, as the Son of man — the holy Child of God, the Ultimate Big Kid, if you please — will set free in the liberation of his death.

And when he senses *that* . . . well, it is simply to laugh. He tacks a "Gone Fishing" sign over the sweatshop of religion, and for all the debts of all sinners who ever lived, he provides exact change for free. How nice it would be if the church could only remember to keep itself in on the joke.

CHAPTER FOUR

Losing as the Mechanism of Grace

THE LOST SHEEP

Admittedly, the coin in the fish's mouth may have struck you as a slightly "bent" episode to choose as an introduction to Jesus' parables of grace; but before proceeding to the first of his "straight" parables on the subject, the story of the lost sheep (Matt. 18:10-14; Luke 15:3-7; Aland no. 169), let me continue just a bit longer in the introductory mode. As you already know, I consider context to be crucial to the treatment of any parable. Accordingly, since I am following Matthew at this point, I want you to look at what occurs immediately preceding the parable in Matt. 18:1-9.

Jesus' disciples come to him (the setting is still Capernaum) and ask, "Who is the greatest in the kingdom of heaven?" The oddity of this question is more obvious in Mark (9:33-37) and Luke (9:46-48) than it is in Matthew. In those two Gospels, the episode (Aland no. 166) comes right after Jesus' second prediction of his passion (Aland no. 164), and it is reported as arising out of an argument among the disciples over which of them was the most important. (Matthew, for his own reasons, interposes the coin in the fish's mouth — Aland no. 165 — between the two events.) In any case, the question they were debating is a prime example of the non-comprehension that bedeviled even the closest followers of Jesus. Observe. Jesus has just finished telling them in so many words that he, the Son of man, is going to die. They, however, unable to make any sense of such depressing talk from the mouth of one they

179

have just recognized as the Messiah, simply change the subject to something happier. "Let's talk instead," they seem to say, "about how things will be when the messianic kingdom is finally accomplished. Who of us do you think will be number one?"

That, of course — given the generally low level of human performances on high subjects — produced more heat than light and degenerated into mere one-upmanship. And Jesus, sensing the friction without even, as far as we can tell, being privy to the contention, brings up the subject by asking the loaded question, "What were you discussing on the way?" (Mark 9:33). Mark observes that the disciples (presumably out of embarrassment) simply didn't answer; but Jesus goes straight to the point anyway. If I may put all three accounts into one, the episode is as follows. Jesus calls the Twelve and says to them, "If anyone would be first, he must be last [*éschatos*] of all and servant [*diákonos*] of all." Then he takes a child *(paidíon)*, puts him in the midst of them, and tells them that unless they turn and become like children, they will never enter the kingdom at all — adding that whoever humbles himself like this child is in fact the greatest in the kingdom of heaven. Finally, he says that whoever receives one such child in his name receives not only him but the one who sent him, and that "he who is the least [*mikróteros*, littlest] among you is the one who is great."

I set this down as yet more evidence that Jesus, as he begins the parables of grace, is preoccupied with the notion that the work of the Messiah will be accomplished not by winning but by losing. Out of the five items in my already often-repeated catalogue of "losing" categories — the last *(éschatos)*, the least *(eláchistos)*, the lost *(apolōlós)*, the little *(mikrós)*, and the dead *(nekrós)* — he has, in a mere handful of verses, just ticked off no less than three. Not only that, but in holding up as his example a little boy (or girl — the Greek word *paidíon* is actually a neuter diminutive), he has included the note of little-childhood I have already alluded to (see above, pp. 165-66 and 175-76) and which Jesus again and again emphasizes (for instance, Matt. 19:13-15 and parallels, and the opening line of the upcoming parable of the Lost Sheep, Matt. 18:10).

Moreover, in Mark 9:38-41 and Luke 9:49-50 (Aland no. 167), he continues in the same vein. The disciples, even after Jesus has just finished exalting losers over winners, still haven't an inkling of what he's getting at. One of them, John, immediately changes the subject, providing yet another example of incomprehension. "Master," he says, "we saw a man casting out demons in your name, and we forbade him because he was not following us." True enough, John probably thought he was picking up on Jesus' words about being "sent"; but most likely, he was in fact dismayed at this man's lack of proper accreditation — at his status as an inferior to the duly authorized Twelve. John's view, in other words, was that anyone who did Jesus' work should be a winner who could pass the merit-badge test for Official Exorcist; he was totally unprepared to give anything more than the cold shoulder to an unlicensed loser.

Jesus, however, simply tells John (Luke 9:50) not to run around forbidding such people. "He who is not against you is for you," he says — implying, as I read it, that none of the acceptability tests John has in mind has any bearing on Jesus' way of going about the business of the kingdom. "So what if the man is an outsider and therefore a loser," Jesus seems to ask; "haven't I just gotten through saying that I myself, the Messiah, am going to be the biggest outsider and loser of all? Don't you think it's about time you stopped being scandalized by what you consider my lack of messianic respectability and just listen to me for a change?"

That thought, logically enough, brings us to the very next bit of context (Matt. 18:6-9; Mark 9:42-50; Aland no. 168). Jesus says that "if anyone scandalizes [*skandalísē*] *one of these little ones* [*mikrón*] who believes in me, it would be better for him to have a great millstone tied around his neck and be sunk to the bottom of the sea." To me, the most natural referent of the *mikrón* in this remark is the unofficial exorcist the disciples have just referred to: he is precisely one of the "little losers" about whom Jesus has been, and still is, talking. The word *skandalísē*, however, needs more attention.

The verb *skandalízein* means, variously, to cause someone to stumble, sin, give up his faith; to give offense or scandal; or to throw difficulties in someone's way. The KJV, for example, renders it "offend"; the RSV, "cause to sin"; the TEV, "cause to turn away." In any case, it seems to me that the precise offense or cause of turning away that Jesus has in mind is the despising of the littleness, lostness, lastness, etc., that he has been working up into a veritable catalogue of redeeming unsuccesses. "Don't go around throwing their littleness or lack of respectability at them," he says in effect, "because those things are my chosen métier. If you spook them away from such things, you spook them away from me. I just can't use you if you insist on behaving like that. You'd be better off dead — which, incidentally, happens to be the only condition I'm ultimately going to bother with anyway."

Furthermore, he follows that up with what I see as variations on the same theme. "Woe to the world," he says (Matt. 18:7), "because of these turnings away [skándala]. Such skándala will always come [because, as I read it, Jesus' insistence on unsuccess will always be radically unacceptable to people in their right, success-loving minds] but woe to the man [and specifically, to the disciple] by whom the skándalon comes." In other words, any disciple of Jesus who enlists on the side of the world's winners will simply have cut himself off from the losers who alone have the keys to the kingdom; worse yet, he himself will inevitably become just another doomed winner.

And Jesus drives that point home with some bizarre imagery. "If your hand or your foot causes you to turn away," he says (that is, if being a winner with success-oriented equipment causes you to forget that I work through losers only), "then cut it off. It's better for you to enter into life maimed or lame [in other words, to live as a loser in this age] than to end up having your whole unredeeming and unredeemed success thrown in the fire of the age to come."

But then, after one more illustration about plucking out an eye if it causes this same turning away, Jesus sums up his argument with a mini-parable on salt (Mark 9:49-50; Luke 14:34-35 — with the parallel passage at Matt. 5:13). "You are the salt of the earth," he says (I am using the Matthean reading), "but if the salt has become insipid [mōranthḗ — literally, become foolish], what in the world is there that can restore saltness to it? It is good for nothing except to be thrown out and trampled on by people [anthrṓpōn, men]."

Consider the imagery. Salt seasons and salt preserves, but in any significant quantity, it is not of itself edible, nourishing, or pleasant. On the basis of Jesus' comparison, therefore, we are presumably meant to understand that neither his paradoxical messiahship nor his disciples' witness to it (assuming they don't betray it with sugary substitutes) will be all that appetizing to the world. People simply do not come in droves to anyone who insists that the only way to win is to lose. Nevertheless, Jesus' teaching is exactly that salty: "The disciple is not above his teacher," he told his followers (e.g., Matt. 10:24-25); "it is enough for the disciple to be like his teacher." And he went on to spell out the meaning of that assertion in his very first prediction of his death (e.g., Matt. 16:24-25): "If anyone wants to come with me, let him deny himself, take up his cross, and follow me. For if anyone wants to save his life, he will lose [*apolései*] it; and whoever loses his life for my sake will find it."

But if the salt of the earth becomes insipid — if a disciple of Jesus forgets that only losing wins, and a fortiori, if the apostolic church forgets it — where in the wide world of winners drowning in the syrup of their own success will either the disciple or the church be able to recapture the saltiness of victory out of loss? The answer is nowhere. And the sad fact is that the church, both now and at far too many times in its history, has found it easier to act as if it were selling the sugar of moral and spiritual achievement rather than the salt of Jesus' passion and death. It will preach salvation for the successfully well-behaved, redemption for the triumphantly correct in doctrine, and pie in the sky for all the winners who think they can walk into the final judgment and flash their passing report cards at Jesus. But every last bit of that is now and ever shall be pure baloney because: (a) nobody will ever have that kind of sugar to sweeten the last deal with, and (b) Jesus is going to present us all to the Father in the power of *his* resurrection and not at all in the power of our own totally inadequate records, either good or bad.

But does the church preach that salty message? Not as I hear it, it doesn't. It preaches the nutra-sweet religion of test-passing, which is the only thing the world is ready to buy and which isn't even real sugar let alone salt. In spite of all our fakery, though, Jesus' program remains firm. He saves losers and only losers. He raises the dead and only the dead. And he rejoices more over the last, the least, and the little than

183

over all the winners in the world. That alone is what this losing race of ours needs to hear, even though it can't stand the thought of it. That alone is the salt that can take our perishing insipidity and give it life and flavor forever. That alone. . . .

But why hammer half-moons into the woodwork when Jesus drives the point home with one square blow? We have arrived at the parable of the Lost Sheep — and as you may suspect, I have very nearly finished my exposition before even starting it. Let me simply comment on the highlights of the parable as they now appear.

In Matthew (18:10-11), Jesus begins the parable with the already cited, "Watch that you don't despise one of these little ones [*mikrōn*], for I tell you that their angels in heaven always behold the face of my Father who is in heaven." (Whatever it may have been that these last words were alluding to in the theology of Jesus' times, they at least say clearly enough that it is precisely the little, and not the big, who have an abiding relationship with God.) Furthermore, Matthew has Jesus continue in the same vein in verse 11: "For the Son of man came to save the lost [*apolōlós*]." This verse, which is absent from the oldest and best manuscripts we have, is still worthy of some kind of inclusion. For the record, the KJV and VgCL put it in the text, the TEV sets it in square brackets, and the RSV, NEB, and JB print it as a footnote. In any case, the verse simply puts one more accent on the "lostness" already stressed throughout the passages at hand.

When Luke introduces the parable of the Lost Sheep (in 15:1-3), he puts the same emphasis on losers in a different but equally definite way. He records that tax collectors *(telōnai)* and sinners *(hamartōloí)* were coming to Jesus to hear him, and that the Pharisees and scribes (winners all) grumbled extensively about such consorting with losers. "This man welcomes outcasts [*hamartōloí*]," they murmur, "and even eats with them" (verses 1 and 2, TEV). And Luke completes his introduction (in verse 3) by saying, "So Jesus told them this parable." In other words, the parable is presented as yet another instance of Jesus' rubbing the salt of lostness on the sensibilities of those who are preoccupied with the sweetness of their own success.

As far as the parable itself is concerned, Matthew and Luke give only slightly differing versions. Jesus begins by proposing to his audience (to the disciples, presumably, in Matthew; to the Pharisees and scribes in Luke) a hypothetical case. Suppose, he suggests to them, a man has a hundred sheep and one of them gets lost (Matthew says it "goes astray" — *planēthē;* Luke says "he loses" — *apolésas* — it). Jesus then asks (expecting, of course, an affirmative answer), "Won't the man leave the ninety-nine on the mountain [Luke says, 'in the desert'] and go and seek the stray [Luke has 'the lost']?"

Time for a pause. While it may or may not be true that shepherds in Jesus' day had that kind of devotion to individual members of their flocks, this parable can hardly be interpreted as a helpful hint for running a successful sheep-ranching business. The most likely result of going off in pursuit of one lost sheep will only be ninety-nine more lost sheep. Accordingly, I think it best to assume that Jesus is parabolically thumping the tub for the saving paradox of lostness. He implies, it seems to me, that even if all one hundred sheep should get lost, it will not be a problem for this bizarrely Good Shepherd because he is first and foremost in the business of finding the lost, not of making a messianic buck off the unstrayed. Give him a world with a hundred out of every hundred souls lost — give him, in other words, the worldful of losers that is the only real world we have — and it will do just fine: lostness is exactly his cup of tea. (Incidentally, the "ninety-nine just persons who need no repentance" whom Jesus adduces later in the parable are strictly a rhetorical device: in fact, there are not and never have been any such people anywhere.)

No matter what we do with lostness, though, the rest of the parable is about one thing and one thing only: joy *(chará),* which is the root and blossom of the shepherd's will to find. This note is clearer, perhaps, in Luke than in Matthew, but it is the whole point of both. Matthew has Jesus say simply that the man rejoices *(chaírei)* more over the one than over the ninety-nine who had not strayed; in Luke, Jesus paints a vivid picture of the joy, complete with the man putting the sheep on his shoulders, coming back to his house, calling together his friends and neighbors, and saying, "Rejoice [*synchárēte*] with me, for I have found my lost [*apolōlós*] sheep."

185

It is at the very end of the parable, however, that Jesus makes his point most strongly. Pushing his comparison all the way to heaven itself, he says (Matt. 18:14), "Thus it is not the will of my Father who is in heaven that one of these little ones [*mikrōn*] should perish [*apólētai*]." These words need no more comment than I have already given them; but in Luke (15:7), Jesus gives his summation in a way that cries out for further exposition. "Thus," he says, "there will be more joy in heaven over one sinner who repents than over ninety-nine just persons who need no repentance." Time out now for a full-scale halt on the subject of repentance as it arises in Jesus' parables of joy at finding the lost.

To begin with, let me enter into the record at this point the parable of the Lost Coin. It appears only in Luke (at 15:8-10; Aland no. 220), and it is presented there as a variation on the immediately preceding parable of the Lost Sheep. Jesus begins in the same hypothetical way ("what woman, if she has ten drachmas . . ."), and he continues with the same suggestion that she will drop everything and hunt energetically for the lost property. When she finds it, Jesus says, she too calls friends and neighbors together and says, "Rejoice [*synchárēte*] with me, for I have found the drachma I lost [*apólesa*]." Finally, Jesus concludes the parable (at verse 10) with substantially the same observation as before: "Thus, I say to you, there is joy before the angels of God over one repentant [*metanooúnti*] sinner."

It is usual, when expounding the word *metanoéein* (repent), to go about the job etymologically. Since the word is a compound of *metá* (after) and *noéein* (think), its root meaning is to change one's mind or, better said, to change one's heart about one's sins. That approach, however, does not serve well here. Neither the lost coin nor the lost sheep was capable of any repentance at all. The entire cause of the recovery operation in both stories is the shepherd's, or the woman's, determination to find the lost. Neither the lost sheep nor the lost coin does a blessed thing except hang around in its lostness. On the strength of this parable, therefore, it is precisely our sins, and not our goodnesses, that most commend us to the grace of God.

Hence if in our interpretations we harp on the necessity of a change of heart — if we badger ourselves with the dismal notion that sinners must first forsake their sins before God will forgive them, that the lost must somehow find itself before the finder will get up off his backside and look for it — we carry ourselves straight away from the obvious sense of both stories. And since that violates not only the parables but also Rom. 5:8 ("while we were still sinners, Christ died for us"), I propose to take a different tack altogether and to look not at etymologies but simply at the stories as Jesus tells them.

Consider the following propositions, all of which I think are true. A lost sheep is, for all practical purposes, a dead sheep; a lost coin is likewise a dead asset. In addition (if I may look forward a bit to the parables of the Unforgiving Servant and of the Prodigal Son), a debtor about to be foreclosed on is a dead duck and a son who has blown his inheritance is a deadbeat. These parables of lostness, therefore, are far from being exhortations to repentance. They are emphatically not stories designed to convince us that if we will wind ourselves up to some acceptable level of moral and/or spiritual improvement, God will *then* forgive us; rather they are parables about God's determination to move before we do — in short, to make lostness and death the only tickets we need to the Supper of the Lamb. In all of them, it is precisely the lost (and thus the dead) who come to the party; in none of them is any of the unlost (and thus the living) in on the festivities. More than that, in none of these parables is *anything* (except the will of God) portrayed as necessary to the new life in joy. Neither the lostness, nor the deadness, nor the repentance is in itself redemptive; God alone gives life, and he gives it freely and fully on no conditions whatsoever. These stories, therefore, are parables of grace and grace only. There is in them not one single note of earning or merit, not one breath about rewarding the rewardable, correcting the correctible, or improving the improvable. There is only the gracious, saving determination of the shepherd, the woman, the king, and the father — all surrogates for God — *to raise the dead*.

That, I think, puts repentance — and confession, and contrition, and absolution, and all their ancillary subjects — in a different light. Confession, for example, turns out to be something other than we thought. It is not the admission of a mistake which, thank God and our better nature, we have finally recognized and corrected. Rather it is the admission that we are *dead* in our sins — that we have no power of ourselves either to save ourselves or to convince anyone else that we are worth saving. It is the recognition that our whole life is finally and forever *out of our hands* and that if we ever live again, our life will be entirely the gift of some gracious other.

And to take the other side of the coin, absolution too becomes another matter. It is neither a response to a suitably worthy confession, nor the acceptance of a reasonable apology. *Absolvere* in Latin means not only to loosen, to free, to acquit; it also means to dispose of, to complete, to finish. When God pardons, therefore, he does not say he understands our weakness or makes allowances for our errors; rather he disposes of, he finishes with, the whole of our dead life and raises us up with a new one. He does not so much deal with our derelictions as he does drop them down the black hole of Jesus' death. He forgets our sins in the darkness of the tomb. He remembers our iniquities no more in the oblivion of Jesus' expiration. He finds us, in short, in the desert of death, not in the garden of improvement; and in the power of Jesus' resurrection, he puts us on his shoulders rejoicing and brings us home.

CHAPTER FIVE

Death, Resurrection, and Forgiveness

THE UNFORGIVING SERVANT

I felt free to raise the topic of forgiveness at the end of the last chapter precisely because the very next parable (the Unforgiving Servant, Matt. 18:21-35; Aland nos. 172-173) is one of Jesus' major treatments of the subject. But my tying of forgiveness to the raising of the dead — my insistence that it is a gift given to the totally incompetent, not a reward bestowed on the suitably disposed — may need more explanation.

When Jesus speaks about forgiveness (and above all, when he acts to bring it about), he bases his most telling words and deeds squarely on death and resurrection. Consider only two examples, the parable of the Prodigal Son and the crucifixion. In the first, Jesus is at pains to point out that the gift of forgiveness proceeds solely out of God's love and is therefore antecedent to any qualifying action on the part of the receiver (before the prodigal gets even a word of confession out of his mouth, the father runs, throws his arms around his son, and kisses him — Luke 15:20). And in the crucifixion, God in Christ acts strictly "for the joy that was set before him" (Heb. 12:2), enduring the cross and despising the shame for an entire race that was stone-cold dead in its sins (cf., e.g., Rom. 5:8, 12, 21). He waits, in other words, for nothing: not for repentance and certainly not for reform. He asks for no response, no life glued halfway back together, before he extends his pardon; he needs only the death that sin has caused, for the simple reason

189

that the power of Jesus' resurrection does everything else that needs doing.

I set this down because while the note of unmerited grace raising the dead is clear enough in the parable of the Unforgiving Servant, it is not nearly so obvious in the sayings of Jesus (Matt. 18:15-20; Luke 17:3-4; Aland nos. 170-171) that immediately precede the parable. In the Lukan version, in fact, forgiveness seems quite simply to be made conditional on repentance: "Be on your guard!" Jesus says. "If your brother sins, rebuke him, and if he repents, forgive him. And if he sins seven times a day against you, and turns to you seven times and says, 'I repent,' you must forgive him."

In fairness, of course, even Luke's version (especially in view of the opening words, "Be on your guard!") should probably be interpreted chiefly as an insistence that Jesus' disciples must set no cutoff point for forgiveness — that they may never allow sin, however protracted or repeated, to have any effect on their determination to pardon. In short, it is unforgivingness, not subsequent sin, that is portrayed here as real abuse of the Gospel of forgiveness. But since Luke includes neither the parable of the Unforgiving Servant nor the Matthean buildup to it, the very brevity of the passage causes repentance-as-a-condition to leap to the eye of the reader.

When we turn to Matthew, however, we initially find ourselves confronted with a passage even more difficult than the one in Luke. For immediately after the parable of the Lost Sheep (with its conclusion, "thus it is not the will of your Father in heaven that one of these little ones should perish"), Matthew (18:15-17) gives us a discourse in which Jesus apparently reneges on everything he's established since chapter 16. "If your brother sins against you," he says, "go and rebuke him just between the two of you. If he listens to you, you have gained your brother. But if he refuses to listen to you, take with you one or two others, so that 'every accusation may be upheld by the testimony of two or three witnesses.' But if he refuses to listen to them, tell it to the church; and if he refuses to listen to the church, let him be to you as a Gentile and a tax collector."

"So much," Jesus seems to be saying, "for the losers of this world.

190

Sure, I seek them as a shepherd seeks his lost sheep. But I'm not about to overdo it. What I really have in mind is that you should give your personal lost sheep — your sinning brother — exactly and only three shots at getting found. If he doesn't make it under that wire, you just tell him, 'Tough luck, Charlie.'"

Indeed, it is precisely on the strength of this and other apparently hard-nosed passages that the church worked up its two-thousand-year love affair with excommunication — its gleeful enthusiasm for running persistent strays off the Good Shepherd's ranch. But since that whole approach makes hash not only of the preceding parable of the Lost Sheep but also of the upcoming one on the Unforgiving Servant — and since I have already expressed my reluctance to conclude that the Gospel writers just dumped pericopes every which where without regard to context — I am not about to take such an interpretation lying down. I invite your attention, therefore, to what strikes me as the crucial bit of context here, namely, Jesus' final words in verse 17: "Let him be to you as a Gentile and a tax collector."

Some people have an odd idea of what constitutes fair exegesis. To them, the only thing you can do with "Gentile and tax collector" is read the words in the sense they presumably had for the average Jew of Jesus' day. Accordingly, such exegetes think that because Jesus' compatriots would have thought "outcast" when they heard the phrase, Jesus himself had to have been thinking about excommunication when he uttered it. But such an approach is a short stack of half-baked waffles.

The first waffle is precisely the failure of this sort of exegesis to pay attention to context: Jesus has just finished talking about actively seeking outcasts, not about giving them the boot. Therefore, even if he was actually thinking "outcast" when he said "Gentile and tax collector," it is quite unwarranted to conclude that he was telling his disciples to shun such types. The other waffle is its failure to pay attention to who is talking: Jesus was *not* an average Jew — and he was, by now, not an average Messiah either. His previous performances (sabbath-breaking, sniping at the establishment, hanging out with undesirables) were unconventional in the extreme. Thus there was at least a strong possibility that "Gentile and tax collector," from his mouth, might have had a non-excommunicatory meaning. Above all, though — and this, to me, clinches the case against these two waffles — who, in fact, were the undesirables Jesus hung around with? Were they not precisely "sinners of the Gentiles" (cf. Gal. 2:15) and tax collectors?

In other words, who says that exegesis is only fair if it's based on some critic's guess about what Jesus might possibly have *thought?* How come what he actually *did* can't govern the interpretation? Even if the critics could prove that Jesus couldn't possibly have thought what I take him to mean, so what? The fact remains that he did more than just think; if I want to understand the significance of his remarks from his life as a whole, what's to stop me? On at least one occasion (when he asked to have the crucifixion called off in the Garden of Gethsemane), his actions spoke louder than his words; who's to say that couldn't have been true on other occasions as well?

Consequently, I am going to let Jesus' actual behavior govern my reading of these verses: since he actively sought out the Gentiles and tax collectors he adduces here as apparent candidates for rejection, *I propose to take his words as ironic.* Consider, if you will, the dynamics of the situation. Jesus has been harping for some time on lostness, lastness, death, and the rest; but he is also acutely aware that his disciples hardly understand him at all. He develops a strategy, therefore: he will sucker them into revealing their incomprehension by giving them, as his own seemingly serious teaching, a string of propositions that will sound like nothing so much as a retraction of what he's been saying. He follows up his story of a really indefatigable seeker of the lost — of a shepherd who risks everything to find a single stray — with a series of "rules for limited forgiveness" that could have been written by the Committee for the Prevention of Wear and Tear on the Righteous. In other words, the whole thing is a setup: what Jesus is about to say is so obviously at odds with what he has just been saying that even apostolic dummies will sense the incongruity. But when they try to respond to his obviously erroneous rules with emendations based on their inadequate grasp of what true forgiveness involves, they will be forced to recognize that they failed utterly to understand him. The gambit, as clever as it is simple, goes like this (White is Jesus; Black, the disciples):

192

White: "... so the shepherd seeks the lost sheep unconditionally."

Black: "You don't really mean that as practical advice, do you?"

White: "Okay, so I'll make it practical. Forget the first story. The shepherd in the new parable gives the stupid sheep three chances to get found; then he gives up on it."

Black: "Hey, maybe that's a little tougher than you meant to be. How about, he gives it seven chances?"

White: "Aha! Gotcha! How about seventy times seven? And how about checkmate? You thought I didn't really mean unconditionally, huh?"

That bit of whimsy, of course, catapults us straight from "Gentile and tax collector" (Matt. 18:17) to the question by Peter (18:21) that leads Jesus straight into the parable of the Unforgiving Servant. The intervening verses, however, while they are every bit as susceptible of hardnosed interpretation as the passage we have just dealt with, deserve at least an attempt to give them a lenient reading.

Take verse 18 first: "Amen, I say to you whatever you bind on earth will be bound in heaven, and whatever you loose on earth will be loosed in heaven." I am sure no one needs reminding that this passage (along with John 20:23) has traditionally been the basis for the idea that the church can not only grant but also withhold absolution. For the record, though, I feel bound to point out that that particular doctrinal development does not seem to be consistent with the church's proclamation in the Nicene Creed that it acknowledges "one baptism for the forgiveness of sins." I take that phrase to mean that in baptism we are clothed, once and for all, with a forgiveness woven for us by Jesus' death and resurrection. The grace of baptism, therefore, is quite fittingly referred to as *habitual* grace (from "habit" as in "a nun's habit") because we wear it, all our lives long, as an irremovable vestment of forgiveness.

Accordingly, the church's creedal teaching seems to be that no matter what sins we commit subsequent to baptism, every last one of them is committed *inside* an effective suit of pardon that we can neither lose nor undo. To be sure, sinners can refuse to believe they are wearing the suit — and they can even, by refusing to forgive others, set themselves at cross-purposes with the suit; but I do not think we ought to talk as if the church, on its own motion, has any power to remove the suit by withholding absolution. (As a matter of fact, the church's own ancient insistence that baptism should never be repeated, even after grave sin, seems to argue for the same conclusion.)

Just what does this passage about binding and loosing mean then? Well, if you accept my view that Jesus was being ironic when he suggested that a sinning brother should be given only three whacks at forgiveness, these words show him dropping the irony and saying, seriously and plainly, what will happen if anyone follows such an unforgiving, unshepherdlike course.

Jesus flags this change of tone by the very first word in verse 18: the "Amen" is his standard trick of speech for calling attention to an utterly serious pronouncement. "Now listen up real good," he says in effect, "because I've been stringing you along. All that plausible advice about excommunicating the recalcitrant is hazardous to your health. Because if you go around binding your brother's sins on him, if you insist that beyond three months or three thousand miles of sinning his warranty of forgiveness will run out — if, in short, you treat him like an outcast instead of joining him in his lostness as I have joined Gentiles and tax collectors in theirs — then the deadly rule of unforgiveness will be all you have, here or hereafter. But if you loose his sins, if you move toward him in unconditional, unlimited forgiveness, then the life-giving rule of grace will prevail, both now on earth and forever in heaven."

The rest of the passage (Matt. 18:19-20), while a bit more obscure, is at least susceptible of the same reading. "Again I say to you," Jesus continues (the "again," I take it, serves as a repetition of the "amen"); "if two of you agree on earth about anything they ask, it will be done for them by my Father in heaven. For where two or three are gathered together in my name, there I am in the midst of them." Since these words stand just before the parable of the Unforgiving Servant — and since they are the capstone of the whole passage (Matt. 18:15-20) immediately following the story of the Lost Sheep — I think it only fair to assume that their primary reference is to the way forgiveness seeks out the lost. (That they can also have other meanings, I do not doubt; I am simply concerned here to put first things first.) Accordingly, I take them to mean that if two of Jesus' disciples — if, that is, his followers in their plural capacity as his witnessing church — agree to forgive rather than to excommunicate, then the Father will ratify and confirm their decision with all the power of his grace. And he will do that precisely because wherever two or three are gathered together in Jesus' name (that is, wherever the witnessing church is), there is Jesus himself, the friend of publicans and sinners, the Good Shepherd who lays down his life for the sheep, the beloved Son in whom the Father sees his whole creation forgiven and made new.

Before proceeding, though, let me add a note about the witnessing church to which Jesus, in my interpretation, has just referred. As I see it, the church's witness is at least threefold: kerygmatic, baptismal, and eucharistic. It is kerygmatic because the church is commissioned to proclaim the original apostolic preaching *(kérygma)*, namely, the announcement to the world of Jesus' resurrection from the dead. It is baptismal because the church is constituted as a living sign of that resurrection by the baptism in which its members die and rise in Jesus. And it is eucharistic because as often as two, or three, or any number of his followers "do this in remembrance of him," he is present among them in all the gracious power of his death and resurrection. At least tangentially, therefore, the passage at hand ends (Matt. 18:20) with a eucharistic note, and so with one more hint of the interrelationship in the Gospels between death-resurrection and grace-reconciliation.

That brings us, both logically and in terms of the text itself, to the parable of the Unforgiving Servant (Matt. 18:21-35). Since I have already commented on Jesus' emphasis (verses 21-22) on unlimited as opposed to limited forgiveness — on his tricking Peter into proposing a generous seven chances for forgiveness and then sending him sprawling with a bizarre insistence on seventy times seven — let me go straight to the story.

Jesus begins it by tying what he is about to say to the unconditional forgiveness he has just called for. *"Diá toúto,"* he says (on account of this, because of this, therefore), "the kingdom of heaven is like a king who wanted to settle accounts with his servants." Jesus, shrewd teacher that he is, begins by setting up law, not grace, as the first element of the parable. This king is a bookkeeper, pure and simple: for the honest, for the upright, and above all, for the solvent, he will have kind words; but for anyone in real trouble, he will have no care at all except to get his money back as best he can. Accordingly, when the stone-broke servant who owes him ten thousand talents is brought in (the amount of the debt is set at an astronomical ten million dollars or so to stress its radical unrepayability), the king orders him to be sold, lock, stock, barrel, wife, and children, and restitution to be made. There is no forgiveness in the story so far and there is no reason to expect it. It is all a matter of cut your losses and get out.

But then the servant falls on his knees before his master and says, "Have patience with me [*makrothýmēson,* be big-hearted] and I will repay you everything." And sure enough, the king's attitude suddenly changes. He goes straight from having had all the mercy of a loan shark to being a softy. "Taking pity," Jesus says (the Greek is *splanchnistheís,* from *splánchna,* the bowels, the seat of compassion), "the lord of that servant released him and forgave [*aphēken*] him the debt." Enter here, therefore, gut reaction rather than head reaction — or if you like, left-handed, right-brain activity as opposed to right-handed, left-brain activity — as the new basis of the king's behavior. But enter here also an even more important principle: the servant has to do nothing more than ask for grace to get grace. It is not that he earns it by extravagantly promising to repay everything at some future date. It is simply that the king cancels the debt *for reasons entirely internal to himself.*

Examine that last point more closely. The servant (closet bookkeeper that he is) no doubt thinks that his master is actually responding to his ridiculous offer of repayment. He has, in other words, not a shred of the notion of grace in his own mind. Like all desperate sinners, he knows only that he is in a tight spot and that he can't escape without outside help. But when he comes to imagine for himself what kind of "outsider" he needs to get him out of his bind, he can't think of anyone who isn't exactly like himself. Hence his con job about repayment: he assumes that the king is not only a bookkeeper interested solely in money, but also a stupid bookkeeper who can't spot a losing proposition when it slithers up to him. The servant knows he needs salvation, but the only savior he can imagine is someone who, except for dumb luck, would long ago have ended up as much in need of saving as himself.

The king, however, responds to nothing that the servant has in mind. He ignores the manifest nonsense about repayment. He makes no calculations at all about profit and loss. Instead, he simply drops dead to the whole business of bookkeeping and forgives the servant. Wipes the debt out. Forgets it ever existed. Does, in short, what the servant couldn't even conceive of doing. And do you know why the king could do that and the servant couldn't? Because the king was willing to end his old life of bookkeeping and the servant wasn't. Indeed, the servant was so busy trying to hold together his own bookkeeper's existence — so unable to imagine anything even vaguely like dropping dead to it — that he never even saw what the king had done. All he knew was that the heat, which formerly had been on, was now off. He hadn't the slightest notion of what it had cost the king to put out the fire.

You complain, perhaps, that I have once again dragged in death and resurrection by the hair of the head. I make no apology; both of them are integral to this parable. For one thing, the king does indeed die to the life he had when the story began: he goes out of the debt-collecting business altogether. For another, the servant's failure to perceive the king's death in the first half of the story is actually the only thing that can make sense of his otherwise incomprehensible mercilessness to his fellow servant in the second half. Consider, therefore, this bizarre unforgivingness that gives the parable its name.

The commonest objection to Jesus' parabolic picture of the servant's pitilessness is that it sets up a cardboard figure of wickedness. "How could anyone outside a comic book," we ask ourselves, "actually fail to see that if you've just been forgiven a multimillion-dollar debt — and freed from slavery to boot — you don't first-off go and try to beat a hundred bucks out of somebody who's still a slave?" The unforgiving servant, however, is anything but a cartoon villain; he is, in fact, exactly what everybody else in the world is, namely, an average citizen totally unwilling to face death in any way. Not only hasn't he paid attention to his lord's death to a lifetime of bookkeeping; he's also totally unwilling to accept the death the king has handed him in setting him free. Note that last point well: in spite of the fact that he was an important enough servant to run up a whopping debt (mere stableboys don't have opportunities like that), his first thought on being released was not how to die to his old life and market himself in a new one. Rather it was to go on with all his bookkeeping as before. Hence, with deathless logic, he puts the arm on his fellow servant. And hence he misses the whole new life he might have lived out of death.

And so do we, when we refuse death. Jesus has not only set Peter up in this passage; he has set us up as well. He has been saying with utter clarity that he, the Messiah, is going to solve the world's problems by dying. His answer to our sins will be the oblivion of a death on the cross. His response to our loss of control over our destinies will be to lose everything himself. What he tells us in this parable, therefore, is that unless we too are willing to see our own death as the one thing necessary to our salvation — unless we can, unlike the unforgiving servant, die to the gimcrack accounts by which we have justified our lives — we will never be able to enjoy the resurrection, even though Jesus hands it to us on a silver platter. If we cannot face the price he has paid to free us, we might as well never have been freed at all.

The remaining details of the parable make that clear. The unforgiving servant's fellow slaves see his unmerciful behavior and are greatly distressed. They understand what the king has done. They know that he has laid down vast royal prerogatives — that, as far as the indebted servant is concerned, he has rolled over and played dead. And they see clearly what an outrage, what a violation of grace it is when the servant is unwilling to lay down even the two-bit prerogatives he himself has. So they come and tell their lord all that has taken place; and the lord summons the servant and confronts him with his refusal to die. "You wicked servant!" he shouts at him in anger. "I forgave you all that debt just because you asked me to. Don't you think you should have had mercy [*eleêsai*] on your fellow servant, as I had mercy [*êleêsa*] on you?"

In other words, the king sets before the servant the two scenes he has just been through and he rubs the salt of them into the wound of the servant's refusal to die. In each, there was a creditor with lawful rights; in each, a plea for patience from the debtor and a promise to repay. But then the king drives home the one, crucial difference. "I *died* for you, for Christ's sake!" he says; "but you were so busy making plans for your stupid life, you never even noticed." And therefore the king pronounces judgment on him. Because the servant has chosen a losing life instead of a gracious death, the king condemns him to just that life: he delivers him to the torturers, to be tormented until he pays the debt — which means, obviously, for his whole life, until death itself does for him what he refused to do on his own.

Jesus then ends the parable with a confirmation of that same judgment: "So also my heavenly Father will do to you, if you do not each forgive your brother from your heart." Interestingly, therefore, this parable of grace ends as a parable of judgment as well — and it makes clear, long before we get to the parables of judgment themselves, the only basis on which anyone will be finally condemned. None of our debts — none of our sins, none of our trespasses, none of our errors — will ever be an obstacle to the grace that raises the dead. At the most, they will be the measure of our death, and as soon as we die, they too will be dead, because our Lord the King has already died to them. But if we refuse to die — and in particular, if we insist on binding others' debts upon them in the name of our own right to life — we will, by not letting grace have its way *through* us, cut ourselves off from ever knowing the joy of grace *in* us.

In heaven, there are only forgiven sinners. There are no good guys, no upright, successful types who, by dint of their own integrity, have been accepted into the great country club in the sky. There are only failures, only those who have accepted their deaths in their sins and who have been raised up by the King who himself died that they might live.

But in hell, too, there are only forgiven sinners. Jesus on the cross does not sort out certain exceptionally recalcitrant parties and cut them off from the pardon of his death. He forgives the badness of even the worst of us, willy-nilly; and he never takes back that forgiveness, not even at the bottom of the bottomless pit.

The sole difference, therefore, between hell and heaven is that in heaven the forgiveness is accepted and passed along, while in hell it is rejected and blocked. In heaven, the death of the king is welcomed and becomes the doorway to new life in the resurrection. In hell, the old life of the bookkeeping world is insisted on and becomes, forever, the pointless torture it always was.

There is only one unpardonable sin, and that is to withhold pardon from others. The only thing that can keep us out of the joy of the resurrection is to join the unforgiving servant in his refusal to die.

CHAPTER SIX

Losing as Winning

THE PROLOGUE TO THE GOOD SAMARITAN

In our study of Jesus' parables up to this point, I have used the Matthean sequence of events and materials as my principal source; now, however, it is time to change guides and follow Luke. The first reason for this change is simply procedural: at the outset, I made a decision to follow the numbering system of the Aland *Synopsis* in establishing the sequence of the parables. To review that sequence briefly, the parables of the kingdom (Aland nos. 122-134 — dealt with in a previous volume) all occur within the larger context of Jesus' ministry in Galilee (Aland nos. 30-173). In addition, the parables of grace we have so far examined in this volume (namely, Aland nos. 144-173) fall into that same, primarily Matthean framework.

But with Aland no. 174 (the decision to go to Jerusalem, Luke 9:51), we begin to follow the predominantly Lukan account of Jesus' leaving Galilee and undertaking his last journey to Jerusalem. Not only does the ensuing collection of materials (which extends all the way to the triumphal entry: Luke 19:28; Aland no. 269) contain the bulk of Jesus' parables of grace, it also shows Jesus "setting his face" to go to Jerusalem. In other words, by the very juxtaposition of sayings and deeds in the Lukan narrative, the rest of the parables of grace are set more and more clearly in the light of Jesus' conviction that his mission will be fulfilled in the mighty act of his dying and rising.

Indeed, it is just that juxtaposition that is the second and substantive reason for the changeover from Matthew to Luke. Up till now, Jesus has mostly *talked* — and talked, as it were, with the clutch of his redeeming death not yet fully engaged. True enough, he has proclaimed a radically left-handed messiahship and he has adumbrated its dark mysteriousness by a constant flow of concepts like lastness, lostness, leastness, littleness, and death. But from now on, it becomes obvious that he is determined to push his insistence on losing-as-winning, on weakness-as-strength, all the way to its logical, *acted-out* conclusion in his own death and resurrection. Accordingly, as we approach the next of the parables of grace (the Good Samaritan: Luke 10:25-37; Aland nos. 182-183), I want to spend a shortish chapter showing how this note of mystery-finally-in-gear manifests itself in Luke's buildup to that parable (Luke 9:51–10:24; Aland nos. 174-181). In particular, I want to demonstrate how, even at this relatively early stage in the final journey to Jerusalem, Jesus himself is already clear that death and resurrection is in fact the key to the operation of grace.

The first passage in this section is a single verse, Luke 9:51. But for all its brevity, it contains not one but two striking references to the mystery of death-resurrection: "And when the days of his being received up [*tás heméras tḗs analḗmpseōs autoú*] drew near, he set his face to go to Jerusalem." The noun *analḗmpsis* (a taking or receiving up) occurs in the New Testament only at this point. There are, however, nine occurrences of the verb *analambánein* (to take up), five of which (Mark 16:19; Acts 1:2, 11, 22; and 1 Tim. 3:16) refer to Jesus' ascension into heaven. Plainly, then, since Luke is the author of Acts (and uses, in Acts 1:22, practically the same phrase, namely, "the day on which he was taken up"), Luke's allusion to the ascension in the passage at hand is a shorthand way of summing up the entire mystery of death-resurrection that Jesus has come to reveal. Similarly, the "setting of his face toward Jerusalem" has the same mystery as its primary reference. It harks back to Luke's account of the transfiguration (9:30-31), in which Moses and Elijah "appear in glory and speak of [Jesus'] *exodus* that he was about to accomplish at Jerusalem." As Luke handles this one-verse introduction to the last journey to Jerusalem, therefore, it is pregnant with the mystery about to be made manifest. It may have been enough for Matthew

(19:1-2) and Mark (10:1) to present the bare details of Jesus' leaving Galilee for Judea. Luke, however, headed as he is for a succession of parables that will positively harp on death-resurrection, cannot let this moment of decision pass without enduing it with the full aura of the mystery.

The next passage we come to (Luke 9:52-56; Aland no. 175) tells of Jesus' rejection by a Samaritan village to which he sent messengers, presumably to make arrangements for a stop during the journey to Jerusalem. "They did not receive him," Luke says, "because he was obviously going toward Jerusalem." Jesus, in other words, having already been rejected by the Jewish authorities because he associated with outcasts (and in particular, with Samaritans — cf. John 4:9), is now rejected by the very outcasts for whom he jeopardized his respectability in the first place.

It is a rerun of the old, disgraceful human story: all of us, even the rankest outsiders, feel better about ourselves if we can keep someone else further outside than we are. The last ethnic group admitted into the volunteer fire department is the very squad that turns, rumps together, horns out, to reject the next group struggling up the social ladder. Jesus came to save a lost and losing world by his own lostness and defeat; but in this wide world of losers, everyone except Jesus remains firmly, if hopelessly, committed to salvation by winning. It hardly matters to us that the victories we fake for ourselves are two-bit victories, or that the losses (and losers) we avoid like the plague are the only vessels in which saving grace comes; we will do anything rather than face either the bankruptcy of our wealth or the richness of our poverty.

And what then is it that we do when we thus disregard our true wealth? We delude ourselves into thinking that our own salvation can be achieved by keeping books on others. The Samaritans wrote Jesus' name down in red ink because he fell short in their religious audit; the Pharisee in Jesus' parable looked down at the publican and thanked God that he himself was not a crook. And we do the same: "I know I'm no prize, but at least I'm better than that lecher, Harry" — as if putting ourselves at the head of a whole column marching in the wrong direction somehow made us less lost than the rest of the troops. It would be funny if it were not fatal; but fatal it is, because grace works only in those who accept their lostness. Jesus came to call sinners, not the pseudo-righteous; he came to raise the dead, not to buy drinks for the marginally alive.

It is not just the Samaritans, though, whose bookkeeping leads them to miss the point of Jesus' determination to go to Jerusalem and death. In Luke 9:54, his disciples James and John turn out to be no better. Even though they have heard everything Jesus has said about lostness — even though they have been the butt of his irony about Gentiles, tax collectors, and other outcasts, and even though they have heard his words to Peter about unlimited forgiveness — they still instinctively resort to salvation by bookkeeping. Confronted with the Samaritan village's rejection of the Jesus they have accepted as the Messiah, the only thing they can think to do is even the score. "Lord," they ask him, "do you want us to bid fire come down from heaven and consume them?" They say in effect, "We're the ones who are winners when it comes to Messiah-watching; let's just get this villageful of losers out of the game with one good, hot blast." Yet they were not winners: they themselves consistently failed to understand Jesus' plain words about his coming death. It would only be much later, after they had seen Jesus himself dead and risen, and after they came to see themselves as dead and risen in him, that they would really be winners. And even at that, most of them would win only by martyrs' deaths — by the very loss, ironically, that they were in such a hurry to inflict on the Samaritans.

But Jesus simply turns and rebukes them (Luke 9:55). The earliest manuscript tradition does not record the substance of the rebuke, but there is a less well attested tradition that gives it as follows: "And he said, 'You do not know what manner of spirit you are of. For the Son of man did not come to destroy men's lives but to save them.'" In either case, Jesus says a firm no to their whole conception of how the plan of salvation works. He tells them they are talking about something one hundred and eighty degrees opposed to what he himself has in mind. In short, he unceremoniously shuts them up, leaving them with yet another proof that they are losers, and yet another invitation to accept their losing status rather than reject it.

The rest of the Lukan prologue to the parable of the Good Samaritan can be dealt with more briefly; I will note only the points at which it reinforces the thrust of the argument I have been making. In 9:57-62 (Aland no. 176), Jesus effectively throws cold water on three would-be followers. The first of them is apparently an enthusiast who thinks that joining up with Jesus on his journey to Jerusalem will land him unambiguously on a winning team. "I will follow you wherever you go," the man tells Jesus — to which Jesus replies, "Foxes have holes and birds of the air have nests, but the Son of man has nowhere to lay his head." Score another point for Jesus as the divine loser, and for lostness as the touchstone of discipleship.

The second and third characters have a slightly different view of what following Jesus will involve. Number two accepts Jesus' invitation but wants permission first to go and bury his father; number three feels he should be allowed to say a proper good-bye to his family before setting out. To both of them, Jesus says that all such behavior is now irrelevant. "Let the dead bury their own dead," he tells the one, "but as for you, go and proclaim the kingdom of God." And he tells the other, "No one who puts his hand to the plow and looks back is fit for the kingdom of God." In other words, it is not only that the human race's business-as-usual desire to be on the side of a winner is inappropriate to Jesus' mission; it's that *none* of our usual bits of business, however virtuous or proper, has the least bearing on the mystery of redemption. "Follow *me*," he says flatly. "Follow me into my death, because it is only in my death and resurrection that the kingdom comes. All the other tickets to the final, reconciled party — all the moral, philosophical, and religious admission slips on which humanity has always counted — have been cancelled. Nothing counts now except being last, least, lost, little, and dead with me. Buy *that,* and you're home free; buy anything else and you're out in the cold."

And Luke follows up that unvarnished advice with an episode that has even less of a sensible, protective coating on it. In 10:1-12 (Aland no. 177), Jesus appoints seventy others and sends them, two by two, into every town and place where he himself is about to come. "The harvest is plentiful," he tells them, "but the laborers are few" (as well they would be, since no one in his right mind would willingly sign on with a Messiah determined to get himself killed). And as if that weren't enough, he tells them that their own mission will be just as useless: "I send you out as lambs in the midst of wolves" (in other words, as *lost sheep* whose most important credentials will be precisely their lostness and their willingness, in the face of the world's unrelenting wolfishness, to end up as somebody else's dinner). All of which he reinforces by his advice to take no money, no suitcase, no shoes, and to talk to no one on the road. Think of it. He sends them out with no more of the trappings of personal status than a corpse has when it's being shipped home for burial. And when they finally do get to someone's house, they are simply to wish it peace and stay there, eating, drinking, and doing whatever comes along. They are, in short, to be empty vessels, personalities whose contents of initiative and self-determination have been poured down the drain of Jesus' own lostness.

But then (in Luke 10:1-16; Aland nos. 177-179), Jesus drives home the coffin nail of lostness with a series of harsh blows. He tells the seventy (in verses 10-12) that in the entirely likely event that their prospective hosts reject them as freeloading losers, they are simply to shake off the dust of the town against their rejectors and tell them, "Tough luck, winners; you just missed the kingdom of God." Next, he follows that up (in verses 13-15) by pronouncing woes on three of the cities — Chorazin, Bethsaida, and Capernaum — that had just rejected Jesus himself as a loser. And finally (in verse 16), he unequivocally identifies what will happen to them with what has happened and will happen to himself: "He who hears you, hears me" (that is, anyone who accepts your lostness accepts mine), "and he who rejects you rejects me, and he who rejects me rejects him who sent me" (in other words, *losing* is the name of God's game and it's the only game in town: follow *me*, or follow nothing).

In the final verses of this section (Luke 10:17-24; Aland nos. 180-181), the seventy return with joy, saying, "Lord, even the demons are subject to us in your name" — thus missing almost completely the point of the saving emptiness he sent them out to manifest. Jesus — used, by now, to such dunderheadedness — calmly corrects them.

"Sure," he says in effect; "I gave you all kinds of power: over snakes and scorpions and over all the power of the enemy. But no matter what you think, kiddies, such right-handed power is not what it's all about. You should be rejoicing only that your names are written in heaven" — which means, if we may push this left-handed, strength-out-of-weakness interpretation all the way to the end of the New Testament, in the *Lamb's book of life,* that is, in the final roster of lost sheep written by none other than the great Lost Sheep Himself.

If that strikes you as an unwarranted extension of Jesus' remarks, consider what comes immediately afterward in verses 21-24. "In that same hour, he rejoiced in the Holy Spirit and said, 'I thank you, Father, Lord of heaven and earth, that you have hidden these things from the wise and understanding and revealed them to babes [*nēpíois*].'" After all the talk and all the grimness of the journey, Jesus reposes himself in the heart of his mission — in that perfect intimacy he has with the one who sent him — and he sings there of the littleness and the leastness by which the Father wills to reconcile all things to himself Then finally, turning to the disciples, he says to them privately (even their incomprehension now seeming to him just one more instance of saving lostness), "Blessed are the eyes that see what you see! For I tell you that many prophets and kings desired to see what you see and did not see it, and to hear what you hear and did not hear it."

There is a stunning Latin prayer to St. Joseph that picks up on this text and provides the perfect conclusion to everything I have been trying to say. *"O felicem virum,"* it begins: "O happy man, blessed Joseph, to whom God was given — whom many kings desired to see and did not see, to hear and did not hear — not only to see and to hear, but to carry, to kiss, to clothe, and to care for." Do you grasp the picture? Joseph is the perfect paradigm of our own blessedness. All the things hidden from the wise and understanding (that is, from all the winners who ever lived) are revealed to babes — to the last, the least, the lost, and the little — in the ultimate littleness of God's Holy Child, Jesus himself. Joseph, therefore, is preeminently an empty vessel. A father who, according to tradition, did no begetting, a simple carpenter who understood almost nothing and who died before he could understand more, he ranks now above prophets and kings precisely because, in his own emptiness, he carried, kissed, clothed, and cared for the one who emptied himself for our sakes.

And we are called to do the same. We are not saved by what Jesus taught, and we are certainly not saved by what we understand Jesus to have taught. We are saved by Jesus himself, dead and risen. "Follow *me*," he says. It is the only word that finally matters.

CHAPTER SEVEN

The First of the Misnamed Parables

THE GOOD SAMARITAN

In its immediate context, the parable of the Good Samaritan (Luke 10:29-37; Aland no. 183) is put forth as Jesus' answer to a question posed by a lawyer (Luke 10:25-28; Aland no. 182). As Luke relates the episode, Jesus is either still in Samaria or perhaps already some distance into Judea; in any case, he is on his way to Jerusalem, and hence to his passion and death. In Matthew and Mark, by contrast, the question is asked in Holy Week, sometime between the triumphal entry and the crucifixion (Matthew has it at 22:34-40, Mark at 12:28-34). In Matthew, it is asked (as in Luke) by a lawyer *(nomikós),* and in Mark, by one of the scribes *(grammatéōn);* only Luke includes the parable of the Good Samaritan as part of Jesus' response.

This difference of placement is of some importance to my interpretation. Holy Week, as far as Jesus' teaching activities were concerned, was the time when he put forth nearly all of his parables of *judgment* as distinct from his parables of *grace.* He was knowingly and deliberately headed for an imminent and unjust death and he found himself engaged in a kind of week-long fencing match with the religious authorities. Their hope was to catch him in some actionable disagreement with the Jewish law; his goal was to provide them with no such grounds — to give them no alternative but to proceed against him illegally. Thus in Matthew, the lawyer tries to trick Jesus (the verb is *peirázein)* into voicing a presumably heterodox view of which commandment in the law was the greatest. In Mark, the scribe (one of the Pharisees) who asks the question has a slightly different and perhaps more kindly program in mind: having just heard Jesus trounce the Sadducees (and thus vindicate the Pharisees) in an argument about the resurrection at the last day, he seems intent on providing Jesus with an opportunity to make yet another respectably pharisaic pronouncement. In both, however, Jesus simply answers from Scripture, quoting Deut. 6:4-5 and Lev. 19:18. Love of God, he says, is the first and great commandment; love of neighbor, the second. The response is correct, minimal, and above all, cagey.

In Luke, however, Jesus does not answer the question directly. Rather, he maneuvers the lawyer *(nomikós)* into the position of answering it himself and then uses the man's predictably orthodox reply as a springboard into the distinctly unorthodox parable of the Good Samaritan. Jesus, in other words, seems to have a different agenda in Luke than he has in the other two synoptics. He apparently feels no need to be guarded about legalities. Rather, he seems bent on leading the lawyer into an understanding of the themes (namely, lastness, lostness, leastness, littleness, and death) that he has been developing ever since he left Galilee for Jerusalem — which themes, obviously, are the very ones I have chosen to put forth as the interpretative touchstones of all the parables of grace. In summary, therefore, I am about to make as much as I possibly can of Luke's remarkable transposition of the lawyer's question from Holy Week to the Jerusalem journey. There will be little or no *judgment* orientation in what follows here; instead, the *grace* that works by finding the lost and raising the dead will govern all.

The lawyer begins (Luke 10:25) by standing up and addressing Jesus. "Teacher," he says, "what shall I do to inherit eternal life?" Jesus' reply, at least at the outset, seems to be every bit as cagey as his reply in Matthew. In the old rabbinic tradition he turns the question back on the questioner. (I cannot resist paraphrasing Woody Allen's classic formulation of the gambit: *Inquirer:* "Why does a Rabbi always answer a question with a question?" *Rabbi, after a long pause:* "Why *shouldn't* a Rabbi always answer a question with a question?") Accordingly, Jesus asks him, "What is written in the law? How do you interpret it?"

Why does he take this tack? Why is he so guarded at this point in the dialogue, when he will so shortly unburden himself of a parable that is unguardedly offensive in its exaltation of a Samaritan hero over two respectable religious types? I think it is because at the beginning of their exchange he detects a certain hostility in the lawyer's motives. Luke, in fact, gives some support to this view when he introduces the man's question: "Behold, a certain lawyer stood up, putting him to the test" (the verb is *ekpeirázein*). Jesus, of course, has long been aware of the establishment's hostility toward him: as early as Mark 3:6, the Pharisees and the Herodians were trying to figure out a way to destroy him. Hence, when yet another establishment type asks him a religious question, he responds instinctively with caution.

Yet the lawyer's motives were possibly not hostile at all. His question about eternal life may well have been sincere; and in any case, Jesus' reply (including, especially, the parable of the Good Samaritan) certainly seems to respond more to a sincere interest than to an implied threat. But what exactly was that interest? On what basis could an expert in the Torah have come to think that Jesus might actually have something religiously important to say? Well, perhaps on the basis of his having heard Jesus' recent and mysterious exaltation of losing over winning, of being last instead of first. Perhaps he overheard Jesus' remarks to would-be followers (Luke 9:57-62) — or possibly, his prayer of rejoicing in the Holy Spirit (Luke 10:21) in which he thanked the Father that he had "hid these things from the wise and understanding and revealed them to babes." Admittedly, Luke does not easily give up his own suspicions: even after the lawyer has answered his own question by quoting the summary of the deuteronomic and levitical law — and even after Jesus has given him a peaceable pat on the back ("You have answered correctly; do this and you will live") — Luke still prefaces the lawyer's next question ("And who is my neighbor?") with the hostile comment, "But he, wanting to justify himself . . ."

In any case, by the time Jesus actually starts addressing the question of neighbor in the parable of the Good Samaritan, he himself seems definitely to have dropped his guard. As I read him, he has decided to deal unsuspiciously, if provocatively, with what he takes to be a mind honestly curious about the mystery of lostness. Needless to say, other interpretations of this sequence are possible. But what convinces me of the validity of the one I am making is the content of the parable itself. The Good Samaritan is a veritable paean to lostness, outcastness, and even, in a certain sense, death.

I suppose I had best lay my cards face up right here. To me, the central figure in the parable is not the Samaritan. He is simply one of the three characters in the story who have the opportunity to display neighborliness as Jesus defines it. The defining character — the one to whom the other three respond by being non-neighbor or neighbor — is the man who fell among thieves. The actual Christ-figure in the story, therefore, is yet another loser, yet another down-and-outer who, by just lying there in his lostness and proximity to death (*hēmithané*, "practically dead," is the way Jesus describes him), is in fact the closest thing to Jesus in the parable.

That runs counter, of course, to the better part of two thousand years' worth of interpretation, but I shall insist on it. This parable, like so many of Jesus' most telling ones, has been egregiously misnamed. It is not primarily about the Samaritan but about the man on the ground (just as the Prodigal Son is not about a boy's sins but about his father's forgiveness, and just as the Laborers in the Vineyard is not about the workers but about the beneficent vineyard-owner). This means, incidentally, that Good Samaritan Hospitals have been likewise misnamed. It is the suffering, dying patients in such institutions who look most like Jesus in his redeeming work, not the doctors with their authoritarian stethoscopes around their necks. Accordingly, it would have been much less misleading to have named them Man-Who-Fell-Among-Thieves Hospitals. But then the medical profession might sense libel in such an attempt at theological correctness. Back to my argument.

What I am most concerned to skewer at this point is precisely the theological mischief caused by the misnaming of this parable. Calling it the Good Samaritan inevitably sets up its hearers to take it as a story whose hero offers them a good example for imitation. I am, of course, aware of the fact that Jesus ends the parable precisely on the note of imitation: "You, too, go and do likewise." But the common, good-works interpretation of the imitation to which Jesus invites us all too easily gives the Gospel a fast shuffle. True enough, we are called to imitation. But imitation of what, exactly? Is it not the *imitatio Christi,* the following of Jesus? And is not that following of him far more than just a matter of doing kind acts? Is it not the following of him into the only mystery that can save the world, namely, his passion, death, and resurrection? Is it not, *tout court,* the taking up of his cross?

Therefore, if you want to say that the parable of the Good Samaritan tells us to imitate the Samaritan in his sharing of the passion and near-death of the man who fell among thieves — if you want to read his selfless actions as so many ways in which he took the outcastness and lostness of the Christ-figure on the ground into his own outcast and losing life — then I will let you have imitation as one of the main themes of the parable. But please note that such an interpretation is not at all what people generally have in mind when the subject of imitating the Good Samaritan is broached to them. What their minds instantly go to is something quite different, something that is utterly destructive of the notion of a grace that works only by death and resurrection. Because what they imagine themselves called upon to imitate is not a mystery of lostness and death graspable only by left-handed faith; rather, it is a mere plausibility — a sensible if slightly heroic career of successful care-giving based on the performance of right-handed good works.

What is wrong with that? Quite simply, it blows the Good News right out of the water. For if the world could have been saved by providing good examples to which we could respond with appropriately good works, it would have been saved an hour and twenty minutes after Moses came down from Mt. Sinai. "For if there had been a law given which could have given life, verily righteousness should have been by the law. But the scripture hath concluded all under sin, that the promise by faith of Jesus Christ might be given to them that believe" (Gal. 3:21-22, KJV). Do you see the problem? Salvation is not some felicitous state to which we can lift ourselves by our own bootstraps after the contemplation of sufficiently good examples. It is an utterly new creation into which we are brought by our death in Jesus' death and our resurrection in his. It comes not out of our own efforts, however well-inspired or successfully pursued, but out of the shipwreck of all human effort whatsoever. And therefore if there is any ministering to be imitated in the Good Samaritan's example, it is the ministry to Jesus in his passion, as that passion is to be found in the least of his brethren, namely, in the hungry, the thirsty, the outcast, the naked, the sick, and the imprisoned in whom he dwells and through whom he invites us to become his neighbors in death and resurrection (see the parable of the Great Judgment, Matt. 25:31-46).

But that dark invitation is so far removed from the glittering generality of salvation by imitating good examples that I think now, perhaps, you can begin to see what I am getting at. Neither the Samaritan nor, a fortiori, Jesus is an example of some broader, saving truth about the power of human niceness. Jesus is an example of nothing of the sort. He is the incarnation of the unique, saving mystery of death and resurrection. We do not move from him to some deeper reality called love or goodness that will finally do the trick and make the world go round. No human virtues, however exalted or assiduously practiced, will ever make that cut. Love, as we so regularly mismanage it, is the largest single factor in making our personal worlds go down the drain: psychiatrists' couches are not kept warm by patients complaining of the depredations of total strangers. And goodness, as we so self-interestedly define it, is the mainspring of all the really great evils of the world. The extermination of six million Jews, for example, was done precisely in the name of a perverse vision of goodness — of a totally Aryan society that would bring in the millennium just as soon as the non-Aryans were weeded out. Rather, we move from the disasters of our loving and the bankruptcies of our goodness into the passion of Jesus where alone we can be saved. Niceness has nothing to do with the price of our salvation.

Besides, as everyone knows, nice guys finish last. Good Samaritans are sued with alarming regularity; and if one of them does manage to stay out of court, he probably goes home and loses all the benefits of his goodness in a fight with his wife over putting some deadbeat's expenses on Visa. Scripture hath concluded — locked up — *all* under sin.

The entail of our sinfulness cannot be broken by good examples, even if, *per impossible,* we could follow them. Quite the contrary, the Gospel says clearly that we can be saved only by bad examples: by the stupid example of a Samaritan who spends his livelihood on a loser, and by the horrible example of a Savior who, in an excruciating death, lays down his life for his friends.

Give me that and I will let you have the Good Samaritan as a model for behavior. But example me no nicer examples. The troops have been confused enough for two thousand years. We don't need even another minute's worth of sermons about good works. On to the parable, then, for a look at its details through fresh eyes.

"A certain man," Jesus says, "went down from Jerusalem to Jericho." Consider first the physical remarkability of the journey. It is downhill all the way. Jerusalem stands 2,500 feet above the level of the Mediterranean and Jericho lies 825 feet below it. That's a drop of the better part of three-fifths of a mile and it takes the man in question down into increasingly depressing territory. Without making too much of it, I am disposed to take Jesus' postulation of such a descent as a parable in itself of his own downhill journey to his passion and death, and thus into the lastness, lostness, etc., that he now sees as the heart of his saving work. And as if to underscore the allusion, he adds a whole string of details that mark the man as a loser par excellence: "he fell among thieves who stripped him and beat him up and went away, leaving him half dead." Score several points for my notion that the man who fell among thieves is the authentic Christ-figure in the parable of the Good Samaritan.

"By chance," Jesus continues, "a certain priest was going down that road and when he saw the man, he passed by on the other side." So too, Jesus says, did a Levite when he came to the place. Note the nature of these first two candidates for the possible role of neighbor to the unfortunate who is this parable's surrogate for the Messiah. Jesus is talking, of course, to a lawyer, an interpreter of the Torah; but the people he adduces at this point do not exactly correspond to the lawyer. True enough, they owe their respective callings to the Torah; but they are far less involved in interpreting it than they are in offering the temple sacrifices it enjoins. Jesus' reference here, therefore, may well be at least a glancing one to the whole sacrificial system conceived of as an instrument of salvation. Consider the picture: two official representatives of atonement as understood by the religious authorities of Jesus' day find themselves unable or unwilling to see a wounded loser as having any claim on their attention or any relevance to their work. In short, they think of themselves as winners. They have all their vocational ducks in a row and they see no point in allowing either their lives or their spiritual, moral, or physical plans for the season to be ruined by attention to some outcast. How like the reaction Jesus himself received! He came to his own country and his own people did not receive him (John 1:11). He was despised and rejected (Isa. 53:3) for dying as a common criminal. He himself, in other words, was as unrecognizable a Christ-figure as the man who fell among thieves. Admittedly, it was eventually claimed of him that on the third day he rose from the dead. But rising from the dead was a totally insufficient apology for the abysmally bad messianic taste he had shown by dying in the first place. Real Messiahs don't die.

Finally, though, Jesus brings on the Good Samaritan. Note once again the nature of the character introduced as the man of the hour: he is an outcast come to deal with an outcast, a loser come to minister to another loser. The man who fell among thieves presumably was a Jew; therefore, if either the priest or the Levite had bothered to make his acquaintance, they would have recognized him as one of their own. But since the shipwreck of his life had made him unrecognizable to them, he might as well (as might Jesus in his dereliction, please note) not have been a Jew at all. He, like Jesus, seemed only reproachable. They could not bring themselves to go forth out of their safe theological and psychological camp to meet him and bear his reproach (Heb. 13:13).

But the Samaritan, already under reproach himself (cf. John 4:9), has no such problem. Instead, he goes to the man on the ground — the surrogate for the Savior — and he involves himself in his passion. He binds up his wounds, pouring in oil and wine — all acts of kindness, to be sure, but also acts that any normal person would find inconveniencing, distasteful, and depriving, not to mention expensive of both time and resources. Moreover, he puts the man on his own animal, thus effectively dying to his own comfort and to whatever prospects he may have had of accomplishing his journey in good time. Next, he brings him to an inn and takes care of him for the whole night, further interrupting his own progress and frustrating his travelling man's dearest wish, namely, a peaceful Scotch in the motel bar and an early, quiet bed after a hard day on the road. And as if all that weren't enough, he gets up in the morning, goes down to the front desk, and books the mugging victim in for an indefinite stay, all expenses paid — room, meals, doctors, nurses, medicines, health club, and limo if needed — and no questions asked. To sum it up, he lays down a very good approximation of his life for someone who isn't even his friend, simply because he, as an outcast, finally has found someone who lives in his own neighborhood, namely, the place where the discards of respectable religiosity are burned outside the camp (again, Heb. 13:11-13) — the dump, in other words, to which are consigned the last, the lost, the least, the little, and the dead.

And having said all that, Jesus invites the lawyer to answer his own question. "Which one of these three," he asks, "seems to you to have been a neighbor to the one who fell among thieves?" It is a setup, of course, and the lawyer gives the only possible reply: "He who showed kindness to him" — which leads Jesus to the punch line of the parable, "You go and do the same."

As I said, I take that to be light-years away from an exhortation to general human niceness. Jesus' whole parable, especially with its piling up of detail after detail of extreme, even irrational, behavior on the part of the Samaritan, points not to meritorious exercises of good will but to the sharing of the passion as the main thrust of the story. What is to be imitated in the Samaritan's action is not his moral uprightness in doing good deeds but his spiritual insight into the truly bizarre working of the mystery of redemption. The lawyer is told by Jesus, in effect, to stop trying to live and to be willing to die, to be willing to be lost rather than to be found — to be, in short, a neighbor to the One who, in the least of his brethren, is already neighbor to the whole world of losers.

As if to underscore the validity of this interpretation, Luke concludes the tenth chapter of his Gospel (in verses 38-42) with the story of Jesus' visit to Mary and Martha — which, if I may use a musical illustration, I take to be a coda to what Jesus has just said in the parable of the Good Samaritan about the centrality of his passion to the whole question of life eternal, and even of life here and now.

Jesus goes into a village and a woman named Martha welcomes him. Martha brings him to her house and immediately gets her nose out of joint because her sister Mary just sits at Jesus' feet and rapturously soaks up every word he says. Finally, when Martha has had all she can take of her sister's calf-eyed preoccupation with Jesus, she simply loses it right in front of everybody. "Lord," she says, "don't you care that my sister has left me to do all the work by myself? Tell her to help me!" Martha's problem is that, for all her welcoming of Jesus, she is just too busy (as the priest and the Levite were too busy) with her own life to pay impractical attention to somebody who isn't about to give her the kind of help she thinks she needs. She has carefully kept her life's books and, like all bookkeepers when their stock in trade is denigrated, she can only lash out with a tirade of blame (aimed at Jesus as well as her sister) against the unproductiveness of just hanging around.

But Jesus (who, as we believe, saves us precisely by just hanging around) puts her — and all the bookkeepers, and all the other captains of their souls and masters of their fates — out of business with the lesson of the Good Samaritan all over again. "Martha, Martha," he says, "you get worried and worked up about so many things. It's a wonder you don't kill yourself with all the effort it's taking you to hold your life together. Let it go. As long as the most important thing in your life is to keep finding your way, you're going to live in mortal terror of losing it. Once you're willing to be lost, though, you'll be home free. Your lostness is the one thing no one will ever be able to take away from you. The only ticket anybody needs is the one ticket everybody already has, and Mary, like the Samaritan, has chosen to use it. Come on. Sit down and let's get lost together."

CHAPTER EIGHT

Grace More Than Judgment

FROM THE FRIEND AT MIDNIGHT TO THE RICH FOOL

The next group of parables in the Lukan sequence runs from 11:1 to 12:21 (Aland nos. 185-200). This section comprises not only two parables generally recognized as such (the Friend at Midnight and the Rich Fool), but also a welter of less formal parabolic teachings and sayings (the kingdom divided against itself, the return of the unclean spirit, the sign of Jonah, the light of the body, the leaven of the Pharisees, the five sparrows, and the hairs of the head).

Even though there is a judgmental aspect to many of these utterances, I shall remain true to my plan of attack and read them primarily as parables of grace. Admittedly, two of the items in this section (the denunciation of the Pharisees and scribes, and the Watchful Servants) are placed by Matthew in Holy Week — where, by my analysis, they are properly parables of judgment. But the rest of this material — in Matthew and Mark as well as in Luke — occurs before the triumphal entry and, accordingly, justifies my insistence that it should all be read in the light of Jesus' final journey to Jerusalem. He is going to his death: therefore death and resurrection must continue to be regarded as the clockwork, so to speak, that makes his parables of grace tick.

Jesus begins these sayings (at Luke 11:1) with the Lord's Prayer, and he segues immediately into the parable of the Friend at Midnight. Take the Lord's Prayer first. As Luke gives it, it is Jesus' response to a request that he should, like John the Baptist, teach his disciples to pray. Furthermore, the Lukan version of the prayer — especially as most modern editors of the text now read it — is far shorter (38 words as against 57 in the Greek) than the one in Matt. 6.

When I put those two facts together, they suggest to me that Jesus' intention in giving such a short prayer is to accede to the request while at the same time denying it, or at least holding up a warning hand against the implied equation of his ministry with that of John the Baptist. As I observed above in chapter two, Jesus has already distanced himself considerably from the program of salvation as envisioned by John. Redemption as the Baptist proclaimed it was largely a matter of placing oneself in a position of ethical, religious, and political uprightness so that membership in the coming kingdom could be insured. As Jesus envisions it, however, inclusion in the kingdom has already happened — and happened for everyone — in the catholic mystery of which he himself is the sacramental embodiment (see my first volume, *The Parables of the Kingdom*, e.g., the Growing Seed, the Yeast, etc.). Furthermore, as Jesus proclaims this mystery on his way to Jerusalem, it calls not for triumphant, upright action but simply for being last, lost, least, little, and dead — all of which, luckily, everyone eventually will be, willy-nilly. In short, it is a gift already given to the world in its dereliction, not a plausibility to be negotiated for with a down payment of good deeds.

Therefore when Jesus is asked to match John the Baptist's programmatic performance on the subject of prayer, he draws back. His disciples want religious training and spiritual formation. But Jesus, apparently convinced by now that no human achievements, either religious or moral, can bring in the kingdom, gives only the barest bones of a prayer. In fact, he gives one in which the only human action held up for imitation is forgiveness — an act that is inevitably linked, in plain human terms as well as in terms of Jesus' eventual ministry, with a willingness to be dead.

I realize that this sounds as if I am assigning Paul's theology to Jesus' consciousness. I am and I am not. I do not think, of course, that Jesus had Paul's categories as such in mind. But I do think that on any serious view of either the inspiration of Scripture or the history of salvation as spelled out in Scripture, the risen and ascended Jesus hired Paul on the road to Damascus precisely for the job of rescuing his essential teaching from misunderstanding. There were far too many in the early church (notably, the authorities of the Jerusalem church) who felt themselves called to peddle the exact opposite of what Jesus had in mind. To them, law — or as we might put it more broadly, religion — was a precondition of acceptance into the fellowship of the Gospel. Therefore it was left to Paul — who saw clearly that only faith in the dead and risen Jesus was necessary to salvation — to oppose that view and thus to become the ultimate scriptural guide to Jesus' teaching. I like to imagine that what Jesus actually said to Paul on the Damascus road was not, "Saul, Saul, why do you persecute me?" but, "Help! I'm a prisoner in a commandment factory." The emendation is a bit of whimsy, of course. But it does underscore the fact that Paul was called to articulate, in other and later words, the very thing that Jesus had been saying earlier and in his own way.

In any case, the Lord's Prayer, which is clearly a preface to the parable of the Friend at Midnight, is exceedingly odd in its content, in its proportions, and in its adequacy as a response to a request for a religious formula. It begins, simply, "Father" — an opening that to me speaks not of someone with whom we will have a relationship after certain pious or ethical exercises but of the One to whom we are already related by sonship. More than that, it suggests that for both the disciples and us, the sonship we have is precisely Jesus' own — that we stand before the Father *in him ("in the beloved,"* Eph. 1:6, to use the Pauline phraseology). We pray, in other words, not out of our own dubious supplicative competencies but in the power of his death and resurrection. Or to put it most correctly, he (and the Spirit as well) *prays in us.* Prayer is not really our work at all.

Then, after no more than a "hallowed be your name" and a "let your kingdom come," he tells them to pray for nothing more by way of human achievement than the food they need day by day. No spiritual attainments, no ethical perfections; just the bare necessities to keep body and soul together so they can get on, presumably, with the one thing really necessary, namely, that "good part" — that quiet union with himself in his death and resurrection — which, just three verses earlier, he chided Martha for derogating in her sister Mary.

And that leads him into the heart of the prayer, the longest single topic in its brief contents. "Forgive us our sins as we forgive every one who is indebted to us." The Gospel truth is that forgiveness comes to us because God in Jesus died to and for our sins — because, in other words, the Shepherd himself became a lost sheep for our sake. And it is just that truth, I think, that Jesus underscores when he holds up the forgiveness of debts as the model for our imitation of his forgiving. A person who cancels a debt is a person who dies to his own rightful possession of life. Unless he does it out of mindlessness or idiotic calculation, he cannot write off what is justly due him without accepting his own status as a loser, that is, *as dead.* Death and resurrection are the key to the whole mystery of our redemption. We pray in Jesus' death and resurrection, we are forgiven in Jesus' death and resurrection, and we forgive others in Jesus' death and resurrection. If we attempt any of those things *while still trying to preserve our life,* we will never manage them. They are possible only because we are dead and our life is hid with Christ in God (Col. 3:3). And they can be celebrated by us only if we accept death as the vehicle of our life in him.

It is just this insistence, as I see it, that leads Jesus to the last phrase of the prayer, "and do not lead us into trial [*peirasmón*]." Life is a web of trials and temptations, but only one of them can ever be fatal, and that is the temptation to think it is by further, better, and more aggressive living that we can have life. But that will never work. If the world could have lived its way to salvation, it would have, long ago. The fact is that it can only *die* its way there, *lose* its way there. The precise temptation, therefore, into which we pray we will not be led is the temptation to reject our saving death and try to proceed on our living own. Like the blasphemy against the Holy Spirit, that is the one thing that cannot be forgiven, precisely because it is the refusal of the only box in which forgiveness is ever delivered.

All of which, for Luke, leads directly into the parable of the Importunate Friend at Midnight. Jesus asks the disciples to suppose that they have a friend who is home in bed at midnight. Note what that means.

He has them posit, as the figure of God the Father in this parable, a person who is deep in the experience of the nearest ordinary sacrament of death available to living people, namely, the daily expiration of falling asleep — that radically uncontrollable, lost state in which all reasonable responses to life are suspended. Next, he invites them to imagine that they break in upon that parabolic death of God with a veritable battering ram of reasonable requests. He gives them a whole rigamarole of plausible arguments with which to persuade their dead friend to rise. They need three loaves; they need them so they can feed a ravenously hungry guest; and they could not have come any sooner because their guest has only just now arrived. They would, of course, have raided their own pantry, but alas, this was not their day to go food shopping and they are fresh out of everything. The sleeper is their only hope.

Astonishingly, though, Jesus has the surrogate for God give them the cold shoulder. The sleeper's first response is a not-really-awake "don't bother me," followed by a more organized list of reasons for them to get lost: "The door is already locked, my children are with me in the bed, and I can't get up to give you anything" (Luke 11:7).

Time for a halt. My reading of death and resurrection into this text may make you suspect that I am guilty of charley-horsing the arm of Scripture. I am not. Consider the evidence. The Greek for "I am not able to get up to give you anything" is *ou dýnamai anastás doúnai soi*. The word *anastás* is from *anasténai* (to raise, to rise), which, along with the verb *egeírein* (to raise, to rouse), is one of the two major roots used in the New Testament to refer to resurrection. Moreover, this is not the only use of resurrection language in this parable: *anastás* appears again in verse 8, as does *egertheís*. This parable tells us, therefore, that it is out of death, not out of life, that God rises to answer our prayers. And note well that he rises not in response to the reasonableness (or the moral uprightness) of our requests but *for no good reason other than to raise the rest of the dead.*

Look at the way Jesus actually puts it (Luke 11:8): "I tell you, even if he will not get up [*anastás*] and give you the bread because he is your friend, yet on account of your shamelessness [*anaídeian*] he will rise [*egertheís*] and give you as much as you need." What is this shamelessness but death to self? People who lead reasonable, respectable lives — who are preoccupied first and foremost with the endless struggle to think well of themselves — do not obtrude upon their friends' privacy at midnight. And why don't they? Because that would display them as thoughtless beggars and make them look bad. But if someone were dead to all that — if he could come to his friend's house with nothing more than the confession that he was a total loss as a host (or anything else) — then precisely because of his shamelessness, his total lack of a self-regarding life, he would be raised out of that death by his rising friend.

I am aware that the usual interpretation of this passage renders *anaídeian* as "shameless persistence" and then goes on to maintain that if we nag God enough, he will come through with the wherewithal for our lives. I have nothing against urging persistence in prayer; but I do think that holding it up as the main point of this particular parable gives, if not a charley horse, then at least an Indian burn to the arm of Scripture. Note that Jesus carefully avoids crediting any of the *content* of the importunate friend's request with efficacy. His reasons, his carefully argued justifications for asking his friend to rise and give him bread, are all sloughed off with a peremptory "I'm dead; go away." To hold, then, that Jesus is telling us that God will rise to our help simply because we go on repeating the same arguments seems to me not only unwarranted here but also perilously contrary to his words in Matt. 6:7, "When you pray, do not use a lot of words [*mē battalogésēte* — don't babble, don't use 'vain repetition'], as the pagans do, who think they will be heard because of their much speaking [*polylogía*]."

No, God rises from his death in Jesus not to satisfy our requests, reasonable or unreasonable, unexpressed or overexpressed, but to raise us from our own deaths. All we need to offer in order to share in the joy of his rising is the shameless, selfless admission that we are dead without him, and the faith to confess that we are also dead with him and in him. The whole parable, therefore, is a conjugation of prayer according to the paradigm of death and resurrection — a footnote to the Lord's Prayer, if you will, in which Jesus tells us that even the daily bread he taught us to pray for comes only out of death. And the rest of the passage (Luke 11:9-13) is more of the same.

Once again, I am aware of the more usual "persistence wins" interpretation given to lines like "Ask and it will be given to you, seek and you will find, knock and it will be opened to you" (Luke 11:9ff.). But in fact, persistence doesn't win anywhere near often enough to be held up as the precondition of God's answering prayer. And I will not let you hand me the cheap, cruel bromide that when persistence doesn't win it probably wasn't real persistence. Tell that to somebody who asked, and sought, and knocked till her knuckles bled for a child who eventually died of leukemia anyway. Or if you don't have the nerve for that, try at least to remember that no matter how persistent or productive your prayers, there will inevitably be, on some dark day, one whoppingly unproductive prayer of yours (the prayer to be spared your death just one more time) that God will answer, "Sorry; the door of your life is already shut; all my real children are with me in the bed of my death; and I'm not about to rise from the dead just to give you back the same old two-bit life you were perishing of. Bring me a shameless acceptance of your death, though, and I'll show you how I really do business."

It is in that light, therefore, that we should look at the last part of the text. "Everyone who asks, receives," Jesus says, "and he who seeks, finds, and to him who knocks, it will be opened." Taken literally as a program for conning God into catering to the needs of our lives, that is pure bunk: too many sincere, persistent prayers have simply gone unfulfilled. But taken as a command constantly to bring our deaths to his death and to find our resurrection in his, it is solid gold. Furthermore, consider the clincher that Jesus adds: "What father among you will give his son a snake when he asks for a fish, or a scorpion when he asks for an egg? If you then, *being evil* [*ponēroí*], know how to give good gifts to your children, how much more will the heavenly Father give *the Holy Spirit* to those who ask him?"

The two italicized phrases sum up my case. "If you then, *being evil* . . .*" "If you," Jesus seems to be saying, " — you who can never manage to be anything more than reasonable, who can make only fallen, sinful sense, and who are trapped in a losing battle to make a radically uncooperative world say uncle — if you whose best is none too good can still care enough to provide kippers and eggs for the condemned — how

225

much more will the heavenly Father give you resurrection from your lifelong death?" For it is precisely resurrection that the Father and the Son have appointed as the principal gift of the Holy Spirit. Listen to Jesus in John. "But when he, the Spirit of truth comes, he will lead you into all truth. He will not speak of himself [*pace* all the self-appointed Spirit promoters], but whatever he hears he will speak, and he will proclaim to you things to come. He will glorify *me*, for he will take *of mine* and proclaim it to you" (John 16:13-14). The work of the Spirit is nothing other than the work of Jesus; and the work of Jesus is the raising of the dead.

This Lukan passage on prayer, then, far from being a pious sop — far from being a promise of spiritual comfort to make up for an inveterate failure to deliver material gifts, whether in full, on time, or at all — this conclusion to the parable of the Friend at Midnight is nothing less than a proclamation of the heart of the Good News. We have died. We do not have to ask for death, or seek it, or work ourselves up to it. We have only to accept the death we already have, and in the clean emptiness of that death we will find the life that all along has been hid for us with Christ in God (Col. 3:3). We are safe, not because of the reasonableness or persistence of our prayers but because he lives in our death. Entombed together with him in baptism, we have already been raised up together in him through faith in the working of God who raised him from the dead (Col. 2:12). While we were dead in our trespasses, he made us alive together in Christ — by *grace* we are saved — and he raised us up together and made us sit together in the heavenly places in Christ Jesus (Eph. 2:5, 6). And all of that *now*. Not just hereafter, and certainly not just a week from some Tuesday.

That, in the last analysis, is why we pray. Not to get some reasonable, small-bore job done, but to celebrate the job beyond all liking and happening that has already been done for us and in us by Jesus. We have a friend in our death; in the end, he meets us nowhere else. Prayer is the flogging of the only Dead Horse actually able to rise.

The next passage in this sequence (Luke 11:14-26; Aland nos. 188-189) deals with Jesus' response (after he had given speech to a dumb man who was possessed) to the charge that he cast out demons by

Beelzebul, the prince of the demons. His parabolic retort ("Every kingdom divided against itself is laid waste, etc.") seems at first to be saying
little more than, "If the devil is behind this, how come he's fighting
against himself?" But what Jesus really seems to be getting at, once
again, is the inability of the world to straighten itself up by any kind of
reasonable, sensible action, human *or* angelic. "If you're going to play
that Beelzebul game," he says in effect, "all you'll ever succeed in doing
is discrediting even the minor cures you yourselves are able to perform.
But if it is by *the finger of God* that I cast out demons, then the kingdom
of God has come upon you."

The Finger of God. In the church fathers — and most notably in the
great Latin hymn, *Veni Creator Spiritus* ("Come Holy Ghost") — the
phrase is taken as one of the titles of the Holy Spirit.

> *Tu septiformis munere,*
> *dextrae Dei tu digitus*
> *tu rite promisso patris*
> *sermone dittans guttura.*

> The sevenfold gifts of grace are thine,
> O finger of the Hand Divine;
> True promise of the Father thou,
> Who dost the tongue with speech endow.
>
> (Stanza 3, Hymnal 1940 translation)

Dextrae Dei Digitus, the Finger of the *right* hand of God. In the previous
volume, *The Parables of the Kingdom,* I took the liberty of indulging myself in a theological lark. I pointed out that in both Greek and Latin,
the ordinary way of saying "right hand" is simply to use the word
"right," omitting any actual mention of "hand." I did that in order to
suggest that when Jesus ascends and sits *ek dexión toú patrós* (on the
right of the Father), it might just be possible to think of him as ruling,
not by virtue of the unparadoxical, straight-line power of the right *hand*
of God but out of the right *side* of God's brain. That only substituted
one analogical formulation for another; but as we now understand the

functioning of the brain, it is precisely the right hemisphere that governs the left hand — and it is by the paradoxical, indirect power of God's left hand that he saves the world in the death and resurrection of Jesus. I take the same liberty now.

It is by the Holy Spirit, the presiding genius of the Gospel — the one who takes of the left-handed work of Jesus and shows it to us — that Jesus does what he does. And what he does is *raise the dead*. His power is not from this plausible, perishing world, nor is it from the prince of this hopelessly divided kingdom. It is from himself in the death and resurrection by which alone the true kingdom comes. "The world," he says in effect (Luke 11:21ff.), "is full of strong-arm, right-handed types; but when the stronger, left-handed arm comes, it takes away all the armor in which the world trusted and divides the spoils of its plausible efforts. He who is not with me, therefore, is against me; and he who does not gather with me [in the field of my death, and there only] scatters." And then, in a solemn warning, he sums up his case: "When the unclean spirit [which I take to mean the plausible spirit of right-handed action] has gone out of a man, it travels through waterless places looking for a place to rest, but it doesn't find one."

Think about that. We have seen, perhaps, the light of the Gospel. We have realized that it is in our lastness, lostness, leastness, littleness, and death — and not in the chewing-gum and baling-wire contraptions of our lives — that we are saved. But that left-handed truth is hard to hold onto, and so by and by, when the unclean spirit returns, it finds us empty, swept, and put in order by the new broom of Jesus' death. And what does it do? It goes and brings seven other spirits more evil than mere right-handed action: it finds ways of standing the Gospel itself on its head. It takes prayer — prayer that was meant to be a standing in Jesus' death — and turns it into right-handed spiritual exercises. It takes forgiveness of sins — forgiveness that can come only by death and resurrection — and turns it into a reward for plausible, convincing repentance. It takes, in short, the grace of God that works by raising the dead and converts it into a transaction available only to those with acceptable lives. And so seven — or seven hundred — spirits enter and dwell in us, and our last state is worse than the first.

228

It is the old, sad story of the errant tendencies of doctrine-producing minds. The saving truth has been gladly found, and then disastrously lost, over and over and over. In spite of it all, though, Jesus' power does not come through anything here except death. Unless we can be content to sit quietly in that clean, empty room, all the evils of the world will come, tracking their reasonable, hopeless grime back in. Our strength, like the strength of the Stronger One who saved us, is literally to sit still.

But you are fidgeting. "If that isn't an out-and-out charley-horsing of Scripture," you say, "I've never seen one." Well, perhaps it is. I make no apologies. On with the text.

Hearing all this from Jesus, a woman in the crowd speaks up and says to him (Luke 11:27, 28), "Blessed is the womb that bore you and the breasts that you sucked." Jesus' mother, she suggests — with all the enthusiasm of a mind that, along with the church, has missed nearly the whole point of his words on this journey to Jerusalem and death — must be very proud of her son's snappy performance. To which Jesus replies, "No; blessed are those who hear the word of God and keep it." If the Blessed Virgin Mary had any blessedness, it showed itself not in babble about "my son, the wonder-working rabbi," but in her own hearing and keeping of the word of his passion and death. She is (credit the church with having gotten at least this much right about her) the *mater dolorosa*, the sorrowful mother. Through her entire life, she was pierced with the sword prophesied by Simeon (Luke 2:35). Her child, as Simeon said in the temple, "was put here for the fall [*ptósin* — the variant, *ptóma*, means corpse] and the rising [*anástasin* — resurrection, yet again] of many in Israel, and for a sign that will be spoken against." Mary is thus the first fruit of him who is the firstfruits of them that slept.

Which brings us nicely to the next passage, the Sign of Jonah (Luke 11:29-32; Aland no. 191). The crowds on the journey are getting bigger, but Jesus is not happy about them. "This generation is an evil [*ponēra*] generation," he says. "They seek a sign, but no sign will be given to them except the sign of Jonah." Not so oddly, from my point of view, he uses here the same word, "evil," that he used only a little while ago to describe us when we answer our children's prayers ("If you then, being evil . . ."). I say not oddly, because he is making the same point, contrast-ing the world's plausible, right-handed way of giving help with God's mysterious, left-handed program of salvation by raising the dead. He knows they have not heard what he is saying, let alone understood what he is proposing to do. But he spells it out for them anyway: *no signs*. No divine responses to ethical probity, religious correctness, or spiritual competency. Only the sign of Jonah, which Matthew (12:40ff.) gives in so many words: "As Jonah was in the belly of the whale three days and three nights, so the Son of man will be three days and three nights in the heart of the earth." He will offer them, as the sign of the mystery of faith, only his resurrection from the dead. "The men of Nineveh," he tells them, "will arise [*anastésontai*] at the judgment with this generation and condemn it." (The entire human race rises in Jesus, please note; but those of us who reject the death out of which resurrection comes will hardly accept our rising.) "And they will condemn it," Jesus continues, "because they repented at the preaching of Jonah, and behold, a greater than Jonah is here." So, too, Jesus says, with the Queen of Sheba, be-cause she came from the ends of the earth to hear the wisdom of Solo-mon, and behold, a greater than Solomon is here.

In the resurrection, we shall finally see that all the signs we asked for in our plausible, evil minds pale into insignificance before the sign actually given. The world is not saved because of its repentance, its wis-dom, or its goodness — and certainly not because of its stumbling ef-forts to become either sorrier, wiser, or better. Rather it is saved because it is a dead world, and because the life of him who is greater than Jonah or Solomon has reigned out of its death. We have always been safe in our deaths. It's just that, until Jesus, we could never see them as the sign of our salvation.

The rest of the parabolic passages in this section can be read partly as comments on that truth, partly as prologue to the parable of the Rich Fool, and partly as a coda to the whole composition. Let me enter them into the record briefly.

In Luke 11:33-36 (Aland nos. 192-193), Jesus says, "No one lights a lamp and then hides it or puts it under a bucket; rather, he puts it on the lampstand that those who enter may see the light." He is speaking principally, I take it, of himself: the light he will not hide is the mystery of his death and resurrection. And he presses the comparison. "Your eye," he says, "is the lamp of your body: when your eye is sound [*haploús*: single, or simple; sometimes, in a pejorative sense, silly; also, clear, doing only what it is supposed to do], your whole body will be full of light [that is, full of the benefits of the eye's single-minded pursuit of light instead of darkness]. But when it is evil [*ponērós*] your body will be full of darkness. Watch therefore lest the light that is in you be darkness. If then your whole body be light, having no part [*méros*] dark, it will be bright all over, as when a lamp shines on you with its light."

Once again, Jesus brings in the word *ponērós*, "evil." And once again, he uses it to stand for the pursuit of all those plausible schemes by which we try unsuccessfully to make our lives come out even. Sadly, though, our bright ideas turn out to be only dim bulbs: our frantic living does not produce life. But if we allow the devastatingly simple, single truth of Jesus' death in our death — even the *silly* truth of his death, for silly is from the German *selig*, "blessed," and it is by the blessed foolishness of the preaching of the cross that we are saved — if we allow that death to be our only light, then we are in the light indeed. Yet one more time, in other words, Jesus exalts the "one thing necessary" — that "good part" *(agathós méros)* he commended to Martha, that quiet sitting at his nail-pierced feet — by which we find his death reigning in ours.

Next follows (Luke 11:37-54; Aland no. 194) a denunciation of the Pharisees and scribes, about which (since it will come up in its Matthean form in my final volume on the parables of judgment) I have only one thing to call to your attention here. I want you to note the recurrence of the words and themes we have been dealing with all through this chapter. He says that the Pharisees are inwardly full of violence *(harpagḗs)* and evil *(ponērías)*. A *harpagmós*, a "thing to be snatched at," is exactly what Paul, in Phil. 2:6ff., says Jesus did not consider his equality with God to be. Rather, he "emptied himself, taking on the form of a slave and coming in the likeness of men; and being found in outward form as a man, he humbled himself, becoming obedient to death, even a death on a cross." Enough said. And likewise enough said about *ponēría*, except to notice that right after he calls them evil, he calls them fools *(áphrones)* as well, thus underscoring the dim view he takes of the plausible, fruitless fuss by which they manage their lives.

And through the rest of his denunciation he continues, if not explicitly to exalt his death over their living, at least to bring death into the discussion. He calls them *unmarked graves.* He says they *build the graves of the prophets.* Then, stigmatizing the way their fathers *killed* the prophets and the way they *build* the prophets' tombs, he sets against all this *ponēría,* all this evil folly, the wisdom *(sophía)* of God, which he quotes as saying, "I will send them prophets and apostles, and some of them they will *kill* and persecute in order that the *blood* of all the prophets shed from the foundation of the world might be required of this generation. . . ." That's a lot of death; and true to form, the Pharisees didn't like it one bit. They set about in earnest to trap him and to do him in — never even imagining that in the death they would provide for him, he would wait to give them life. Meanwhile, he tells his disciples to "watch out for the leaven of the Pharisees, which is hypocrisy" (Luke 12:1). Precisely because their eye is *not* single — precisely because it is full of the yeasty festering of their dark, plausible designs for living — they have made themselves blind to the death that is their only source of life.

This emphasis on the darkness of human lives and on the true light that shines only out of death continues in Luke 12:2-10 (Aland nos. 196-197). Death may now be an inaccessible mystery to the world, but "nothing is covered up that will not be revealed, or hidden that will not be known. Whatever you have said in the dark [in your acceptance of the mystery of my death in yours] will be heard in the light, and what you have whispered in closed rooms [in your tomb and mine] will be proclaimed from the housetops. I tell you, my friends, do not be afraid of those who *kill* the body and after that have no more that they can do. I will show you whom to fear: fear him who, after he has *killed,* has power to cast into hell."

Once again, it is death that is safe. Hell is only for those who insist on finding their life outside of Jesus' death. Nothing, therefore, is out of control. Every sparrow counts, all the hairs of your head are numbered. "I have a whole new creation in my death and resurrection," Jesus

232

says in effect. "So stop with all this evil, foolish pretense that you have life. Just acknowledge me before the world — confess by faith that my death is all you need — and I will acknowledge you before the angels of God. But if you won't do that, I'm afraid you're out of luck. Death and resurrection is the only game we're playing here. You can talk against *me* all you like [Luke 12:10: 'Everyone who speaks a word against the Son of man will be forgiven'], but don't knock my methods, because the Holy Spirit is groaning himself hoarse to convince you of them ['but he who blasphemes against the Holy Spirit will not be forgiven']."

Then, after two brief warnings against trying to live by getting our act together rather than by letting our passion and death happen, Jesus turns to the parable of the Rich Fool (Luke 12:16-21; Aland no. 200). Both of the warnings are about wealth. In the first (Luke 12:11-12; Aland no. 198), Jesus says the disciples are not to be anxious when they are brought before the synagogues and the rulers and the authorities. They are not to worry about what they are to answer or what they are to say. They are, in short, to be poor, and lost, and as good as dead: without the riches of a well-prepared case, without the luxury of knowing what's going to happen, and, above all, without any comforting sense that their lives are triumphantly in their own hands. And they are to be all of that because the Holy Spirit will teach them in that very hour, and not one minute before, what needs to be said. It is a warning, needless to say, that we hardly heed. Of all the desires for wealth, practically the last one we will give up is the desire for mental and spiritual richness. Yet Jesus is only urging his disciples, and us, to do what he himself did in his own trial and passion: to lay down his life and to let God raise it up in his own good time. For our comfort, even Jesus blinked at the prospect. In Gethsemane, he prayed that God would "let this cup pass" from him. But he also prayed, "nevertheless, not my will but yours be done." Poverty, not wealth — death, not life — is the only material God uses to save us.

The second warning (Luke 12:13-15; Aland no. 199) is against our less refined desire for material wealth. Someone comes to Jesus out of the crowd and says, "Teacher, tell my brother to give me my fair share of our inheritance." To which Jesus snaps back, "Hey, man, who made me a judge or divider over you people?" The man's case, no doubt, was good enough; but Jesus' ministry is not the incidental patching up of injustices. Rather it is the bearing of the final injustice — death — and the raising up from it of an entirely new and reconciled creation. Therefore he adds, "Guard yourselves against all covetousness [*pleonexía*, much-having], for a person's life does not consist in the rafts of goods that belong to him." So much for the IRAs, and the second homes, and the retirement plans that are the hope of the well-off and the envy of the poor who will never have them. Our world runs on avarice. Wealthy, poor, or in-between, we are all of us, in Jesus' eyes, nothing but unreconstructed rich people. We clutch at our lives rather than open our hands to our deaths. And as long as we do that, the real life that comes only by resurrection remains permanently out of reach.

The whole case, as I see it, is summed up in the parable of the Rich Fool. "The land of a certain rich man," Jesus tells them, "bore plentifully. And he thought to himself, 'What shall I do? I'll tear down my barns and build bigger ones, where I'll be able to store all my grain and other goods. And then I'll say to my life [*psyché*] . . .'" But stop right there. Time for a major point about scriptural wordplay.

Traditionally, the word *psyché* is translated here as "soul." But *psyché* also happens to be one of the major words in the New Testament for "life." In the immediately preceding passage, for example, Jesus says that a person's *psyché*, his life, does not consist in abundance of goods. Likewise, in the Sermon on the Mount (Matt. 6:25), he says, "Don't worry about your *psyché*, fussing about what you shall eat. . . ." The instances are too many even to begin to list them all.

Accordingly, since Jesus has, just before the Rich Fool, used *psyché* in the sense of life — and since, in this chapter, I am positively harping on his exaltation of the clean emptiness of our deaths over the messy clutter of our lives — I am taking the liberty of giving the word the odd-sounding (but, I think, tolerable) translation of "life" as it comes from the mouth of the fool. (Modern translators get around the inappropriateness of "soul" in various ways. The TEV, for instance, reads "I will say to *myself: Lucky man!*" The NEB and NIV read ". . . to *myself: Man . . .*" Such translations get the sense of the passage pretty much right, but they fail to pick up Jesus' repetitions of the word *psyché* as he works his way through the passages at hand. Hence my preference for "life.") Back to the text.

"I will say to my life," gloats the Fool, "Life, you have ample goods laid up for many years. Take your ease, eat, drink, and be merry." Jesus, in other words, is having the Fool do what we all do in our avarice: congratulate ourselves on our lifestyle whenever possible. He sets him up as the paradigm of our whole plausible, reasonable, right-handed, wrongheaded struggle to be masters of an operation that is radically out of our control — to be captains of a ship that, all our life long, has been taking on water faster than we can bail. And then Jesus delivers the Sunday punch: "But God said to him, 'Fool! [the word is *áphrōn*, the same word he uses in denouncing the Pharisees and scribes back in Luke 11:40]. This night your life [*psyché*] is required of you; then who will own all this stuff you've spent so much time preparing?'"

In a quiet last line, Jesus adds, "This is how it is with one who lays up treasure for himself and is not rich in God's sight [*eis theón*, literally, 'into God']." Jesus — upon whom the Father looks and says, "This is my beloved Son" — is the only rich man in the world; we, who spend our whole lives in the pursuit of wealth, come in the end only to the poverty of death. And we complain bitterly, unable to make head or tail of such a cruel reversal. But in Jesus — who made his grave with the wicked in their moral poverty and with the rich man in the death of all his possessing — all the pointless pursuing and all the sad incomprehension are turned to our good. He waits for us in our deaths. Quite literally, there is nothing we need to do except die.

CHAPTER NINE

Fruitfulness out of Death

THE WATCHFUL SERVANTS AND THE BARREN FIG TREE

T he parables of the Watchful Servants (Luke 12:35-48; Aland no. 203) and of the Barren Fig Tree (Luke 13:6-9; Aland no. 207) are further illustrations of how Jesus, at this point in his ministry, uses judgment-oriented imagery but gives it a resolutely grace-governed presentation. Once again, both stories also occur later on, in Holy Week, as frankly judgmental parables (cf. Matt. 24:45-51 for the first and Matt. 21:19, as an acted parable, for the second). Here, however, Jesus' continued emphasis on death as the modus operandi of the kingdom makes them unquestionably parables of grace.

By way of a bridge from the parable of the Rich Fool with his unusable goods to the Watchful Servants and their faithful waiting, Luke gives us (in 12:22-34; Aland nos. 201-202) a catena of short, parabolic utterances. Jesus says to his disciples, "on account of this I say to you, don't worry about your life [*psychē*], what you shall eat, etc. . . ." Jesus, as I hear him, is about to contrast the Fool's frenetic attempts at living well with the behavior of crows, lilies, and grass-creatures who quietly trust God to work in and through their mortality. He is, in other words, about to take the death that is an unqualified terror to all of us fools and display it as our only safety, our only source of the true life *(psychē)* that is "more than food." And the governing phrase — the one that specifies death as the touchstone of all these sayings — comes at the end of them (12:28). Let me put it down first, therefore, as a kind of headline: "For if God so clothes the grass in the field, which is *alive to-day* and *tomorrow is cast into the oven,* how much more will he clothe you, O *you of little faith?"* (italics mine).

He begins (12:24) with the ravens, who plainly are unencumbered by the kind of "life-plans" we constantly make ("they neither sow nor reap") and who, unlike us, have "neither storeroom nor barn" (*apothḗkē* — Jesus uses the same word in the parable of the Fool). "God nourishes them," he says; "how much different are you than birds?" Then, casti-gating our efforts to hold our lives together by our own devices, he says, "Which of you by worrying can add a *day to his life?"* (the phrase, as it oc-curs in verse 25, is *epí tḗn hēlikían autoú péchyn:* it can mean either a "foot to his height" or "a day to his age"). "If you," he continues, "are not able to do even such a little thing, why do you worry about the rest?"

Then, after instancing the lilies that neither work nor make clothes for themselves, he says that "not even Solomon in all his glory was clothed like one of these." The reference to Solomon, while it can be ex-plained simply as a convenient example of royal splendor, suggests something more profound to my ear. Back when he spoke of the Sign of Jonah (see chapter eight above) — when he said that the only sign to be given this generation would be his own death and resurrection — he added that the Queen of Sheba would "rise up [*egerthḗsetai*] in the judg-ment with the people of this generation because she came halfway around the world to hear the wisdom of Solomon, and behold, a greater than Solomon is here." Solomon's greatness lay in his life and in his lifestyle; but the greatness of the One who is greater than Solo-mon lies precisely in his death. Therefore when Jesus conjoins Solomon and the mortal lilies of the field, it is at least possible to take it as yet an-other adumbration of the theme of death and resurrection. Indeed, Je-sus himself seems to have sensed the connection. He follows up the ref-erence to Solomon with the words I quoted as a headline to this section, namely, "the grass in the field that is alive today and tomorrow is cast into the oven."

Jesus ends these comments to his disciples on the note of faith, be-cause faith is the only thing they need once they understand that grace works entirely by raising the dead. He rebukes their care and anxiety to make a life for themselves, calling them people of "little faith." And he rebukes our faithless fussing as well.

"Everything that is not of faith is sin," says Paul in Rom. 14:23. In the last analysis, what the New Testament sets up as the opposite of sin is not virtue; it is faith. And how lucky that is for us. Precisely because virtue is not an option for the likes of us — precisely because we can no more organize our lives on good principles than we can on bad ones, and even more precisely because all the really great acts of human wickedness *(ponēría)* have always been done in the name of virtue — we are not to trust either in virtue or in our efforts to achieve it. All of that is just our life *(psychē)*, and for us as for the Fool, life is not something we can guarantee.

But death we can; and if we will trust him to work through it in the mystery of his death, we will find that, like the ravens and the lilies and the Queen of Sheba and the men of Nineveh, we have always been home free by the power of his resurrection. It is not a matter of our knowing it or feeling it — or of our working up plausible, right-handed devices for laying hold of it. "No man," Luther said, "can know or feel he is saved; he can only believe it." Therefore it is by faith alone that we can lay hold of our true life out of death — faith in him who is the resurrection and the life. All we have to do is trust Jesus and die. Everything else has already been done. The ravens and the lilies bear mute testimony to that trust; our joy waits until we give voice to what they already express.

Our death, therefore, is the one "purse that will never wear out," the true "treasure in heaven that will never decrease." We are rich only in our mortality; everything else may safely be sold (Luke 12:33). For our death is the only thing the world cannot take away from us. The goods on which our heart now reposes can be removed from us, or we from them, in a night: the thief, the moth, and the changes and chances of this mortal life are always and everywhere one giant step ahead of us. But if we repose our hearts upon the faith that he works in our death, we cannot lose. The astonishing graciousness of grace is that it takes the one thing you and I will never lack — the one thing, furthermore, that no one will ever want to beg, borrow, or steal from us — and makes it the only thing any of us will ever need. It was, I think, precisely because the martyrs bore witness to this saving supremacy of death that they were the first saints commemorated by the church. Indeed, the days of their deaths were commonly referred to as their *natales,* their birthdays. It was one of the church's happier insights. For as in our first birth into this world we did nothing and triumphed gloriously, so in the second birth of our death we need do even less to triumph more. By Jesus' death in ours, and by our death in his, we have laughingly, uproariously, outrageously beaten the system. It is a piece of wildly Good News: what a shame we don't let the world of losers hear it more often.

Indeed, it is this very note of stewardship of the Gospel of grace — of readiness to comply with and to proclaim its absurdly minimal demands — that is evident in the way Jesus begins the immediately following parable of the Watchful Servants (Luke 12:35-48, Aland no. 203). "Let your loins be girded about and your lamps burning," he says to the disciples. "You have," he tells them in effect, "an incredibly cheerful piece of intelligence to impart to the desperate winners out there who are panicked at the thought of their inevitable losing. I don't want you bumbling around in their darkness with the pants of your trust down around your ankles for lack of the girding of faith in my death." But he opens the parable itself with an even more pregnant bit of imagery: "And you yourselves must be like men who are waiting for their lord [*kýrion*] to come back from a wedding [*ek tōn gámōn*]. . . ."

Time for another halt. One of my convictions about interpreting Jesus' parables is that it is always a mistake to say too quickly what we think is their "main point." Had he wanted to give us glittering generalities, he could no doubt have unburdened himself of them in plain Aramaic and avoided the bother of having to make up artful stories. But in fact he did tell stories; and since he was no slouch at crafting them, we should spend more time than we do on their details — especially when the detail is as rich a one as the wedding Jesus sketches in here.

Let me illustrate by introducing two other New Testament uses of the imagery of the wedding: the Marriage at Cana where Jesus performed his first sign *(sēmeíon),* turning water into wine (John 2:1-11); and the Marriage of the Lamb to his Bride, the New Jerusalem, at the very end of the Bible (Rev. 19:7-9 and 21:1–22:17, passim). These two passages — in which a wedding reception is used to delineate major events in the history of salvation — make me suspicious of interpretations that dismiss the wedding party in the parable of the Watchful Servants as nothing more than a minor detail. Had Jesus wanted simply to get the lord of the servants home unpredictably late, he could have arranged for him to be tied up in traffic on the freeway, or stuck in an all-night diner with a boring friend. But Jesus says it was precisely a wedding that delayed the lord's coming. And he uses that device, I think, because of a bizarre connection in his mind — or at least in the mind of the Spirit who presides over the Scriptures — between weddings and death.

Consider the Cana story first. When Jesus' mother tells him that the party they are both attending has just run out of wine, he gives her a cryptic reply: "What's that to me and you, woman? *My hour* [*hē hóra mou*] has not yet come." In the literary shorthand of John's Gospel, *hóra* (hour, time) is one of the words used to refer to the climactic events of Jesus' ministry, namely, his passion, death, and resurrection. Furthermore, in the peculiarly transposed time-sequence of John, the Wedding at Cana is followed immediately by the cleansing of the temple — which, in all the other Gospels, occurs in Holy Week. Somebody therefore (either Jesus, John, the Spirit, or all three) saw a connection between the two events. So much so, that in the Johannine version of the casting out of the money-changers, Jesus actually makes a parabolic reference to his coming death. When asked what sign he is showing by thus cleansing the temple, he replies, "Destroy this temple and in three days I will raise it up." The reference, of course, is to his own body's death and resurrection — in other words, to nothing less than the Sign of Jonah all over again.

As for the second passage, the Marriage of the Lamb to his Bride in the Book of Revelation is equally fraught with death. Notice the details. The Lamb is none other than the *Lamb Slain:* the crucified, risen Redeemer. In addition, the saints — the citizens of the New Jerusalem that comes down from heaven as a bride prepared for her husband — have "washed their robes and made them white in the blood of the Lamb" (Rev. 7:14).

And as if those two passages were not enough importing of death into the imagery of marriage, consider Jesus' parable of the King's Son's Wedding (Matt. 22:1-14), in which death is liberally poured over all the proceedings: the first-invited guests *kill* the messengers bringing the King's invitation; the King himself, in response, *destroys* those *murderers* and *burns up* their city.

You may, of course, have your doubts as to whether Jesus had all that in mind when he began the parable of the Watchful Servants. But since you can't prove he didn't any more than I can prove he did, your argument, so dear to critical minds, ends in a draw. In any case, I am not so much concerned to guess what Jesus may have had in mind as I am to comment on what the church, in the Scriptures, has preserved of what he actually said. But since I believe the Holy Spirit presided effectively over the formation of Scripture, I do feel at least a bit free to try guessing what the *Spirit* may have had in mind when he fingered in all this imagery of the wedding.

Let your mind *play* with the scriptural parallels therefore. The lord of the servants — who is, after all, the Christ-figure in this parable — comes to them from a nuptial feast. Correspondingly, the Lord Jesus — whom the Book of Revelation (22:20) asks to "come" — comes to the consummation of history from his own nuptials as the Lamb Slain. The servants, to take another parallel, are described as waiting expectantly to open to the lord when he comes and knocks; we, their counterparts, are to be ready to welcome the Lamb Slain when he "stands at the door and knocks" (Rev. 3:20). Finally, when the lord comes and finds his servants watching, they are blessed because "he will gird himself with a servant's towel and make them sit down *and he will come and serve them.*" Their great good luck is that he will come home in a hilarious mood. He will not come with sober assessments of past performances or with grim orders for future exertions; rather he will come with a song in his tipsy heart, a chilled bottle of Dom Perignon in each tail of his coat, and a breakfast to end all breakfasts in his hands: bacon, sausage, grits, homefries, and eggs sunny-side up. We too, then, are blessed in the risen Jesus, for he comes to us from his nuptials in death, and asks only that we wait in faith for him. He will knock at the door of

241

our own death, and he will come in and throw us a party (Rev. 3:20; 19:7-9).

The imagery of the coming of the Lord in this parable, therefore, is party imagery: Jesus comes to us from a party, and he brings the party with him. Moreover, he has made it clear that he will keep the party going both now and forever: now, in the mystery of the Lord's Supper by which we celebratively "show forth the Lord's death till he comes" (1 Cor. 11:26); and forever, at the "Supper of the Lamb" (Rev. 19:9) where we will "sit together with him in heavenly places" (Eph. 2:6) as his "Bride" (Revelation, passim).

Whether that sort of commentary is exegesis, eisegesis, both, or neither, I don't know and don't care. My only reason for offering it is that it has the virtue of letting Scripture comment on Scripture. For it is only when that happens that you begin to get a hint of the richness of biblical imagery. In fact, I am disposed to press the wedding image even harder and say that the whole of Scripture, from Genesis to Revelation, is one long development of the theme of boy meets girl, boy loses girl, boy gets girl.

Watch. The Word — who in response to the Father's good pleasure woos creation into being out of nothing — meets the world in the first and second chapters of Genesis and falls head over divine heels in love with it. But in Genesis 3, the world turns its back on the Word and wanders lost in death. Then, in most of the rest of Scripture, the Word unceasingly seeks in death for the beloved he lost: he seeks for her in the passion and defeat of Israel in the Old Testament and in the death of the incarnate Lord in the New. Finally, in the Book of Revelation, by his winsome power as the Lamb Slain, the Word courts the world once and for all: at the end of the story, Boy gets girl, makes her his bride, and takes her home to his Father's house forever.

It is a consummation eminently worth waiting for; and it is the joyful safeness of that waiting that is the principal burden of the parable of the Watchful Servants. For as Jesus tells the story, even if the lord of the servants comes at midnight or later, they are blessed because his will is only to come in and sup with them. And as the parable applies to us, no one who waits for Jesus in faith can ever wait too long for him to come or ever be in any danger of missing the bus on which he comes. For he comes, not on the uncertain bus of our lives but on the absolutely certain bus of our death. He comes, to ring a change on the phrase, in the utterly dependable act of our *missing the bus* altogether. All we need to watch out for is that we take no other buses, however plausible — that we be content to sit still at the bus stop of his death in ours. And that, if you will, is what the word "ready" means at the end of this parable (Luke 12:40). "The Son of man," Jesus says, "comes at a time you don't think" (*hḗ hṓrą ou dokeíte,* in an hour that seems like nothing to you). To be "ready" for that, therefore, all you have to do is wait in faith for *nothing* — that is, for death. And the only way of being unready is to cut short that waiting by unfaith — to dash off on material or spiritual excursions we think will give us life. But our life does not consist in the abundance of things we possess (Luke 12:15). Rather our life is hid with Christ in God (Col. 3:3) in the mystery of Jesus' death and resurrection. He who loses his life for Jesus' sake, therefore, will find it (Matt. 10:39).

Hearing all this, Peter says to Jesus, "Lord, are you telling this parable to us, or to everybody?" Jesus answers him with yet another parable: "Who then is the faithful [*pistós*] and wise [*phrónimos*] steward whom the lord will set over his household to give them their share of food at the proper time? Blessed is that servant, if the lord, when he comes, finds him so doing. Truly I tell you, that he will put him in charge of all his property."

While Jesus' reply can no doubt be given a reading that extends it to the "everybody" Peter asked about, it seems to me the most natural interpretation is to take it as referring to the disciples and, by extension, to their successors, the clergy: that is, to all the stewards of the Gospel in their several generations.

In the light of this text, then, preachers of the Word labor under three distinct requirements. First, they are to be faithful *(pistoí)*. They are called to believe, and they are called only to believe. They are not called to know, or to be clever, or to be proficient, or to be energetic, or to be talented, or to be well-adjusted. Their vocation is simply to be faithful waiters on the mystery of Jesus' coming in death and resurrection. What the world needs to hear from them is not any of their ideas, bright or dim: none of those can save a single soul. Rather, it needs to hear — and above all to see — their own commitment to the ministry of waiting for, and waiting on, the only Lord who has the keys of death (Rev. 1:18).

Second, the clergy are to be wise *(phrónimoi)*. They are not to be fools, rich or poor, who think that salvation can come to anyone as a result of living. The world is already drowning in its efforts at life; it does not need lifeguards who swim to it carrying the barbells of their own moral and spiritual efforts. Preachers are to come honestly empty-handed to the world, because anyone who comes bearing more than the folly of the *kérygma* — of the preaching of the word of the cross (1 Cor. 1:21, 18) — has missed completely the foolishness *(mōrón)* of God that is wiser *(sophóteron)* than men. The wise *(phrónimos)* steward, therefore, is the one who knows that God has stood all known values on their heads — that, as Paul says in 1 Cor. 1:26ff., he has not chosen the wise, or the mighty, or the socially adept, but rather that he has chosen what the world considers nonsense *(tá mōrá)* in order to shame the wise *(sophoús)*, and what the world considers weak *(tá asthené)* in order to shame the strong. The clergy are worth their salt only if they understand that God deals out salvation solely through the klutzes *(tá agené)* and the nobodies *(tá exouthenéména)* of the world — through, in short, the last, the least, the lost, the little, and the dead. If they think God is waiting for them to provide classier help, they should do everybody a favor and get out of the preaching business. Let them do less foolish work. Let them sell junk bonds.

But it is the third of these clerical requirements that strikes me as the most telling: preachers are stewards whom the Lord has "set over his household servants to provide them with food at the proper time." After all the years the church has suffered under forceful preachers and winning orators, under compelling pulpiteers and clerical bigmouths with egos to match, how nice to hear that Jesus expects preachers in their congregations to be nothing more than faithful household cooks. Not gourmet chefs, not banquet managers, not caterers to thousands, just Gospel pot-rattlers who can turn out a decent, nourishing meal once a week. And not even a whole meal, perhaps; only the right food at the proper time. On most Sundays, maybe all it has to be is meat, pasta, and a vegetable. Not every sermon needs to be prefaced by a cocktail hour full of the homiletical equivalent of Vienna sausages and bacon-wrapped water chestnuts; nor need nourishing preaching always be dramatically concluded with a dessert of flambéed sentiment and soufléed prose. The preacher has only to deliver food, not flash; Gospel, not uplift. And the preacher's congregational family doesn't even have to like it. If it's good food at the right time, they can bellyache all they want: as long as they get enough death and resurrection, some day they may even realize they've been well fed.

So much for the faithful preacher. Jesus, however, does not end his answer to Peter there. "But if," he continues, "that servant says in his heart, 'My lord is certainly taking his own sweet time about coming,' and if he begins to smack his fellow waiters and waitresses around, and to eat and drink and get drunk . . ." If, that is, the preacher gets tired of the foolishness of the Gospel and begins to amuse himself with his own versions of intelligible fun and games — whether by exploiting his fellow servants' bodies, or by intellectually devouring their souls like cheese puffs — then the Lord of that preacher "will come on a day he does not expect and at a time [*hóra* again] he does not know, and he will cut him up in little pieces and appoint his portion [*méros*] with the unfaithful [*apístōn*]."

Only one thing is necessary, therefore, and that is the "good part" (*agathós méros*) that Mary chose and Martha despised. All that preachers need to do is sit at the feet of Jesus on the cross and preach out of their fidelity to that sitting. But if they will not do that, the only thing left for them is the "part of the unfaithful": the slow or sudden falling to pieces of their lives by virtue of their very efforts to live them. Because they will not choose the emptiness of being faithful (*pistós*), the only thing left for them is to live by what they think they know. But because they are not wise — not *phrónimoi*, not aware that the only thing that counts any more is the foolishness of the cross — then all the two-bit pomposities they substitute for the saving simplicity will simply bore them and everyone else to tears. They will, like Ahimaaz (2 Sam.

245

18:19ff.), be nothing but breathless messengers who never figured out what the message was supposed to be.

Jesus therefore wraps up the parable of the Watchful Servants with a warning that needs almost no comment: "That servant who knew the will of his lord but did not ready himself [*mḗ hetoimásas*], or act [*poiḗsas*] according to that will, will be skinned royally [*darḗsetai pollás*]. But he who did not know, even if he did things worthy of a real beating [*plēgṓn*], will be skinned only lightly [*darḗsetai olígas*]. For from the one to whom much has been given much will be required; and from the one to whom people have committed much they will demand the more." Jesus came to raise the dead; he saves by no other means. If the clergy cannot be faithful to the muchness of that little, they really would be better off selling junk bonds.

Between the parable of the Watchful Servants and the parable of the Barren Fig Tree, Luke interposes some sayings of Jesus that continue his emphasis on death rather than living as the means of salvation. For brevity's sake — and since the point has already been belabored — let me give you only some notes on the passages in question (Luke 12:49–13:5; Aland nos. 204-207).

Luke 12:49-53 (Jesus as Cause of Division): "I came to cast fire on the earth; and what do I care if it's already kindled! I have a baptism to be baptized with and how distressed I am until it is consummated [*telesthḗ*]! Do you think I came to give peace on earth? No, I tell you, rather division." And Jesus continues in the same vein, listing samples of the way his ministry will disrupt all our efforts at normal, proper living: households divided two against three, father against son, daughter against mother, and so on.

This is quite plainly death-talk. *Item: Baptism.* John baptizes only with water; Jesus will baptize with the Holy Spirit and with fire (Matt. 3:11). *Item: Jesus refers to his death as his baptism.* James and John (Mark 10:35ff.) want to sit on his right and his left in glory; Jesus says they don't know what they're asking for. "Are you able," he asks, "to drink the cup I drink [an anticipation of 'let this cup pass from me' in Gethsemane: e.g., Matt. 26:39], or to be baptized with the baptism with which I am baptized?" *Item: "Until it is consummated"* [*telesthḗ*]. The root

246

of the Greek word reappears dramatically at the very point of Jesus' death on the cross: *"Tetélestai,"* he says (John 19:30), "it is finished, *consummatum est." Item: "Not peace but division."* God's insistence on death-resurrection as the method of salvation will play hob with all sensible approaches to life. People will fight rather than switch from the prudent wisdom of ordinary living to the scandal and the foolishness of a crucified Messiah (1 Cor. 1:21-25).

Luke 12:54-56 (Interpreting the Times): Item: Jesus tells the crowds, "when you see a cloud rising in the west, you say, 'A rainstorm is coming,' and that's what happens; and when the south wind is blowing you say, 'It's going to be a scorcher,' and it is." He compliments them, in other words, on their ability to read — and to accept and adjust to — the signs of the natural disruptions of their designs for ordinary living. They will cancel a picnic, for example: they will accept the death that the rainstorm imposes on their plans for the day and they will rise out of it into something totally new, like an afternoon with a good mystery. But then he calls them hypocrites: "How come," he asks them, "you can be so discerning about these natural signs of disruption in earth and sky, but you can't discern this present time?" He is going to Jerusalem and his death. And he is going there in order to make death and disruption safe — to make it the very means of grace and salvation. But when he says in plain words that he's going, nobody really hears him (Jesus has already predicted his death and resurrection twice, e.g., Luke 9:22 and 9:43-45), and when he talks to them in parables about it, all their native intelligence evaporates. *Item: "This present time" (tón kairón toúton).* The word *kairós* means "time" in the sense of "due season" or "high time," as opposed to "clock time" (which in Greek is *chrónos). Kairós* here, therefore, echoes the significance of the word *hóra*, "hour," as used in the Watchful Servants, and of the words *hē hóra mou*, "my hour," "the time of my death," as used throughout the Gospel of John.

Luke 12:57-59 (Settling with One's Accuser): Jesus holds up litigiousness as an example of the way people's lives are in fact made worse by their efforts to get the due rewards of their living. He says they would be better off dropping their suit on the way to court — advice which, to determined plaintiffs, is tantamount to telling them to drop dead. The whole passage, in fact, anticipates another saying from the passion narrative, namely, Jesus' words in Gethsemane: "those who take the sword will perish by the sword" (Matt. 26:52).

Luke 13:1-5 (Jesus on Current Horror Stories): Some enthusiasts of the kind of journalism featured at supermarket checkout counters ("Mom Ices Baby in Freezer!" "Scoutmaster Goes Berserk with Bazooka!") regale Jesus with an atrocity story. Pilate, they tell him, killed some Galileans and poured their blood on their own altars. "So?" Jesus replies. "You think that because these Galileans suffered such a horrible death, they were some kind of super-sinners? No way! But unless you repent, you will all likewise perish." Then he adds an item of his own from the tabloids ("Siloam Tower Collapses; Kills Eighteen!"). His point? Well, I hardly think he was saying that if they could manage to repent of their sins, they wouldn't die: the way the Gospel works out, even being sinless can't guarantee that. In fact, it guarantees just the opposite: a still more horrible death on the cross. Maybe what he was telling them to repent of was actually their rejection of death — a rejection they compensated for by whistling in the dark and telling horror stories. Maybe they were supposed to stop pretending death was something God sent only to bad guys and realize it was his chosen way of saving even people with lives as carefully lived as theirs. "You're *all* going to die," Jesus tells them in effect. "But since I'm going to die for you and with you, maybe you should stop trying to keep death at arm's length. You have nothing to lose but your horror."

In any case, it is just this acceptance of death that Jesus continues to press in the next parable, the story of the Barren Fig Tree (Luke 13:6-9; Aland no. 207). The episode of the fig tree appears in all three synoptic Gospels. Only in Luke, however, is it presented as a story told by Jesus on the way to Jerusalem; in Matthew and Mark, it appears in Holy Week as an *acted parable* — with Jesus himself actually cursing the fig tree and the fig tree withering away.

According to my division of the parables, therefore, the actual cursing of the fig tree should turn out to be a parable of judgment; and the story version, by its placement well before the events of Holy Week, should turn out to be a parable of grace. Not that the two categories are

248

mutually exclusive: the parable of the Barren Fig Tree, by its very nature, is about judgment, crisis, the time of decision. But it is also about the unique way in which the judgment is, for now at least, suspended in favor of grace. In this, the Barren Fig Tree is a companion piece to Jesus' earlier parable of the Wheat and the Weeds. In both stories, a perfectly correct *judgment* on a bad situation gives way to a *letting be*, to a *suffering* of the badness — to an *áphesis,* that is, that both permits and forgives the evil (the Greek *aphiénai* variously means to let, allow, permit, suffer, pardon, forgive).

Consider the story, then. A certain man has a fig tree planted in his vineyard and he comes to it looking for figs and finds none. So he says to his vinedresser, "Three years I've been trying to get figs from this tree and it hasn't produced even one. Cut it down. Why should it use up ground?" But the vinedresser says to him, "Let it be, Lord [*kýrie áphes autén*], for one year more, till I dig around it and put on manure. If it bears fruit next year, so much the better; if not, then you'll cut it down."

Look first at the details of the parable. It may not be wise to put too much weight on the fact that the fig tree is planted in a vineyard: people probably planted both in the same space, and Scripture certainly seems to consider "vines and fig trees" companion plantings. But there is at least a suggestion here that the lord in the parable is principally a grape grower (he has, apparently, a full-time vinedresser) and that he has planted the fig tree more out of personal delight than out of entrepreneurial practicality. Plainly, then, since the fig tree stands for the human side of the parabolic picture (for the Jerusalem Jews, or for Judaism in general, or for the whole human race: take your pick), Jesus seems to be saying that the world is more God's hobby than his business, that it exists more for pleasure than for profit. God's attitude toward the world, therefore, involves *favor* from the start; grace is not something he drags in later on just to patch up messes. Unnecessary, spontaneous delight is the very root of his relationship with the world.

There is a complication, however, in the next set of details. Not, of course, in the part about seeking figs and finding none: that simply stands for God's disappointment with whatever it is you decide to let the fig tree represent. But when Jesus introduces the vinedresser into the parable — and then proceeds to make *him* the source of the decision to exercise grace instead of judgment — he takes a new tack. It would have been just as easy for Jesus to make the lord of the vineyard himself the originator of the gracious beneficence (as he did, for example, in the parable of the Laborers in the Vineyard, Matt. 20:1-16). At this point, though, Jesus is not content to leave things that simple. As he does in a few other places, he casts two characters in the divine role: one to represent the Father (the divine beneficence in its judgmental aspect) and the other to represent the Son (the divine beneficence as grace). Needless to say, it is the second of these characters that turns out, somewhat bizarrely, to be the Christ-figure in the parable (see the Unjust Steward, chapter fourteen below, for the most bizarre instance of all).

In any case, it is the vinedresser who is the Christ-figure here. It is precisely because he, underling though he is, invites the owner of the vineyard into forbearance and forgiveness that the barren fig tree continues to live by grace. *"Áphes,"* he says to his lord: *"Let it be."* And it is just that word that makes him one of the clearest Christ-figures in all the parables. For on the cross, in the very teeth of death, Jesus himself says, *"Áphes,* forgive."

Note, too, the vinedresser's last line: he says to his lord, "If it doesn't bear fruit next year, then *you* will cut it down." I'm not sure what that says about God the Father, but I'm certain it says that God the Son — who is the only one who offers the reconciled creation to the Father, and to whom the Father has in fact committed all judgment (John 5:22) — will never go back on the *áphesis* he has pronounced over the world. "I did not come to judge the world," Jesus said, "but to save the world" (John 12:47).

The world lives, as the fig tree lives, under the rubric of forgiveness. The world, of course, thinks otherwise. In its blind wisdom, it thinks it lives by merit and reward. It likes to imagine that salvation is essentially a pat on the back from a God who either thinks we are good eggs or, if he knows how rotten we actually are, considers our repentance sufficient to make up for our unsuitability. But by the foolishness of God, that is not the way it works. By the folly of the cross, Jesus becomes sin for us, and he goes outside the camp for us, and he is relegated to the dump for us, and he becomes garbage and compost, offal and manure for us. And then he comes to us. The Vinedresser who on the cross said *"áphes"* to his Lord and Father comes to us with his own body dug deep by nails and spears, and his own being made dung by his death, and he sends our roots resurrection. He does not come to see if we are good: he comes to disturb the caked conventions by which we pretend to be good. He does not come to see if we are sorry: he knows our repentance isn't worth the hot air we put into it. He does not come to count *anything*. Unlike the lord in the parable, he cares not even a fig for any part of our record, good or bad. He comes only to forgive. For free. For nothing. On no basis, because like the fig tree, we are too far gone to have a basis. On no conditions, because like the dung of death he digs into our roots, he is too dead to insist on prerogatives. We are saved gratis, by grace. We do nothing and we deserve nothing; it is all, absolutely and without qualification, one huge, hilarious gift.

And all because there is indeed a Vinedresser. I can love Jesus. As I said, I don't know about his Father. The only thing I can say about God the Father is that he's lucky to have such a lovable Son. Sometimes I think that if I had to go by his track record instead of just taking Jesus' word for his good character, I wouldn't give him the time of day. And I don't know about the Holy Spirit either. So much hot air has been let off in his name that if Jesus hadn't said he was sending him, I'd write him off too. But Jesus I can love. He does everything, I do nothing; I just trust him. It is a nifty arrangement, and for a deadbeat like me, it is the only one that can possibly work. As long as I am in him, I bear fruit. As long as his death feeds my roots, I will never be cut down.

> Jesus, Jesus, Jesus:
> Jesus, Jesus, Jesus;
> Jesus, Jesus, Jesus, Jesus,
> I love you, I love you, I love you.

CHAPTER TEN

Interlude on an Objection

WHY NOT LIFE RATHER THAN DEATH?

If I assess your mood correctly, it is time to take a break. You have listened for a long time now to what must seem like a monomaniacal insistence on death, and you have just about had it with all this talk about free grace. "What ever happened," you want to object, "to the positive idea of Christian *living?* If all we have to do to be saved is drop dead, why bother even trying to live — especially, why bother to be good, loving, or moral? Why not just go out and sin all we like? What role have you left for religion in the world, if everybody is going to get home free for nothing?"

Let me interrupt your train of thought right there, because you are beginning to drift away from the point of your most telling objection, namely, my failure to deal with the legitimate subject of living. I shall get to that in a moment. First, though, I want to lay to rest the last two ghosts you just let loose.

What role have I left for religion? None. And I have left none because the Gospel of our Lord and Savior Jesus Christ leaves none. Christianity is not a religion; it is the announcement of the end of religion. Religion consists of all the things (believing, behaving, worshiping, sacrificing) the human race has ever thought it had to do to get right with God. About those things, Christianity has only two comments to make. The first is that none of them ever had the least chance of doing the trick: the blood of bulls and goats can never take away sins (see the

Epistle to the Hebrews) and no effort of ours to keep the law of God can ever succeed (see the Epistle to the Romans). The second is that everything religion tried (and failed) to do has been perfectly done, once and for all, by Jesus in his death and resurrection. For Christians, therefore, the entire religion shop has been closed, boarded up, and forgotten. The church is not in the religion business. It never has been and it never will be, in spite of all the ecclesiastical turkeys through two thousand years who have acted as if religion was their stock in trade. The church, instead, is in the Gospel-proclaiming business. It is not here to bring the world the bad news that God will think kindly about us only after we have gone through certain creedal, liturgical, and ethical wickets; it is here to bring the world the Good News that "while we were yet sinners, Christ died for the ungodly." It is here, in short, for no religious purpose at all, only to announce the Gospel of free grace.

Your other ghost can be laid to rest just as quickly. The reason for not going out and sinning all you like is the same as the reason for not going out and putting your nose in a slicing machine: it's dumb, stupid, and no fun. Some individual *sins* may have pleasure still attached to them because of the residual goodness of the realities they are abusing: adultery can indeed be pleasant, and tying one on can amuse. But betrayal, jealousy, love grown cold, and the gray dawn of the morning after are nobody's idea of a good time.

On the other hand, there's no use belaboring that point, because it never stopped anybody. And neither did religion. The notion that people won't sin as long as you keep them well supplied with guilt and holy terror is a bit overblown. Giving the human race religious reasons for not sinning is about as useful as reading lectures to an elephant in rut. We have always, in the pinches, done what we damn pleased, and God has let us do it. His answer to sin is not to scream "Stop that!" but to shut up once and for all on the subject in Jesus' death.

Furthermore, the usual objection to God's silence, namely, that people will take such graciousness on his part as *permission* to sin, is equally nonsensical. For one thing, he made us free, so we already have his permission — not his advice, mind you, nor his consent, nor his enthusiasm — but definitely his promise not to treat us like puppets. For another, few of us, at the point of sinning, actually run around trying to get someone to sign a permission slip for us; we just go ahead full steam on our own. And for the final thing, the whole idea of people actually being *encouraged* to seduce maidens, or water stock, or poison wells by the agony and death of Jesus on the cross is simply ludicrous. We ourselves, thank you very much, are all the encouragement we need for dastardly deeds.

I am left, therefore, with the unhappy suspicion that people who are afraid the preaching of grace will encourage sin are in fact people who resent the righteousness they have forced themselves into. Having led "good" lives — and worse yet, having denied themselves the pleasures of sin — they seethe inwardly at any suggestion that God may not be as hard on drug pushers and child molesters as they always thought he would be on themselves.

But enough of religion and morality, those two doughty substitutes for living. What about your really considerable objection? What about the charge that in exalting death as the means of grace, I have utterly neglected the subject of the Christian life? I plead guilty. I have neglected it. But only because I think that Jesus, at this point in his career, is neglecting it too. Still, I shall meet you halfway: I shall give you a few assurances that I still consider living a genuine possibility for faithful Christians; and then I shall give you an example of the kind of living I have in mind when I say we are to be "dead" even before our final death.

Life is good. God invented it, and when it is lived according to his designs, it can be terrific. And the designs of God — the laws, physical and moral, by which life is meant to be governed — are nothing less than his specifications for the beauties of his several creatures. The law, therefore — moral law in particular, but physical law as well — is precisely our beauty; and insofar as we succeed in living lawfully, we enjoy our own gorgeousness just as God enjoys it. Moreover, even in our present fallen world, the goodness of good living (physical or moral) is still available to us. Christians therefore, in gratitude to God, continue to live and to pursue goodness of all sorts: the pleasures of sports, the delights of the mind, the joys of mutual affection, the consolations of nature, the satisfactions of virtuous and kindly acts — no lawful action, high or low, great or small, is ever an inconsiderable thing to a Christian.

However. But. Still. Nevertheless. In spite of all that. The Gospel truth is that neither we nor the world can be saved by efforts at living well. If the human race could have straightened up its act by the simple pursuit of goodness, it would have done so long ago. We are not stupid; and Lord knows, from Confucius to Socrates to Moses to Joyce Brothers, we've had plenty of advice. But we haven't followed it. The world has taken a five-thousand-year bath in wisdom and is just as grimy as ever. And our own lives now, for all our efforts to clean them up, just get grimier and grimier. We think pure thoughts and eat wheat germ bread, but we will die as our fathers did, not noticeably better.

Once again, the world cannot be saved by living. And there are two devastatingly simple reasons why. The first is, we don't live well enough to do the job. Our goodness is flawed goodness. I love my children and you love yours, but we have, both of us, messed them up royally. I am a nice person and so are you, except for when my will is crossed or your convenience is not consulted — and then we are both so fearful that we get mean in order to seem tough. And so on. The point is that if we are going to wait for good living to save the world, we are going to wait a long time. We can see goodness and we can love it. We can even love it enough to get a fair amount of it going for us on nice days. But we simply cannot crank it up to the level needed to eliminate badness altogether.

The second reason is more profound. The world's deepest problem is not badness as opposed to goodness; it is *sin,* the incurable human tendency to put self first, to trust number one and no one else. And that means that there is nothing — no right deed, however good, noble, lawful, thrifty, brave, clean, or reverent — that cannot be done for the wrong reason, that cannot be tainted and totally corrupted by sin. As I observed earlier, the greatest evils are, with alarming regularity, done in the name of goodness. When we finally fry this planet in a nuclear holocaust, it will not have been done by a bunch of naughty little boys and girls; it will have been done by grave, respectable types who loved their high ideals too much to lay them down for the mere preservation of life

255

on earth. And lesser evils follow the same rule. When I crippled my children emotionally (or when my parents crippled me) it was not done out of meanness or spite, it was done out of love: genuine, deeply felt, endlessly pondered human love — flawed, alas, by a self-regard so profound that none of us ever noticed it.

Life, therefore, for all its goodness — the act of living, for all its lawfulness and even occasional success — cannot save. I am sorry to disappoint you, but we are back at death — faith in Jesus' death — as the only reliable guide, the only effective opposite to *sin,* which otherwise can play havoc with goodness and badness alike. But let me take the edge off that by giving you an illustration of what death as a way of living might be like. The temptation, of course, is to imagine it as a doing of nothing at all, a profound quietism, a deadly, boring wait for death itself finally to turn up and end the nag. To help you get around that view, I want you to hold out your right hand, palm up, and imagine that someone is placing, one after another, all sorts of good gifts in it. Make the good things whatever you like — M & Ms, weekends in Acapulco, winning the lottery, falling in love, having perfect children, being wise, talented, good-looking, and humble besides — anything. But now consider. There are two ways your hand can respond to those goods. It can respond to them as a live hand and try to clutch, to hold onto the single good that is in it at any given moment — thus closing itself to all other possible goods; or it can respond as a dead hand — in which case it will simply lie there perpetually open to all the goods in the comings and the goings of their dance.

When I talk about being dead, accordingly, I have in mind not the absence of interest in the dance of living, but the absence of clutching at our partners in the dance — not *not-dancing,* if you will, but *not-trying-to-stop-the-dance.* In a way, that is nothing more than gurus and spiritual advisers the world over have been saying for millennia. But it is also, I think, quite specifically the way the Gospel invites us to live. Jesus, obviously, was not without an interest in life: his reputation as a glutton and winebibber was not gained by sitting at home eating tofu and drinking herb tea. But equally obviously, Jesus did not count his life — either human or divine — a thing to be grasped at. He was open at all times to what God put into his hand and he remained faithful in that openness until death — at which point God, by the power of the resurrection, put the whole world in his hand.

Think "dead hand," then: it is the only way, here or hereafter, that life can safely be enjoyed.

CHAPTER ELEVEN

Back to Death, Lastness, and Lostness

THE MUSTARD SEED, THE YEAST, AND THE NARROW DOOR

The next group of parables runs from Luke 13:10 to 13:30 (Aland nos. 208-211) and includes the Mustard Seed, the Yeast, and the Narrow Door. In these, Jesus not only continues his emphasis on death but also returns with considerable force to the themes of lastness and lostness as touchstones of the operation of grace.

The section begins with Jesus' healing of a crippled woman (Luke 13:10-17; Aland no. 208). This story, which is parabolic only to the extent that it contains Jesus' usual sprinkling of colorful comparisons, nonetheless has a bearing on my interpretation of the parables. The healing, we are told, took place in a synagogue on the sabbath — to the annoyance of the authorities of the congregation. Jesus, of course, violated the sabbath in various ways right from the start of his ministry; but it is worth asking whether his breaking of it now sheds a light different from that of earlier occasions.

I think it does. In those first violations of the injunction to do no work on the sabbath, Jesus was at pains to vindicate his own authority. Justifying his "hand-milling" of grain on the sabbath, for example, he said, "the Son of man is lord even of the sabbath" (Mark 2:28). But in the developed Christian imagery of the sabbath, a new emphasis, above and beyond the original one of rest, comes to the fore. It is an emphasis on death; and I want to enter it into the record here as Jesus comes closer and closer to the death he is courting on this final journey to Jerusalem. Let me give you, therefore, a few notes about the sabbath — remembering, if you will, that I am using the word, even in Christian contexts, to refer to Saturday. (Sunday, for Christians, is not the sabbath; it is the First Day of the Week, the Lord's Day, *Dies Dominica,* celebrated in honor of the resurrection. In the Romance languages, the name for Saturday comes from the Hebrew — e.g., the Italian *Sabbato;* the name for Sunday comes from the Latin for Lord's Day — e.g., the French *Dimanche*).

Item. In the old covenant, the sabbath is a day of rest in honor of God's work of creation; in the new covenant, the sabbath becomes a day of death — the day Jesus' body lay in the tomb, the day *Christ lag in Totesbanden.*

Item: Christian liturgical terminology. Jesus dies on *Good Friday,* which, in addition to being the eve of the sabbath, is also the preparation of the Passover. And he rises on *Easter Sunday,* which is the first day of the working week. But the day in between is called, variously, *Easter Even, Holy Saturday,* or *The Holy Sabbath, Sabbato Sancto.*

Item: Easter Even. The great service on this day is the *Easter Vigil,* whose theme is the renewal of creation by the resurrection of Jesus from the dead (the entire first creation story, Gen. 1:1-2:3, is the first of many lessons recapitulating the history of salvation from the old covenant to the new). In other words, as the church on Holy Saturday sits quietly in the tomb with the dead Christ, it also sits joyfully, believing that, in Jesus, death has been made twice as creative as the act of creation ever was. The death of Jesus, therefore, is not just something that lasted through a single sabbath day in the spring of A.D. 29. Precisely because he who was dead that day was the Incarnate Lord, the Second Person of the triune God, his death is an eternal as well as a temporal fact. Jesus is not only risen forever; he is also dead forever. The heavenly sabbaths we look forward to celebrating will be a perpetual renewal of creation, proceeding by a perpetual resurrection out of a perpetual death.

O quanta qualia sunt illa sabbata,
quae semper celebrat superna curia,

quae fessis requies, quae merces fortibus,
cum erit omnia Deus in omnibus.

O what their joy and their glory must be,
Those endless sabbaths the blessed ones see;
Crown for the valiant, to weary ones rest:
God shall be all, and in all ever blest.

(Peter Abelard; translation by J. M. Neale)

We too, therefore, will live endless sabbaths out of our death in him. When the weariness of all our living is over, we shall receive the reward of our faithfulness unto death (Rev. 2:10). The Lamb Slain (5:6, 9, 12; 13:8), who makes all things new (21:5), will give us the crown of his eternal life (2:10).

Item: The personal significance of the Christian celebration of Holy Saturday — of the Holy Sabbath. What we celebrate is precisely death, not dying. Dying, if you think about it, is simply the world's worst way of living: it is tag-end living, minimal living, hardly living. And dying, besides being no fun, is also totally unfruitful: nothing grows out of it because the common reaction to it is a continuous attempt, physically and mentally, to *reverse* it — to go counter to the direction that the universe in this particular instance wants to take. But death, precisely because it is an arrival at an accomplished fact, and above all because Jesus rises gloriously out of that fact, is the most fruitful thing there is. Death, therefore — nothingness, *no thing* — is the *only thing* we need.

Item: Nothingness. On Holy Saturday, the Holy Sabbath, the Easter Vigil begins in a darkened church. The symbolism is obvious: we are dead in Christ's death. But then, in honor of the resurrection, the new fire is struck, the paschal candle is lit, and we begin the celebration of a new creation out of the nothingness of death. People often say they are afraid of death — about, as they sometimes put it, having to be *nothing* after all these lovely years of being *something.* When they tell me that, I try to focus the problem more tightly. "Let me see if I understand you," I say. "You're bothered by the thought that you will be non-existent in, say, the year 2075. But tell me something. Has it ever occurred to you to worry about the fact that you were likewise non-existent in 1875? Of course it hasn't: for the simple reason that, by the forces of nature alone, you got bravely over that first attack of nothingness and were born. Well, all the Gospel is telling you is that your death — your second bout of nothingness — is going to be even less of a problem than your first. By the power of Jesus' death and resurrection, you will get bravely over that too, and be reborn. In fact, you already have been; so go find something more dangerous to worry about."

Final Item: Only death is usable in the new creation. Jesus came to raise the dead. He did not come to raise the living; and he especially did not come to raise the dying (remember Lazarus: John 11:1-16). As long as you and I are just hanging onto life, Jesus cannot do a thing for us. He saves the dead, not the moribund; the lost, not the detoured; the last, not the middle of the line. It is only when we go all the way into death — past living and past dying — that we can experience his power.

I have already dealt (in *The Parables of the Kingdom*) with the parables of the Mustard Seed and of the Yeast as Mark and Matthew locate them in the earlier part of Jesus' ministry. All I am going to offer here are a few reflections based on the fact that in Luke (Luke 13:18-21; Aland nos. 209-210) Jesus tells these parables a second time during his final journey to Jerusalem. A mustard seed, or any seed for that matter, must end its career as a seed before something can come of it. It must, that is, go all the way into death. Therefore, while Luke's placement of this parable may be singular, there is nonetheless a certain thematic appropriateness about it: Jesus, too, must end his career before anything can come of his messianic program.

One other observation on the mustard seed: it becomes a tree (*déndron*). I think it worth noting that the imagery of the tree is not only central to the shape of the Scripture but also inseparably involved with death. Mankind falls into sin and death by a tree in Genesis, is saved by a tree through the death of the Incarnate Lord on the cross, and lives forever in the New Jerusalem in the shade of the tree of life that yields twelve fruits and whose leaves are for the healing of the nations. True enough, the Greek word for "tree" in these instances is *xýlon,* not *déndron:* it means "wood" — originally, lumber or firewood.

261

But in the later Greek of the New Testament, it quite plainly means "tree" (*"xýlon* of life," for example, Rev. 22:2); and from that usage, it easily becomes a metonym for the cross: Jesus "hung upon a *xýlon*" (Acts 5:30) and "bore our sins on the *xýlon*" (1 Pet. 2:24), etc.

About the yeast *(zýmē)*, only one comment. While yeast cannot be said to die when it is mixed into dough, it can legitimately be said to get lost in the mixture. Jesus, in fact, says that the woman "hid" it *(enékrypsen)* in three measures of flour. Consequently, even though the yeast is not an image of death, it is nonetheless an image of the saving lostness that Jesus, at this juncture, talks about almost as much as he does about death (see the Good Samaritan, for example — and especially the upcoming parables in Luke 15: the Lost Sheep, the Lost Coin, the Lost Son).

For the present, however, Luke proceeds to the parable of the Narrow Door (Luke 13:22-30; Aland no. 211) — but not without a reminder (verse 22) that Jesus is saying all these things precisely on his way to Jerusalem. For both Luke and Jesus, in other words, death hangs over this entire proceeding; to me, therefore, the verse is yet another justification for my use of death as the touchstone of the parables of grace.

Someone comes up to Jesus on the road and says to him, "Lord [*kýrie*], will only a few be saved?" In one sense, it is easy to understand how such a presumption of exclusivity could arise in the questioner's mind, considering the harsh-sounding, apparently judgmental parables he may have heard during this journey: the Good Samaritan, the Friend at Midnight, the Sign of Jonah, the Rich Fool, the Watchful Servants, the Barren Fig Tree. On the other hand, it must have been exasperating to Jesus to have his main point so completely missed: he was, after all, laying down a program of salvation (namely, faith in his death and resurrection) that would make eternal life available to absolutely everybody — and on a give-away basis at that. "All you have to do is be dead and trust in my death," he said in effect; "I do all the rest."

Jesus' difficulty, of course, was that such a program was simply unintelligible to his hearers. As every preacher knows, people hear not what is said but only what they are prepared to hear. Consequently, since no one in Jesus' audience (the disciples included) was in any way prepared to comprehend the idea of a Messiah who would die, it is not surprising that his parabolic intimations of his death and resurrection — not to mention his literal prediction of it — went totally unheard.

Accordingly, Jesus' hearers fastened their minds on something they could at least partially grasp, namely, the notes of judgment and even of condemnation in his parables of grace; and they skipped blithely over death and resurrection by which alone grace works. And Jesus himself (who by no means had the world's longest fuse) seems simply to have become monumentally annoyed with them. Almost out of spite, he gives no direct answer to the question of whether only a few will be saved. Instead, he deliberately perpetuates their confusion by giving his answer in the ham-fistedly judgmental imagery of the Narrow Door. It is a prime example of Jesus positively encouraging misunderstanding.

Straight off, he responds in the plural, thus answering his questioner by playing to the crowd: "Strive [*agōnízesthe*] to enter through the narrow door [*stenês thýras*]." What he is doing, of course, is the old rhetorical trick of setting up a straw man by confirming the worst case. Because insofar as an eschatology maven like his questioner could hear him at all, the only thing Jesus could possibly mean by "striving" and "narrow door" would be, "You bet there'll be only a few, sonny; and if you're smart, you'll knock yourself out studying for the entrance exam. Because I've made it so tough that most of you are going to flunk."

I realize, of course, that there are a fair number of Christian preachers who would be more than happy to stand up and say that's exactly what Jesus meant. But I have trouble with such a failure to spot the irony Jesus is using here. So much so, that when I put their cheerfully exclusivist interpretation of his words against something like John 12:32 ("I, if I be lifted up, will draw *all* [*pántas*] to me"), the circuit breakers in my mind simply pop. And by the same token, when I put that dire interpretation against what I think Jesus is actually saying in these parables of grace, I am forced to look for another, more catholic interpretation of the Narrow Door.

So here it is. The narrow door — the tight squeeze in front of absolutely free salvation — is faith in Jesus' death. Jesus does not set up ten thousand tricky wickets and threaten to admit to heaven only the aces

263

who can negotiate every one of them. Jesus has simply put, smack in the front of his Father's house of many mansions, the one, scant doorway of his death and ours. Its forbidding narrowness lies not in the fact that it is so small it is hard to find; rather it lies in the fact that it is so repulsive it is hard to accept. Let me, in all reverence, repeat the last assertion as plainly as possible: to anyone in his right mind, the program of salvation via death, as proposed by Jesus, simply stinks on ice. It lets in the riffraff, since all they have to be is dead; and it offends the classy, since they wouldn't even be caught dead entertaining such a proposition. Besides, in Gethsemane, Jesus himself said it was a terrible idea and he warned us over and over again that the number of people who would be willing to buy it would be undamned few. He did not, however, say either that it was his heart's desire that the number actually be few, or that he was going to sit up in his private tower cheering every time somebody turned away in disgust from such a forbidding front door. In fact, he says that he himself, hanging dead on the cross, is the front door ("I am the door," John 10:9); and far from turning up his nose at the world's rejection, he insists on trying forever to convert it to acceptance — "I, if I be lifted up from the earth, will draw all to myself" | (John 12:32).

Do you see what that does for the details of this parable? It abolishes the exclusivity of the imagery of narrowness and makes the parable susceptible of an inclusive interpretation. Watch. All the suction in the universe — all the "drawing" by which the Word woos creation back to be his bride — is through the narrow door of death. You may run from it, you may fight it, you may protest it, you may hate it — all in the name of what you call life. But if ever just once you slip up in your frantic struggle to live your way to your eternal home — if just once you simply drop dead — well then, sssslurrrp!!! . . . the suction will get you, and home you go. Not because you deserve to; only because that's the way the universe is built. Good Friday and the Holy Sabbath are the tip of the iceberg of redeeming death that lies under all of history. It was the Lamb Slain *from the foundation of the world* (Rev. 13:8) who said, "I, if I be lifted up, will draw all to me."

Salvation is hard, therefore, and salvation is easy — and the hardest thing about it is its easiness. It uses such cheap, low-down methods that only the last, the lost, the least, the little, and the dead will ever be able to cotton onto it. Moreover, that is exactly what Jesus says at the end of his introduction (Luke 13:24) to the parable of the Narrow Door: "For many, I tell you, will seek to enter and will not be able" (*ouk ischýsousin*, will not have the strength for it).

But then he takes a tack that seems to undo everything I have been saying — a tack that has given editors of the Greek text a punctuation problem. If you put — as most of them do — a full stop (that is, a period) after "will not be able" at the end of verse 24, then you put at least some distance between those words and the actual beginning of the parable in verse 25, to wit, "Once the master of the house has risen up and closed the door . . ." In other words, you leave open the possibility that the inability to enter is not necessarily due solely — or even at all — to the master's closing of the door. But if you put a half stop (a comma, in this case) between the verses, then you have practically necessitated two conclusions: first, that the householder's door in verse 25 is the same as the narrow door in verse 24; and second, that the reason why only a few are ever going to make it to their final home is that our Lord and Master's idea of how to throw a good party is to keep out as many people as possible. Obviously, since I don't believe that the second conclusion is Gospel, and since I am convinced that the first is not the case, I myself am delighted to put a full stop after verse 24. (For the record, the KJV, RSV, NEB, NIV, and many others opt for the full stop. Examples of the effect of the half stop may be seen in the English Revised Version [marginal reading] and in J. B. Phillips's translation.) In any case, let me put a full stop to textual criticism and get back to what should probably now be called the parable of the Narrow Door versus the Other Door.

Jesus says: "Once the householder [*oikodespótēs*] has risen up [*egerthê*] and closed the door [*thýran*], you will begin to stand outside and knock [*kroúein*] on the door, saying, 'Lord, open up for us'; and he will answer and say to you, 'I don't know where you're coming from.' Then you will begin to say, 'We ate and drank right in front of you and you taught in our streets.' And he will say to you again, 'I don't know where you're coming from; get away from me, all you workers of iniquity.'"

Far enough for the moment. Look carefully at the words I have given the Greek for. *Oikodespótēs* (I am shifting to the milder translation, "householder") is a word that has appeared before and will appear again. Jesus uses it twice during the parables of the kingdom (see my previous volume, *The Parables of the Kingdom*): once in referring to the householder in the parable of the Wheat and the Weeds (Matt. 13:24-30) — which householder, please note, was the very one who said *áphete* (forgive, let them be) concerning the weeds; and he uses it a second time in referring to the householder who "brings forth out of his treasure things new and old" (Matt. 13:51-52) — the one whom Jesus holds up as a model for the instructed disciple. He also applies the word to three other significant characters: to the lord of the vineyard, the gracious Christ-figure in the parable of the Laborers in the Vineyard (Matt. 20:1-16); to the party-giver in the parable of the Great Supper (Luke 14:15-24) who goes to heroic lengths to fill his house with guests; and perhaps most remarkably, to the figure of God the Father in the parable of the Vineyard and the Tenants (Matt. 21:33-44) — that is, to the vineyard owner whose son was killed for the sake of the vineyard. (The Vulgate, incidentally, translates *oikodespótēs* as *paterfamilias* in all these instances — thus suggesting, whether in the case of the Christ-figure or the Father-figure, the desirability of a familial, rather than a coldly judicial, interpretation.)

In the light of all these usages, what can be said about the force of *oikodespótēs* in the parable of the Doors? I think it has the effect of making this a parable about the divine housekeeping — about the way God provides for and manages the whole house of creation — about (to use the correct theological term) the divine *economy*. And it implies that while the managing of his house may well require certain exclusionary measures, those measures are not the divine *oikodespótēs'* idea of how to run a home. In short, I think it only fair to import into the interpretation of this parable all the freight of grace and leniency carried by the word *oikodespótēs* in Jesus' other parables. Accordingly, I am going to take the householder here not only as a Christ-figure but also as a figure of some gentleness. I am not at all disposed to follow the usual interpretation and make him out to be a tough customer.

Two factors lead me to take that approach: the general thrust of the imagery of the parable, and the specific presence of the words *egerthē* (has risen) and *thýran* (door). Consider the significance of the imagery first.

What Jesus is doing here is very like what he did in the parable of the Friend at Midnight: he is painting a parabolic picture, using nighttime behavior as his model. But in this case, he prefaces his parable with the apparently forbidding image of a narrow door. That image, though, is by no means an entirely negative one. Unless we are going to make Jesus out to be a trickster daring us to do the impossible, this first door he speaks of must be seen as an unlocked door, a usable door, an open door. Nevertheless, when he begins the parable itself in verse 25, he seems to confuse the imagery: he sketches a picture of a householder getting up and *closing* a door. As I said, my way of resolving the confusion is to conclude that he is talking about two different doors; otherwise, what would be the point of his telling us to strive to enter what he has slammed shut? Actually, I don't think there is any real confusion here at all: I think that Jesus used the word "door" in verse 24 as a variant of "gate" (see Matt. 7:13-14 — the "narrow" imagery could well have been repeated many times by Jesus, with occasional alterations for variety's sake). But then, I think, his use of the word "door" suggested — on the analogy of the Friend at Midnight — the possibility of yet another parable.

In any case, the picture seems to me to be as follows. It is evening, after supper. The householder has been reading *The Wall Street Journal* or watching the ten o'clock news, and he has fallen asleep in his recliner. Suddenly the clock strikes midnight. He awakes with a jolt, realizes the time, gets up *(egerthē)*, and does all the things he should have done earlier. He locks the door *(thýran)*, turns off the lights, and goes to his proper bed. But on his way to some solid sleep at last, he is interrupted by insistent banging on his front door: a mob of people, claiming to be his friends, want to come in and to . . . well, what might they want to do? Go to bed with him and sleep the whole night? Hardly. Jesus postulates far too hyper a crowd for such quiet behavior. Perhaps what they want is a chance to bend his ear with the latest gossip, or perhaps just a chance to prove to the neighbors they are important enough to be let into his house any hour of the day or night. Whatever it is, it will be something based entirely on *their* concerns, *their* convenience, their problems — in short on *their* lives. At any rate, as Jesus portrays them, they talk like a bunch of selfish parvenus: after the householder's first snub, they come back at him with indignation disguised as bonhomie. "But we've *lunched* with you! We've had *drinks* with you at the club! We've even attended your *fabulous* lectures!" Despite their social-climbing cajolery, though, Jesus has the householder tell them they simply don't fit in with his plans: "I don't know where you're coming from," he says. For all he can understand of their idiotic lives and preoccupations they might as well be from another planet. They certainly haven't the foggiest notion of how *he* wants to operate.

Now then. Having thus extrapolated the parable, let me exegete my extrapolation. The *nap* out of which the householder/Christ-figure rises is Jesus' three days in the tomb. The *door* he closes is the door to the exchanges of ordinary living. And the *sleep* to which he finally goes is the endless sabbath of the death of Jesus, which is the perpetual basis of the resurrection to eternal life.

And what, at that rate, is the *narrow door* the householder has still left open? Well, it is the remote possibility that, instead of noisily insisting on their own notions of living their way to salvation, they might just join him in the silence of his death and wait in faith for resurrection.

Is that forcing the original text? On balance, I don't think so. But even if it is, I'm not worried: no one ever gets through Scripture without occasionally putting the arm on one passage in favor of another. Accordingly, because I really do think the *oikodespótēs* is a Christ-figure — and because I really don't think Jesus will ever close the door of grace — I think the closing of the *oikodespótēs'* door should be interpreted not as the locking out of the damned but as the closing of the door of ordinary living as a way to eternal life. Jesus our *oikodespótēs* rises out of his three-day nap in the grave and he closes all other doors to salvation except faithful waiting in the endless sabbath of his death. He leaves us, that is, no entrance into life but the narrow door of our own nothingness and death — the Door, in fact (John 10:9), that is Jesus himself.

Please note carefully what I am saying. I am not saying there is no such thing in Scripture as God's slamming the door on the damned: there is plenty of it, and I am not about to say that he won't, in the end, do something awfully similar. (I might, of course, make a few qualifications about the subject — I might even be accused of qualifying the hell right out of it. But yes, Virginia: if you have to know, I really do think there is a hell.) What I *am* saying is that this parable of the Door is not one of the places where the final disposition of the damned is being talked about. For my money, it is yet another grace parable in judgment clothing — a phenomenon we have seen much of already, and will see more of in the parable of the Great Supper. And as with all such parables, it should be interpreted as gracefully as possible; it should not be used as an excuse to preach sermons on the tight security of the eschatological slammer.

What confirms me in that opinion is the fourth of the Greek words I have flagged, namely, *kroúein,* to knock. In the Book of Revelation (3:20), Jesus says, "Behold, I stand at the door and knock" *(kroúō).* Do you see what that says about this parable? It says that while all the world's winners are out there knocking their knuckles bloody on the locked doors of their lives, Jesus is knocking quietly at the narrow door of their deaths trying to get them to let him in. It says, in other words, the exact opposite of what most people think: not that he is busy dreaming up ways to keep sinners out but that he is actively and forever committed to *letting himself in.* (Don't worry, Virginia, that still leaves you a terrific hell: if they never open up and he never stops knocking, that's the hell of it all.) It says, in short, that this is a parable of grace, even though it manages to be that only by the desperate expedient of demanding to be stood on its head.

One last point before proceeding. The parallels between this parable and the Friend at Midnight (Luke 11:5-13) are worth noting. In both, there is a door *(thýran)* that has been closed by the householder — who in the case of the Friend at Midnight says also, "my children [*paidía*] are with me in bed; I cannot rise [*anastás*] to give you anything." In the light of where we have come in this book, that seems to me to say that God's real children — those who trust only in Jesus, who is the *paída* whom God raised (*anastésas*: see Acts 3:26) — are with him in the bed of Jesus' endless death. And it says that Jesus will never get out of that bed, since it alone is the root of his resurrection. Nevertheless, there is definitely a rising in the Friend at Midnight. Though the householder in that case "will not rise [*anastás*] and give to him because he is his friend [that is, because of the merits of ordinary living], still, because of his shamelessness [his acceptance of his death as the only thing he's got], he will rise [*egertheís*] and give him as much as he needs [that is, life abundant in the resurrection]." Finally, the verb *kroúein*, to knock, also appears in the Friend at Midnight — but with the reverse assurance that our knocking will not be in vain. For this knocking is not the clamor of those trying respectably to live their way to salvation; rather it is the shameless, faithful acceptance of Jesus in his death as the Way, the Truth, and the Life. It is a knocking at God's door with nothing more to commend us than the Door himself, the dead Christ on the cross.

To return to the parable of the Narrow Door, then, Jesus continues by having the householder say (after the second "I don't know where you're coming from"): "get away from me, all you workers of iniquity. There will be weeping and gnashing of teeth when you see Abraham, Isaac, and Jacob in the kingdom of God, and you yourselves thrown out of it. People will come from east and west and from north and south and they will sit down to eat [*anaklithésontai*] in the kingdom of God. And behold, those who are now last will be first and those who are now first will be last."

This is the summation of the parable. Jesus says that those who are knocking at the door of ordinary, plausible, right-handed living — all of them, mind you, "good" people trying to live decently — are nothing but workers of iniquity *(adikías)*, that is, of the unrighteousness that springs from unfaith. Good living is no more capable of justifying us than bad living is of condemning us. Only faith in Jesus dead and risen has anything to do with the case. And Jesus drives that home by citing specific examples of faith — of blind, even stupid, obedience to the God who works by raising the dead. He holds up Abraham, Isaac, Jacob, and the prophets and he says that they will be the ones who are in the kingdom, while all the types who are trying to climb their way into the eternal social register will be out in the cold.

Finally, though, he says something that I think vindicates the frankly catholic interpretation I have given the Narrow Door. He says that people (the Greek simply says "they") will come from all over creation and sit down *at supper* — which means, as I read it in the light of the finished imagery of Scripture, at nothing less than the *Marriage Supper of the Lamb*. That imagery suggests not a trickle of guests who, after heroic efforts, will find their way to some slow leak of a house party, but a flood of billions upon billions who — free, for nothing — will be drawn by the love of Jesus into the ultimate wedding blowout. True enough, they will be drawn through strait gates and narrow ways; but they will be drawn by the Narrow Door himself, and they will be drawn inexorably. All they need is the willingness to be last — and lost and least and little and dead — for by his grace upon their deaths, they will be first in the resurrection of the dead.

271

CHAPTER TWELVE

Death and the Party

THE TRANSITION TO THE GREAT BANQUET

Fascinatingly — considering in particular that Jesus at this point is consciously and deliberately on his way to death — the fourteenth and fifteenth chapters of Luke (Aland nos. 214-221) have, as their principal motif, the image of the party. Chapter 14 begins with a sit-down dinner in the home of a leading Pharisee — a dinner at which Jesus does a number of bizarre things: he performs an unacceptable healing on the sabbath, he criticizes his fellow guests' social behavior, he dispenses odd, if not nonsensical, advice on party-giving, and he tops off the occasion by confusing everyone with the parable of the Great Banquet. In the rest of the chapter, he lectures the crowds that follow him on the cost of the paradoxical "party" he is about to give the world in his death and resurrection; and in chapter 15, he regales us with no fewer than three parties: one each for the Lost Sheep, the Lost Coin, and the Lost Son. All in all, he clearly links the theme of the party, both explicitly and implicitly, with the mystery of death, lastness, and lostness that he has been adumbrating all through this final journey to Jerusalem.

This combining of "death-talk" with party imagery is not uncommon in Scripture (to recall only the climactic instance of it, think of the Marriage Supper of the Lamb Slain in the final chapters of Revelation). But it occurs most frequently as a twist that Jesus gives to certain of his parables. He has already included a wedding reception in the parable of the Watchful Servants, and he has introduced the notion of an eschatological dinner party at the end of the parable of the Narrow Door. And in the Prodigal Son and the King's Son's Wedding, he will make a completely literal connection between death/lastness and the party. But before moving on to the parties at hand in Luke 14, I want to say a few words about the material at the end of chapter 13 that forms the bridge to them.

Immediately after he has told the parable of the Narrow Door, some of the Pharisees warn Jesus to get out of town: Herod, they tell him, wants to kill him. This is crocodile solicitousness on their part, of course: they themselves have been after Jesus' scalp for almost as long as he has been preaching (since Mark 3:6, in fact). Nor does Jesus respond in any worried way to their rattling of his cage. He is on his way to Jerusalem for the express purpose of being killed; his first reaction to their fake concern, therefore, boils down to little more than a snappish "So what?" "Go and tell that fox," he says, "'Look, I cast out demons and do cures today and tomorrow, and on the third day I shall finish my work [*teleioúmai,* be brought to my completion: coupled as it is here with "the third day" the word is a clear reference to Jesus' death]. Still, I have to continue on my way today, tomorrow, and the next day, because it is not fitting for a prophet to be killed outside of Jerusalem'" (Luke 13:32-33).

But Jesus' snappishness changes abruptly to tenderness and pity. At the thought of his own death — and in particular, I suppose, of its radical unrecognizability as a messianic act — he laments over the Holy City which he now knows will not accept him. "O Jerusalem, Jerusalem, killing the prophets and stoning those sent to you! How often would I have gathered your children together as a hen gathers her chicks under her wings, and you would not! Behold, your house is taken away from you. [The Greek verb behind 'taken away' is, once again, the multivalent *aphiénai:* forgive, permit, let be, leave, forsake, let go, dismiss, divorce.] And I tell you, you will not see me until the time comes when you say, 'Blessed is he who comes in the name of the Lord!'"

I find this whole passage to be a vindication of my insistence on using death as a touchstone for the interpretation of the parables of grace. It shows quite clearly how close to the surface of Jesus' mind the

273

subject really was. All it took was one mention of Herod's antipathy (just a little political gossip, really, with a nasty edge to it) and out came a flood of messianic utterances couched in relentless death-talk. And the specific words he uses make the death-resurrection character of his messiahship plainer than ever. "Today and tomorrow," he says (that is, for the time being, for now, for the time before the mystery is revealed — for the time, if you will, of the *signs* of his messianic program rather than of the *program* itself), "I cast out demons and do cures" (in other words, he acts like a recognizable, interventionist Messiah); "and on the third day [*tȩ̄ trítȩ̄ hēmérą:* as noted, these words are a clear reference to resurrection out of death; compare, for example, Matt. 16:21 and parallels; Mark 9:31 and parallels; Luke 18:33 and parallels] I shall finish my work" (*teleioúmai:* be perfected, that is, bring my actual messianic program, and not just the signs of it, to accomplishment — compare the use of the same verb by Jesus on the cross in John 19:30: *tetélestai,* "it is finished").

So too, I find the imagery of his lament over Jerusalem vindicative of my interpretation. Jerusalem deals out death but will not accept a Messiah who works by death. Jesus has longed to gather his people under his wings in love; but now the only way he will accomplish that is by the very death they will inflict upon him. They will be healed by his stripes; death and not living will be the instrument of their salvation. The net effect of all the plausible, right-handed schemes the city has concocted in the name of living has not been life, it has been the corruption of life — and it will very shortly be nothing less than disaster. And as with Jerusalem, so with us. The human race's efforts to get its act together have resulted in many things, a lot of them plain, unvarnished messes; but the one thing we have never succeeded in doing is getting our act together. And therefore for us, as for Jerusalem, the house of our life — the ramshackle agglomeration of bright ideas, old stupidities, good intentions, and ill will in which we have for so long tried to live our way to some semblance of wholeness — is put away from us, divorced from us, set permanently out of our reach. The only home left for us now is Jesus' death.

Far from being a tragedy, though, this divorce, this *áphesis,* this separation from the house of our own life is, by the very word Jesus uses, an absolution for all the failings of that house. *"Aphíetai hymín ho oîkos hymôn,"* he says. In a good half of its many uses in the New Testament, the verb *aphiénai* means simply *forgive;* accordingly, this *áphesis* is not just the loss of our life, it is also, by a great mercy, the loss of the garbage of our life. All the clutter that, like decrepit bachelors, we have allowed to pile up in the house of our living, all the hates, the lies, the lusts, and the lunacies — the whole lifetime's accumulation of irretrievable mistakes — has been forgiven, absolved, put away, carted off.

If then we accept that absolution, that housecleaning that is a house-removal — and if we take up residence in the clean emptiness of Jesus' death — we will have his life and have it abundantly. But if we try to hang onto the old house of our living we will have only hell. Because that Collier brothers' mansion, that Charles Addams monstrosity, is *gone. We are dead,* and our life is hid with Christ in God (Col. 3:3). To go back to that life is to go back to nothing. The only real dwelling we have now is the Father's house of many mansions: hell is simply the stupid pretense that *nowhere* really would be a nicer place to spend eternity.

But enough of the bridge to Luke 14; time to let a whole series of parties begin. Jesus goes to the h

ouse of a certain Pharisee to have dinner on the sabbath day . . . but since you probably know this story of healing on the sabbath in its straight form, let me try to make it more accessible by updating a few details. Imagine a modern house for this prosperous Pharisee — one with a dining room grand enough to hold a fourteen-foot table. Make the meal to which he invited Jesus a sit-down dinner for twelve; and make the guests Episcopalians or Presbyterians — pleasant but a bit shirty is the effect you want. Then bring on Jesus.

He gets through the soup and the fish well enough, but just as the roast is brought in, he discovers that the gentleman next to him has a back problem. Being not only kindhearted but good with his hands (perhaps he has studied Healing Touch at a holistic health center), he suddenly decides to help the man, right there in front of everybody. "May I have your attention just a minute, folks?" he says. "Old Waldo here has a real bad back. Hurts him worse than a toothache. So if it's okay with you all, I'm just going to plop him down right here on the dinner table and do a little healing on him. Er, Mrs. Terwilliger, do you think you could move that roast down to the other end? Waldo's a pretty big old boy, you know. There! Up you go now, Waldo. And mind your feet so you don't get your shoelaces in the cauliflower."

Do you see? The crime of healing on the sabbath is no mere technical violation of the law. It is a crime against civility, against decency, against common sense — against, in short, the received wisdom about how life should be lived. It is proof that the person who commits it has lost all sense of conformity and manners and is therefore dangerously impervious to the glue that holds everybody else's life together. And Jesus' curing of the man's dropsy at a sabbath dinner is as alarming as the hypothetical treatment of old Waldo in the midst of the Limoges: normal people would "rather die" than do, or even watch, something like that — they would be, as they say revealingly, "mortified." Therefore when anyone actually does behave that way, what alarms them is precisely the appearance, in the midst of all their fearful living, of someone who has been liberated from the fear of death.

Jesus, of course, challenges his host and fellow guests to accept his liberation. He asks them "Is it lawful to heal on the sabbath or not?" But as with Waldo, he doesn't bother to wait for an answer. When he's done with the healing — during and after which all present have bitten their tongues and uttered not one complaining word about such an imposition — he gets up on his high horse and criticizes them for *thinking* he's a boor. His words, "Which of you, if his son or his ox falls into a pit, will not pull him out on the sabbath day?" are in about as good taste as would be, "Well, Waldo's just fine now, but don't any of you dare start thinking unkindly of me for fixing him up, because you'd do exactly the same thing, if your child or your favorite dog came in here all smashed and bloody."

Jesus' behavior, you see, is simply unpardonable: besides being tasteless, it presumes his fellow guests are worse than they are. Nobody present wants him not to heal the sick. They simply can't understand why he has to turn the healing into a sideshow of bad manners. What they are probably thinking is something quite mild — like, "Oh, come now; heal all you like, but can't you make us all just a bit more comfortable and put off the actual treatment till after dinner?" The scribes and Pharisees, you see, are being neither unreasonable nor heartless. What time, after all, was the sabbath meal? Noon? One? Three-thirty? *Tops,* all they're asking Jesus to do is wait six hours: the sabbath ends at sundown, for crying out loud! After that he can turn Waldo into Superman, for all they care. But the fact that he has to do it right now on the sabbath, between dinner and dessert, with Waldo's feet in the host's face, means only one thing: loony or sane, Jesus is bad news. Either way, he's just too unafraid to be safe company.

Which brings us to Jesus' side of the question. He did a good deal of healing on the sabbath. You might even say that healing on the sabbath was his favorite way of livening up an observance he felt had been unnecessarily toned down by the scribes and Pharisees. But there was more to it than that. Jesus was unique; and he perceived his uniqueness with increasing clarity as his life went on. The trouble with uniqueness, though, is that practically no one can see it as anything but craziness. All they see when they meet somebody truly one-of-a-kind is the electric sign inside their own heads that keeps flashing, "Not Like Us! Not Like Us!" Therefore, since one of Jesus' main points was that his method of salvation (namely, death and resurrection) would be like nothing any sane person could have a kind word for, he probably figured that healing on the sabbath was as good a way as any to introduce the world to its, and his, uniqueness.

In any case, healing on the sabbath is just as repugnant to the church nowadays as it was to the scribes and Pharisees in Jesus' time. Furthermore, if we insist on emulating him by doing a bit of it on our own, we will find ourselves just as despised and rejected as he was. Some modern instances of this aversion to healing on the sabbath? Helen decides she wants to start an AIDS support group in the local church. Response? "Well sure, Helen, sick people need help. But these guys are *queer!* We've got to think of the young kids. Better try someplace else." Or: Cynthia, drunk, calls her pastor at 3:00 A.M. and wants to talk about the problems she has with men. Response? "Now listen, Cynthia. I know this all seems very important to you right now, but:

you woke me up out of a sound sleep; you've kept me on the phone for an hour; and now my wife is sitting next to me with smoke coming out of her ears because I'm being nice to another woman at four in the morning. I'm going to unplug the phone, Cynthia. I promise I'll call you, but I just have to get some sleep." Or finally, consider the pastor who divorces his wife, marries his mistress, and then suggests to the Official Board of the church that their allowing him to remain in the pulpit would be a splendid example of grace and forgiveness in action. Response? "No way, José."

But back to the text. Having offended everybody in sight by his willingness to toss aside the conventions of living — having given them, that is, a whiff of the freedom of death in the prison of their days — he finds himself on a roll. Not content with giving them a mere hint, he tells a parable that flings open every window in the jailhouse. Having noted how this crowd of snobs has clucked and sniffed about the seating arrangements, he begins, "When you are invited by someone to a wedding reception, don't sit down in the best place, because somebody more important than you may have been invited by your host. And then the host will have to come and say, 'Give your place to this man,' and you will be ashamed and have to sit in the lowest [*éschaton*, last] place. Instead, when you are invited, go and sit in the lowest [*éschaton*] place, so that when your host comes he will say to you, 'Come on up, friend, to a higher place'; then there will be honor [*dóxa*, glory] for you in the presence of all those who sit at the table with you. For everyone who exalts himself will be humbled and he who humbles himself will be exalted."

Unfortunately, that last line always manages to cast a pall over the rest of the parable. People hear "humble yourself" and they immediately think of the bitter pill of moral effort. But this parable is not about a cure that is worse than the disease; it's about the liberating joy that comes from letting the party happen instead of trying to put personal body English all over it. It's about, in other words, the "letting go" of Jesus himself who "for the joy that was set before him, endured the cross, despised the shame, and is set down on the right hand of God" (Heb. 12:2).

That connection between humility and death is reinforced by the symbolism of the entire parable. For insofar as we insist on taking what we have decided is the best place, we effectively close ourselves to all the other places at the table. It's like the illustration of the hand in chapter ten above: clutch the gift that you have in your palm at the moment and no other gifts can get in; hold it in a dead hand, though — in a flat, open hand — and the dance of gifts can proceed unimpeded. But note, too, how this parable expands that image. Jesus tells us that in life, as at the dinner table, we are to take the lowest seat. As already noted, the word used here for "lowest" is actually *éschatos,* the Greek for "last." That suggests, accordingly, that the precise seat we are invited into, the seat specifically reserved for each one of us, is death. For not only is death our last and lowest state but it is also the state that is the sole condition of our resurrection. Jesus speaks often of "the last day" *(hē eschátē hēméra)* as the day of resurrection and the day of judgment; here he simply develops the same theme.

Look next, though, at the Christ-figure in this parable. Obviously, it is the host; but notice how the image of host here is refracted and reflected by other places in Scripture. First, just as the host is the source of the invitation to the wedding, so Jesus calls the whole world to the Marriage Supper of the Lamb. "Go out into the highways and hedges," he says, "and *compel* them to come in" (Luke 14:23); "I, if I be lifted up from the earth, will draw *all* to me" (John 12:32). Second, with Jesus as with the host, whatever judgment is issued, favorable or unfavorable, it is issued precisely upon people who are *already guests* — that is, who have already been *invited into* and *accepted at* the party. Their right to be members of the party is never in doubt; only their acceptance of it is questioned. Finally, the host pronounces *favorable* judgment on those who accept the last and lowest place — namely, death — and who are willing to wait there for the fulfillment of his promise (John 6:39-40), "I will raise him up [*anastḗsō autón*] at the last day." (The resurrection, incidentally, is at least hinted at by the *aná* [up] words of the host in the parable, "Friend, come up higher": *prosanábēthi anóteron.*)

One last verbal connection in this parable: I find in the phrase "with shame" (verse 9) an echo of the parable of the Friend at Midnight.

Here as there we are told that death and loss rather than life and success are the instruments of our salvation. For if we hope to be saved by our talent for lifting ourselves into first place by our own bootstraps, then we will, by the very impossibility of the enterprise, "begin with shame [*aischýnēs*]" to take the lowest place — that is, to have lastness, lostness, and death thrust upon us without our acceptance. But if we are shameless enough to accept death as the instrument of our salvation — if, with a shamelessness (*anaídeian*) like that of the friend who came as a beggar at midnight, we will drop our pretenses of success and come to Jesus in our failure — then Jesus our Friend will rise, and Jesus our Host will come, and he will raise us up at the last day and bid the endless party to begin.

Meanwhile, however, Jesus continues to add to the tension of the party by criticizing his host as well: he suggests that the Pharisee who gave the dinner should not have invited the successful, healthy, competent guests who are present; rather he should have invited the poor, the maimed, the halt, and the blind.

It is easy to sympathize with the people who had to put up with Jesus — especially with this Pharisee who is only trying to have a decent sabbath meal. First it was Waldo on the table with the main course, then it was critical comments about his guests, and now it's a lecture about how he should have invited all the losers in town. Jesus was never even a candidate for the congeniality award. I have a theory that maybe he hung around with publicans and sinners because polite society found itself less and less interested in giving him houseroom.

On closer examination though, Jesus' remarks to his host are less personally attacking than they seem. He is at pains, as he has been all through his final journey to Jerusalem, to set forth death and lostness, not life and success, as the means of salvation. And at this dinner party he has found himself in the presence of a bunch of certified, solid-brass winners: establishment types who are positive they've got all the right tickets, religious and otherwise, and who think a fun evening consists of clawing your way to the top of the social heap. Therefore when he addresses his host, he is principally concerned to redress the imbalance he feels all around him, to assert once again his conviction that a life lived by winning is a losing proposition.

"When you give a luncheon or a dinner [*deípnon*, supper]," Jesus says to the Pharisee, "don't invite your friends or your brothers or your relatives or your rich neighbors, because they'll just reciprocate your invitation. But when you give a feast, invite the poor, the crippled, the lame, and the blind, and you will be blessed [*makários*, happy] because they don't have any way of paying you back. Rather, everything will be repaid to you in the resurrection [*anastásei*] of the just [*dikaíōn*]."

There are a number of ways of interpreting this passage; most of them, frankly, you can keep. If, for example, you take it as advice on how to run your social life, it is simply a formula for ruining an evening. Guests chosen only because they won't invite you to their house in return are less than likely to be scintillating dinner company. Alternatively, if you take it simply as an instance of oriental hyperbole — that is, if you interpret it as nothing more than a "don't forget the handicapped," phrased in the form of "don't waste your time on the healthy" — you reduce it to an unnecessarily complicated version of an ethical commonplace.

But as I take this text, I see in it yet another major theme poking its nose into the interpretative tent. Watch. Jesus has already been critical of the following items taken from everybody's list of Favorite Things To Be: Being First, Being Found, Being Big, Being Important, and Being Alive. Now however, he castigates the one item that holds all these futilities together and gives them power over us, namely, Being a Bookkeeper. The human race is positively addicted to keeping records and remembering scores. What we call our "life" is, for the most part, simply the juggling of accounts in our heads. And yet, if God has announced anything in Jesus, it is that he, for one, has pensioned off the bookkeeping department permanently.

It is bookkeeping, therefore — our enslavement to it and God's rejection of it — that seems to me to be the burden of the closing lines of this parable of the Chief Seats. Jesus warns his host not to consult any records he has kept on people: not the Friend/Foe ledger, not the Rich/Poor volume — and none of the other books either; not Nice/Nasty,

Winners/Losers, or even Good/Bad. And he warns him because, as far as God is concerned, that way of doing business is over. It may be our sacred conviction that the only way to keep God happy, the stars in their courses, our children safe, our psyches adjusted, and our neighbors reasonable is to be ready, at every moment, to have the books we have kept on ourselves and others audited. But that is not God's conviction because he has taken away the handwriting that was against us (Col. 2:14). In Jesus' death and resurrection, God has declared that he isn't the least interested in examining anybody's books ever again, not even his own: he's nailed them all to the cross. Accountability, however much it may be a buzzword now, is not one of his eschatological categories.

That, I take it, is the point of Jesus' words against reciprocation and repayment. Jesus is saying, "Listen, you are absolutely mired in your scorekeeping, bookkeeping lives. You are so busy trying to hold the world together by getting your accounts straight that you hardly have time to notice that it's falling apart faster than ever. Why don't you just let go? Thumb your nose at the ledger! Drop dead to the accounting! Because it's not just one more thing that can't save you; it's the flypaper that catches everything else that can't save you and leaves you stuck with it forever. Look, I'm on my way to Jerusalem to die so you can be saved, free for nothing. I'm going up there to give you a dramatic demonstration of shutting up once and for all on the subject of the divine bookkeeping. What's the point, then, of your keeping records when I'm not?"

Do you see? He who was sent not to judge the world but to save the world (John 3:17) *will not count our records against us.* What the Son will offer the Father at the last day is the silence of his death on the subject of our sins and the power of his resurrection on the subject of our life. Therefore we are to stop — right now — living as if we could have the least influence on that happy outcome by fussing about who owes what to whom. That, if you will, is why Jesus tells his host to invite people who can't invite him back: to get him to stop doing everything in his life on the basis of debit and credit and to open his eyes to the way God does business. Jesus says to him: "Forget about making a social buck by

282

inviting the right people — and forget about making a spiritual buck by doing the right thing. Invite the wrong people! Do the wrong thing! You want to have a dinner party? Have a stupid dinner party! You want to have a life? Have a loser's life! Spit in the eye of the accounting department! Invite anybody you don't like and be anything you don't like; but don't for a minute mess with anything that isn't last, lost, least, little, and dead. Because that's where the action is, not in your Guinness Book of Spiritual Records."

At the end of his speech to the host, Jesus specifically ties this condemnation of bookkeeping to the resurrection. "You will be happy [*makários*]," he tells his host in verse 14, "precisely because these losers and deadbeats you invite won't be able to repay you." He says, in other words, that happiness can never come in until the bookkeeping stops, until the hand that clutches at the dance goes dead and lets the dance happen freely. And he says that the place where that happy consequence will burst upon us is at the resurrection *(en tễ anastásei)* of the just *(dikaíon)*. And the just, please note, are not stuffy, righteous types with yard-long lists of good works, but simply all the forgiven sinners of the world who live by faith — who just trust Jesus and laugh out loud at the layoff of all the accountants.

And the unjust? Well, the unjust are all the forgiven sinners of the world who, stupidly, live by unfaith — who are going to insist on showing up at the resurrection with all their record books, as if it were an IRS audit. The unjust are the idiots who are going to try to talk Jesus into checking his bookkeeping against theirs. And do you know what Jesus is going to say to them — what, for example, he will say to his host if he comes to the resurrection with such a request? I think he will say, "Just forget it, Arthur. I suppose we have those books around here somewhere, and if you're really determined to stand in front of my great white throne and make an ass of yourself, I guess they can be opened (Rev. 20:12). Frankly, though, nobody up here pays any attention to them. What will happen will be that while you're busy reading and weeping over everything in those books, I will go and open my *other book* (Rev. 20:12, again), the book of life — the book that has in it the names of everybody I ever drew to myself by dying and rising. And when

I open that book, I'm going to read out to the whole universe every last word that's written there. And you know what that's going to be? It's going to be just *Arthur*. Nothing else. None of your bad deeds, because I erased them all. And none of your good deeds, because I didn't count them, I just enjoyed them. So what I'll read out, Arthur, will be just *Arthur!* real loud. And my Father will smile and say, 'Hey, Arthur! You're just the way I pictured you!' And the universe will giggle and say, 'That's some Arthur you've got there!' But me, I'll just wink at you and say, 'Arthur, c'mon up here and plunk yourself down by my great white throne and let's you and me have a good long practice laugh before this party gets so loud we can't even hear how much fan we're having.'"

CHAPTER THIRTEEN

The Party Parables

THE GREAT BANQUET AND THE PRODIGAL SON

Meanwhile, back at Luke 14, the image of the party continues to dominate the proceedings. Jesus' next parable, the Great Banquet (Luke 14:15-24; Aland no. 216), is told at the very dinner table where he has been regaling everyone with his upside-down notions of what constitutes proper social behavior. But the Parable of the Great Banquet does not simply arise out of that awkward meal; it also anticipates the festivities yet to come in chapter 15 — in particular, the definitive party in the parable of the Prodigal Son. As a matter of fact, I think a case can be made that the Prodigal Son's perfect embodiment of what I have been calling the "grace" themes — its exaltation, for example, of losing over winning, its utter disdain for bookkeeping, its flatfooted references to death and resurrection, and, most notably, its celebration of them all with a blowout compared to which all previous Parties look like slow leaks — made it, for Luke, the organizing principle of the entire sequence of passages in chapters 14 and 15.

Look at the evidence of the text. Much of what is included here appears nowhere else: the healing at the Pharisee's dinner party, the lecture to guests and host, and the parables of the Lost Coin and the Lost (Prodigal) Son are found only in Luke. The rest of the items, of course, appear in other Gospels as well. The Great Banquet, the lecture on the cost of discipleship, and the parable of the Tasteless Salt are found in Matthew; and the Lost Sheep is in Mark. But whereas in those Gospels

285

these materials are scattered about in diverse contexts, in Luke their proximity to the story of the Prodigal Son makes their common themes fairly leap off the page. Consider. For one thing there is a party in almost every one of them. For another, the last, the lost, and the dead are held up as God's chosen vessels. And for good measure, the first, the unstrayed, and the alive — all the best and brightest — are displayed as being in no way God's cup of tea. As far as I am concerned therefore, the parable of the Prodigal is the sun around which Luke has made the rest of these materials orbit.

On then with the Great Banquet, beginning with its relationship to the Prodigal Son. This story, about a man whose invited guests refuse to come to his party and who then pressgangs the riffraff of the town into filling up his house, appears twice in the Gospels: in Luke 14, where it occurs during the final journey to Jerusalem; and in Matthew 22, where it occurs between Palm Sunday and the crucifixion. By my classification, therefore, the Lukan version is a parable of grace and the Matthean one (the King's Son's Wedding), a parable of judgment. Moreover, the respective versions bear that out. As Jesus tells the parable in Luke, the governing consideration is the host's gracious desire that his house be filled. The note of judgment is struck only lightly: the host is angry when his invitations are refused and declares at the end that none of those who were invited will taste of his supper. By contrast, the story in Matthew is full of judgment, not to mention savagery: the invited guests murder the servants who bring the king's invitation; the king sends out his armies, destroys those murderers, and burns up their city (social life in this parable seems definitely more urgent than gracious); and at the end of the parable, the man without the wedding garment is cast into outer darkness. Therefore, leaving Jesus' telling of the story in its Matthean form for consideration in the following volume on the parables of judgment, let us look at the present, grace-oriented version in Luke.

Note how it begins. "When one of those who sat at table with him heard this [Jesus' discourse in Luke 14:1-14], he said to him, 'Blessed is he who shall eat bread in the kingdom of God!'" As I read them, those words are pure gush. The gentleman in question has been just as mystified as everyone else by the idea of giving dinner parties for the poor, the maimed, the lame, and the blind. But since Jesus ends his remarks with a reference to the "resurrection of the just," this fellow does what so many of us do when confronted with paradox: he takes the first spiritual bus that comes along and gets out of town. In effect he says, "Ah, resurrection! I can't say that I follow your odd little ideas about dining with cripples, but I do agree with what you say about heaven. It's so comforting to hear that everything's going to work out perfectly in the end."

Jesus, in other words, finds himself confronted with a lazy mind. He has said almost nothing about "the end," yet his hearer fastens on it as if he'd talked of nothing else. So Jesus does what he so often does with lazy minds: he applies a rude shock. He launches straight into a story that bumps his hearers off the bus bound for the heavenly suburbs and deposits them back in the seediest part of town.

It's tempting, of course, to take the parable of the Great Banquet as a mere recasting in story form of what Jesus already said discursively at the Pharisee's table. But it is more than that. It begins with a much stronger condemnation of "living" than the actual dinner party did. Earlier in the evening, when Jesus saw the guests vying for the best seats, he gave them a little lecture (appealing to enlightened self-interest) about how their efforts at being winners could very well spoil their enjoyment of the party. But now, in the parable, he portrays the pursuit of a sensible, successful life as something that will keep them — and us — out of the party altogether.

That is the first point about the beginning of the Great Banquet (Luke 14:16): all the excuses given by the first-invited guests are sensible, legitimate excuses. Going to inspect a newly purchased field is as respectable a thing to do with your life as flying out to the coast to discuss the screenplay for a TV special: one is as good a reason as the other why you can't have lunch in New York on Wednesday. And the same is true of test-driving your new fleet of pickup trucks or honeymooning with your latest wife: no host in his right mind would be seriously miffed if you responded to his invitation with such legitimate regrets.

Yet in the parable, the householder not only reacts with anger at their refusals; his anger becomes the moving force behind the party that finally does take place. What are we to make of that? Well, my disposition is to take the vehemence of this party-giver as Jesus' way of dramatizing the futility of "living" as a way of salvation. He is saying that God works only with the lost and the dead — that he has no use for winners. Therefore God will be as furious over legitimate excuses as he would be over phoney ones, since in either case the net result is the same: we keep ourselves out of reach of his gracious action.

There is, of course, a more specific way of interpreting this kind of passage. Whenever Jesus' parables include the note of judgment — of distinguishing who is really "in" and "out" — it is always possible to take them as referring to Jew and Gentile. I find some drawbacks to that, though. The first is that while Jesus was certainly critical of the Jewish establishment of his day, he can hardly have been on the Gentile side of a Jew/Gentile split; he cannot, therefore, legitimately be taken to be as anti-Jewish as this kind of interpretation makes him out. The second is that if you don't ascribe this supposed anti-Jewishness to Jesus himself, you usually end up blaming it on the church. The parables, you say, were probably heavily doctored by the (mostly Gentile) ecclesiastical community of the second century and thus reflected that community's views rather than Jesus'. But to me, that's even less helpful: it drains the authority of Jesus right out of the parables.

My major objection, however, is that I simply do not like bandying about the Jew/Gentile distinction. For one thing, it is so deeply infected by anti-Semitism as to be beyond return to healthy use. Furthermore, it is in the long run irrelevant. Jesus did not save the world as a dead Jew — or as a risen Gentile — he saved it as dead and risen, period. He saved it in our humanity *tout court*, not in any special classification of it. Therefore, whatever his apparent strictures against the Jews — whatever parabolic characters he may have made possible stand-ins for the Jews — he does not intend seriously to suggest that judgment will go against the Jews just because they are Jews, or for that matter, in favor of Gentiles just because they are Gentiles. To me, the fundamental distinctions in Jesus' parables are loser/winner, last/first, dead/alive — not Jew/Gentile. Accordingly, insofar as Jews can legitimately be viewed as objects of judgment in Jesus' parables, it is because, as individuals or groups of individuals, they insist on salvation by winning rather than losing. They are not the enemy: the most that can legitimately be said is that some of them are examples of cooperating with the enemy — which, of course, can be said of every group on earth.

In any case, since the true enemy is "winning" and "living," Jesus proceeds straight to the losers and the dead ducks who form the heart of the parable of the Great Banquet. Here are people who are having the time of their lives — free food, free drinks, free costumes, a Peter Duchin orchestra to dance to — and all on a day when they woke up expecting nothing, if not worse. There was no way they could even have imagined themselves as they are now, the social equals of the winners the host first invited. These are the poor and the handicapped. They don't drive BMWs, they don't own Dior gowns, and they don't tear open their mail in breathless anticipation of yet another gala. These people walk (some of them); they drive, if anything, shopping carts; and they don't get invited anywhere for one simple reason: they are a disgrace to polite, successful society. It's crucial to notice this point, because Jesus is not telling the parable to enforce a moral about being nice to those less fortunate than ourselves. We already knew about that obligation. Rather, he is telling the parable to stand all known values on their heads: hence this bizarre story in which a well-known socialite throws a party for people he found sitting in doorways drinking muscatel out of brown paper bags.

Do you see? The point is that none of the people who had a right to be at a proper party came, and that all the people who came had no right whatsoever to be there. Which means, therefore, that the one thing that has nothing to do with anything is rights. This parable says that we are going to be dealt with in spite of our deservings, not according to them. Grace as portrayed here works only on the untouchable, the unpardonable, and the unacceptable. It works, in short, by raising the dead, not by rewarding the living.

And it works that way because it has no reason outside itself for working at all. That, I take it, is the point of the *two* frenzied searches for extra guests (one into the "streets and lanes" and one into the "highways and hedges"), on which the servant in the parable was sent. They establish that the reason for dragging the refuse of humanity into the party is not pity for its plight or admiration for its lowliness but simply the fact that this idiot of a host has decided he has to have a full house. Grace, accordingly, is not depicted here as a response; above all, it is not depicted as a fair response, or an equitable response, or a proportionate response. Rather it is shown as a crazy initiative, a radical discontinuity — because God has decided, apparently, that history cannot be salvaged even by its best continuities. The world is by now so firmly set on the wrong course — so certain, late or soon, to run headlong into disaster — that God will have no truck with responding to anything inherently its own, whether good or evil. The ship of fools is doomed: if its villains do not wreck it, its heroes will. Therefore there is no point in any continuance, whether of punishment of the wicked or reward of the righteous — no point, that is, in further attempts to redeem the world by relevancy. And therefore in the parable, Jesus has the host make no relevant response at all to the shipwreck of his party; he has him, instead, throw a shipwreck of a party.

In other words, just as the only constant factor in the whole story is the host's monomaniacal determination that his house be full (a determination, please note, that leads him into the curious folly of trying to get even with his first guests by jury-rigging a party they wouldn't be caught dead at anyway), so also the only constant factor in the history of salvation is God's equally monomaniacal commitment to grace. It is precisely that commitment that leads him into the corresponding weakness and foolishness of insisting that being caught dead is the only ticket to the Supper of the Lamb.

Indeed, it seems to me that it is just this foolishness and weakness of God — and the consequently high price of death-resurrection it puts on the otherwise free party — that leads Luke to introduce Jesus' words about the cost of discipleship (Luke 14:25-35; Aland nos. 217-218) immediately after the parable of the Great Banquet. For in this passage, Jesus gathers up all the threads of his teaching about losing and death as the way of salvation. He tells the crowds that if anyone comes to him and does not hate father, mother, wife, children . . . even his own life, he cannot be his disciple. He talks about the necessity of bearing the cross. And then he gives them three short parables to drive home the reality of what he is saying. To convince them he is not just a guru mouthing spiritual truths but a dangerous and expensive operator inviting them into his own dangerous and costly operation, he first tells the parable of the Tower ("Who in his right mind starts a building project without first toting up the cost?"). Next, he adduces the parable of the King Going to War ("If your army is only half the size of your enemy's, you negotiate for peace before he gets to your borders"). Finally, to underscore his meaning, he says plainly (Luke 14:33), "Therefore whoever of you does not renounce his entire substance [*hypárchousin:* possessions, goods] cannot be my disciple."

Jesus, in other words, gives them the hard sell. "Listen," he says. "I don't want to waste your time here. What I'm laying out for you is not only the best offer of salvation you've ever seen; it's the only one that will actually work when you get it home. This is the real thing, not some $27.00 fake Rolex Oyster you can pick up on the sidewalk in New York. But unfortunately, even with my spectacularly low overhead, it'll still cost you a bundle. How much? Well, J. P. Morgan said, 'If you have to ask, you can't afford it.' But that was about a yacht, which you could get along without; what I'm selling, you really need. So I say, 'You better ask, because you don't want to be handed the bill on one of your tight-wad days and find yourself looking around for a cheaper outfit to deal with.' How much does it cost then? Everything you've got. The works. The whole farm. With no pocket money left over. There are no pockets in a shroud."

Jesus' point, however, is not simply that discipleship in the way of death-resurrection is expensive; more important, it's that it is liberating once the price is paid. For the very next thing he says is the parable of Salt ("Salt is wonderful; but if salt has become insipid, how can you make it salty again?"). I have already dealt with other aspects of this parable above in chapter four; here I want simply to underscore its note of liberation. Think about what Jesus is actually saying. On the one hand, it is terrifying and unreasonable: in order to gain salvation, life, and reconciliation, you have to lose every amenity, every relationship,

291

every last scrap of the good life you might have. In short, you have to be dead. On the other hand, the deal is a bargain to end all bargains: sooner or later, you're going to have to lose all those things anyway — willy-nilly, the death that is your wherewithal for buying a new world is already in the bank.

What has that to do with salt? Just this: the saltiness of Jesus' disciples — the taste, zip, and zing that the church at its best can give to the world — derives precisely from our recognition that the Good News is one huge, inside joke. Because it really is a divine comedy. Sure, the price of salvation is high. And sure, you should sit down and count the cost. But do you see what you come up with when you get done counting? You come up with the absolute certainty that *everything you've got* turns out to be exactly the right amount to cut you in on the deal: you have one (1) life, and the price is one (1) life. Even more hilarious than that, you would have to shell out everything anyway, even to get nothing for it. And funniest of all, even if you shell out only because you have to, your total loss will still get you one (1) ticket to the final party. It's exactly like the Great Banquet, in fact: all you have to be is a certified loser and God will send his servant Jesus to positively drag you into his house. And that's the saltiness of the joke: salvation (root: *sal,* which is *salt*) really is free — inconvenient, but free. Which is exactly what salt is: not worth buying for its own sake, but dirt cheap considering the way it perks up everything else.

The only sad thing is that so often the church looks as if it never heard the joke. Either it's afraid to talk about losing and blathers on instead about salvation through moral success, intellectual competence, and spiritual triumph; or if it does finally get around to telling people that death-resurrection is the name of the game, it puts on a long face and acts as if the whole deal is a crying shame. But the Gospel is not a tragedy; it's precisely a hilariously salty story — so flavorful it's in positively bad taste — in which schoolteachers, crane operators, models, bag ladies, arbitrageurs, tennis pros, drug addicts, bankers, lawyers, lechers, and pimps all get away with murder just by dropping dead.

Salvation offered on any other basis is bad news, not Gospel. We are raised, reconciled, and restored not because we are thrifty, brave,

clean, and reverent but because we are dead and our life is hid with
Christ in God — because, that is, Jesus has this absolute *thing* about raising the dead. In the Gospels, he never meets a corpse that doesn't sit up
right on the spot. "I, if I be lifted up, will draw *all* to me." And if the
church can't remember that Good News, then like unsalty salt, it isn't
fit to be put anywhere — not on the land, not even on the dunghill; it
should simply be thrown as far away as possible. Which, when you
think of it, is pretty much what the world has done with the church in
the late twentieth century. Maybe the children of this world really are
wiser in their generation than the dim-bulb children of light who can't
recognize a joke when they hear one.

In any case, all these elaborate appetizers from chapters 14 and 15
having been served up, Luke now brings on the main course, the parable of the Prodigal Son (Luke 15:11-32). He prefaces it, of course (in
15:1-10), with the parables of the Lost Sheep and the Lost Coin, but
since I have dealt with those in chapter four above, I shall underline
only one thing in them here: they, too, are about a party. Each ends
with a celebration, a calling together of friends and neighbors — a rude
interruption, mind you, of whatever laundering, housekeeping, bookkeeping, or gardening they may have thought constituted their lives —
for a whole afternoon of wine, roses, and laughs. And why? Because by
the hilarious constitution of the universe — by the extension of the
salty joke into the ultimate shaggy dog story — it turns out that what
makes history come out in triumph is some dumb sheep that couldn't
find his way home.

But then, to make both the hilariousness and the tastelessness of
the joke abundantly clear, Jesus moves on to the parable of the Prodigal
Son — and to the biggest, tackiest party yet thrown. George Balanchine
was a great choreographer; but if you want to see, in one dramatic presentation, a roundup of all the godawful things that have ever been
done with this parable, take a good look at his *The Prodigal Son* next
time you have a chance. The father is a forbidding terror; the son comes
groveling home; and forgiveness comes only after Baryshnikov has
danced his way through enough *tsouris* to keep the entire population of
New York depressed for a year. So let me simply expound the story it-

self, making no effort to hide my enthusiasm for what I think it really says.

The parable is an absolute festival of death, and the first death occurs right at the beginning of the story: the father, in effect, commits suicide. It took me years to notice this fact, but once you see it, it's as plain as the nose on an elephant. The younger son comes to his father and says, "Give me the portion of goods that falleth to me" (I quote from the KJV for heightened contrast). In other words, he tells his father to put his will into effect, to drop legally dead right on the spot. Obligingly enough, the father does just that: he gives the younger son his portion in cash, and to the elder brother, presumably, he gives the farm. Thus, just two sentences into the parable, Jesus has set up the following dynamics: he has given the first son a fat living; he has made the brother, for all the purposes of the parable yet to come, the head of the household; and he has put the real paterfamilias out of business altogether.

Next, of course, Jesus tells us that the younger son went to a far country where his rich boy's life turned rapidly into a lost cause — where he "wasted his substance with riotous living." We are free, naturally, to supply any specific forms of riotousness that appeal to us: boys or booze, girls or drugs, or gambling casinos at $10,000 a night. But whatever the details, the denouement of this part of the story is that the prodigal finally wakes up dead. Reduced to the indignity of slopping hogs for a local farmer, he comes to himself one dismal morning and realizes that whatever life he had is over. (One note about the words for "life" in this parable. The "living" the father divided was *tón bíon*, one of the Greek words for "life." The "goods" that the son requested, and that he wasted intemperately, were *tén ousían*, which is the Greek for "substance" or "being." In any case, what the father gave away and what the son wasted was not just some stuff that belonged to them; it was their whole existence, their very being, their lives.)

Having thus introduced death into the parable a second time, Jesus proceeds to have the prodigal come face to face with it. He sits him down next to the hog trough and has him look at his life and find . . . nothing. "How many hired servants of my father's," he says, "have bread enough and to spare, and I perish with hunger." And so, in desperation over his own inarguable death — over the end of everything that could possibly be called a life — he formulates the first version of his confession: "I will arise and go to my father, and will say unto him, Father, I have sinned against heaven, and before thee, and am no more worthy to be called thy son: *make me as one of thy hired servants.*"

I have italicized the words at the end of this confession because they show that while the boy may have come face to face with death, he is still far from being able to admit he is in fact already dead. He may understand that he has died as a son — that he has, by his prodigality, lost all claim to his former status as his father's loyal child. But what he does not yet see is that, as far as his relationship with his father is concerned, his lost sonship is the only life he had: there is no way now for him to be anything but a dead son. And because he does not grasp that fact, he formulates a bright new plan of his own for faking out a quasi-life for himself: a life as a hired hand. In short, precisely because he cannot admit he is utterly out of business, he puts himself back in the one business that never ceases to amuse and console the lifeless, namely, the bookkeeping business. He strikes a trial balance, using figures he just fudged in, and prepares himself a trumped-up spreadsheet: sonship he may not be able to claim, but hired-handship . . . ah, there's a possibility. Maybe the old man will be senile enough to make a deal. So in one sense, the second death in the parable — the death of the prodigal — occurs in the far country. But in the most important sense, in the sense in which he admits it to himself, it does not occur until he comes home. Watch closely, therefore, the details that Jesus now unfolds. "And he arose, and came to his father. But when he was yet a great way off, his father saw him, and had compassion, and ran, and fell on his neck, and kissed him."

Time for a major pause. All the fearsome histrionics Balanchine assigns the father notwithstanding, this is the moment of grace. But to give Balanchine a little credit, it is, like all the moments of a grace that works by raising the dead, a moment of judgment as well — an uttering of the irrevocable sentence of death before resurrection. From the father's point of view, of course, Balanchine is just plain wrong. The father simply sees this corpse of a son coming down the road and, because raising dead sons to life and throwing fabulous parties for them is his favorite way of spending an afternoon, he proceeds straight to hugs, kisses, and resurrection. But from the son's point of view, Balanchine is onto something. In the clarity of his resurrection, the boy suddenly sees that he is a dead son, that he will always be a dead son, and that he cannot, by any efforts of his own or even by any gift of his father's, become a live anything else. And he understands too that if now, in this embrace, he is a dead son who is alive again, it is all because his father was himself willing to be dead in order to raise him up.

And so he makes his confession for the second time: "Father, I have sinned against heaven, and in thy sight, and am no more worthy to be called thy son." Period. Full stop. No hired-hand nonsense at all. End of the subject insofar as the subject lies in his hands.

Time for a pause within the pause. What this parable is saying first of all is that, as far as Jesus is concerned, repentance involves not the admission of guilt or the acknowledgement of fault but the confession of death. Let me quote from myself in *Between Noon and Three*:

> Confession is not a medicine leading to recovery. If we could recover — if we could say that beginning tomorrow or the week after next we would be well again — why then, all we would need to do would be apologize, not confess. We could simply say that we were sorry about the recent unpleasantness, but that, thank God and the resilience of our better instincts, it is all over now. And we could confidently expect that no one but a real nasty would say us nay.
>
> But we never recover. We die. And if we live again, it is not because the old parts of our life are jiggled back into line, but because, without waiting for realignment, some wholly other life takes up residence in our death. Grace does not do things tit-for-tat; it acts finally and fully from the start. (*Between Noon and Three* [San Francisco: Harper & Row, 1982], p. 77)

And that brings us to the second thing this parable is saying: as far as Jesus is concerned, all real confession — all confession that is not just a fudging of our tattered books but a plain admission that our books are not worth even a damn — is *subsequent to forgiveness*. Only when, like the prodigal, we are finally confronted with the unqualified gift of someone who died, in advance, to forgive us no matter what, can we see that confession has nothing to do with getting ourselves forgiven. Confession is not a transaction, not a negotiation in order to secure forgiveness; it is the after-the-last gasp of a corpse that finally can afford to admit it's dead and accept resurrection. Forgiveness surrounds us, beats upon us all our lives; we confess only to wake ourselves up to what we already have.

Every confession a Christian makes bears witness to this, because every confession, public or private, and every absolution, specific or general, is made and given subsequent to the one baptism we receive for the forgiveness of sins. We are forgiven in baptism not only for the sins committed before baptism but for a whole lifetime of sins yet to come. We are forgiven before, during, and after our sins. We are forgiven before, during, and after our confession of them. And we are forgiven for one reason only: because Jesus died for our sins and rose for our justification. The sheer brilliance of the retention of infant baptism by a large portion of the church catholic is manifest most of all in the fact that babies can do absolutely nothing to earn, accept, or believe in forgiveness; the church, in baptizing them, simply declares that they have it. We are not forgiven, therefore, because we made ourselves forgivable or even because we had faith; we are forgiven solely because there is a Forgiver. And our one baptism for the forgiveness of sins remains the lifelong sacrament, the premier sign of that fact. No subsequent forgiveness — no eucharist, no confession — is ever anything more than an additional sign of what baptism sacramentalizes. Nothing new is ever done, either by us or by God, to achieve anything. It was all done, once and for all, by the Lamb slain from the foundation of the world — by the one God in the Person of the Word incarnate in Jesus. We may be unable, as the prodigal was, to believe it until we finally see it; but the God who does it, like the father who forgave the prodigal, never once had anything else in mind.

All of which takes us straight out of the pause mode and into the party. The father puts no intermediate steps between forgiveness and celebration. There is none of that, "Well, Arthur, you're forgiven; but let's have some good behavior now to make the deal stick" — none of that ungracious talk by which we make the house of forgiveness into a penitentiary. Instead, he turns to his servants and, bent on nothing but the party that life in his house was always meant to be, he commands the festivities to begin: "Bring forth the best robe, and put it on him; and put a ring on his hand, and shoes on his feet: and bring hither the fatted calf, and kill it; and let us eat, and be merry; for this my son was dead, and is alive again; he was lost, and is found."

And there is the third and, if you will, the crucial death in the story: the killing of the fatted calf. Indeed, as far as I am concerned, the fatted calf is actually the Christ-figure in this parable. Consider. What does a fatted calf do? It stands around in its stall with one purpose in life: to drop dead at a moment's notice in order that people can have a party. If that doesn't sound like the Lamb slain from the foundation of the world — who dies in Jesus and in all our deaths and who comes finally to the Supper of the Lamb as the pièce de resistance of his own wedding party — I don't know what does. The fatted calf proclaims that the party is what the father's house is all about, just as Jesus the dead and risen Bridegroom proclaims that an eternal bash is what the universe is all about. Creation is not ultimately about religion, or spirituality, or morality, or reconciliation, or any other solemn subject; it's about God having a good time and just itching to share it. The solemn subjects — all the weird little bells, whistles, and exploding snappers we pay so much attention to — are there only because we are a bunch of dummies who have to be startled into having a good time. If ever once we woke up to the fact that God finally cares only about the party, then the solemn subjects would creep away like pussycats ("Thank God! I thought they'd never leave!") and the truly serious subjects would be brought on: robes, rings, shoes, wines, gold, crystal, and precious stones ("Finally! A little class in the act!").

So now, if we were to sum up the parable thus far, it would be nothing but hilariously good news: the father, the prodigal, and the fatted calf are all dead; they are all three risen (the calf, admittedly, as a veal roast — but then, you can't have everything); and everybody is having a ball. As Jesus put it succinctly: "They began to be merry."

But then comes on (*solemn music:* enter here, in grand procession, the Departments of Ethics and Moral Theology, the Faculty of the School of Religion, the Deans and Trustees of the Law and Business Schools, and the Representatives of the Bursar's Office) the only live character in the parable, the Elder Brother. Mr. Respectability. Herr Buchhalter. Monsieur Comptabilité. The man with volumes and volumes of the records he has kept on himself and everyone else. "And as he came and drew nigh to the house, he heard musick and dancing."

He makes a stagey *contrapposto:* nostrils flared, eyes closed, back of right hand placed against his forehead. He gasps: Music! Dancing! Levity! Expense! And on a working day, yet! "And he called one of the servants, and asked him what these things meant." He is not happy: Why this frivolity? What about the shipments that our customers wanted yesterday? Who's minding the store? "And he [the servant] said unto him, Thy brother is come; and thy father hath killed the fatted calf, because he hath received him safe and sound." He rants: The fatted calf! Doesn't the old fool know I've been saving that for next week's sales promotion when we show our new line of turnips? How am I supposed to run a business when he blows the entertainment budget on that loser of a son? "And he was angry, and would not go in." Finally, therefore, he makes a proclamation: I will not dignify this waste with my presence! Someone has to exercise a little responsibility around here! And Jesus, willing to oblige him with an important audience for all this grousing, sends him one: "Therefore came his father out, and intreated him." It is easy to stray from the main thrust of the parable at this point. The temptation — since the father has been grace personified to the prodigal — is to read his reply to the elder brother's next words as more of the same tender concern. But since grace works only on the dead, that is a false start. This boy's precise problem is that he refuses to be dead, that he is frantically trying to hold what passes for his life in some kind of gimcrack order. Therefore, since grace cannot possibly work on him, the only proper way to read his father's reply is as judgment — as the brandishing before him of the free saving grace of resurrection from the dead, and the condemnation of all his laborious attempts at living. Watch.

"And he answering said to his father, Lo, these many years do I serve thee, neither transgressed I at any time thy commandment: and yet thou never gavest me a kid, that I might make merry with my friends: But as soon as this thy son was come, which hath devoured thy living with harlots, thou hast killed for him the fatted calf." All of which is pure, unsauced, self-serving tripe. Take *"thy living,"* for example: it wasn't the father's living *(bíon)* any more, because the father died to all that life at the beginning of the parable. Or, take *"wasted"*: while it was indeed wasted, it was probably, on balance, less of a waste than the elder brother's boring life of turnip-counting. Or take *"with harlots"*: as for its having been spent on steamy one-night stands with torrid bar pickups . . . well, that may have been the case, but Mr. Upright here probably wasn't getting himself all worked up like this on the basis of hard information about his brother's habits; more likely, he was getting this stuff straight out of his own two-bit sexual fantasies which, with great interest, he made sure he told God about every day. And as for the *"I've* always been a good boy" line, and the "He gets veal but I never even got to eat goat" nonsense. . . . But enough; time to let the father speak in judgment.

"And he said unto him, Son, thou art ever with me, and all that I have is thine."

You little creep! his father says. What do you mean, *my* living? I've been dead since the beginning of this parable! What your brother wasted was his, not mine. And what you've been so smug about *not* wasting has actually been yours all along. Don't bellyache to me. You're in charge here; so cut out the phoney-baloney. If you were really dying for veal, you could have killed the fatted calf for yourself any day of the week. And if you really wanted to be ready to entertain customers at all hours of the day and night, you would have kept a dozen fatted calves on hand, not just a single measly one you have to have a fit over every time it gets cooked. And as far as your brother's sexual behavior is concerned, listen, Mr. Immaculate Twinkletoes, you've got a lot to learn. I have no idea how much fun he had getting himself laid, drunk, and strung out, but even if it was only marginal, it was probably more than you've had sitting here thinking.

But see? the father continues, you even get me off the track. The only thing that matters is that fun or no fun, your brother finally died to all that and now he's alive again — whereas you, unfortunately, were hardly alive even the first time around. Look. We're all dead here and we're having a terrific time. We're all lost here and we feel right at home. You, on the other hand, are alive and miserable — and worse yet, you're standing out here in the yard as if you were some kind of beggar. Why can't you see? You *own* this place, Morris. And the only reason you're not enjoying it is because you refuse to be dead to your dumb rules about how it should be enjoyed. So do yourself and everybody else a favor: drop dead. Shut up, forget about your stupid life, go inside, and pour yourself a drink.

The classic parable of grace, therefore, turns out by anticipation to be a classic parable of judgment as well. It proclaims clearly that grace operates only by raising the dead: those who think they can make their lives the basis of their acceptance by God need not apply. But it proclaims just as clearly that the judgment finally pronounced will be based only on our acceptance or rejection of our resurrection from the dead. The last judgment will vindicate everybody, for the simple reason that everybody will have passed the only test God has, namely, that they are all dead and risen in Jesus. Nobody will be kicked out for having a rotten life, because nobody there will have any life but the life of Jesus. God will say to everybody, "You were dead and are alive again; you were lost and are found: put on a funny hat and step inside."

If, at that happy point, some dumbbell wants to try proving he really isn't dead . . . well, there is a place for such party poopers. God thinks of everything.

CHAPTER FOURTEEN

The Hardest Parable

THE UNJUST STEWARD

The parable of the Unjust Steward (Luke 16:1-13; Aland nos. 222-224) may well be the most difficult of all the parables of Jesus. This story, in which a business manager's crooked attempts to feather his bed after having been fired are first held up for admiration and then made the occasion of obviously critical comments, probably spooks more interpreters into more false starts than any other. Let me list just a few of the devices, desperate and otherwise, that suggest themselves to me as I confront the parable's built-in contradictions.

The first, and worst, is to try to make the whole problem go away by maintaining that Jesus never said these words. This approach — even though it is frequently used to get Jesus off the hook of teaching things his commentators find intellectually disreputable — has two fatal flaws. The first is that there is no way of proving Jesus *didn't* say something when the only source we have says he *did*. Aggressive critics, of course, can always claim they base their conclusions not on other sources but on considerations of "form criticism"; but even for them, the Unjust Steward just sits there in the text stubbornly insisting that Jesus told it. The second flaw in this approach, however, is the really devastating one: if Jesus didn't say this, who did? You might possibly get away with assigning an item like his remarks about divorce and fornication to the hand of some second-century ecclesiastical morality maven, but the Unjust Steward? Derivative minds like that cook up only derivative intellectual concoctions, bland and predictable; they do not produce wildly original dishes like this one.

Admittedly, there is a variation on the "Jesus didn't say it" approach that is less silly — and that is, if you will, more or less inevitable with this parable: I call it the "give Jesus credit for the words but blame every other thing you can on somebody else" gambit. In the case of the Unjust Steward, it works nicely to separate the moralism of the epilogue to the parable from the obviously intended immorality of the parable itself. Here is how you put it into effect.

In your mind's eye, you have Luke sit down at his Gospel-writing desk the morning after he has finished the Prodigal Son, and you have him reach for the pack of index cards containing his so far unused notes on the final journey to Jerusalem. He slips the rubber band off, and what does he find? He finds a whole collection of moralistic bits and pieces about fidelity, covetousness, the law, divorce, scandal, forgiveness, faith, duty, and the coming of the kingdom, plus one miracle (the cleansing of the ten lepers) and four parables: the Unjust Steward, the Rich Man and Lazarus, the Unjust Judge, and the Pharisee and the Publican. How is he to hang all this together? Well, maybe the imagery of the big country house he's just used in the Prodigal Son at the end of chapter 15 can be carried over into the beginning of chapter 16 by starting it off with the Crooked Major Domo story. And then, let's see . . . since that material ends with a crack about unrighteous mammon, maybe he can tuck in some of these scraps about money and trustworthiness and stuff. And then . . . terrific! While he's on the subject, the Rich Man–Poor Beggar story will slide in nicely, and. . . .

But you see the point. He was making an author's decision; and as such choices go, he did remarkably well. His only mistake, probably, was hanging onto all those moral bits and pieces until this late in his Gospel. They sound far more like the early Jesus — the wonder-working rabbi of the Sermon on the Mount — than like Jesus on his way to death and resurrection. And as a matter of fact, when Matthew looked at *his* pack of index cards, he decided that Jesus' warning against trying to serve both God and mammon (Luke 16:13) should, in his own Gospel, go precisely into the Sermon on the Mount at chapter 6, verse 24. In other words, there is actually a textual reason for suspecting that at least the last line of the long version of the Unjust Steward does not necessarily belong to the parable as originally told. So just to lay *my* cards face up for you, here is the way I divide the passage: Luke 16:1-8 is the parable of the Unjust Steward as such; 16:13 is totally extraneous material attracted to this place because of "mammon"; 16:10-12 is possibly extraneous material attracted for the same reason; and 16:9 is the verse that did all the attracting to begin with and therefore the *crux interpretum* of the whole passage. (I am of two minds about whether verse 9 should be considered part of the actual parable. On the one hand, it shouldn't: verse 8 makes a wonderfully crisp, snappy, Jesus-style ending all by itself. On the other hand, there is so little connection between verses 8 and 9 that I sometimes suspect that no one other than Jesus himself would ever have dreamt of putting them back to back. My solution? In months with 31 days, I read the parable as verses 1-8; in months with 30 days, I read it as verses 1-9; on February 29th, I read it as verses 1-13; and for the rest of February, I thank God it really doesn't matter much how *I* read it anyway.)

In any case, it all boils down to the fact that there are basically just two ways of interpreting this parable: you can make the steward out to be a hero or you can make him out to be a villain. Obviously, if you decide to read the parable as verses 1-8, the white-hat interpretation will be your natural choice; but if you read it as verses 1-13, the black hat will seem to fit better. It's worth noting, though, that each interpretation has a price to it. If you make the steward a bad guy, several things don't make sense. In the first place, the heavily moralized parable that that gives you consists ill not only with the preceding parables in Luke but with the entire tone of the final journey to Jerusalem. Jesus has been on a grace trip for seven chapters now: he has been talking lastness, lostness, death, and resurrection, and he has again and again made it clear that the bookkeeping department's heyday is a thing of the past. Why then, at this stage of the game, would he poke in a parable that has none of the above as its main point — that amounts to little more than a surgeon general's warning that "shady dealing is hazardous to your soul's health"? Above all, why on earth would he put into the parable verse 8 ("And the Lord praised the unjust steward because he had acted shrewdly . . .") — a verse which, unless it is taken as pure sarcasm, makes no sense whatsoever if you take the steward as a plain old bounder?

On the other hand, if you make the steward a good guy, verse 8 becomes the principal support for your interpretation — so much so, that you are willing (as I am) to lop off the rest of the passage in order to do justice to its decisiveness. Even at that price, though, the steward-as-hero interpretation seems preferable: it is, as you will see, consonant with the whole thrust of the parables of grace; in particular, it allows the parable to voice once again the theme of forgiveness-by-resurrection-from-the-dead that is the burden of so much of what Jesus has been saying. It even allows you to entertain the most bizarre and fruitful notion of all, namely, that of the unjust steward as Christ-figure. But more of that shortly. Time now to expound the parable in order.

It begins with some nameless informant telling a certain rich man that his steward has been wasting *(diaskorpízōn)* his money *(hypárchonta,* possessions). Score one fascinating point right there for a "grace" rather than a "morality" interpretation of this parable: *diaskorpízein* is the same verb used in the Prodigal Son to describe the boy's "wasting" of his substance in the far country. From Jesus' very choice of words, therefore, we are given a hint of continuity. Next, the master — without any trial or even fair inquiry — simply reads the steward the riot act: "What's this I hear? You're a disgrace! Turn in your books! You're fired!" Score yet another point for continuity: just as with the Prodigal Son, death enters this parable early, and as a pivotal consideration. The son found himself dead in the far country; the steward comes out of his master's office with none of his old life left at all.

But at this point, the parable of the Unjust Steward diverges from the Prodigal Son and begins to look more like an upside-down version of the Unforgiving Servant. Watch. "So the steward said to himself, 'What shall I do now that my master has taken away my managership? I'm not strong enough to work as a laborer. I'm too proud to be a beggar. Aha! I've got it! I'll use my brains and ace out that unforgiving tyrant. So he wants to play letter-of-the-law games, does he? He would like me to turn in my books, eh? Well, I'll do just that — after I've made a few . . . adjustments.'"

What he does, of course, is call in his master's debtors and settle accounts with them at considerable write-offs: he knocks the bill of one of them down by half, the bill of another by a fifth. All of which might produce a number of different results, depending on how you estimate it. On the one hand, it might at one and the same time make him look bad to his master and good to the debtors. If the master ever remembers any of the originally owed amounts he could be so furious over being gypped that the presence of cash in the till would hardly be enough to mollify him. But then, if the debtors thought kindly of the steward's write-offs, they might, as he hoped, "receive him into their houses" after he was officially fired. On the other hand, his sharp dealing could, with even more logic, be read as making him look good to his master and bad to the debtors. For all we know, the master may have been overjoyed to get even fifty cents on the dollar from deadbeats like those. Likewise, for all we know, deadbeats like those could very likely have spotted the steward as no better than themselves and refused to give him office space.

But whichever of those readings or combination of them you decide to go with, the deciding factor remains verse 8: "And the Lord praised the unjust steward, for the children of this age are wiser in their generation than the children of light." Somehow, between verse 2 ("What's this? You're fired!") and verse 8 ("My beamish boy! You're a genius! I never thought I'd see even a nickel from those accounts!"), the master of the steward has turned from an unforgiving bookkeeper to a happy-go-lucky celebrator of any new interest that comes along. And what has happened to him, can, as I have said, be best understood by comparing this parable with that of the Unforgiving Servant.

In that parable, forgiveness starts from the top down: the lord, who is owed ten million dollars by one of his servants, simply drops dead to his own claim and absolves the debt. His intention, of course, is that the servant will take the hint and likewise drop dead to the hundred dollars owed to him by a fellow servant. But as Jesus tells the story, things do not work out that way — the forgiven servant chooses a bookkeeper's life rather than a spendthrift's death and thus short-circuits the working of forgiveness. Still, the point of the parable remains unchanged: grace works only on those it finds dead enough to raise.

Exactly the same point is made in the parable of the Unjust Steward, but by a reversal of the story's device: forgiveness in this parable starts from the bottom up. Here, it is the lord of the steward who starts out unwilling to drop dead to any of his bookkeeping: he will not die to the steward's peculations, and he will not die to the accounts past due that he has never succeeded in collecting. The steward, however, does die; and because he is freed by his death to think things he could not have thought before, he is the one who, from the bottom of the heap, as it were, becomes the agent of life for everybody in the parable. He becomes life from the dead for his lord, because somehow the sight of a loser bringing off a coup like this in the very thick of his losses finally loosens the old boy up: "My God!" the master says. "My whole life has been a joke, and only now I learn to laugh at it!" But the steward is also able to be the resurrection of his lord's debtors because they wouldn't consent to deal with anyone but a crook like themselves: they would never have gone near him if they hadn't been convinced he was dead to all the laws of respectable bookkeeping.

As far as I am concerned, therefore, the unjust steward is nothing less than the Christ-figure in this parable, a dead ringer for Jesus himself. First of all, he dies and rises, like Jesus. Second, by his death and resurrection, he raises others, like Jesus. But third and most important of all, the unjust steward is the Christ-figure because he is a crook, like Jesus. The unique contribution of this parable to our understanding of Jesus is its insistence that grace cannot come to the world through respectability. Respectability regards only life, success, winning; it will have no truck with the grace that works by death and losing — which is the only kind of grace there is.

This parable, therefore, says in story form what Jesus himself said by his life. He was not respectable. He broke the sabbath. He consorted with crooks. And he died as a criminal. Now at last, in the light of this parable, we see why he refused to be respectable: he did it to catch a world that respectability could only terrify and condemn. He became sin for us sinners, weak for us weaklings, lost for us losers, and dead for us dead. *Crux muscipulum diaboli*, St. Augustine said: the cross is the devil's mousetrap, baited with Jesus' disreputable death. And it is a mousetrap for us, too. Jesus baits us criminals with his own criminality: as the shabby debtors in the parable were willing to deal only with the crooked steward and not with the upright lord, so we find ourselves drawn by the bait of a Jesus who winks at iniquity and makes friends of sinners — of us crooks, that is — and of all the losers who would never in a million years go near a God who knew what was expected of himself and insisted on what he expected of others.

You don't like that? You think it lowers standards and threatens good order? You bet it does! And if you will cast your mind back, you will recall that is exactly why the forces of righteousness got rid of Jesus. Unfortunately, though, the church has never been able for very long to leave Jesus looking like the attractively crummy character he is: it can hardly resist the temptation to gussy him up into a respectable citizen. Even more unfortunately, it can almost never resist the temptation to gussy itself up into a bunch of supposedly perfect peaches, too good for the riffraff to sink their teeth into. But for all that, Jesus remains the only real peach — too fuzzy on the outside, nowhere near as sweet as we expected on the inside, and with the jawbreaking stone of his death right smack in the middle. And therefore he is the only mediator and advocate the likes of us will ever be able to trust, because like the unjust steward, he is no less a loser than we are — and like the steward, he is the only one who has even a chance of getting the Lord God to give us a kind word.

"And the lord praised the unjust steward because he had dealt shrewdly": *"This is my beloved Son, hear him"* (Mark 9:7).

"For the children of this world are shrewder in their generation than the children of light": *"And the Word became flesh and dwelt among us . . . full of grace and truth [John 1:14] . . . and his own people did not receive him [John 1:11]. He emptied himself, taking the form of a servant . . . and finding himself merely human, he humbled himself, becoming obedient to death — death on the cross. Therefore God himself exalted him and graced him with a name that is above any other name, so that at the name of Jesus, every knee will bow . . . and every tongue confess that Jesus Christ is Lord, to the glory of God the Father"* (Phil. 2:7-11).

Lucky for us we don't have to deal with a *just* steward.

CHAPTER FIFTEEN

Death and Faith

LAZARUS AND DIVES

There are only two other passages in Luke 16: a short intermezzo containing a diatribe against the Pharisees that occasions some comments about the law and about divorce (verses 14-18; Aland nos. 225-227), and the parable of the Rich Man and the Poor Man (Dives and Lazarus: verses 19-31; Aland no. 228). The parable, as will be seen, slips effortlessly into the thematic flow of the final journey to Jerusalem; but the intervening material (more of those moralistic bits and pieces that Luke delayed inserting into the narrative) needs a bit of nudging to get it into the stream. Watch.

Luke's reason for putting in the passage about the Pharisees at this point seems fairly obvious: its opening verse mentions in passing that they were "lovers of money" *(philárgyroi),* and that they "were making fun" *(exemyktérizon)* of Jesus. After the material about mammon Luke had just added to the parable of the Unjust Steward, these words no doubt struck him as at least marginally consequential, particularly in view of what appears in verse 15. Jesus tells the Pharisees, "You are the ones who make yourselves look right in men's sight, but God knows your hearts. For what is exalted among men is an abomination before God." This last remark returns Luke neatly to some of the major themes of Jesus' Jerusalem journey: human respectability as contrasted with the divine disreputability and successful living as an ineffective substitute for the lastness and lostness that alone can save. It brings him back, in short, to the subject of "life" as the chief impediment to the resurrection of the dead.

Then, because the Pharisees were nothing if not devotees of the law, Luke finds that some of Jesus' words about John the Baptist and the law will fit in at verse 16: "The law and the prophets [the whole previous revelation of God] were in effect up to the time of John; since then, the kingdom of God is proclaimed as good news and everyone enters into it violently." Once again, Luke is on target: it is not success of any kind that saves — not even success in keeping the law; it is only the violent disruption of all success proclaimed by the Gospel of death and resurrection that can lead to true life in the kingdom.

Finally, though, Luke is confronted with two bits of material whose relevance at this point seems vague to say the least. He includes, at verses 17 and 18, the words "It is easier for heaven and earth to pass away than for the smallest detail of law to be done away with. Every one who puts away his wife and marries another commits adultery; and he who marries a woman thus put away, also commits adultery." I can, I think, give a fairly simple rationale for the inclusion of verse 17: it is one of those "if you take the sword, you will perish by the sword" utterances. Jesus, after stigmatizing the Pharisees' reliance on successful law-keeping, simply reminds them — as Paul was to do at length in Romans and Galatians — that the law is not the great, smiling friend they think it is. Since its demands remain perpetually holy, just, and good — and since we are none of those things — the law can only condemn those who rely on their keeping of it to save them.

I am less sanguine, however, about verse 18. Frankly, I think the only reason it appears here is that Jesus, for his own reasons, actually said these words at this point in his ministry (Matthew and Mark also include them in roughly the same time period). In the other two synoptics, they come as part of a response to a question about "putting away a wife" proposed to Jesus by Pharisees; hence they do not seem as "off the wall" as they do in Luke. Accordingly, the question becomes: what conceivable rationale did Luke have for thinking they formed a logical sequence to the verses that precede them? Certainly, there is no way of taking them, in their Lukan context, as *ex professo* teaching about matrimony: that would leave them not only off the wall but totally out of the universe of discourse. All I can conclude is that Luke tucked them in as an illustration of one of the things about the law that so easily condemns. Consider. The Pharisees thought that with a little logic-chopping about "putting away" and "bills of divorcement" they could remarry and still be successful lawkeepers. Jesus simply reminds them that the law's dictate about marriage making two people "one flesh" still stands and thus condemns them as failures. Note, however, that in this verse he does not condemn their failure as much as he does their pointless attempts at success. There is a lesson here for the church: if we are serious about proclaiming a grace that works precisely in failure, collapse, and death, we ought to be charier than we are about excluding matrimonial failure, collapse, and death from the ecclesiastical dispensation of grace. Excommunicating divorced persons on the basis of this passage is a mischievous missing of the very point that Luke makes by including it in this unusual place.

As I said, though, the parable of Dives and Lazarus (Luke 16:19-31) needs no arm-twisting to make it consistent with the larger context of Jesus' teaching at this juncture. It adduces not only the themes of death and resurrection but also those of lastness, lostness, leastness, and littleness; and it also adumbrates — as did the parables of the Prodigal Son and the Unjust Steward — the theme of judgment that will be the burden of Jesus' later parables. Specifically, it enshrines all these themes in a telling story about the contrast between rich and poor. Living well may be the world's idea of the best revenge, and it is certainly the human race's commonest criterion for distinguishing the saved from the lost. But in the mystery of the kingdom, it is precisely living badly — being poor and hungry and covered with repulsive sores — that turns out to be the true vehicle of saving grace. Even a minute's consideration will serve to make that clear.

As I have observed a number of times now, if the world could have been saved by successful living, it would have been tidied up long ago. Certainly, the successful livers of this world have always been ready enough to stuff life's losers into the garbage can of history. Their program for turning earth back into Eden has consistently been to shun the sick, to lock the poor in ghettos, to disenfranchise those whose skin was the wrong color, and to exterminate those whose religion was inconvenient. Nor have they been laggard in furthering that program. On the whole, they have been not only zealous but efficient: witness, to name only a handful of instances, the AIDS crisis, the South Bronx, the apartheid policy in South Africa, and the death camps under Hitler.

But for all that, Eden has never returned. The world's woes are beyond repair by the world's successes: there are just too many failures, and they come too thick and fast for any program, however energetic or well-funded. Dives, for all his purple, fine linen and faring sumptuously, dies not one whit less dead than Lazarus. And before he dies, his wealth no more guarantees him health or happiness than it does exemption from death. Therefore when the Gospel is proclaimed, it stays light-years away from reliance on success or on any other exercise of right-handed power. Instead, it relies resolutely on left-handed power — on the power that, in a mystery, works through failure, loss, and death. And so while our history is indeed saved, its salvation is not made manifest in our history in any obvious, right-handed way. In God's time — in that *kairós,* that due season, that *high time* in which the Incarnate Word brings in the kingdom in a mystery — all our times are indeed reconciled and restored *now.* But in *our* time — in the *chrónos,* the sequential order of earthly events, the *low time* of days, years, centuries, and millennia — the shipwreck of history drags on unchanged and unchangeable *now.* And the only bridge between the *now* in which our times are triumphantly in his hand and the *now* in which they are so disastrously in our own is *faith.* The accomplished reconciliation can only be believed; it cannot be known, felt, or seen — and it cannot, by any efforts of ours, however good or however successful, be rendered visible, tangible, or intelligible. Like the servants in the parable of the Wheat and the Weeds, we can only let both the reconciliation and the wreckage grow together until the harvest — until the judgment in which the resurrection finally displays God's time as victorious over ours and allows history to become the party it always tried but never managed to be.

In a way, I feel like apologizing for coming at Dives and Lazarus backwards like this — for putting the cart of the meaning of the parable

313

before the horse of the parable itself, but let it stand. At least you will know where I'm going as I take up the details of the story.

Jesus begins the parable (which appears only in Luke) without preface or explanation. There was a certain rich man, he says, who had a very good life indeed: handmade suits, custom-tailored shirts, a daily menu not a notch below *Lutèce,* and, presumably, a portfolio to bankroll the whole operation indefinitely. Like Nubar Gulbenkian, the legendary financier, he wore out three women, three horses, and three stockbrokers before noon every day.

But outside the heavily guarded gate of Nubar's chateau (shall we call the unnamed rich man Nubar instead of Dives? Let's — just for fun) there was a certain poor man named Lazarus who was covered with sores and rummaged in the garbage for food. Jesus says the dogs came and licked his sores. Those were no doubt Nubar's children's cocker spaniels; Nubar's dobermans probably took delight in forcibly reminding Lazarus of just whose garbage he was rummaging in.

In any case, the poor man died and was carried by the angels to the bosom of Abraham; Nubar, finally worn out himself in spite of Brooks Brothers and French cooking, died and was buried; and the scene, as in so many of the best old jokes, shifts to the hereafter. From hell, where the accommodations are well below his accustomed standards, Nubar sees Abraham and Lazarus enjoying an intimate little chat. And he cries out for Abraham to have pity on him and send Lazarus with a nice, cool Campari and soda to take the curse off the infernal heat. Like the Bourbons, Nubar has learned nothing and forgotten nothing. Send Lazarus, indeed! He still thinks of himself as a winner who by divine right can command lackeys like this beggar to fetch him drinks.

So Abraham carefully explains to him the realities of the situation. One: Nubar had a whole lifetime's worth of good things while Lazarus was up to his eyebrows in misery. Two: just in case he hasn't noticed, things have definitely been reversed; score at the end of this last game of his heretofore winning season: Nubar, zero; Lazarus, one thousand. And three: the rules of the league are such that, far from being able to demand overtime in which to even the score, he isn't even going to be allowed to punt. Between us and you, Abraham tells him, there is a great gulf fixed: it's fourth down and ten million yards to go, Nubar. I don't make the rules here, I just call the plays as I see them. The game is over.

Nubar, however, never once having had to take no for an answer in his whole life — never having been at a loss for some way of making a buck out of even the most unpromising situation — falls back on his winner's instincts. Maybe Abraham will give him at least a brownie point if he does a *mitzvah* and arranges to have Lazarus deliver a singing telegram to his five equally rich brothers warning them about the possible disastrous consequences of their present investment programs. Abraham, though, is unenthusiastic. Having Lazarus schlep all over the Middle East ringing doorbells is just another of Nubar's bossy, "when you care enough, send a lackey" ideas. Besides, why should Abraham interrupt the resurrection tête-à-tête he's having, when none of the brothers will listen to advice anyway? Listen, Nubar, he says. They've already had a whole Bibleful of telegrams; they should get them out of the wastebasket and try reading them.

But Nubar, not to be defeated, comes up with one last, desperate play: if he can't make a commercial buck, he'll make a spiritual one. Speaking of resurrection, he says to Abraham, you folks up there are missing out on a good thing. You send Lazarus to my brothers, and guaranteed, you'll get results. This would not be your ordinary phone-it-in message; this would be in-person-from-the-other-side-of-the-grave service. Believe me, Nubar says, I know what impresses a client.

So Abraham takes a deep breath and delivers the punch line of the parable. Look, Nubar, he says. I'm going to tell you something. When we talk resurrection up here, we're not talking about some dumb, corpse-revival scheme in which the dead get up and go back to the same old life they had before. We're talking about a whole new order that actually works through death, loss, and failure. And in order to give people even a hint of that, the one thing we don't do is send back revived corpses. The way we've got it worked out, even when the incarnate Word himself gets raised from the dead, he only hangs around for forty days: then . . . pffft! Because you know what would happen if we left him there? They'd never in a million years get the idea that the resurrec-

315

tion was a new order they could get in touch with only by faith — only by *trusting* it; instead, they'd figure it was just one more funny wrinkle in the grimy face of history and they'd try to sell it as something that was merely interesting — as news, for crying out loud! If we left the risen Word on earth, they'd right away get him on *Good Morning America* and *Sixty Minutes,* then on *Carson* and *Donahue* — and then, for all I know, on *Hollywood Squares.* After that, probably, it would be *Jesus, The Movie,* followed by *Jesus, I through VI.* They're dumb, Nubar. Dumb, dumb, dumb. Just like you. So this is how it stands. Your brothers have Moses and the prophets, and they'll also get the risen and ascended Word. That's enough for anybody who's willing to *believe.* But for people who are hanging around, waiting to be *convinced* . . . Listen, Nubar; I'm sorry, but we've got a bad connection here. Must be the great gulf. I'm hanging up.

But enough. Death-resurrection stands forth as clearly in this parable as it does in any of the others. And the successful life is just as roundly condemned. Lazarus starts out as a loser, plays out his allotted hand, and then, in one stunning throw, wins the game with the last trump of an accepted death. Dives starts out as a winner, but because he never accepts death (witness his incessant *handeling* with Abraham, his cooking up of one life-saving deal after another), he loses, hands down. Jesus is anticipating the parable of the Pharisee and the Publican here. In that story, too, both main characters are dead: the difference between them is simply that while the publican accepts his death and is justified, the Pharisee rejects his and is condemned.

And the ending of the parable of Dives and Lazarus makes this point once and for all: "If they will not hear Moses and the prophets, neither will they be persuaded, though one rose from the dead." For those convinced that living is the instrument of salvation, death is such an unacceptable device that they will not be convinced, even by resurrection. From the point of view of those who object to the left-handedness of the Gospel, you see, Jesus' mistake was not his rising in an insufficiently clear way and then sailing off into the clouds. That, if anything, was only a tactical error. His great, strategic miscalculation was dying in the first place: after such a grievous capitulation to

316

lastness and loss, no self-respecting winner could even think of doing business with him.

It is not, of course, that we are to run out and actively seek a miserable life like Lazarus's. Contrary to the misreading of the spiritual advice of earlier centuries (for example, the go-hunt-for-trouble interpretation of Donne's "Be covetous of crosses, let none fall"), we are not to go searching for loathsome diseases and rotten breaks. Life in this vale of tears will provide an ungenteel sufficiency of such things (witness Keble's, "The trivial round, the common task/Will furnish all we ought to ask"). The truth, rather, is that the crosses that will inexorably come — and the death that will inevitably result from them — are, if accepted, all we need. For Jesus came to raise the dead. He did not come to reward the rewardable, improve the improvable, or correct the correctible; he came simply to be the resurrection and the life of those who will take their stand on a death he can use instead of on a life he cannot.

And so Lazarus is the Christ-figure in this parable. Like Jesus, he lives out of death. For those willing to trust the left-handed working of God already disclosed in the law and the prophets (it is the passion of Israel, not its success, that is the *leitmotiv* of Scripture), the mere assertion of Lazarus's triumph, like the mere proclamation of Jesus' resurrection, is all the evidence they are going to get. For those who are unwilling to make a decision to trust such a proposition, however, nothing will be enough to persuade them. But then, that was obvious all along: because like Dives, they will always be in the untenable position of insisting on *something* in a universe where it is precisely out of *nothing* (at the end as well as at the beginning) that God brings all things into life and being.

Death, you see, is absolutely all of the resurrection we can now know. The rest is faith.

CHAPTER SIXTEEN

The Scandal of the Gospel

THE RETURNING SERVANT, THE TEN LEPERS, AND THE VULTURES

In chapter 17 of his Gospel (Aland nos. 229-235), Luke continues stitching in the remaining bits of material — many of them parabolic in nature, if not actually parables in their own right — that he has marked for inclusion in Jesus' final journey to Jerusalem. At first glance, it looks like mere patchwork, one small pericope following another with no particular design; but on closer examination, I find it to be as consistent a tissue of lastness, littleness, and death as any of the preceding chapters.

He begins (Luke 17:1-2) with Jesus' saying that "It is inevitable that *skándala* will come, but woe to the one by whom they come. It would be better for him if a millstone were hung around his neck and he were cast into the sea than that he should *skandalísę* one of these little ones." Obviously, the crucial word here is *skándala*: scandals, causes of offense, temptations to sin, things that make people fall into sin. I have deliberately left it untranslated in order to allow the context to dictate its meaning.

In many of the root word's uses in the New Testament, *skándalon* (and its verb form, *skandalízein*) refers simply to something that occasions sin or temptation. Look, for example, at Matt. 13:41 (in Jesus' interpretation of the parable of the Wheat and the Weeds), where it is said that "the Son of man will send his angels . . . and they will gather out of

318

his kingdom all the *skándala,* along with those who do lawless things."
See also Matt. 16:23 (right after Peter's confession and Jesus' first prediction of his death and resurrection), where Jesus replies to Peter's refusal to listen to this death-talk by saying "Get behind me, Satan; you
are a *skándalon* to me." On other occasions, however, the word is used to
refer to what Paul, in Gal. 5:11, calls "the *skándalon* of the cross,"
namely, the weakness, foolishness, and general offensiveness of the left-
handed method of salvation at work in the death and resurrection of Jesus. This usage also occurs not only in Rom. 9:33, "I will set in Zion a
stone of stumbling and a rock of *skandálou*" (he is referring to the dead
and risen Christ), but also in Rom. 11:9, "Let their table [Israel, that is,
in their rejection of the dying/rising Messiah] be to them . . . a snare and
a *skándalon,*" as well as in 1 Cor. 1:22-23, "the Jews seek a sign and the
Greeks, wisdom; but we preach Christ crucified, to the Jews a *skándalon*
and to the Greeks, foolishness."

The question comes therefore: in which of these two senses — as a
general *occasion of stumbling* or as the specific *offensiveness of Jesus' left-
handed salvation* — is the word *skándalon* used in this passage and in its
parallels at Matt. 18:6 and Mark 9:42? To my mind, the answer has to
be the latter sense. I am persuaded of that by the inclusion, in all three
places, of the concluding reference to *scandalizing* "one of these little
ones." Once again, we are back at the saving littleness — the lostness
and the lastness that Jesus continually contrasts to the pointless pursuit of greatness and the vain effort to win that characterizes the
world's efforts to save itself. Taken in context, therefore, what this passage says is that the scandal of the cross is inescapable: it would be
better for someone to meet a violent end than to be guilty of making
one of these "little ones" — one, that is, who already has a grip on the
operative device of grace — think that his littleness is itself a *skándalon,*
an occasion of failure to be avoided rather than embraced.

That much established, the rest of the section (Luke 17:3-10)
makes eminently consistent sense. Verses 3 and 4, about forgiving a repentant brother even if he sins against you seven times a day (a variant
on the preface to the parable of the Unforgiving Servant in Matt. 18),
turn out to be about the same subject as that parable, namely, the truth

that only those willing to lose can ever really win: if you insist on being a success and on admitting only certifiable moral successes into your circle of friends, you are simply going to be out of luck as far as the process of salvation is concerned.

Verses 5 and 6 likewise become consequential. The apostles say to Jesus, "Increase our faith." They sense, apparently, that he is inviting them yet again to adopt an outlook on life that is contrary to all their right-handed notions of how life ought to be lived. They hear, in these remarks about saving littleness and unlimited, life-laying-down forgiveness, a command to act contrary to all their normal instincts. And they conclude, quite naturally, that they haven't got the spiritual resources to sustain such a program. Jesus' reply, though, is a shocker. In spite of the fact that his words ("If you had faith as big as a mustard seed, you could say to this mulberry tree, 'Pull yourself up by the roots and plant yourself in the sea,' and it would obey you") have been given all kinds of "make-a-greater-spiritual-effort" interpretations, they seem on balance to mean just the opposite. The apostles ask for more faith; Jesus tells them that if they had even less than they have now (faith "like a mustard seed" has got to be very little faith) the preposterous and the impossible would seem as easy as pie and as sensible as shoes.

He tells them, in other words, that even when it comes to faith, they don't have to be winners. One of the most iniquitous ways of expounding the Gospel is to say that while we will no doubt have to put up with physical or financial failure for Jesus' sake, we are nonetheless entitled to expect moral and spiritual success. But that is itself a snare and a *skándalon*. It says that we are only half fallen — that even though the ratty old cocoon of our physical being may fail us, there is hidden within it a spiritual butterfly of a soul that is capable of beauty, competence, and success. And it usually goes on to add that what we need to actualize all that gorgeousness is not a redeemer who dies — not a paradoxical savior who expects us too, physically *and* spiritually, body *and* soul, to die with him — but only a guide, a teacher, a guru, a dispenser of some slick, esoteric *gnósis* who will, with no death at all, enable us to realize our potential as spiritual beings.

Don't get me wrong. I am not against saying that the realization of

320

our spiritual potential is one of the promises of Christ; I just want to add two footnotes to what spiritual fast-talkers usually have to say on the subject. The first is that the Gospel holds up before us the promise of a realization of our physical potential as well: as we maintain in the creed, we believe in the resurrection of the *body* — of the *flesh*. The second is that whether we hope for physical *or* spiritual perfection, the Gospel promises us neither except by death and resurrection. Golgotha and the empty tomb are not just some guru's shtick. They are not the incidental stage business of a swami's mock exit into some blue empyrean we all have inside us anyway. They are, in and as themselves, the very sacrament — the real presence — of the unique mystery of salvation. And no man or woman — however burdensomely physical or magnificently spiritual — comes to the Father except by him who died on the cross and rose from the grave.

So but me no spiritual buts. And above all, faith me no faith that needs to be made greater, or purer, or warmer. It is not as if we have a faith meter in our chests, and that our progress toward salvation consists in cranking it up over a lifetime from cold to lukewarm to toasty to red hot. We cannot be saved by our faith reading any more than by our morality reading or our spirituality reading. All of those recipes for self-improvement amount to nothing more than salvation by works; and none of them is any better than the idea that you might be saved by being able to go twenty hours nonstop on a Nautilus machine. If we have anything in our chests, it is not a metaphysical pulse register or an ethical pressure gauge but a simple switch: *on,* for *yes* to Jesus in our death; and *off,* for *no.* The head of steam we work up in throwing the switch, either way, has nothing to do with the case.

As a matter of fact, I am willing to push my interpretation of "faith like a mustard seed" all the way to an absurdity that matches Jesus' absurdity of the mulberry tree jumping into the ocean. Even faith is not the essential thing. Even if your switch is off — even if you say no to Jesus all your life, and forever after as well — you still die; and out of your death, Jesus still raises you. *That* is how the universe works, not by the endless refinement of spiritual gas. "I, if I be lifted up, will draw *all* to myself": he gets every last one of us, willy-nilly. True enough, we will never enjoy the eternal Supper of the Lamb unless we say yes to it: unless we put on the wedding garment of our acceptance of his acceptance of us, we will spend eternity gnashing our teeth in the darkness outside the party. But the party remains unpoopable: the precise hell of hell is that even if we never go back into the wedding reception, his endless, nagging invitation to the celebration will beat forever like hailstones on our thick, self-condemned heads.

I apologize for all that time on faith like a mustard seed — but not very seriously, because of the verses that follow. In Luke 17:7-10, Jesus ties off the threads of this tissue of littleness and leastness with a demi-parable. Just to make sure the apostles understand clearly that they must not turn faith into a work, he sets them a mental exercise. Suppose, he says, one of you has a slave who comes in from twelve hours hard labor in the field. What do you say to him? Have a seat, Mischa, and let me get you some chopped liver and a little chicken soup? You do not! You say, Mischa, rattle those pots and pans and serve me some supper; then you can eat. And do you thank him when he does it? You do not! It was his job. Remember that the next time you want some kind of super faith or expect me to be super happy because you think you've got it. You've got only one job to do and that's to drop dead for me. That's all I need from you, because everything else that needs doing, *I* do. And I'm not going to thank you for what you do, or reward you for what you achieve, because no matter how nifty any of it may be, it's all useless for my purposes — all tainted, like even your faith, with your boring commitment to winning. I'm just going to come to you in your death, and raise you up with my life, and then say, Mischa, c'mon up here with Arthur and Lazarus and all the rest and let's you and me have a ball.

In any case, the next thing that Luke records is Jesus' cleansing of ten lepers (Luke 17:11-19). The time and place of the action are given only loosely: the healing takes place "on the way to Jerusalem" at the outskirts of "a certain village" somewhere "between Samaria and Galilee." Luke puts the story here, I think, because he reads it as an *acted* parable illustrating the same general points that Jesus' spoken parables have been making: it is about losers who, because of their ostracizing affliction, were dead to ordinary social life; and it is about the fact that resurrection from the dead cannot be recognized, let alone be enjoyed, except on the basis of the acceptance of death.

The episode, however, has a number of twists and turns in it. Ten lepers, standing well away from Jesus as they were supposed to, call out, "Jesus, Master, have mercy on us." He looks at them, and then tells them to go and "show themselves to the priests." This is the first twist. Jesus is referring to Lev. 14:2-3 — a passage that specifies the ceremonies for the removal of *ritual* defilement from a leper who is already physically clean. In other words, he is telling them — while they are still lepers, still losers, still dead to ordinary life — to act as if they were healed and no longer outcasts. They, however, say nothing; they simply go. Luke leaves it unclear whether they took Jesus seriously and were on their way to the priests, or just went away in confusion over such a bizarre reply to their plea for mercy. Whichever it was, though, "as they went, they were healed." Nine of them, of course, just kept going. Apparently, they made no connection between Jesus' "spacey" reply and their recovery. This is the second twist in the story; and it's hard to blame them for what they did. From their point of view, Jesus didn't do anything like what they may have had in mind: no touching, no commanding words, not even the simple "I will; be healed" that he used at other times. For them to have concluded that Jesus himself was responsible for their cleansing was no easy matter of putting two and two together: their leprosy was a *two* and their healing, a *four;* but where the other *two* came from was not at all clear.

The tenth leper, though, when he sees that he is healed, comes back loudly praising God and falls at Jesus' feet, saying, Thank you, thank you, thank you. "And he," Luke says, "was a Samaritan." Which makes twist number three: this man is a twofold outcast, a double loser, a duck twice dead. But Jesus' reply to him is no less perplexing than anything else in the story so far: he says (to the bystanders, it appears, not to the leper), "Hey, weren't there ten who were healed? Where are the other nine? How come we can't find anybody who came back and thanked God except this foreigner?" Only then, finally, does he speak to the Samaritan himself. "Get up and go," he says; "your faith has saved you."

What are we to make of this? The nine, who presumably had no such faith as the Samaritan, were not one bit less healed than he. What difference is Jesus trying to pinpoint between him and them with this terse, if not gruff, reply? Well, I can think of two ways of coming at it, one more or less doctrinal and the other based on the parable of the Prodigal Son.

The doctrinal approach looks at the lepers as an illustration of the resurrection of the dead: just as *all* the dead (not merely the just, the holy, and the good) are raised by Jesus, so all the lepers (not just the perceptive and thankful) are cleansed. But for the lepers to enjoy, to accept, to celebrate the power of their resurrection from the disease . . . well, that cannot happen until they see themselves not simply as returned to normal life by some inexplicable circumstance but precisely as lepers cleansed by Jesus — that is, as living out of their death by the gift of someone else's life. So too with the resurrection of the dead: it is not the return of corpses to their previous living state; it is an eternally new creation arising out of an equally eternal *death* — just as, if you will, our old, natural existence is a perpetual, moment-by-moment emergence out of an equally perpetual *nothing*.

Which brings me to the approach based on the Prodigal Son. The nine lepers in this story are like the son when he formulates the first version of his confession to his father. Like him — as he sits by the hog trough in the far country — they realize they are dead. But also like him, their idea of resurrection is just a matter of revival, of return to some form of ordinary life. The prodigal makes plans to get himself hired on as a servant; the nine lepers, possibly, propose to go back to the garment district and find work as pressers.

The Samaritan leper, however, is like the prodigal when he makes his confession the second time and leaves off the part about "make me a hired servant." For just as the prodigal suddenly sees — when his father kisses him *before* he confesses — that he can only be a dead son who has been raised to a new life, not a hired hand trying to fake out an old-style life of his own, so the Samaritan realizes that it is by his relationship to Jesus, and by that alone, that he now has a new life out of death as a leper. It is not, you see, that either of them is told to forget about the death out of which he has been raised, or to put it behind him, or to "get on with his life." That was what the nine lepers, and the prodigal in his first self-examination, had in mind — and it is, unfortunately, what far too many Christians think about their risen life in Jesus. But the prodigal's startlingly new life (Party! Party! Party!) is, by the very words of the parable, based squarely and only on his death ("Let us eat and be merry: for this my son was dead and is alive again"). Death, in other words, remains the perpetual reason for the party and the abiding ground of the new creation — for the prodigal, for the Samaritan leper, and for us.

And what a gift that is! It means that contrary to all the cartoons of heaven as a place where we shall sit on clouds wearing bedsheets and flapping irrelevant angel wings — as a place, that is, where none of our real history, and certainly none of the diseases, defeats, derelictions, and deaths of our history can find a home — contrary to all that, *everything* about us goes home, because everything about us, good or evil, dies in our death and rises by his life. The son's prodigality goes home, the Samaritan's leprosy goes home; and so does your lying, my adultery, and Uncle Harry's embezzling. We never have to leave behind a scrap! Nothing, not even the worst thing we ever did, will ever be anything but a glorious scar.

And that *is* a gift, because it means we don't have to deny one smitch of our history. The nine lepers go away with their lives unsaved precisely because their lives as lepers have been put behind them and denied. All those years . . . just *gone* — into unsalvageable oblivion, into irretrievable discontinuity: "Who, me? A leper? You must be kidding, buddy. I'm a pants presser." But the Samaritan goes away with his life saved because, like the prodigal, he has not put his derelict life into the forgettery. At Jesus' feet he sees himself whole: dead *and* risen, an outcast *and* accepted, a leper *and* cleansed. And he sees himself that way because, like the prodigal, he has not hated the light and he has not lived the lie of trying to keep his wretchedness away from the light; rather he has *done the truth* (John 3:21), and *come to the light* with the whole sum of his life, so that it might be clearly seen, in the light of Jesus' resurrection, that everything he ever did, good or bad, *was done in God.*

And just to round out this rhapsody of death and resurrection — of the saving, rather than the trashing, of our history — Luke puts in, as the concluding section of chapter 17, Jesus' longish reply to a short question from the Pharisees. Why this apocalyptic material, and why here? Well, because it follows logically: presumably, the Pharisees have been part of Jesus' audience since at least Luke 16:14; and they have been less than happy with all his mumbo jumbo about the lost, the little, and the dead. "Enough with these paradoxes!" they say. "Let's get this show on a road we can understand. Tell us, Master, in twenty-five words or less: *When will the kingdom of God come?*" (Luke 17:20).

They don't, of course, get what they asked for. Instead, they get still more paradox and mystery. "The kingdom of God," Jesus says, "does not come in such a way as to be seen [*metá paratēréseōs,* with watching]. Nobody's going to say, 'Here it is!' or 'There it is!' Because from what I've been saying, it should be obvious to you that the kingdom of God is *already here in your midst* [*entós hymón:* among you, or within you] — hidden, that is, in your lostness and death."

Then, turning to the disciples who are going to have to peddle this mystery after he's dead, risen, and ascended, Jesus tries to give them a bit more of a handle on it. "The days are coming," he says, "when you will absolutely ache [*epithymésete,* desire strongly] to see one of the days of the Son of man, but there won't be anything to see. You may have an overpowering urge to point to something, anything, that might be a visible proof that I have some more marketable plan than the apparent do-nothing-nowhere-nohow program I've given you to sell; but in fact I have no other plan. And the program I do have will not, *in your time,* give you a shred of evidence other than your faith to offer the world. So everyone else will have a field day running around and shouting, 'Look! *There's* the action of God, right over there in Scranton, PA,' or '*Here's* where the action is, right here on this wonderful TV healing show brought to you live from the diving board of the original pool of Siloam.' But when they start that nonsense, for God's sake don't go running after them or follow their example, because it's not going to be like that at all. Actually, the coming of the Son of man will be more like lightning: sort of everywhere at once, lighting up the whole world — not just Scranton or somebody's swimming pool."

"But first," Jesus says, "the Son of man is going to suffer a lot and be rejected by everybody." You know what it's going to be like? he says to them. It's going to be like it was in the days of Noah. Noah was one of the first to be in on the mystery of death and resurrection, but people paid no attention whatsoever to him. He was a sign that the whole world was going down the drain of death and that God had plans to use that death to save it; but they wouldn't think about anything but their precious little lives, their two-bit plans for the season. They had dinner parties to go to, weddings to plan, swimming pools to get the algae out of. And they went right on doing all that, clear up to the very day that Noah got into the ark and the flood came and destroyed them all. The same thing was true in the days of Lot in Sodom. Everybody just went crazily on, living for all they were worth, until the fire and brimstone came pouring down on them from the sky.

Don't you see? Jesus asks them. The message I'm sending you out to proclaim is that death is safe for those who trust in me; but for those who are committed only to what they call "life" . . . well, they just can't accept that. So when the Son of man is finally revealed — when my hidden working in the deaths of the world is made manifest at the last day — all those folks are going to be very unhappy. Still, since I'm going to raise them all anyway, they'll always have a shot, as long as they're willing to cut out the "life" malarkey and accept death and resurrection. For instance. If somebody's up on the roof replacing shingles and he sees me risen from the dead, he should definitely not go down into the house to get his Visa card and splash on a little cologne. And if somebody's out plowing the south forty, he shouldn't go back to the old homestead and finish his tax return. Remember Lot's wife: when the action was finally out in the open and it was time for her to go with the flow, she decided to have a nostalgia binge and look back at the scene of all her lovely alfresco suppers with the Sodom social set. What did it get her? It got her turned into a pillar of salt, that's what. So keep her in mind: you try to save your life like that and all you'll do is lose it. But if you're willing to go with the action in my death and yours — which is the only action in town — you'll get your life back in spades. But I'll tell you something. It's not going to be easy for people to accept that, and it certainly won't be easy for you to figure out why one person buys it and another doesn't. You'll see two buddies on a hunting trip zipped into the same sleeping bag: one of them will say yes to death and resurrection and one of them will say no. You'll see two women having a nice kaffeeklatsch in a sunny kitchen: one of them will go for the deal, the other will say she has to think about it forever.

But now Jesus makes up for his long answer to a short question with the punch line of the whole chapter. The disciples — just as confused by all this as the Pharisees — come back at him with the very same question. "But *where*, Lord?" they ask. And Jesus says, "Where the corpse is, that's where the vultures will congregate."

Of all the big-help, thank-you-for-nothing answers Jesus ever gave, this one takes the cake. At least it seems to until you see it in the light of my paraphrase of Luke 17:20-36: then it becomes as clear as . . . lightning. Because when you take that whole passage as a rhapsody on death, his words about corpses and vultures say only one thing. Jesus says to them in effect, Don't worry about *where* when it comes to resurrection: you put a dead sheep anywhere, and the vultures will find it. Don't you see what that means? You can put the dead of the world anywhere — some of them even in Scranton — and the Son of man will zero in on every last one. The dead are my *dish*, kiddies. They're where I work. Raising them is what I *do*. The living, unfortunately, I can't do much for; but the nice thing is that even they're not a total loss. Because even they die sooner or later and . . . well, as I said, wherever the corpses are, this old vulture's going to find them and raise them up.

So skip all the *where* business, Jesus concludes, and forget about the *how* and the *when* part too. All that matters is that you trust me to do the job, and that you get yourselves out there beating the bushes and inviting everybody else to trust me too. It really is all safe, you know: nobody's got anything to lose but a life that's a loser anyway. Where there's death, there's hope.

Death — to say it once again — is absolutely all of the resurrection we can now know. The rest is faith.

CHAPTER SEVENTEEN

God as Anti-hero

THE UNJUST JUDGE

The last two parables of grace I shall deal with in this book are Jesus' stories of the Unjust Judge (Luke 18:1-8; Aland no. 236) and the Pharisee and the Publican (Luke 18:9-14; Aland no. 237). For two reasons. First and simplest, Luke 18:14 is the point at which the Aland chronology leaves the Lukan account of the last journey to Jerusalem and switches back to Matthew for the account of Jesus' final ministry in Judea before Palm Sunday. But more important than that, Jesus' gradual shift from the theme of grace to that of judgment has now become pronounced enough to warrant tying off the parables of grace as such.

Admittedly, my choice of these two parables as the place for the final knot is a bit arbitrary: the note of grace will continue to sound for a while after this point, and the theme of judgment has already been introduced before it. Grace, for example — with its operative devices of lastness, lostness, littleness, and death — will still be featured in passages yet to come: in Jesus' blessing of little children (Matt. 19:13-15), in the acted parable of the Rich Young Man (Matt. 19:16-30), in the Laborers in the Vineyard (Matt. 20:1-16), in the acted parable of the Raising of Lazarus (John 11), and in Jesus' third prediction of his passion and death (Matt. 20:17-19). But by the same token, judgment has been an element in his parables since at least chapter 14 of Luke: the Great Banquet, the Prodigal Son, the Unjust Steward, Dives and Lazarus, the acted parable of the Cleansing of the Ten Lepers, and the discourse on the coming of the kingdom — all of which I have already dealt with in chapters twelve through sixteen above — have judgment as a notable sub-theme. Between the Aland chronology and the co-presence of the two themes, therefore — not to mention the already considerable length of this volume — I feel reasonably justified in my decision to make an end after just two more parables.

The Unjust Judge, like the Good Samaritan and the Unjust Steward, is another notable example of Jesus' use of an anti-hero. Never having been to a theological seminary, he was blessedly free of the professional theologian's fear of using bad people as illustrations of the goodness of God. There is an old seminarians' joke that stigmatizes this don't-let-God-be-disreputable attitude perfectly: You go to seminary to learn about all the things God couldn't possibly have done, and then you go to church to ask him to do them anyway. In the spirit of that healthy skepticism, I proceed straight to the exposition of the parable itself.

The parable is prefaced with a comment by Luke that Jesus told it as a lesson to people that they ought always to pray and not become discouraged. While this is by no means an unfair or irrelevant hint as to the parable's meaning, I still think that on balance it is a case of Homer nodding. Luke is still using up his last few index cards here; and while his decision to insert the Unjust Judge at this point puts it brilliantly in context (whether you take it as dealing with either grace or judgment), he really should not simply have copied into the text the rather general, early-Jesus-style introduction he originally jotted down for it in his notes.

Be that as it may, the parable itself begins at Luke 18:2: "There was a certain judge [*kritēs*] in a certain city who neither feared God nor respected public opinion." This is a bold stroke on Jesus' part. He is about to take two subjects that most people find diametrically opposed — the grace business and the judging business — and expound them conjointly. Here is a jurist, a practitioner of the law, whom Jesus will portray as a barefaced agent of grace — and whom he will portray that way precisely because he breaks the rules of his profession and puts himself out of the judging business. All of which, Jesus implies without apology, makes him a perfect stand-in for God. He suggests, in other words, that God is not cowed by the supposed *requisita* and *desiderata* of the God-business any more than he is impressed by the rules that people (especially theologians) have dreamt up for him to follow.

Jesus then continues by saying there was a widow *(chéra)* in that city who came to the judge asking him to render her a favorable judgment *(ekdíkēsón me)* against her adversary. The choice of a widow for the other character in this parable is a stunning device for displaying the antithesis between losing and winning that recurs constantly in the parables of grace. On the one hand, the woman is a twenty-four karat loser: widows, especially in ancient times, were people who had lost not only their husbands but their social standing — they had, in a word, lost their life as they knew it. But this particular widow is also a compulsive winner. Like so many of us who, while we may be poor, still go blithely on rejecting our poverty and trying to fake out some kind of wealth — who are, in the last analysis, just high rollers who happen to be unaccountably and embarrassingly broke — she is still committed to making a buck out of her loss. Like the prodigal son when he first formulates his confession, she is dead and she knows it, at least to some degree; but she has not really accepted her death because she still hopes she can ace out the system and get some old-style, if marginal, satisfaction from it.

For a while *(epí chrónon)*, Jesus says, the judge tells her to go fly a kite. Her suit, no doubt, strikes him as having nothing but nuisance value to anyone but herself: he will not have his calendar clogged up with a case that no self-respecting jurist would give even the time of day. (Note here, in passing, the word *chrónos* in the phrase "for a while." I am at least a little tempted to lean on it briefly. *Chrónos,* I take to refer to *our* time: *historical* time, *sequential* time, the *low* time in which we so disastrously try to win by winning. But in the parable, Jesus goes on to say that *afterward* [*metá taúta*] the judge had a change of heart. I suggest that this *after time* might possibly stand for the *kairós,* the *high time of God* in which alone our time is finally reconciled.)

Then, however, Jesus goes on to give the judge's reasoning for his change of heart. "Even though I don't fear God or respect public opinion," the judge says to himself, "still, simply because this widow is giving me such *tsouris,* I will grant her a favorable judgment — just so she doesn't finally wear me out [*hypōpiázę me*] by her constant showing up in my courtroom." He arrives at his judgment, you see, not on the merits of the case but simply on the basis of his own convenience. He is willing to be perceived as a bad judge just so he can have a little peace of mind.

And what does that say about God? It says that God is willing to be perceived as a bad God — and for no better reason than that he wants to get the problems of a worldful of losing winners off his back. It says he is willing — while they are still mired in their futile pursuit of the spiritual buck, the moral buck, the intellectual buck, the physical buck, or the plain ordinary buck — to just shut up about whatever is wrong with them and get the hassle over with. It says in fact what Paul said in Rom. 5:8: "While we were yet sinners, Christ died for us." It says, in short, that God doesn't even wait for us to accept our losing: he simply goes ahead with his own plans for the season, for the *kairós,* the *high old time* he has in mind for himself. Like the father in the Prodigal Son, he just runs, falls on all our necks — the widow's and yours and mine — and showers us with injudicious kisses simply because he wants to get the wet blankets off his back and let the party begin.

The prodigal, of course, responded positively to the father's ungodly behavior: he left out of his actual confession the silly, life-preserving gesture of asking to be made a hired servant and he frankly accepted his status as a dead son who had been raised. The widow does not seem to have responded so favorably to the judge's gift of grace, but the outcome is the same: the son is justified and she is justified. And the words she uses to ask the judge for a favorable verdict (*ekdíkēsón me,* justify me) and the words the judge uses to announce his intention to do precisely that (*ekdikḗsō autḗn,* I will justify her) both contain the root *dik-.* This root enters into a whole string of major New Testament words: *díkaios* (the just), *dikaioún* (to justify), *dikaiosýnē* (justice, justification), *dikaíōma* (justification, justice, judgment), *dikaíōs* (justly), and *dikaíōsis* (justification). Taking those words into account, therefore, ask yourself a leading question: how in fact does the New Testament say we are justified? The answer of course is: by grace through faith (Eph. 2:8) — that is, by our simple trust in the graciously disreputable thing that God did when he fixed up his own insides by the death of Christ.

So Jesus ends the parable by saying, "Listen to what the unjust judge says: 'And will not God judge in favor [*poiésẹ ekdíkēsin,* do favorable judgment] of his own people who cry to him for help day and night? Will he not have mercy [*makrothymeí,* be big-hearted] upon them?'" Pay attention to what I'm telling you, Jesus says in effect. Do you think it makes the least difference to God whether anyone's cause is just? Do you think it matters at all to him that they, even in their loss and death, still try to function like winners? I tell you, none of that amounts to a hill of beans with him. He finds all the lost whether they think they're lost or not. He raises all the dead whether they acknowledge their death or not. It's not that they have to make some heroic effort to get themselves to cooperate with him, and it's certainly not that they have to spend a lot of time praying and yammering to get him to cooperate with them. Don't you see? It's the bare fact of their lostness and death, not their interpretation of it or their acceptance of it, that cries out to him day and night. Lost sheep don't have to ask the shepherd to find them. Lost coins don't have to make long prayers to get the housewife to hunt for them. And lost sons — who may think that they are only allowed to ask for some plausible, sawed-off substitute for salvation — are always going to be totally surprised by the incredible, unasked-for party that just falls in their laps. All they have to be is lost. Not fancy lost, perceptively lost, or repentantly lost; just plain lost. And just plain dead, too. Not humbly dead, engagingly dead, or cooperatively dead; just dead. "I, if I be lifted up," Jesus says, "will draw all to me": the sheep, the coin, the son, the widow — the whole sorry lot of you. You don't have to do a blessed thing, make a single prayer, or have a legitimate case. I do it all.

Finally, though, Jesus answers the rhetorical question he proposed when he first began to point the moral of the parable of the Unjust Judge, namely: "Will not God judge in favor of his people . . . and have mercy on them?" His answer is: "You bet he will — and soon" *(en táchei)*. Forget, if you will, all the hopeless arguments over what Jesus, in his first-century Jewish mind, might have meant by the word "soon." And forget especially all the critics' assertions of what he couldn't possibly have meant. For my money, none of that matters: at the very least, he said *soon* because, for some reason unknown to us, he felt like saying *soon*. In any case, both in terms of the parable of the Unjust Judge and in terms of what Jesus rather shortly did on the cross, I opt for the crucifixion and resurrection as the most likely *scriptural* referents of that *soon*. (At the risk of having even my temporary work permit withdrawn by the New Testament Critics' Union, let me say plainly what I mean by a scriptural referent. For my money, the *scriptural* meaning of a passage is the one it has in the entire context of the biblical revelation of God, not just what it might mean in its particular time and place. And that meaning is the overarchingly important one, since it takes into account not only the licks that the Holy Spirit, the Scriptures' presiding genius, got in at the time the passage was originally composed but also all the other scriptural licks he got in before, during, and after its composition. It even includes the consummate lick of getting the church finally to agree about just which Scriptures he actually presided over.)

In any case, what Jesus actually did *soon* was die and rise — and that, for me, governs everything. Like the unjust judge, he went out of business. He issued a totally disreputable verdict of forgiveness over an entire race of unrepentant, unreconstructed nuisances just because he didn't want to be bothered with the unnecessary job of proving what they had already proved, namely, that they were a bunch of jerks. All that mattered to him was that they were *pitiful* jerks. And because he was willing to drop dead to give them a break — because, like the judge who was tired of the widow's hassling, he was tired of having his cage rattled by a worldful of idiots — he destroyed himself rather than have to destroy them. And that, Virginia, is why "There is therefore now no condemnation to those who are in Christ Jesus." There is no condemnation because there is no condemner. There is no hanging judge and there is no angry God: he has knocked himself clean off the bench and clear out of the God Union. Nobody but a bad judge could have issued a favorable judgment on our worthless cases; and nobody but a failed God — a God finally and for all out of any recognizable version of the God business — could possibly have been bighearted enough to throw a going-out-of-business sale for the likes of us.

Jesus concludes the parable, however, with a warning in the form of yet another rhetorical question. "Still," he says (*plén:* nevertheless, notwithstanding, in spite of all the lovely good news I've just given you), "when the Son of man comes, will he find faith [*pístin*] on the earth?" The implied answer, of course, is no: a dead God is no more acceptable to a world of respectable winners than a corrupt, self-pleasing judge would be to the members of the ABA Ethics Committee. As they would not trust such a judge to sit on the bench, so we will do almost anything to avoid putting our faith in a God who doesn't come up to our standards for divinity.

And there, if you will, is the ultimate dilemma of the church. The one thing it doesn't dare try to sell — for fear of being laughed out of town — turns out to be the only thing it was sent to sell. But because it more often than not caves in to its fear of ridicule, it gives the world the perennial spectacle of an institution eager to peddle anything but its authentic merchandise. I can stand up in the pulpit and tell people that God is angry, mean, and nasty; I can tell them he is so good they couldn't possibly come within a million miles of him; and I can lash them into a frenzy of trying to placate him with irrelevant remorse and bogus good behavior — with sacrifices and offerings and burnt offerings and sin offerings, all of which are offered by the law (Heb. 10:8); but I cannot stand there and tell them the truth that he no longer cares a fig for their sacred guilt or their precious lists of good deeds, responsible outlooks, and earnest intentions. I can never just say to them that God has abolished all those oppressive, godly requirements in order that he might grant them free acceptance by his death on the cross. Because when I do that, they can conclude only one of two things: either that I am crazy or that God is. But alas, God's sanity is the ultimate article of their non-faith. Therefore, despite Scripture's relentless piling up of proof that he is a certifiable nut — that he is the Crazy Eddie of eternity, whose prices are *insane* — it always means that I am the one who gets offered a ticket to the funny farm.

Which is all right, I guess. After the unjust steward, the unjust judge, and the God who hasn't got the integrity to come down from the cross and zap the world into shape, it's a nice, rough approximation of justification by grace alone, through faith.

CHAPTER EIGHTEEN

Death and Resurrection One Last Time

THE PHARISEE AND THE PUBLICAN

— which, in turn, is exactly the right note on which to begin my finale on the parable of the Pharisee and the Publican. Since I have mentioned my suicidal tendencies as a preacher, let me offer you a full-blown example of such self-destructiveness:

> *An ordinary sermon on the two men who went up to the temple*
> *Luke, chapter 18, verses 9-14:* "Jesus also told this parable to some who trusted in themselves that they were righteous [*díkaioi*] and despised everybody else. Two men went up to the temple to pray: one, a Pharisee, the other, a tax collector. The Pharisee stood apart by himself and prayed thus: 'God, I thank you that I am not like others are, greedy, unjust [*ádikoi*], adulterers — and I thank you especially that I am not like this tax collector. I fast two days every week and I give you a tenth of all my income.' But the tax collector stood a long way off and would not even raise his eyes to heaven. Instead, he beat on his breast and said, 'O God, be merciful [*hilástheti*] to me, a sinner.' I tell you, this man went to his house justified [*dedikaiōménos*] rather than the other: for everyone who exalts himself will be humbled, but he who humbles himself will be exalted."

In the Name of the Father and of the Son and of the Holy Spirit. Amen.

Now then. The first thing to get off the table is the notion that this parable is simply a lesson in the virtue of humility. It is not. It is an instruction in the futility of religion — in the idleness of the proposition that there is anything at all you can do to put yourself right with God. It is about the folly of even trying. The parable occurs after a series of illustrations of what Jesus means by faith, and it comes shortly before he announces, for the third time, that he will die and rise again. It is therefore not a recommendation to adopt a humble religious stance rather than a proud one; rather it is a warning to drop all religious stances — and all moral and ethical ones, too — when you try to grasp your justification before God. It is, in short, an exhortation to move on to the central point of the Gospel: faith in a God who raises the dead.

Consider the characters in this parable. Forget the prejudice that Jesus' frequently stinging remarks about Pharisees have formed in your mind. Give this particular Pharisee all the credit you can. He is, after all, a good man. To begin with, he is not a crook, not a time-server, not a womanizer. He takes nothing he hasn't honestly earned, he gives everyone he knows fair and full measure, and he is faithful to his wife, patient with his children, and steadfast for his friends. He is not at all like this publican, this tax-farmer, who is the worst kind of crook: a legal one, a big operator, a mafia-style enforcer working for the Roman government on a nifty franchise that lets him collect — from his fellow Jews, mind you, from the people whom the Romans might have trouble finding, but whose whereabouts he knows and whose language he speaks — all the money he can bleed out of them, provided only he pays the authorities an agreed flat fee. He has been living for years on the cream he has skimmed off their milk money. He is a fat cat who drives a stretch limo, drinks nothing but Chivas Regal, and never shows up at a party without at least two $500-a-night call girls in tow.

The Pharisee, however, is not only good; he is religious. And not hypocritically religious, either. His outward uprightness is matched by an inward discipline. He fasts twice a week and he puts his money where his mouth is: ten percent off the top for God. If you know where to find a dozen or two such upstanding citizens, I know several parishes that will accept delivery of them, no questions asked and all Jesus' parables to the contrary notwithstanding.

But best of all, this Pharisee thanks God for his happy state. Luke says that Jesus spoke this parable to those who trusted in themselves that they were righteous. But Jesus shows us the Pharisee in the very act of giving God the glory. Maybe the reason he went up to the temple to pray was that, earlier in the week, he slipped a little and thought of his righteousness as his own doing. Maybe he said to himself, "That's terrible, I must make a special visit to the temple and set my values straight by thanking God."

But what does Jesus tell you about this good man — about this entirely acceptable candidate for the vestry of your parish? He tells you not only that he is in bad shape, but that he is in worse shape than a tax-farmer who is as rotten as they come and who just waltzes into the temple and does nothing more than say as much. In short, he tells you an unacceptable parable.

For you would — I know I would — gladly accept the Pharisee's pledge card and welcome him to our midst. But would you accept me for long if I had my hand in the church till to the tune of a Cadillac and a couple of flashy whores? Would you (would the diocesan authorities) think it was quite enough for me to come into church on a Sunday, stare at the tips of my shoes, and say, "God, be merciful to me a sinner?" Would the bishop write me a letter commending my imitation of the parable and praising me for preaching not only in word but in deed? Jesus, to be sure, says that God would; I myself, however, have some doubts about you and the bishop. You might find it a bit too . . . vivid. There seems to be just no way of dramatizing this parable from our point of view. That being the case, turn it around and look at it from God's.

God is sitting there in the temple, busy holding creation in being — thinking it all into existence, concentrating on making the hairs on your head jump out of nothing, preserving the seat of my pants, reconciling the streetwalkers in Times Square, the losers on the Bowery, the generals in the Pentagon, and all the worms under flat rocks in Brazil. And in come these two characters. The Pharisee walks straight over, pulls up a chair to God's table, and whips out a pack of cards. He fans them, bridges them, does a couple of one-handed cuts and an accordion shuffle, slides the pack over to God, and says, "Cut. I'm in the middle of a winning streak." And God looks at him with a sad smile, gently pushes the deck away, and says, "Maybe you're not. Maybe it just ran out."

So the Pharisee picks up the deck again and starts the game himself. "Acey-Ducey, okay?" And he deals God a two of fasting and a king of no adultery. And God says, "Look, I told you. Maybe this is not your game. I don't want to take your money."

"Oh, come on," says the Pharisee. "How about seven-card stud, tens wild? I've been real lucky with tens wild lately." And God looks a little annoyed and says, "Look, I meant it. Don't play me. The odds here are always on my side. Besides, you haven't even got a full deck. You'd be smarter to be like the guy over there who came in with you. He lost his cards before he got here. Why don't you both just have a drink on the house and go home?"

Do you see now what Jesus is saying in this parable? He is saying that as far as the Pharisee's ability to win a game of justification with God is concerned, he is no better off than the publican. As a matter of fact, the Pharisee is worse off; because while they're both losers, the publican at least has the sense to recognize the fact and trust God's offer of a free drink. The point of the parable is that they are both dead, and their only hope is someone who can raise the dead.

"Ah but," you say, "is there no distinction to be made? Isn't the Pharisee somehow less further along in death than the publican? Isn't there some sense in which we can give him credit for the real goodness he has?"

To which I answer, you are making the same miscalculation as the Pharisee. Death is death. Given enough room to maneuver, it eventually produces total deadness. In the case of the publican, for example, his life so far has been quite long enough to force upon him the recognition that, as far as his being able to deal with God is concerned, he is finished. The Pharisee, on the other hand, looking at his clutch of good deeds, has figured that they are more than enough to keep him in the game for the rest of his life.

But there is his error. For the rest of his life here, maybe. But what about for the length and breadth of eternity? Take your own case. Let us suppose that you are an even better person than the Pharisee. Let us assume that you are untempted to any sin except the sin of envy, and that even there, your resolve is such that, for the remainder of your days, you never do in fact fall prey to that vice. Are you so sure, however, that the robustness of your virtue is the only root of your unjealous disposition? Might not a very large source of it be nothing more than lack of opportunity? Have you never thought yourself immune to some vice only to find that you fell into it when the temptation became sufficient? The lady who resists a five-dollar proposition sometimes gives in to a five-million-dollar one: men who would never betray friends have been known to betray friends they thought were about to betray them. The reformer immune to the corruption of power finds corruption easier as he gains power.

Take your dormant envy then. From now till the hour of your death, you may very well not meet that one person who will galvanize it into action. But in eternity — in that state where there are no limits to opportunity, when you have a literal forever in which to meet, literally, everybody — is your selflessness so profound that you can confidently predict you will never be jealous of anyone? Is the armor of your humility so utterly without a chink?

There, you see, is the problem as God sees it. For him, the eternal order is a perpetual-motion machine: it can tolerate no friction at all. Even one grain of sand — one lurking vice in one of the redeemed — given long enough, will find somewhere to lodge and something to rub on. And that damaged something, given another of the infinite eternities within eternity itself, will go off center and shake the next part loose. And then the next; and so straight on into what can only be the beginning of the end: the very limitlessness of the opportunity for mischief will eventually bring the whole works to a grinding halt.

What Jesus is saying in this parable is that no human goodness is good enough to pass a test like that, and that therefore God is not about to risk it. He will not take our cluttered life, as we hold it, into eternity. He will take only the clean emptiness of our death in the power

341

of Jesus' resurrection. He condemns the Pharisee because he takes his stand on a life God cannot use; he commends the publican because he rests his case on a death that God can use. The fact, of course, is that they are both equally dead and therefore both alike receivers of the gift of resurrection. But the trouble with the Pharisee is that for as long as he refuses to confess the first fact, he will simply be unable to believe the second. He will be justified in his death, but he will be so busy doing the bookkeeping on a life he cannot hold that he will never be able to enjoy himself. It's just misery to try to keep count of what God is no longer counting. Your entries keep disappearing.

If you now see my point, you no doubt conclude that the Pharisee is a fool. You are right. But at this point you are about to run into another danger. You probably conclude that he is also a rare breed of fool — that the number of people who would so blindly refuse to recognize such a happy issue out of all their afflictions has got to be small. There you are wrong. We all refuse to see it. Or better said, while we sometimes catch a glimpse of it, our love of justification by works is so profound that at the first opportunity we run from the strange light of grace straight back to the familiar darkness of the law.

You do not believe me? I shall prove it to you: the publican goes down to his house justified rather than the other. Well and good, you say; yes indeed. But let me follow him now in your mind's eye as he goes through the ensuing week and comes once again to the temple to pray. What is it you want to see him doing those seven days? What does your moral sense tell you he ought at least try to accomplish? Are you not itching, as his spiritual adviser, to urge him into another line of work — something perhaps a little more upright than putting the arm on his fellow countrymen for fun and profit? In short, do you not feel compelled to insist on at least a little reform?

To help you be as clear as possible about your feelings, let me set you two exercises. For the first, take him back to the temple one week later. And have him go back there with nothing in his life reformed: walk him in this week as he walked in last — after seven full days of skimming, wenching, and high-priced Scotch. Put him through the same routine: eyes down, breast smitten, God be merciful, and all that.

Now then. I trust you see that on the basis of the parable as told, God will not mend his divine ways any more than the publican did his wicked ones. He will do this week exactly what he did last: God, in short, will send him down to his house justified. The question in this first exercise is, do you like that? And the answer, of course, is that you do not. You gag on the unfairness of it. The rat is getting off free.

For the second exercise, therefore, take him back to the temple with at least some reform under his belt: no wenching this week perhaps, or drinking cheaper Scotch and giving the difference to the Heart Fund. What do you think now? What is it that you want God to do with him? Question him about the extent to which he has mended his ways? For what purpose? If God didn't count the Pharisee's impressive list, why should he bother with this two-bit one? Or do you want God to look on his heart, not his list, and commend him for good intentions at least? Why? The point of the parable was that the publican confessed that he was dead, not that his heart was in the right place. *Why are you so bent on destroying the story by sending the publican back for his second visit with the Pharisee's speech in his pocket?*

The honest answer is, that while you understand the thrust of the parable with your mind, your heart has a desperate need to believe its exact opposite. And so does mine. We all long to establish our identity by seeing ourselves as approved in other people's eyes. We spend our days preening ourselves before the mirror of their opinion so we will not have to think about the nightmare of appearing before them naked and uncombed. And we hate this parable because it says plainly that it is the nightmare that is the truth of our condition. We fear the publican's acceptance because we know precisely what it means. It means that we will never be free until we are dead to the whole business of justifying ourselves. But since that business is our life, that means not until *we* are dead.

For *Jesus came to raise the dead.* Not to reform the reformable, not to improve the improvable . . . but then, I have said all that. Let us make an end: as long as you are struggling like the Pharisee to be alive in your own eyes — and to the precise degree that your struggles are for what is holy, just, and good — you will resent the apparent indifference to your pains that God shows in making the effortlessness of death the touch-stone of your justification. Only when you are finally able, with the publican, to admit that you are dead will you be able to stop balking at grace.

It is, admittedly, a terrifying step. You will cry and kick and scream before you take it, because it means putting yourself out of the only game you know. For your comfort though, I can tell you three things. First, it is only one step. Second, it is not a step out of reality into noth-ing, but a step from fiction into fact. And third, it will make you laugh out loud at how short the trip home was: it wasn't a trip at all; you were already there.

Death — for the third and last time — is absolutely all of the resur-rection we can now know. The rest is faith.

In the Name of the Father and of the Son and of the Holy Spirit. Amen.

THE PARABLES
OF JUDGMENT

CHAPTER ONE

Introduction

INCLUSION BEFORE EXCLUSION AS THE
TOUCHSTONE OF THE PARABLES OF JUDGMENT

The theme of judgment — of crisis, of decisive, history-altering and history-fulfilling action on the part of God — is present in Jesus' teaching from the earliest days of his ministry. At first, his pronouncements about judgment are couched in more or less traditional language: like the stock apocalyptic scenarios of the later prophets and the revivalist movements of Jesus' time, their imagery implies that God will intervene in history at some final day and settle its score not only with a bang but with plenty of whimpering on the part of the world. In a word, Jesus starts out sounding like John the Baptist. But as he develops the theme, this judgment, this *krísis*, gradually becomes more complex. Simple intervention on God's part is replaced by puzzling images of nonintervention. Direct, right-handed action that rewards the righteous and punishes the wicked is downplayed in favor of a mysterious, left-handed dispensation that indiscriminately exalts the last, the lost, the least, and the little — a dispensation, in fact, that achieves its goal by the vast leveling action of a universal resurrection of the dead. So much so, that when Jesus finally comes to deliver his formal parables of judgment, he tells them all in the last few days before the crucifixion. Therefore, if there is a single, major subtext to his developed teaching about judgment — if he has in mind any unifying, governing principle in these parables — it is sure to be something closely linked to his own death and resurrection.

I say no more at this point about what that subtext might be. The burden of this book will be to discover it — not only by a detailed examination of Jesus' parables of judgment as they appear in the Gospels of Matthew, Mark, and Luke but also by a comparison of those parables with other judgment passages from the Gospel of John to Revelation. Naturally (since the synoptic Gospels sometimes differ in their sequences of events and parables), this will require a harmonizing of the biblical accounts into a single order. I shall not, however, foist on you a harmony of my own; instead, I shall adopt the numbering system for Gospel passages devised by Kurt Aland in the Greek-English edition of the *Synopsis Quattuor Evangeliorum* (United Bible Societies).* Beyond that, only a few housekeeping details need mentioning here. I shall be working from the original Greek — principally from the text employed by Aland in the *Synopsis,* but also from the second edition of the Aland, Black, Martini, Metzger, Wikgren text, from the twenty-second edition of the Nestle text, and from the Schmoller Concordance to the Nestle text. The translations offered will be largely my own, but they will take into account the versions I habitually consult: the King James Version (KJV), the Revised Standard Version (RSV), Today's English Version (TEV), the New International Version (NIV), and, to a lesser degree, the Clementine Vulgate (VgCL), the Jerusalem Bible (JB), the New English Bible (NEB), and the New Testament in Modern English by J. B. Phillips (JBP).

Let us begin, then. We have three sources for assessing the note of judgment in Jesus' early teaching, all of them to be found on the pages of the synoptic Gospels. They are: the Jewish establishment of his time (most commonly instanced by the Gospel writers as the Pharisees, the scribes, or the Herodians); the disciples and/or the apostles; and, of course, Jesus himself. I take them up in that order.

There is no question that, almost from the first, the religious authorities of the day perceived Jesus' words and deeds as a judgment of

---

*An English edition of *Synopsis of the Four Gospels* is available from the American Bible Society. It is the ideal companion to this book for study purposes.

their trusteeship of the revelation of God. It never seems to have occurred to them to write him off as a maverick. They automatically assumed he was a danger and, as early as Mark 3:6, they were canvassing the possibility of destroying him. From our point of view, of course, the scribes and Pharisees are almost characters in a hiss-and-boo melodrama: the moustache-twirling, cloak-and-dagger parts that the Gospel writers assign them seem overwrought. But from their own point of view, they were quite correct. Powers that be are always expert sniffers of the wind and testers of the waters. They can spot a threat to their system a mile off: all they need is half a sentence from a professor or the odd gesture from a political figure and their heresy-alarm goes off like a klaxon. And Jesus provided them with far more cause for alarm than that. The common people may have been "astonished at his teaching because he taught them as one who had authority *(exousía)* and not as the scribes" (Mark 1:22). And the crowds may have been captivated by his healings and titillated by his consorting with publicans and sinners. But the experts knew better: he was, pure and simple, a menace. Not only was he shaking the foundations of the Torah; he was also certain to make political trouble and bring down the wrath of Rome on their heads. In other words, he threatened to precipitate a judgment they were unable to see as the work of God — to bring about the crisis that would put an end not only to their stewardship of the divine dispensation but also, as they saw it, to the dispensation itself.

The disciples, by contrast, displayed a less critical but still keen perception of the judgmental aspect of Jesus' ministry. For the most part, they were ordinary people, with ordinary people's enthusiasm for anything that promises to even scores and administer comedowns to the mighty. They were, if you will, downright eschatology buffs: they positively itched to hear the note of judgment, and they supplied it full force even in contexts where Jesus barely mentioned it. When I expounded the parable of the Wheat and the Weeds in my previous book, *The Parables of the Kingdom,* I took the view that Jesus' ham-fisted, judgment-loaded allegorization of the parable (Matt. 13:36-43) was not so much a considered expression of his own ideas on the subject as it was a sop thrown to their inordinate fondness for hellfire and brimstone. Indeed, so enamored were they of their own rockem-sockem, right-handed notions of divine crisis management that Jesus had a hard time getting through to them his essentially left-handed, noninterventionist view of the authentic judgment of God. Three times, for example, he predicted his coming death and resurrection (in Matt. 16; 17; and 20 — see also the parallel passages in Mark and Luke). But even though he did so in plain Aramaic, with not a smitch of parabolic obfuscation — and even though those predictions bore witness to his conviction that judgment operates more by God's going out of the judging business than by staying in it — they never moved an inch beyond their conviction that judgment simply had to work by retribution, and in their time at that. In fact, their expectation of direct intervention was so strong that even at the point of Jesus' ascension (Acts 1:6), they still felt compelled to ask him whether he would *now* finally cut out the indirection and get on with some intelligible tidying up of history.

And subsequent generations of disciples have not done much better than they did, even though we have had the rest of the New Testament and two thousand years of reflection to lend us a hand. The church, by and large, has always been more receptive to judgment-as-settling-scores than to judgment as proceeding out of, and in accordance with, the reconciling grace of resurrection. Christian preachers regularly blow the Gospel of grace clean out of the water with sermons that make reward and punishment, not resurrection with its sovereign pardon, the touchstone of judgment. And Christians generally — every day of the week and twice on Sundays in some cases — hear them gladly. The church has found that plain old hanging-judge sermons sell, but that grace remains a drug on the market. As a preacher, I can with the greatest of ease tell people that God is going to get them, and I can be sure they will believe every word I say. But what I cannot do, without inviting utter disbelief and serious doubts about my sanity, is proclaim that he has in fact taken away *all* the sins of the world and that he has, accordingly, solved all the problems he once had with sin. I cannot tell them, as John does, that he "did not come to judge the world but to save the world" (John 12:47). Nor can I ask them, as Paul does, to believe the logical consequence of that statement, namely, that "there is

350

therefore now no condemnation to those who are in Christ Jesus" (Rom. 8:1). Because if I do, the same old questions will come pouring out: "What about Hitler?" "What about child molesters?" "What about my skunk of a brother-in-law?" Their one pressing worry is always, "What have you done with the hell we know and love?"

But that gets us ahead of the story; it is time to turn to the third and most considerable source we have for assessing the nature of judgment in the Gospels: Jesus himself.

The usual view is that Jesus' early teaching about the subject is traditional — that he started out, as I have said, sounding like John the Baptist and identifying himself with customary apocalyptic notions of a forcible and fiery settling of the world's hash. But even at the beginning, his teaching was more complex than that. In his first telling of the parable of the Wheat and the Weeds (Matt. 13:24-30), for example, he spends almost all of his time (verses 24-30a) indicating that God's way of dealing with sin is by forbearance — by an *áphesis,* a forgiveness of evil, a letting-be of the badness of the world, even a permission of sin. Only in verse 30b does he introduce the image of the harvest *(therismós)* at which the weeds will be separated from the wheat and burned in the fire. True enough, in the interpretation of the parable he does speak (Matt. 13:40) in traditional terms of the judgment as the end, the wrap-up of the age *(hē syntéleia toú aiōnos)*. But elsewhere in the synoptic Gospels as well as in the rest of the New Testament other words come to the fore. John habitually uses the word *krísis* (judgment) and its verb *krínein* (to judge) when Jesus speaks on the subject; Paul commonly uses another variant of the same root, *kríma* (judgment, condemnation), to express his own views. As a matter of fact, it will be precisely to those usages that I shall look for the fully developed scriptural notion of judgment. In the next chapter, I shall try to explicate their significance. Here, let me just continue working from the Gospels: even in them there is an evident development of the left-handed view of judgment.

Consider the passage toward which not only the synoptics but also the Gospel of John build: the passion narrative. It is impossible to make too much of its presence as the climactic portion of all four books. The sheer, disproportionate length of the accounts of Jesus' trial and death argues conclusively for their paramount importance in the Gospel writers' minds. The events themselves occupied less than twenty-four hours of Jesus' life (from Maundy Thursday night to three o'clock on Good Friday afternoon); yet they are given an inordinate amount of space in the Gospels. For the record, the figures are: in Matthew, two chapters out of twenty-eight; in Mark, two chapters out of sixteen; in Luke, two chapters out of twenty-four; and in John, seven chapters out of twenty-one. To me, that says plainly that there is no way of leaving what Jesus actually did as the final act of his ministry out of our assessment of what he thought and taught about the ultimate action of God in judgment. It says that the *krísis,* the judgment, is precisely one of forgiveness, of a saving grace that works by death and resurrection. For at the consummate moment of God's mysterious intervention in history, he operates by nonintervention — by a hands-off rather than a hands-on policy. On the cross, with nails through his hands and feet, he does all that he judges needs doing; and he does it all by doing precisely nothing. He just dies. He does not get mad. He does not get even. He just gets out.

For me, nothing else holds a candle to that. The words of Jesus on the subject of judgment may be debatable (though I hope to show in this book that they are not nearly as debatable as some think). But the action of Jesus in his passion — his saving, judging *inaction,* if you will — governs everything. And not just for us who sit here in the community of faith with twenty centuries' worth of theology to guide (or confuse) us. Jesus himself made the crucifixion/resurrection the governing center of his developed teaching. From the feeding of the five thousand onward (that is, beginning at Matt. 14; Mark 6; Luke 9; and John 6), death is uppermost in his mind. Not only does he predict his own death three times after that point, and not only does he undertake his final journey to Jerusalem (Luke 9–18) specifically as a going to the cross; to clinch the case, he makes death (and its cognates, lastness, lostness, leastness, and littleness) the touchstone of all of his parables during that journey. (I have dealt with those parables at length in my previous volume, *The Parables of Grace;* there is neither space nor need to say more about them here.)

In any case, it is the imminence of Jesus' passion and death that gives his parables of judgment their singular force and supplies them with their most profound interpretative principles. Fascinatingly, the most memorable of them occur on the four days between Palm Sunday and Good Friday; and all the rest of them are to be found just prior to that time. This juxtaposition means first of all that the parables of judgment are hot, not cool. They are paradoxical stories told by a Savior on his way to a dreadful yet fully chosen death; they are not eschatological chitchat dispensed by a theology professor sauntering to a lecture. A death sentence, as Doctor Johnson noted, focuses the mind mightily. The fairest and most natural reading of all these parables, therefore, will always be one that makes death and resurrection the principal clue to what Jesus is talking about. It is a mistake to come at them as if we already understood what judgment is all about and were simply trying to see how they can be made to confirm what we think. Come at them that way and you will get only what so many preachers have gotten: a Messiah playing cops and robbers, a vindictive God bent on putting all the baddies under flat rocks. But come to them as the words of a Savior who has just spent weeks or months making death the principal device of his parables of gracious love — and who is now, under the compulsion of the same gracious love, about to die in order to activate the device once and for all — and you will see something new. You will see Gospel, not law; good news, not bad; vindication, not vindictiveness.

At the beginning of my study of Jesus' parables I divided them into three groups: the parables of the kingdom, which run from the start of his ministry to the feeding of the five thousand; the parables of grace, which run from the feeding of the five thousand to Palm Sunday; and the parables of judgment, which are compressed for the most part into Holy Week. I want to add a note to that division now. If I were asked to assign a *color* to each of the three groups, I would call the parables of the kingdom green, the parables of grace purple, and the parables of judgment white. Consider.

The kingdom parables are green because so many of them are about growing — about seeds and plants. They are about the mystery of a kingdom already planted, a kingdom at hand, a kingdom in our midst — a kingdom, above all, that grows and prevails as a seed does: by its own sovereign power and not by any efforts of ours. In the parable of the Sower, for example (Mark 4:1-9), the seed sown succeeds in doing its proper thing despite the circumstances: what falls by the road successfully attracts birds; what falls on the shallow or the thorny ground grows as best it can; and what falls on the good ground bears fruit on the basis of its own peculiar power, some thirty-, some sixty-, some a hundredfold. Or take the Seed Cast by the Farmer on his Field (Mark 4:26-29): the man lies down and gets up night and day, but the seed sprouts and grows "he knows not how" — from an earth that "bears fruit of itself," quite apart from his instrumentality. Or, finally, take the Yeast (Matt. 13:33): the woman puts it into three measures of flour at the very creation of the lump of dough and the yeast grows until the whole is leavened. Let us make green, then, the color of these early parables of the mysterious, already present, catholic kingdom of God.

Purple, though, for the parables of grace. Purple, because they are about passionate, selfless love (the Good Samaritan, the Prodigal Son); but purple above all because they are about a love that works by death. "Greater love has no one than this," Jesus said, "that he lay down his life for his friends" (John 15:13). Death is the mainspring of the parables of grace. For example, the Prodigal Son (Luke 15:11-32) is practically a festival of death: the father dies at the beginning of the parable by putting his will into effect; the prodigal dies in the far country when his life as he knew it comes to an end in bitter poverty; the prodigal dies again — fruitfully, this time — when he comes home, confesses that he is a dead son, and wisely leaves out of his confession the irrelevant, life-protracting request that he be taken back as a hired hand; finally, the fatted calf dies to make possible the party that is the point of the whole parable. Or consider the Lost Sheep (Luke 15:1-7): a lost sheep wandering in the wilderness is, for all intents and purposes, a dead sheep; ninety-nine abandoned sheep are, for the period of the shepherd's absence at least, likewise in danger of death; and a shepherd who puts all of his efforts into a search for a single lost sheep virtually dies to the sheep-ranching business, exposing himself to the loss of *all* his sheep. Moreover, even the parables of grace that do not directly express this theme of love operating by death still embody it: they are, all of them, spoken by a Savior consciously on his way to die for love. Death, therefore — and in particular, death as the fountainhead of grace — is what colors these parables purple.

The parables of judgment, however, are white. I said that they were hot, not cool; and of all the colors that can represent heat, white is the hottest. Red-hot passion scarcely rises above the level of sexual excitement; white-hot passion is love to the ultimate degree. More than that, white is the color of light; in John's Gospel it is precisely the light of the world, Jesus himself, who brings on the judgment — who provokes the *krísis* of the world. Jesus says, "This is the judgment, that light has come into the world, and people loved the darkness rather than the light because their deeds were evil." But above all, the parables of judgment are white because, like white light, they contain all the colors of the other parables and will, if refracted through the prism of a sound interpretation, manifest them with perfect clarity.

If I have anything to contribute to the interpretation of the parables of judgment, it is my steadfast refusal to separate them from the rest of Jesus' parables. I find in them, again and again, not only the green, growing, mysterious, catholic kingdom but also the purple, passionate grace that saves by death. Therefore I am convinced that anyone who interprets them as if Jesus had decided simply to abandon his previous palette — who takes the view, in other words, that Jesus had gotten over his penchant for painting kindly kingdoms and gracious loves and was now getting down to depicting the grim "final solution" in which God gets even with sinners by marching them into the gas chambers of an eternal Dachau — is making a crashing mistake. The Gospel of grace must not be turned into a bait-and-switch offer. It is not one of those airline supersavers in which you read of a $59.00 fare to Orlando only to find, when you try to buy a ticket, that the six seats per flight at that price are all taken and that the trip will now cost you $199.95. Jesus must not be read as having baited us with grace only to clobber us in the end with law. For as the death and resurrection of Jesus were accomplished once and for all, so the grace that reigns by those mysteries reigns eternally — even in the thick of judgment.

Accordingly, while I am playing my cards face up, let me give you what I consider to be the master key to the parables of judgment. As growth-in-a-mystery was the governing device in the parables of the kingdom, and as death-resurrection was the governing device of the parables of grace, so *inclusion before exclusion* is the chief interpretative principle of the parables of judgment. As a general rule — and especially in his specific parables of judgment — Jesus is at pains to show that *no one is kicked out who wasn't already in.* The corroboration of that principle, of course, will be the burden of this entire book; but just to whet your appetite for the labor of exposition, let me give you a few instances of how it manifests itself.

In the parable of the King's Son's Wedding (Matt. 22:1-14), the guest who was cast into outer darkness for not having on a wedding garment was already, by the very terms of the parable — by the host's insistence on dragging in everybody and his brother — a member of the wedding: he was booted out only after he had been invited in. Likewise, in the parable of the Ten Virgins (Matt. 25:1-13), the five foolish girls were every bit as much a part of the wedding reception as the five wise ones; the distinction between the two groups is based on what the wise or the foolish did in response to their already granted acceptance, not on anything they did to earn it. Similarly, in the parable of the Talents (Matt. 25:14-30), all three servants — the one who received a single talent as well as the ones who received two and five — were already in their master's favor. He had laid down his possessions, his whole living; he had died, as it were, for all of them by giving up control over his life. The unfavorable judgment finally pronounced on the one who hid his talent in the ground was based not on whether he was good enough to "earn grace" (a contradiction in terms, please note) but solely on what he did in response to the grace already granted.

But enough specifics for now. I propose to show that judgment, as it is portrayed in the parables of Jesus (not to mention the rest of the New Testament), never comes until *after* acceptance: grace remains forever the sovereign consideration. The difference between the blessed and the cursed is one thing and one thing only: the blessed accept their acceptance and the cursed reject it; but the acceptance is *already in place*

356

for both groups before either does anything about it. To put it another way, heaven is populated by nothing but forgiven sinners and hell is populated by nothing but forgiven sinners: the Lamb of God takes away the sin of the *kósmos,* not just of the chosen few (John 1:29); Jesus said, "I, if I be lifted up, will draw *all* to me" (John 12:32). The difference between heaven and hell, accordingly, is simply that those in heaven accept the endless forgiveness, while those in hell reject it. Indeed, the precise hell of hell is its endless refusal to open the door to the reconciled and reconciling party that stands forever on its porch and knocks, equally endlessly, for permission to bring in the Supper of the Lamb (Rev. 3:20).

But as I said, enough. Time to turn to some of the broader New Testament background of judgment before taking up Jesus' parables themselves.

CHAPTER TWO

The Sovereign Light

JESUS AS THE UNCONDEMNING JUDGE

In this chapter, I am going to do three things that in certain circles are considered suspect. I shall quite seriously use the Gospel of John as a source for Jesus' teaching about judgment; I shall expound that teaching by arguing from some words attributed to Jesus in the book of Revelation; and most alarmingly of all, I shall maintain that the usual distinction between the historical Jesus and the Christ of faith (a distinction that almost always ends up boosting the former and knocking the latter) is historically inaccurate, scripturally pointless, and fundamentally mischievous.

Since it promises to be the most fun, let me undertake the last project first. The practice of giving the "simple Jesus" of the synoptic Gospels primacy over the "complex Christ" of, say, Paul or John — of saying, in effect, that it is the church, and not the Jesus of history, that is the source of what finally became the Christian view of judgment — is a fast shuffle followed by a misplayed card. To begin with, it dates mostly from the nineteenth century, a period whose most publicized theological fracas was the war between science and religion. This conflict, which in some quarters is still thought to be raging full force, was misapprehended, misguided, and misreported from the start. Except in the minds of partisans and publicists, it should never have been fought at all.

On the secular side, it was provoked by philosophico-theological extrapolations from certain scientific "discoveries" — among them the then new findings of paleontology and comparative biology — and it was fueled by a philosophical theory of upward evolutionary progress that had been gaining acceptance since the end of the eighteenth century. The notion that creation was developing and improving quite on its own had been around for some time before Darwin. Evolutionism was not cooked up as a necessary conclusion of Darwin's work; his work, rather, came to be seen as a serendipitous proof that the already popular doctrine of evolutionary progress had some basis in fact. But this in turn produced a standoff. On the one hand, the partisans of the secular view decided that the biblical accounts of creation simply had to be wrong; on the other hand, the defenders of the faith went to the opposite extreme and maintained that the Scriptures were correct in every detail.

Both sides were mistaken. The "scientific" position in no way necessitated positing the absence of God: philosophically speaking (and this was precisely a philosophical war, not a religio-scientific one), God could just as well have presided over an evolving creation as over an instantaneous one. Nor was the religionists' position any better: their taking refuge in the notion that the Scriptures were literally true in every respect would have come as a shock to almost all pre-nineteenth-century Christians — to Paul, for example, or to Augustine, or to Aquinas, or to Luther — all of whom assigned to Scripture far more senses than just the literal one. Neither side, in short, was above making strategic blunders.

But coupled with this mistaken joining of battle on the field of evolution was a philosophical false start: a deistic notion of God that had been around even longer than evolutionism and that had infected the troops of God's champions as well as those of his enemies. Deism — the doctrine that says that God made a perfectly adequate, self-managing world and that, on principle, he does not ever obtrude himself upon it by special interventions (miracles, for example) — had been around for a good part of the eighteenth century. When the nineteenth century opened, there were more than a few religionists who were quite ready to cave in to the secularists' objection to the miraculous. By the time the twentieth century began, their numbers were vastly increased: throughout the Christian intellectual community there was a strong bias against anything that even vaguely resembled a divine finger in the pie.

That bias, however, tricked the Christian strategists into fighting the war between science and religion with their opponents' weapon, namely, a deistic God who didn't interfere in the history of the world. In the hands of the secularists, of course, that weapon was a natural one; but in the hands of Christians it was an odd gun indeed. Not only were the Scriptures embarrassingly well stocked with miraculous interventions; the very notion of a revelation that worked ultimately by incarnation should have made them suspect they were shooting with a rifle that might blow up in their faces. But they didn't; and as a result, the whole course of biblical criticism was altered by their reliance on the faulty weapon of deism.

For in order to wage an intellectually respectable war, they simply assumed (fundamentalists excepted, of course) that their only hope of winning lay in downplaying the familiar, theologized Christ of Paul and John in favor of a hitherto unrecognized "historical" Jesus whom they then proceeded to discover, not to say invent. This "quest for the historical Jesus" (the phrase itself is an example of publicists' hype: the original title of Schweitzer's landmark book was *Von Reimarus zu Wrede*) has been a millstone around the neck of biblical criticism ever since. Not that the quest was all bad: what Jesus might actually have thought in his first-century, Jewish mind is by no means irrelevant; it deserves, in fact, all the attention we can give it. But to act as if it is the only legitimate base for Christian biblical study is to overlook some crucial facts.

For one thing, the sources we have for determining the mind of the historical Jesus generally postdate the sources we have for the Christ of faith. In the words of a memorable tag line, "the Gospels were written for the sake of the epistles." Consider. The authentic Pauline corpus was completed before Paul's death in A.D. 64; Mark may have existed in its present form before then, but Matthew, Luke, and John are, by common agreement, later productions. That alone should have given critics pause. It means that the early church got its hands on the so-called simple Jesus of the Gospels only *after* it had been living comfortably with the complex Christ of Paul. But it also means that, without any serious evidence of disgruntlement with the eventually canonical Gospels, the church *perceived no discrepancy between those two purported brands of Savior.* At the very least therefore, the nineteenth- and twentieth-century penchant for opposing a "historical" construct of Jesus to the wider scriptural view of him that in historic fact appeared first — for setting Matthew and Luke, say, against Paul — should be suspect.

But for another thing, it must be remembered that we have the four Gospels we now accept only because the early church, for its own sufficient reasons, winnowed them out from among others and chose to pass them on to us. On any sane view of the inspiration of Scripture, the Holy Spirit did not preside over its composition simply by chloroforming its several authors and then guiding their ballpoint pens into automatically writing what he wanted to say. His presidency over the process of forming Scripture involved not only authors in all their conscious individuality and peculiarity; it also involved, in an equally conscious way, their audience. In the last analysis, as a matter of fact, it was *the community of faith* — the early church — that he used to decide which books were, and which were not, to be considered Scripture.

I say all this (which possibly may not have been as much fun for you as I promised) because the history of biblical criticism in the twentieth century has been a long, painful, and not wholly conclusive struggle to rid itself of the nineteenth century's unfortunate disregard of the early church's role in determining who and what Jesus might be. We have come a good way beyond all that by now, of course; yet the legacy of the false opposition between science and religion — and in particular of the deistic prejudice against untoward manifestations of divine activity — still persists. We have even managed, in certain circles, to concede the pivotal role of the primitive Christian community and still, because of our undiscarded prejudices, turn it against the very faith that led that community to hand us the Gospels to begin with.

To this day, it is a commonplace of much biblical criticism to assume that Jesus of Nazareth could not possibly have done or thought many of the things the Gospels quite plainly assign to him. We are told, for example, that he never meant (or even said — his words are taken as "second-century ecclesiastical glosses") that he was the Messiah, or the

Son of man. Or, to take a different example of the same tendency, we are told that while his death may be a thoroughly creditable proposition, his resurrection and ascension must be viewed as the fabricated trappings of a nonhistorical "Christ-event" assignable only to the realm of faith — as if, that is, they were on the pages of Scripture not because they actually happened but because the early church concocted the "happenings" in order to give concrete expression to otherwise uncorroborated beliefs.

Such assertions, of course, cannot be proved or disproved; but they can certainly be shown to be suspicious. They proceed not out of scriptural evidence but out of the still present, and to this day still unexamined, deistic prejudice against miracles. To be sure, the resurrection and the ascension are not *simply* miraculous events. They are not just divine irruptions into an otherwise unchanged order; rather they are manifestations — sacraments, real presences — of a mysterious new creation that was, equally mysteriously, present from the foundation of the world. But for all that, it is totally unnecessary to deny that they were *real* presences — *physical* sacraments, *actual* occurrences — unless, of course, you happen to be a deist. For who else, other than a deist, would think it necessary to assign the risen Lord's sailing up into the clouds to Luke's fertile mind rather than to Jesus' decision literally to do so? Why give Luke the credit for *thinking up* the acted parable of the ascension, yet refuse Jesus credit for *acting it out?* Only because you have an a priori principle that Jesus couldn't or wouldn't have done such a thing. But that principle, please note, is based entirely on philosophical prejudice and not at all on scriptural warrant.

I say all this partly to distance myself from what I take to be a mistaken sort of biblical criticism but mostly to alert you to the fact that you must not expect me to be a biblical critic's biblical critic at all. I am a theologian by trade, not a biblical scholar; long ago (for the historical reasons I have already adduced in this chapter), I despaired of the kind of biblical study in which I, along with so many others, was trained. I bring to this exposition of Jesus' parables of judgment a theologian's free-ranging regard for the whole of Scripture, not a critic's narrow attention to what might have been the content of Jesus' teaching only.

362

And I do that because, as I said, we would never have had Jesus' teaching to begin with if it had not been for the church that the Holy Spirit used to give us the rest of the New Testament's teaching about Jesus. I will not set the one against the other. I insist on seeing them as of a piece, and I will not explain or apologize for that insistence any further.

Except to alert you to one more fact you should bear in mind. All trades have their blind spots: if the biblical-criticism fraternity has, for a good century now, suffered from a form of tunnel vision that prevented it from seeing philosophical errors out of the corner of its eye, the theologians' union has, for a lot longer than that, had an inordinate fondness for system. By the very nature of their craft, theologians are dedicated to making things philosophically tidy. If you want (as who doesn't?) a neat synthesis in which all the diverse pieces of revelation are gracefully tied together with a single ribbon of coherent principle, then they are the people to send for. But you must watch them like a hawk, because they can twist almost any two facts, however incompatible, into a thread — and with that thread, they can weave wonderfully. Fair warning then. Even if I am good, I am no better than the rest of my fellow workers on the theological loom. Always feel the goods: it's you, after all, who have to wear the suit.

To work, therefore. Let me try to make clear my thoughts on judgment by noting the way in which the Greek words for judgment are used in the New Testament. Take *kríma* (judgment, condemnation) first. While the word is used in a few places in the Gospels and elsewhere, the passage that unquestionably contains its most difficult and pregnant uses lies in chapters 2 and 3 of Paul's Epistle to the Romans. The difficulties, by and large, stem from a peculiarity in the way Paul wrote his epistles; the pregnancy of meaning, though, derives from the very heart of his thinking.

With no biblical writer more than Paul is it necessary to bear in mind where his argument is going; it is never enough simply to take what he says before he reaches that point and run with it as if it were his final word on the subject at hand. He dictated his letters. He worked, that is, from notes, proceeding through his argument more as an orator on a podium than as a writer at his desk. That means that he had both the freedom and the drawbacks of a speaker. He was free to expand at length on points that were incidental to the progress of his argument; but by the same token, he often expanded at such length that he said things which, taken out of the overall context, can seem to run counter to the argument itself.

Two examples will suffice. For the first, consider what presumably was contained in Paul's dictation notes for 1 Cor. 1. The items might well have been as follows: (1) Open with general greeting. (2) Thank God for the Corinthian church. (3) Warn them against partisan tendencies. (4) Begin main point about Foolishness and Weakness of God. He got through points (1) and (2) nicely; but when he got to point (3), he bogged down. In the course of warning the Corinthians not to say things like "I belong to Paul's party," or "I belong to Apollos," or "I belong to Cephas," he dropped the remark, "Thank God I didn't baptize any of you. . . ." His intention, of course, was simply to say, ". . . otherwise, you'd probably just use that as an excuse for more partisanship." But he immediately remembered that he had indeed baptized Crispus and Gaius; and in the next breath he remembered baptizing the entire family of Stephanus. So, since he was dictating this letter — speaking it rather than writing it — he had to make his corrections as a speaker rather than as a writer. He could not just erase his words or move the cursor back and zap them out; he had to add his corrections as he went along and then get out of his unfortunate digression with a resounding, "But let's get off that subject and on to the main point." Which is exactly what he did. After weaseling out of the question of how many people he actually baptized with "I just don't remember if I baptized anyone else" (1 Cor. 1:16), he began verse 17 with "But Christ didn't send me to baptize but to preach the Gospel" — and leapt decisively to point (4), the Power of Christ crucified.

You see the danger, of course. Paul was wandering down a byroad. An unwary interpreter could easily try to make a large point of his baptismal activities; but that would be a false start because it had only a tangential connection with what he actually set out to say. Thus my second example of Pauline digression: chapters 9–11 of Romans. Paul had begun chapter 8 with the glorious statement that "There is therefore now no condemnation *(katákrima)* to those who are in Christ Jesus"; and he ended it with the even more glorious assertion that "nothing can separate us from the love of God in Christ Jesus our Lord." This is the climax of his argument thus far, and his notes now tell him that, after dealing for a bit with the relationship of Israel to all this grace and mercy, he is to make the point (which he finally gets to in Rom. 11:26ff.) that "all Israel will be saved." But on the way to that point, he talks himself into one of the most memorable (and for the unwary interpreter, disastrous) detours in the whole of Scripture. All of the raw materials for double predestination — for God's right to condemn whoever he damn well pleases — come pouring out of him: the pot that can't speak back to the potter, the potter who is free to make vases or chamberpots, and so on. The dreadful doctrine of divine reprobation, therefore, is based on a misreading — not, admittedly, of Paul's actual words, for he did indeed say all those hard things, but *of the force of his words in the context of his whole argument.*

I introduce those examples because the same kind of theological detour is to be found in his uses of *kríma* (and of the verb *krínein*) in chapters 2 and 3 of Romans. In chapter 1 of that epistle, he has spoken of the power of the Good News; he has set down the general principle of justification by faith alone; and he has established the general guilt of all mankind, Jew and Greek alike, before God. He has, in other words, headed himself for chapter 3, in which he will say clearly that *no one* is righteous — that *no one* keeps the law — and that, when righteousness does come to the world, it will not come by the law but will be a gift from God through faith in Jesus Christ. On his way to that conclusion, however, he spends an inordinate amount of time talking about the *kríma tou theoú*, the judgment, the condemnation of God, that rests upon all human beings. Once again, the unwary interpreter is tempted to misread him. The difficult notion of a judgment that regards only the righteousness of Christ enjoyed by faith (a notion, admittedly, that will not receive its definitive statement until Rom. 8) slips away from the reader and only old-style, reward-and-punishment judgment seems to be on Paul's lips. Nevertheless, Rom. 2:1–3:8 remain essentially a detour. They are a parenthesis within his argument, not the main point of it. That comes only when he reaches Rom. 3:9ff., and in particular, 3:22-24: "For there is no difference [no difference, that is, that can be seen as proceeding out of old-line, tit-for-tat *kríma*]; for all have sinned and fallen short of the glory of God, but they are all justified by his grace through the liberating action of Christ Jesus." And Paul then continues in the same, gracious vein: this liberating action is effective for all because God has appointed Jesus a propitiation *(hilastérion)* through faith in his blood in order that God might show his own righteousness *(dikaiosýnes)* by the forgiveness *(páresin)* of past sins through his forbearance *(anochę̃)* — in order, that is, to manifest his righteousness right now *(en tǫ̃ nýn kairę̃*, in the present time) and to prove not only that he himself is righteous *(díkaios)* but that he makes righteous *(dikaioúnta)* those who have faith in Jesus (Rom. 3:25-26).

Romans 2–3, therefore, must be read as an argument in progress. And because the argument does not reach its conclusion until late in chapter 3, it is a mistake to start making conclusions about judgment *(kríma)* in chapter 2. True enough, as you read your way through the passage, your customary view of judgment as God's way of getting even with sinners will tempt you to decide that Paul is coming down hard on the side of that view. But on any fair reading of the entire section you will see that, at the most, he is simply setting you up for a deliverance from that view by means of his favorite subject, grace *(cháris)* — a subject that, for him, remains sovereign over anything you might have thought he was saying about *kríma*.

Admittedly, it takes a bit of doing (perhaps even of fine slicing) to see that. Nevertheless, the fact remains that Paul's view of judgment proceeds *out of* his notion of grace, not *contrary to it*. It is far less difficult, however, to see this radically nonjudgmental character of judgment when you come to Jesus' words about *krísis* (judgment) as they appear in the Gospel of John. I give only a single example: the passage that appears in chapter 3 at the end of Jesus' dialogue with Nicodemus, the Pharisee who came to him by night.

Everyone knows and loves John 3:16: "For God so *(hoútōs*, thus) loved the world that he gave his only Son that everyone who believes *(pás ho pisteúōn)* in him should not perish but have eternal life." To be sure, that verse alone establishes the primacy of faith *(pístis)* over any rewardable or punishable works; but the rest of the passage (John 3:17-21) expands upon the theme mightily and deserves far more attention than it gets. Let me comment on its verses in order.

Verse 17. "For God did not send his Son into the world that he might judge *(krínē)* the world, but that the world might be saved *(sōthḗ)* through him." Jesus repeats the substance of these words in John 12:47, and they are perhaps his most definitive statement on the subject of judgment. To me, they indicate that contrary to all our guilty expectations, God is not mad at the world. Even when he sends his Son to it — the same Son, incidentally, whom he has appointed to do all his judging for him (John 5:22: "the Father judges no one, but has given over all judgment to the Son") — this Son, strangely, does not judge, but rather saves. Not only in this verse, therefore, but throughout the Gospel of John, there lurks the image of the rigged trial, of a judgment at which the judge is shamelessly in cahoots with the guilty world and utterly determined to acquit it no matter what.

Verse 18. "He who believes *(ho pisteúōn)* in him is not judged *(ou krínetai);* but he who does not believe *(ho mḗ pisteúōn)* has already been judged *(ḗdē kékritai)* because he has not believed *(pepísteuken)* in the name of the only Son of God." All that the world has to do to escape judgment is *believe* — for the simple reason that, by the gracious work of Jesus, it has in fact *already escaped* it. It need do nothing to earn that escape, and it certainly need not compile questionable lists of good works to prove that it deserves to escape. It need not negotiate with God, or be afraid of God, or try conning God into being lenient. It has only to believe that God in Jesus has settled all his problems of sin and to laugh loud and long at how graciously easy the whole business always was. But for those who do not believe — who will not trust the gracious order of the universe revealed in Jesus, who go on insisting on responsibility and accountability and all the other dreadful, losing subjects with which the world beats itself over the head — for them, there is deep trouble. For they have been judged and condemned already by the very fact of their refusal to believe in the nonjudgment already pronounced

— in the noncondemnation under which they actually stand — all of which, but for their estranged, stubborn faces, they could be enjoying free of charge.

Verse 19. "And this is the judgment *(krísis):* that the light has come into the world and people loved the darkness rather than the light because their deeds were evil." Yes, Jesus says; there is indeed a judgment, and that judgment still stands because the law and the prophets I came to fulfill still stand. There is a judgment because the law remains forever your beauty, and when I come to you in my fulfillment of all its righteous demands, I will only make the ugliness of your disobedience look a thousand times worse. But *I* do not judge you. You judge yourself by taking your stand on the law's demands rather than on my righteousness which is yours for the believing. *I* do not condemn you. The law does; but I have lifted the curse of the law and given you a yoke that is easy and a burden that is light: all you need is simply to trust my word that I do not in fact condemn. But if you insist on running from the light of that word into the darkness of your own guilt — if you will not come to me and let me transform your ugliness into my beauty, if you fear my beauty because you dread its contrast with your ugliness — well, then, I cannot help you. Or, better said, you cannot receive the help I have already delivered to you because you choose not to trust my assurance that you already have it. I wish we could do business, Jesus says; and as a matter of fact, I have gone ahead and done all the business that needs doing. But as long as you keep yourself out there in the dark, my doing of it might just as well never have happened: I have put a billion-dollar deal in your left hip pocket and you won't even move your hand to check it out.

Verse 20: "For every one who does evil *(phaúla,* bad things, vile things) hates the light and does not come to the light lest his deeds be exposed." Out in the darkness of our unbelief, we fear God and we hate God. Because we will look only at our own ugliness and not at Jesus' gracious, transforming beauty, we keep ourselves from the one thing that can save us — that has in fact saved us, even though we will not trust it. But . . . .

Verse 21. ". . . but he who does [___ _____] comes to the light that it may be clearly seen that his deeds have been done in God." As you can see, I have left out two words on purpose. What do you suppose they were? What is it that we all, sitting in the darkness with our *phaúla*, our vile deeds, our evil, our ugliness, naturally assume Jesus to have said? Do not you, do not we all, bizarrely expect him to return, at the end of this rhapsody of gracious nonjudgment, to the old bait-and-switch offer of which we always suspected him? Are we not, in our guilt, fully prepared to hear him take back grace and reinstate law by saying, "but he who does *the good* comes to the light . . ."? But what does Jesus actually say? He says, "He who does *the truth (tḗn alḗtheian)* comes to the light. . . ."

Do you see what that means? It means that we can come to the light no matter what our deeds have been. We are not required to clean up our act beforehand, and we are certainly not required to submit proof that the act will stay clean henceforth and forever. We are only required to *do the truth*, to bring our ugliness out of the dark into the light and to let the absolving acceptance of Jesus shine upon it. And we are to do that precisely in order that it may be clearly seen — by us, please note, because it was we, not God, who were in the dark — that *all* our deeds, good *and* bad, were done in God. Even our sins were committed in the Light who lightens everyone. Even in the moment of their commission, they were absolved by that Light. And except for our fearful, groundless hatred of the Light, we could have seen that all along.

To which fact, every Christian worship service bears witness. Sunday after Sunday we come into church with the same list of tiresome sins: our lust, our laziness, our anger, our jealousy, our pride. And Sunday after Sunday we begin our worship by confessing them. Why? What is the real purpose of Christian confession? Is it to present them to a God who doesn't know about them, or to haggle over them with a God who might possibly be talked into forgiving them? No. It is only to bring them to the light of Jesus and to see clearly that they were forgiven all along. It is only (to put it in the startling terms of the *Exultet,* the old Latin proclamation sung on Easter Eve) to force ourselves to rejoice over our sin because it has become the occasion of his grace — to see it as a *felix culpa,* a happy fault — and to wash away the whole sorry history of the world's transgressions in the absolving blood of the

369

Lamb. *"O certe necessarium Adae peccatum,"* the *Exultet* sings, "O certainly necessary sin of Adam," *"quae talem et tantum meruit habere redemptorem"*: "which deserved to have such and so great a Redeemer." We have always been home free, lightened even in the house of our sins by the Light of Light in whom they were all wrought. The only thing we do in confession is drag ourselves back in out of the dark that never was.

Let me end this chapter by delivering the third item I invoiced at the beginning, namely, verse 20 of chapter 3 of the Book of Revelation: "Behold, I stand at the door and knock. If any one hears my voice and opens the door, I will come in to him; and I will have supper *(deipnḗsō)* with him, and he with me."

I choose this passage not because I intend to make a full commentary on the letters that Jesus, in a vision, told John the Divine to write to the seven churches in Asia but because it enables me to ring some changes on the image I just introduced of the house set in illusory darkness. In those early sections of Revelation, Jesus speaks to John in a vision of light: he is holding seven stars in his right hand and he is walking in the midst of seven golden lampstands. So much for the outer darkness: even as he stands out there on the world's front step and knocks — even there, outside the door of the swept and ordered house (Luke 11:25) he has provided for us in his death and resurrection, there is light; even those of us who perversely choose to love the darkness are standing in the Light. And so much for the threat of the seven devils worse than our first uncleanness (Luke 11:26) whom we might possibly invite in to make that house dark again: the judge of the world is on the doorstep and there isn't room for a single one of them.

For the judge who stands there is not alone. There is a crowd with him, and it isn't the cops. It is a party. It is all the guests at the Supper *(deípnon)* of the Lamb — plus the chefs and the caterer's crew and the musicians and the stars of the evening — all making an eternal racket, all pleading to bring the party into the house. And they have found our address not because they looked it up in the "books that were opened" at the last judgment before the great white throne (Rev. 20:12) — not because they examined our records and found us socially acceptable —

370

but only because he showed them our names in the "other book that was opened" (Rev. 20:12, again): the Lamb's book of life.

Do you see? If he had looked us up in those *books,* we would all have been judged *according to our works* (Rev. 20:12, still), and the eternal party would never even have come down our street. But because he looked us up only in *the book* — because he came to save and not to judge, because in the Lamb's book we are all okay, all clothed with his righteousness, all drawn infallibly to himself by his being lifted up in death and resurrection — because of that and only because of that, he finds the door of every last one of us and lands the party on our porch. All we have to do is say yes to him and open the door. We do not have to earn the party; we already have the party. We do not have to understand the party, or conjure up good feelings about the party; we have only to enjoy the party. Everything else: the earning, the deserving, the knowing, the feeling — our records, our sins, even our sacred guilt — is irrelevant. "No man," Luther said, "can know or feel he is saved; he can only believe it." And he can only believe it because there is nothing left for him to do *but* believe it. It is already *here.* There is therefore *now* no condemnation. The Light *has come* into the world.

Even at the judgment, therefore, the gracious Light — the *Phôs hilarón* — is still the only game in town. When the Lamb stands at the door and knocks, only an inveterate nonsport would say, "Darkness, anyone?"

CHAPTER THREE

Death as the Engine of Judgment

THE MAN BORN BLIND
THE GOOD SHEPHERD
JESUS ON DIVORCE AND CELIBACY
JESUS AND THE LITTLE CHILDREN
THE RICH YOUNG MAN

For me, the parables of judgment begin at Matt. 19:1 (Aland no. 251) — the point at which the Matthean account of Jesus' final ministry in Judea supersedes the Lukan account of his last journey from Galilee to Jerusalem (Luke 9:51–18:34; Aland nos. 174-237). Nevertheless, the intervening passages (John 7:1–10:21) that Aland includes at nos. 238-250 deserve at least a few words, especially in view of my comments in the preceding chapter on the Johannine view of judgment.

This lengthy section of the Gospel of John deals with a visit Jesus made to Jerusalem for the feast of Tabernacles, and it buttresses nicely what I have been trying to establish as the gist of his teaching about judgment. In briefest outline, it goes as follows. At John 7:1, Jesus is in Galilee (as he is in Matt. 19:1 and Luke 9:51). His unbelieving brothers urge him to leave there and go to Judea in order to make a public demonstration of his ministry at the feast; but Jesus refuses, saying his time has not yet come. After his brothers depart without him, though, Jesus goes up to Jerusalem secretly and remains in hiding until the feast is about half over, at which point he begins to teach openly in the temple.

372

He charges the Judean authorities (John 7:14-39) with not keeping the law and with trying to kill him; they, in turn, accuse him of having a demon. Since he knows they do not seriously think he is crazy but rather are furious over his heterodox assertions of authority — particularly over his healing of a sick man on the sabbath (John 5:9) — he flaunts that healing and tells them not to judge *(mé krínete)* by appearances but to judge right judgment *(dikaían krísin)*. The crowds listen eagerly to all this, but the chief priests and the Pharisees send officers to arrest him. Still, nothing happens at this point: the officers, just as impressed and/or confused by Jesus as the crowds are, return to their superiors without him. The authorities then debate the issue among themselves (John 7:40-52; fascinatingly, it is Nicodemus, the Pharisee whose visit to Jesus evoked the discourse in John 3:16ff., who stands up and defends him), and the arrest scheme goes temporarily into abeyance.

Jesus then speaks again (John 8:12), calling himself the light of the world and saying, "He who follows me will not walk in darkness but will have the light of life." (I make no comment here: the congruence of this entire passage with what I have so far set forth in this book should be obvious.) He accuses the authorities once again of judging *(krínete)* according to the flesh, but insists that he himself judges *(krínō)* no one. Yet even if he does judge *(krínō)*, he says, his judgment *(krísis)* is true *(alēthés)* because it is nothing less than the judgment of the Father himself. The Judean authorities continue to bait him, but they still do not arrest him because, as John says, "his hour had not yet come" (8:20). Jesus then says plainly (8:26-28) that he has much to say about them and much to judge *(krínein)*, but that they will understand it all only when they have "lifted up the Son of man" — that is, only at his ultimate, gracious act of judgment, namely, the crucifixion. At these words, oddly, many believe *(epísteusan)* in him (8:30-36), and Jesus assures them that if they continue in his word, they will know the truth *(alētheian)* conveyed in his being lifted up, and that that truth will make them free.

Still, Jesus' argument with the authorities continues (John 8:37-47). He says they are seeking to kill him, but that if they were the children of Abraham, they would not act in such an un-Abrahamic way; they object that they are so Abraham's children — and God's too, for that matter. He says they are of their father the devil (8:48-59); they say again that he is the one who has a demon. He replies that he is not possessed — that he does not seek his own glory — but that there is One who does seek it, and it is that One who will be the ultimate judge (*ho krínōn*). But then Jesus solemnly declares, "If any one keeps my word, he will never see death" (8:51). They say that proves he has a demon: even Abraham and the prophets died; who does he think he is? Jesus says they simply have not known God and he adds that Abraham himself, as a matter of fact, "rejoiced to see my day." They say he is too young to have known Abraham; he says, "before Abraham was, I am." They try to stone him for blasphemy; he, mysteriously, hides himself and goes out of the temple (8:52-59).

The next passage after these exchanges about judgment, light, and death is the vivid Johannine account of Jesus' acted parable of the Healing of the Man Born Blind (John 9:1-41; Aland no. 248). Once more, Jesus recurs to the theme that he is the light of the world; and once again — practically the minute after he restores the man's sight — the objections of the Pharisees resume in full force. They positively grill both the man and his parents, trying to prove the healing a fraud. In the end, though, when Jesus delivers his peroration to the healing (9:39), he does so by tying together, yet one more time, the themes of judgment and light: "For judgment *(kríma)* I came into the world," he says, "that those who do not see may see, and that those who see may become blind."

Then, in John 10:1-18, he goes on to tie the knot between judgment and death: he speaks of himself as the good shepherd who lays down his life for the sheep. He proclaims, in other words, that his death is the operative device by which the reconciling judgment of God works — that the crucifixion is God's last word on the subject of sin, the final sentence that will make the world one flock under one gracious shepherd. Nevertheless, as John notes in the concluding paragraph (10:19-21) of this entire section, the net result of everything Jesus has said and done at the feast of Tabernacles is a continuing division among the

Judean authorities. Some still say he is possessed; others are disposed to take him seriously. But those who favor getting rid of Jesus are about to prevail. The long narration has admirably advanced the plot: after only a few more confrontations — and in particular after the raising of Lazarus from the dead (11:1-53) — the authorities will be ready to arrest him as a threat to public safety. Because they love darkness more than light, they see Jesus' preaching of judgment only through the dark glasses of their fear that he will provoke the Romans to take action and destroy both the temple and the nation. As Caiaphas the high priest later says in unwitting prophecy (11:50), they decide that "it is better that one man die for the people than that the whole nation perish." And so John himself ties the ultimate knot in this paradoxical tapestry of judgment: even though they will not accept the light that Jesus brings them, their very effort to extinguish that light on the cross will become an instrument of grace. Even they themselves, therefore, will have in some sense "done the truth": their worst will have been done in the Light that brings everything to its best.

With that much (or that little) said about the Johannine intermezzo, it is time to return to Matt. 19:1. Jesus, as I noted, is in Galilee; but he departs immediately for the region of Judea beyond the Jordan and large crowds follow him. This passage corresponds, of course, with Luke 9:51, where Jesus leaves Galilee to begin his last journey to Jerusalem. But in Luke, it takes many chapters — nine, in fact, all devoted to the parables of grace I have expounded in *The Parables of Grace* — to reach the point (Luke 18:18) that Matthew arrives at only verses later at Matt. 19:16. At first, therefore, it might seem that there is a large discrepancy here between the Lukan and the Matthean chronologies. Nevertheless, it is possible to argue that Luke's nine chapters do not represent as long a time period as they seem to. Since only *two* sabbaths (Luke 13:14 and 14:1) are recorded in the whole section, it just might be that the entire passage represents a space of three weeks or less. If that is so, it fits in nicely with my choice of colors for the parables of grace and the parables of judgment. Because in both Matthew and Luke, we are now very nearly up to Palm Sunday (it occurs in Luke 19 and Matt. 21): we are, in short, only days away from Jesus' death and resurrection.

Accordingly, just as Jesus' certainty of an early crucifixion colored the parables of grace with the purple of passion and death, so that same sense of the imminence of the cross produces the white heat of the parables of judgment.

As a matter of fact, there is even an image in Scripture that corroborates this dominance of death over the parables. In the Lukan account of the transfiguration (Luke 9:28-36), Moses and Elijah appear in glory and speak with Jesus about his *éxodos* (that is, his death and resurrection) which he was about to accomplish *(hén émellen pléroún)* in Jerusalem. Do you see? It is as if Jesus has gone up on the mountain to consult not one but two doctors — two specialists in the dispensation of the mystery — who tell him he has less than a month to live. From that point on, therefore, his mind has only one thing uppermost in it: death and resurrection. To my way of thinking, that has two tremendous consequences for the study of the parables. Not only does death-resurrection become the most likely *leitmotiv* — the sovereign recurring theme — in his composition of both the parables of grace and the parables of judgment; it also becomes (or should become) the principal interpretative device for their exposition.

I note those consequences here for a reason. At this point in the Gospel narrative, all three synoptic writers are doing two things. Principally, of course, they are preparing to head into the passion/resurrection narrative which, as I have said, is the *terminus ad quem* of all four Gospels. But incidentally, they are also trying to work in the remaining bits and pieces about Jesus they have not so far included. They have on hand, as it were, a slim packet of index cards with unused words and actions of Jesus noted on them, and they are concerned to put check marks on as many of them as possible. Accordingly, as I come in the course of my exposition to what seems to be extraneous, or at least arbitrarily inserted material (which I shall do very shortly indeed, in Matt. 19:3-12), I shall make every effort to give it a death-resurrection interpretation. And I shall do that on two grounds. The first is that Jesus (with the cross uppermost in his mind) may well have said or done the very things the Gospel writers attribute to him at those very points in his ministry. The second is that even if he did not, the writers themselves may well have inserted them where they did for the same reason: they may have seen, in these apparently moralistic or otherwise out-of-synch passages, a death-resurrection coloring that warranted their inclusion.

In any event, Matt. 19:3-12 becomes the first instance of a seemingly irrelevant passage that turns out, on examination, to be more germane than it looks. Some Pharisees come to Jesus and ask him (*peirázontes autón:* tempting him, putting him to the test) a leading and tricky question. "Is it lawful," they inquire, "for a man to put away his wife for any and every reason?" It is not clear from the text just why they put the question this way. Perhaps the most likely interpretation is that they suspected Jesus of being a "liberal" about the law (he did, after all, break the sabbath) and hoped he would say something incriminatingly loose on the subject of matrimony.

Whatever their reason, Jesus comes back at them with a reply that is devastatingly strict. Quoting Genesis, he attacks *them* for the very tampering with the law of which they hoped to convict him. By the decree of the Torah, he tells them, a man and his wife are one; what therefore God has joined together, let no one put asunder. Jesus knows (see Matt. 5:31) that they have long taken the view that giving a wife a "letter of putting away" (an *apostásion*) was permissible — that the inconvenience of the law could be mitigated in cases where the inconvenience of the wife became excessive. And sure enough, they take the bait. They quote the Torah back at him from Deut. 24:1: "Why then," they ask, "did Moses command us to give a wife who is put away a letter of *apostasíou?*" But Jesus, shrewd rabbinical controversalist that he is, is ready for them. "I quoted from Genesis," he tells them, "and since Genesis comes first in the Torah, that means that my quote shows God's intention from the beginning. What you gave me from Deuteronomy comes later: it's nothing more than an accommodation to your resistance to the truth (*tḗn sklērokardían hymṓn,* your hardness of heart)."

Jesus then adds a verse that has always been one of the most difficult and problematical in Scripture: "And I say to you that whoever puts away his wife, *except for harlotry (mḗ epí porneíą),* and marries another, commits adultery" (Matt. 19:9). I have nothing to say about this so-called Matthean exception, other than to note that it is indeed an exception. For one thing, it is at odds with the rest of what Jesus is saying at this point (the parallel passages in Mark 10:11-12 and Luke 16:18 offer no such exception to the uncompromising strictness of his reply to the Pharisees); for another, the church's occasional, and foolish, enactment of it into canon law has served almost no purpose beyond providing an excuse for cashiering marriages that a little Christian forgiveness might have saved. Because whatever it means and wherever it came from, the phrase itself is exceptionally ill-suited to its context. Throughout this passage, Jesus is intentionally taking a hard line; therefore it is precisely the hardness of his reply, not this inconsistent exception to it, that must occupy the interpreter's attention.

What then is my interpretation? Simply this. Jesus is zeroing in on the Pharisees' desire to establish their own righteousness — to be winners, successful livers of lawful lives — by whittling the law down to the size of their own less-than-successful obedience. But that, he tells them in effect, just won't wash. The law still stands in all its righteous, unflinching obligation. And he goes on to imply what Paul was to say later and more fully in Romans, namely, that if they take their stand on the law they will simply be condemned by the law because no one can ever really keep it. But not to worry, he tells them in effect; because if you take your stand on my saving cross — if you will only believe me when I say I came not to judge but to save, not to examine records but to erase them, not to enforce the charges contained in the law of commandments and ordinances but to nail them all to my cross (Eph. 2:15; Col. 2:14) — then you will be out of the court system forever. For you will have taken your stand on the truth about yourself — on the truth that all your deeds, whatever they were, were done in the light of my absolving death and resurrection — and that truth, by your simple trust in my word that it is already true, will make you free.

Do you see what that means? It means that we are saved not by our successes but in and through our failures — not by our lives but in our deaths. For our so-called lives and our vaunted successes cannot be saved. They are nothing but suits of obsolete armor, ineffective moral and spiritual contraptions we have climbed into to avoid facing the one thing that *can* save us: our vulnerability. Jesus is not the least bit interested in saving the President of the United States or the Archbishop of Canterbury or the Duchess of Kent; he is not even interested in saving the Father of Six Children, or the Mother on Welfare. He does not care beans about the titles and roles we assign to ourselves in our successes, any more than he cares beans about the names we call ourselves in our failures. It is *us* he saves, not our lives. It is the *person* he dies for, not the suit of clothes in which the person hides from the bare truth about himself. He does not save you or me as we dress ourselves up at high noon on a good day; he saves us only as we stumble naked and uncombed from lumpy mattress to cold shower after a long, hard night — as, that is, we limp in faith from the bed of our death, through the blood of the cross, to the joy of his resurrection.

If you find that a bit much to wring out of Jesus' *obiter dicta* on the subject of matrimony, you have plenty of company. It isn't only you and the Pharisees who found less in his remarks than I claim to have discovered. Jesus' own best friends are with you all the way. In Matt. 19:10-12 — after the Pharisees have presumably walked off in disgust — the disciples proceed to miss his point by a country mile. "Gee whiz, Lord," they say to him in effect, "if that's how tough your marriage standards are, shouldn't we just advise people not to get married at all?" Their literal minds, you see, have gone to the only destination they can think of: celibacy. But Jesus refuses to let them stay there. He does the old, master-teacher's trick of dividing himself in two and quietly crouching down behind them before shoving them over from the front — and then he sends them sprawling. "Dummies!" he says to them. "Haven't you heard what I've been saying? Not getting married is no solution either. That's just more fiddling with the law — more of the same, silly business of trying to win the game by shaving the rules. Don't you see that I'm not going to save winners at all? Besides, who would volunteer for the job of being eunuchs like that just to make a moral buck? Only one more little club of losers who thought they had figured out a way of winning — only a bunch of select types who were either born without *cojones* or cut them off because they thought that society, or maybe even God, had decided it was a neat idea. Well, if you like that sort of thing, more power to you; me, I've had it with all these private success clubs

379

and their nifty admissions requirements. What I'm into now is a *catholic* salvation: one that's going to work on *failure only* — one that's going to include the whole world because the only thing it's going to need will be the one thing that everybody has, namely, death. Not life. Not success. And certainly not the ability to draw to some moral inside straight. Just the *cojones* to admit the truth that they're dead, and to trust me to take care of everything else."

That, I gather, you finally find a bit more than too much. I apologize. But not for myself alone. I had help: Jesus, after all, was the one who brought up the subject of castration to begin with. Relax, though: time now for a return to seemliness on both our parts: Jesus' Blessing of Little Children (Matt. 19:13-15).

The brief account of this often-portrayed episode is found in all three synoptic Gospels. Moreover, it is present in all three in the same context: it occurs not long before Palm Sunday and Good Friday. Therefore, in line with my principle that what was uppermost in Jesus' mind should be uppermost in ours as we interpret him, I ask you to set aside all the sentimental Victorian depictions of this episode that you may have in your head and think about it solely in terms of Jesus' death as the gracious judgment rendered by the Light of the world.

For Victorian sentimentality is precisely what all those intellectually loosey-goosey pictures of Jesus blessing a mixed bag of tiny tykes are actually about. The modern world's wishful view of childhood as a blessed, innocent state — and thus of children as fundamentally unfallen creatures — is a late-nineteenth-century invention. Prior to that time, children were not only seen (wisely) as no less sinful than anyone else; they were also seen (sadly) as imperfect, sawed-off adults who needed little more than to have their imperfections beaten out of them and their education beaten into them. Children were seen as losers, in other words — and childhood was considered a state that no sane child (or adult) would choose to stay in for one minute more than was necessary.

I bring that up again (I made the same point in my previous book, *The Parables of Grace*) because it is crucial here. Jesus is not simply being the gentle Scoutmaster in this passage; he sees an opportunity to make a death-forgiveness-judgment-light buck and he takes it. Watch.

"Children *(paidía)* were brought to Jesus," Matthew says (19:13), "that he might lay his hands on them and pray." So far, so good. But then the disciples — sharing the perennial, pre-Victorian view that children are little losers with whom the Important Rabbi should not be bothered — rebuke the people who brought them. "C'mon," they seem to be saying to the importunate parents, "get these kids out of here; the Master has bigger fish to fry." But Jesus, in effect, rebukes *them* (19:14) for being the same thickheaded point-missers they had just been on the subject of eunuchs. Little losers, he tells them — the last, the least, and the dead (of which children are the perfect paradigm) — are what his plan of salvation is all about. "Let *(áphete)* the children come to me and do not hinder them," he says, "for to such belongs the kingdom of heaven." But what he is thinking is, How many times do I have to say this? How long is it going to take you to catch on to the fact that I don't work with winners? I am not in the business of saving people's questionably successful lives. I am in the business of being a loser myself and of offering them, in my crucifixion, a chance to turn the absolutely certain unsuccess of their death into pure gold. So what am I going to do now? I am going to *show* them, that's what. Right now. With these very children. And so, as Matthew notes, "he laid his hands on them and went away."

Notice the details of the account. The word he uses to rebuke the disciples, "Let *(áphete)* the children come . . . ," is one of the most weighty in the New Testament. The verb *aphiénai* (root, *aph-;* noun, *áphesis*) is not only the ordinary word for *let, permit, allow, suffer, dismiss;* it is also, in the other half of its many uses, the ordinary word for *forgive*. It is the word Jesus uses when he has the farmer in the parable of the Wheat and the Weeds tell the servants to "let *(áphete)* both grow together until the harvest"; it is the word he utters from the cross when he says, "Father, forgive *(áphes)* them"; and it is the word he tells us to use when we pray his prayer: "Forgive *(áphes)* us our trespasses as we forgive *(aphḗkamen)* those who trespass against us." The word, in short, carries within itself a profound pun by which forgiveness and permission constantly dog each other's steps. Even if Jesus did not intend the pun, therefore, it still lurks in the passage at hand by the inspiration of the Spirit — and it tempts the interpreter mightily.

But that is not all. The rebuke is also a judgment. "Let the children (*paidía*) come" is a condemnation of all those — disciples, Pharisees, you, me — who love the darkness of our success more than the light of failure that streams from the Holy Child (*país:* Acts 4:27). The judgment, you see, is precisely what Jesus said it was in John 3:19: that the light of death and resurrection has come into the world but that hardly anyone wants it because we are all busy rubbing the wet sticks of our lives together in the dark. Grace doesn't sell; you can hardly even give it away, because it works only for losers and no one wants to stand in their line. The world of winners will buy case lots of moral advice, grosses of guilt-edged prohibitions, skids of self-improvement techniques, and whole truckloads of transcendental hot air. But it will not buy free forgiveness because *that* threatens to let the riffraff into the Supper of the Lamb. And therefore the world of winners is judged already (*édē kékritai,* John 3:18) because it will not believe in the name of the only begotten Child (*país,* again: Acts 4:27) whom God raised from the dead — in the Loser of God who, in the fullness of his permitting, forgiving love, goes ahead and lays his hands on a bunch of grubby little kids and says, "There! That's what I have in mind."

So the Blessing of the Children becomes an acted parable second to none: a parable of grace and forgiveness and light — and a parable, above all, of the inescapable judgment that Mercy pronounces on a world that won't even put mercy on the bottom of its list. In addition, though, it becomes the totally apposite, utterly logical preface to the next passage in Matthew, namely, the acted parable of the Rich Young Man.

This episode (Matt. 19:16-22) likewise appears in all three synoptics. Matthew and Mark identify the man who eagerly comes to Jesus as young and rich — a yuppie if there ever was one. Luke introduces him simply as "a ruler" (*árchōn*) and leaves the reader in the dark as to his age. In any case, they all agree on the question that this go-getter has in mind (I conflate the accounts): "Good Teacher," he asks, "what good deed must I do to inherit eternal life?" The man, you see, is already a success as far as this world is concerned. But now . . . well, let us supply him with some adapted lines from Auden's *Caliban to the Audience* to flesh out his innermost thoughts.

He feels a call to higher, finer things. "Oh, yes," he sighs, "I have had what once I would have called success. I moved the vices out of the city into a chain of reconditioned lighthouses. I introduced statistical methods into the Liberal Arts. I revived the country dances and installed electric stoves in the mountain cottages. I saved democracy by buying steel. . . . But the world is no better and it is now quite clear to me that there is nothing to be done with such a ship of fools adrift on a sugarloaf sea in which it is going very soon and suitably to founder. Deliver me, dear Teacher, from the tantrums of my telephones and the whispers of my secretaries . . . deliver me from these helpless agglomerations of dishevelled creatures with their bed-wetting, vomiting, weeping bodies, their giggling, fugitive, disappointing hearts, and their scrawling, blotted, misspelled minds, to whom I have so foolishly tried to bring the light they do not want . . . translate me, bright Angel, from this hell of inert and ailing matter, growing steadily senile in a time forever immature, to that blessed realm, so far above the twelve impertinent winds and the four unreliable seasons, that Heaven of the Really General Case where, tortured no longer by three dimensions and immune to temporal vertigo, Life turns into Light, absorbed for good into the permanently stationary, completely self-sufficient, absolutely reasonable One."

Now do you see the man's problem as Jesus saw it? This fellow is a winner who will not give up trying to win. To be sure, he has gotten beyond mere worldly winning to a desire for Something Better; but he cannot for the life of him imagine the pursuit of that Spiritual Something by any other means than still more winning. He is sure there must be techniques for making a spiritual profit just as there were for making a temporal one, and he has come to Jesus to study them.

Jesus, however, has his number. "What's with all this talk about good?" he asks him (Matt. 19:17). "Nobody's good, and nobody's going to be. Maybe I'm good; but my goodness looks so much like badness that people can't even stand the thought of it. And God, of course, really is good, but not in any way you can hope to imitate. So just knock off this goodness routine and listen to what I'm trying to tell you."

Time to shift for a moment here to Mark 10:19 and Luke 18:20.

Matthew's version of what Jesus says next has an element of unparadoxical moralism in it — an element that the other two Gospels (with greater logic, I think) leave out. For what I think Jesus sets out to do after saying that goodness eludes us all is to challenge the young man. He wants him to take an honest look at just how successful he has actually been at practicing the goodness he thinks is the answer to his problems. In other words (if you will pardon the anachronism), Jesus is hoping for a little Pauline insight from him — hoping he will see that the law can save no one because the law can be kept by no one. So he says to him, "Hey! You know the commandments: 'Don't kill; Don't commit adultery; Don't steal; Don't bear false witness; Don't defraud; Honor your father and mother.' Why don't you take a really good look at them?" Jesus, you see, is handing the rich young man a straight-line. And the yuppie is supposed to respond with something like, "Oh, I get you: I haven't really been a winner even at those things, so why should I run around looking for even more good things I can be a failure at?"

Alas, though, the gambit doesn't work. This young man cannot even conceive of losing, so he simply cuts Jesus off with, "Oh, Teacher, I've done all those things perfectly ever since I was a kid. Why don't you give me a really hard, grown-up assignment?" But then, as Mark says (10:21), "Jesus looked at him, and loved him." You poor, amiable sap, he thinks to himself. I like you a lot, Harry. More than you'll ever know. But it just doesn't work that way. You try to save your life like that, you'll only lose it. You have to lose, l-o-s-e, lose your life to save it. Still, I'll give you a shot at what I mean, just to prove I love you.

And so, with consummate understatement, Jesus gently breaks the Good News to him. "You only have to do one simple little thing, Harry: sell everything you have and give it to the poor. That will take care of getting your treasury of merits off your back. Then come and follow me into my death." And at that saying, Mark says, the young man got very gloomy in the face and went off in a deep depression because "he had great possessions" — because, that is, he just couldn't bear the thought of being a loser.

The saddest part of the whole thing, though, is that he turned his back on the only really good piece of news he would ever hear, because in something under threescore years and ten, all that great stuff of his — all those *ktémata pollá,* those many goods, worldly or spiritual, physical or intellectual — would be taken from him anyway. And so would all his terrible stuff as well: the whole pile of his unacknowledged failures, the ratty tissue of his irretrievable relationships and second-rate loves. *All* of his achievements — his successful virtues as well as his success-loving vices — would someday go whistling into the ultimate no-win situation, the final, redeeming unsuccess of death. And the next saddest part of it is that in spite of this acted parable of the Rich Young Man — in spite of Jesus' clear insistence that no winner will ever do anything but lose — you and I go right on blithely trying to win. If it is not financial success that keeps us from the saving emptiness of Jesus on the cross, it is moral success, intellectual success, emotional success, or spiritual success. We simply will not lose; and without losing, we will never, ever, win.

Which is why, in terms of both Matthew's Gospel and this book, it is time to start a fresh chapter. Matthew is headed for the great parable of losers who win, the Laborers in the Vineyard (Matt. 20:1-16; Aland no. 256); and I want to use his next section (19:23-30; Aland no. 255: On Riches and the Rewards of Discipleship) as a bridge to it.

So as they say in books designed for the little children to whom the kingdom of heaven belongs, turn the page.

CHAPTER FOUR

A Rhapsody of Unsuccess

THE CURSE OF RICHES
THE EYE OF THE NEEDLE
THE LABORERS IN THE VINEYARD

After the rich young man leaves the scene, Jesus makes a remark that needs more careful exposition than it often gets. The Gospel accounts (Matt. 19:23; Mark 10:23; Luke 18:24) differ in some significant details, so I take the liberty of giving you all three. In Matthew, he says to his disciples, "Amen, I say to you, it will be hard *(dyskólōs)* for a rich man *(ploúsios)* to enter the kingdom of heaven." In Mark, he "looks around" and he says to the disciples, "How hard it will be for those who have riches *(hoi tá chrémata* — goods — *échontes)* to enter the kingdom of God." But in Luke, Jesus "looks at *him*" (that is, at the young man going sadly into the sunset of his successful life) and he says, to no one in particular, "How hard it is for those who have riches [the words are identical with Mark's version] to enter the kingdom of God."

On the whole, I am disposed to soft-pedal the Matthean account at this point. I find Mark more convincing as far as the words of Jesus are concerned, and I think Luke is more nearly right about the stage business with which Jesus delivers them. In all three Gospels, of course, this saying has judgmental aspects not only on its face but also in its general context, namely, as part of the buildup to Holy Week and to the specific parables of judgment that Jesus will deliver before his death. But in Matthew, it seems not only judgmental but unfairly so: "Amen, I say to you, *it will be hard....*" When the saying is put that way, it sounds as if Jesus is little more than a new Moses issuing a new and harsher law to the effect that the mere possession of wealth is offensive enough to warrant exclusion from the kingdom. His words, in short, seem a bit too sermon-on-the-mountish for this late in his ministry. (Not that I think that either these words or the Sermon on the Mount must necessarily be taken simply as legislation imposing a new morality; even in Matthew, both are more paradoxical than that. It's just that the prescriptive tone he gives them tactically shoves the interpreter into a legalistic corner.)

In the other two synoptics, though, Jesus' words sound more like lament than law. "How hard it is . . ." is not an edict that says, "I will make it tough on the rich"; it is a sad, loving commentary on how tough the rich make it for themselves. It is indeed a judgment; but it is a judgment that is precisely parallel to his lament over the city in Matt. 23:37-39 and Luke 13:34-35: "O Jerusalem, Jerusalem, killing the prophets and stoning those who are sent to you! How often would I have gathered your children together as a hen gathers her brood under her wings, and you would not! Behold, your house is forsaken!" It is a judgment, in other words, utterly in line with the principle of inclusion before exclusion that I set down at the outset as the key to the parables of judgment: it is gracious, loving acceptance mourning the rejection of acceptance. Jesus has already included both the city and the rich young man within the grace of his saving death: except for their own self-estrangement, both are loved and both are uncondemned. It is only their rejection of his acceptance — which, please note, is the sole Gospel basis for condemnation — that puts them in darkness rather than light.

But that is not the only reason I prefer Mark's and Luke's recounting of words and stage business at this point; I also think that their versions make the best sense of the next remark that all three Gospel writers assign to Jesus, namely, "It is easier for a camel to go through the eye of a needle than for a rich man to enter the kingdom of God."

It is common expository practice to suggest that in these words Jesus is referring to some actual narrow gate or passageway in the city of Jerusalem. If that is so, the meaning is plain enough: a fully loaded camel, with bundles of goods strapped to its sides, cannot get through the Eye of the Needle Gate without being unloaded; likewise, a rich young man has to get rid of his baggage before . . . etc. Still, the passage makes just as good sense if it is taken as plain old Oriental hyperbole: just as you can't stuff a camel through an opening designed to take only a thread, so you can't get someone who has a great, fat, successful life to volunteer to go through the narrow eye of lastness and death. Both interpretative gambits, therefore, come to the same point: Jesus' plan of salvation works only with the last, the lost, the least, the little, and the dead; the living, the great, the successful, the found, and the first simply will not consent to the radical slimming down that Jesus, the Needle of God, calls for if he is to pull them through into the kingdom.

Actually, therefore, this strict-sounding pronouncement of Jesus turns out to be more descriptive than prescriptive — as do a good many others. In Matt. 7:13-14, for example, he says, "Enter in by the narrow gate; for wide is the gate and easy is the road that leads to destruction (*apóleian*), and many there are who travel it. But narrow is the gate and difficult the road that leads to life, and few there are who find it." These words, like the words "how hard it is . . . ," have often been read as a new, wrenching turn of the law's screw intended to keep nearly everybody out of the kingdom. But on a wider and fairer reading, neither they nor the remark about the camel and the eye of the needle should be given such an interpretation. Both should be read under the grand rubric of John 13:22: "I, if I be lifted up from the earth, will draw *all* to me." Jesus the Needle is willing to sew up the salvation of every last son of Adam and every last daughter of Eve by threading them into the eye of his death — into the spear-wound in his side, if you will — just as Jesus the Divine Vacuum Cleaner will suck everyone who isn't obsessed with the wide gate of success right smack into the kingdom through the narrow slot of his failure on the cross. Accordingly, all we have to do is *let go* — let go of everything that is not the slim thread of our lastness and lostness, and let go of every effort to walk the easy road of winning — and upon that letting go, he will draw us home.

Thus, while the sentence he pronounces on those who will not let go is indeed a judgment, it describes and mourns their condition more than it prescribes and gloats over their fate. It is sadder than it is stern, more loving than it is condemning. "Oh, damn!" Jesus says, stamping a lover's furious foot: "Why won't you come? Why won't you let me draw you? Why do you insist on loving the darkness when you're already standing in the light? How can you not know the things that belong to your peace?" (Luke 19:42). And therefore Hell (*apóleia*, destruction — the ultimate destination of overloaded camels and fatheaded finders of the wide road of success) is as real as it is unnecessary and as eternal (so it seems, God help us) as the Love that will not let go even of those who won't stop hanging on to the successes that are destroying them. It is a perpetual Mexican standoff between the Loser who has won it all and the Winners who cannot stand the thought of losing. It is, in short, *hell*.

The disciples, however, are no more ready to think about such things than the rest of us are. "They were exceedingly astonished," the Gospel says (Mark 10:26), and they said to him, "Then who can be saved?" But then, Mark adds, "Jesus looked at them."

Once again, the stage business is no less important than the lines. The *looks* that Jesus uses or implies in this scene are worth a thousand words. He looks at the young man walking dejectedly away; he looks at the disciples in their incomprehension; and all the while, in his mind's eye, he looks at his own impending death. Moreover, in every one of these looks, the attentive watcher of the play senses the sad wrath of his love. Perhaps for the first time, Jesus hints at his growing realization that what he is asking of the world is simply too much — that it really is an impossible invitation. "You're right," he says after he has held the look for the extra beat needed to convey an inward resignation; "with men, this is impossible" (Matt. 19:26). Grace, he realizes, is the last thing the world will buy.

But grace, he also realizes, is the only thing that will work on the world as it so sadly is. "An eye for an eye" won't work because all it does is double the number of eyeless people. Retribution won't take evil out of the world; it will simply perpetuate it in spades. A judgment that works only by punishing sinners and rewarding the righteous produces all hell and no kingdom: there are just too many sinners, and there are no righteous. The only thing that's going to get evil out of the world is for him to take it into himself on the cross — to drop it down the black hole of his death — and to make a new creation by the power of his resurrection. And so after thinking it all through, he adds, "but with God, all things are possible" — even the impossibility of grace.

Most of the disciples, apparently, remain stymied by all this; but Peter — dear old dim, bright Peter — suddenly gets at least a glimmer of what Jesus is talking about. Not a clear vision, mind you, for Peter goes nowhere with it at this point and he forgets it almost completely at the trial and crucifixion. But he does see for a moment that Jesus is talking about losing, not winning, as the touchstone of salvation. He says (Mark 10:28), "Look, we have left *(aphēkamen!)* everything and followed you." Matthew has him add, "what will that get us therefore?" but since Mark and Luke leave this out, I think we can give him credit for just a tad less denseness than Matthew suggests. However dimly he perceives it, Peter does sense that saving lives is not what Jesus is up to. He smells, if you will, the reek of death; and he notices, in a way he never noticed before, that it does not seem to bother Jesus — that, in fact, Jesus is convinced it smells like roses. And therefore when he says, "We have left everything . . . ," he is not just looking for a payback. Rather, he is saying — in the very thick of all the impossibilities his conscious mind perceives — something much more like, "Look, I can't say I understand you, but I'm with you all the way." He is anticipating, in other words — with just as much sincerity and just as little self-knowledge — what he will say later, shortly before his denial of Jesus: "Lord, I am ready to go with you to prison and to death" (Luke 22:33).

Jesus, grateful for his sincerity and going gently on his lack of insight, gives him a soft answer with a hard core. Not budging an inch from his insistence that grace works only by loss, he says to Peter and to all the disciples (I am following Mark 10:29-31 here), "Amen, I say to you, there is no one who has left *(aphēken)* house or brothers or sisters or mother or father or children or lands for my sake and for the Gospel, who will not receive a hundredfold now in this time, houses and brothers and sisters and mothers and children and lands, *with persecutions* [italics mine], and in the age to come, eternal life. But many that are first shall be last, and the last first."

I shall resist (almost) the temptation to read those italicized words back into the preceding list of goods to be restored "now in this time." I shall not spend more than this one sentence reminding you that twentieth-century psychology has taught us only too well that it is precisely our possession, gained or regained, of mothers and fathers, children and siblings and stuff, that lies at the root of most of our problems. I simply point out that, in Mark, the awfulness of saving grace — the dreadfulness of a Love that will not take us *out* of our troubles, but instead insists on saving us *in and through* them — is succinctly conveyed by the phrase "with persecutions." The other two Gospels, of course, introduce that awfulness just as definitely when they quote Jesus' words about the first and the last; but they do so out of the blue, as it were, without the preparation that Mark supplies. Why they left them out (both, after all, had access to Mark) is a puzzle. Matthew, perhaps, felt that the upcoming parable of the Laborers in the Vineyard more than made up for the omission; Luke's reasons are simply a mystery. In any case, it is to that very parable that Matthew turns next; so let me get straight to it, expounding it as the rhapsody of unsuccess that I, along with him, take it to be.

THE LABORERS IN THE VINEYARD (MATT. 20:1-16)

(Classroom Teacher's Version)

Since you have all read the assignment . . . (much eye-rolling, some guilty looks) . . . I shall tell you the story anyway.

There was a man who owned a vineyard. His operation was not on the scale of E & J Gallo, but it was quite respectable: let us put him in the Robert Mondavi class. We first see this gentleman on the evening of the second Sunday in October. September has been a perfect month — hot and dry, bringing the grapes to 20° Brix — but his meteorological service tells him that the weather is about to turn into cold soup. So what does our friend Robert do? He gets up first thing Monday morning, goes down to what passes for the local hiring hall and contracts for

391

as much day labor as he can pick up. Unfortunately, every other grower in the neighborhood uses the same weather reports, so he has to promise higher pay to attract the workers he needs: $120 for the day is the figure that finally guarantees him a crew.

I see a hand up. Yes, Virginia?

No, Virginia, $120 is not a ridiculous figure. A *denarius* was a day's pay; I have simply taken the liberty of making it a good day's pay. A penny a day may have been alright for the translators of the KJV, but this is 2000.

Anyway, Robert loads his crew into a couple of old school buses and puts them to work, chop-chop. Just before nine A.M., though, he gets another weather bulletin. They have moved the start of the three weeks of rain from Wednesday back to Tuesday: he has one day, not two, to get the harvest in. Out he goes at nine, therefore — and with increasing panic at noon and at three — to hire on still more hands. Each time he succeeds in rounding up all the available help, giving them the by now practiced line that he is Robert Mondavi, the famous payer of top dollar who is also Mr. Fairness himself: whatever is right, they will get.

It's a huge harvest, though, and with only one hour left before dark, Robert realizes he won't get it in on time without still more help. So out he goes again, but the hiring hall is closed by now and the village square has only its usual crowd of up-to-the-minute losers hanging out in a haze of smoke. You know the types: lots of leather, some girls (and their boyfriends) with more mousse than brains, six-packs everywhere, and music that ruptures eardrums. What the hell, Robert thinks in desperation: it's worth at least a try. So he walks up to the group, ostentatiously switches off the offending ghetto-blaster, and goes into his spiel: he's Robert Mondavi; he's famous and he's fair; they could probably use a buck; so what do they think? What they think, of course, is also What the hell: whatever he wants them to do, it won't take long; and whatever he pays, at least it's a couple more six-packs for the night. Off they go.

Now then: run your mind over the story so far. I'm sure you know exactly what happens each time one of those new batches of workers

392

gets dropped off at the vineyard. Before they pick even a single grape, they make sure they find out from the workers already on the job the exact per diem amount on which Robert Mondavi is basing his chances at the Guinness Book of World Records. And since they are — like the rest of the human race — inveterate bookkeepers, they take the $120 figure, divide it by twelve and multiply it by the number of hours they'll be working. Then and only then do they lay hand to grape, secure in the knowledge that they will be getting, respectively, $100, $70, $40, and $10.

Robert, however, has a surprise for them. At the end of the day, he is a happy man. With his best and biggest harvest on its way to the stemmer-crusher, he feels expansive — and a little frisky. So he says to his foreman, "I have a wild idea. I'm going to fill the pay envelopes myself; but when you give them out, I want you to do it backwards, beginning with the last ones hired."

Once again, I'm sure, you know what happens. When the first girl with purple hair gets her envelope and walks away opening it, she finds six crisp, new twenties inside. What does she do?

No, Virginia, put your hand down. She does *not* go back and report the overage; she just keeps on walking — fast.

But when her shirt-open-to-the-waist boyfriends catch up with her and tell her they got $120, too . . . well, dear old human nature triumphs again: they cannot resist going back and telling everybody else what jerks they were for sweating a whole day in the hot sun when they could have made the same money for just an hour's work.

The entail of Adam's transgression being what it is, however, the workers who were on the job longer come up with yet another example of totally unoriginal sin. On hearing that Robert Mondavi is now famous for paying $120 *an hour,* they put their mental bookkeeping machinery into reverse and floor the pedal. And what do they then come up with? O frabjous joy! They conclude that they are now about to become the proud possessors of, in order, $480, or $840, or even — bless you, Robert Mondavi — $1,440.

But Robert, like God, is only crazy, not stupid. Like God, he has arranged for their recompense to be based only on the weird goodness he is most famous for, not on the just deserts they have infamously imagined for themselves: every last envelope, they find, has six (6) twenties in it; no more for those who worked all day, and no less for those who didn't.

Which, of course, goes down like Gatorade for the last bunch hired, like dishwater for the next-to-the-last, like vinegar for the almost-first, and like hot sulfuric acid for the first-of-all. Predictably, therefore — on the lamebrained principle that those who are most outraged should argue the case for those who are less so (wisdom would have whispered to them, "Reply in anger and you'll make the best speech you'll ever regret") — the sweatiest and the most exhausted decide to give Robert a hard time. "Hey, man," they say; "you call this a claim to fame? Those punks over there only worked one hour and we knocked ourselves out all day. How come you made them equal to us?"

Robert, however, has his speech in his pocket. "Look, Pal," he says. (Incidentally, the Greek word in the parable is *hetaíre,* which is a distinctly unfriendly word for "friend." In three of its four uses in the New Testament — here, and to the man without the wedding garment in the King's Son's Wedding, and to Judas at the betrayal — it comes off sounding approximately like "Buster.") "Look, Pal," he tells the spokesman for all the bookkeepers who have gagged on this parable for two thousand years, "Don't give me *agita.* You agreed to $120 a day, I gave you $120 a day. Take it and get out of here before I call the cops. If I want to give some pot-head in Gucci loafers the same pay as you, so what? You're telling me I can't do what I want with my own money? I'm supposed to be a stinker because you got your nose out of joint? All I did was have a fun idea. I decided to put the last first and the first last to show you there are no insiders or outsiders here: when I'm happy, everybody's happy, no matter what they did or didn't do. I'm not asking you to like me, Buster; I'm telling you to enjoy me. If you want to mope, that's your business. But since the only thing it'll get you is a lousy disposition, why don't you just shut up and go into the tasting room and have yourself a free glass of Chardonnay? The choice is up to you, Friend: drink up, or get out; compliments of the house, or go to hell. Take your pick."

Do you see now? Jesus' story of the Laborers in the Vineyard is every bit as much a parable of grace as it is of judgment, and vice versa. It is about a grace that works by raising the dead, not by rewarding the rewardable; and it is about a judgment that falls hard only upon those who object to the indiscriminate catholicity of that arrangement. On the pattern of the Pharisee and the Publican, this parable takes a flock of dead ducks and makes them not only equal to the live wires who worked all day, but a lot happier in the end. If I had to give them a heraldic description, I would say that grace *couchant* — insouciant grace, grace with her hair down, grace sprawled on the chaise lounge with a bottle of champagne — is *sinister* on their coat of arms. And conversely, on the pattern of the Prodigal Son, this parable takes a herd of industrious turtles and whacks them over the head with the bad news that there is only Good News: judgment *rampant,* therefore, stands *dexter* on their device — judgment that lights into everyone with a universal vindication and then sticks its tongue out at anybody who finds that more than he can take.

In the last analysis, though, it is indeed the tiger of judgment rather than the lady of grace that is the main theme of the Laborers in the Vineyard: my purpose in retelling it classroom-style was precisely to dramatize its unique contribution to the judgment side of the equation. When the lord of the vineyard finally laces into the bellyachers — when he finally gives them, in a rhetorical question, the precise reason why judgment falls not on the unacceptable but only on those who will not accept acceptance — he says: "Is your eye evil because I am good?"

It is the evil eye, you see — the *ophthalmós ponērós,* the eye that loves the darkness of its bookkeeper's black ink, the eye that cannot stand the red ink of unsuccess as it appears in the purple light of grace — that is condemned here. Bookkeeping is the only punishable offense in the kingdom of heaven. For in that happy state, the *books* are ignored forever, and there is only the *Book* of life. And in that book, nothing stands against you. There are no debit entries that can keep you out of the clutches of the Love that will not let you go. There is no minimum balance below which the grace that finagles all accounts will cancel your credit. And there is, of course, no need for you to show large amounts of black ink, because the only Auditor before whom you must finally stand is the Lamb — and he has gone deaf, dumb, and blind on the cross. The last may be first and the first last, but that's only for the fun of making the point: everybody is on the payout queue and everybody gets full pay. *Nobody is kicked out who wasn't already in;* the only bruised backsides belong to those who insist on butting themselves into outer darkness.

For if the world could have been saved by bookkeeping, it would have been saved by Moses, not Jesus. The law was just fine. And God gave it a good thousand years or so to see if anyone could pass a test like that. But when nobody did — when it became perfectly clear that there was "no one who was righteous, not even one" (Rom. 3:10; Ps. 14:1-3), that "both Jews and Gentiles alike were all under the power of sin" (Rom. 3:9) — God gave up on salvation by the books. He cancelled everybody's records in the death of Jesus and rewarded us all, equally and fully, with a new creation in the resurrection of the dead.

And therefore the only adverse judgment that falls on the world falls on those who take their stand on a life God cannot use rather than on the death he can. Only the winners lose, because only the losers can win: the reconciliation simply cannot work any other way. Evil cannot be gotten out of the world by reward and punishment: that just points up the shortage of sheep and turns God into one more score-evening goat. The only way to solve the problem of evil is for God to do what in fact he did: to take it out of the world by taking it into himself — down into the forgettery of Jesus' dead human mind — and to close the books on it forever. That way, the kingdom of heaven is for everybody; hell is reserved only for the idiots who insist on keeping nonexistent records in their heads.

One last comment. Just before Jesus launches into the payout sequence in this parable, he says, *"opsías dé genoménēs,* when it was evening, the lord of the vineyard said to his steward. . . ." I have an image for that. On Shelter Island, where I used to live, there is an odd local custom. Every Friday evening, at exactly five minutes of five, the fire siren goes off. For years, I wondered about it. What was the point? They tested the siren every day at noon, so it couldn't be that. I even asked around, but nobody seemed to know a thing about it. Then one day it finally dawned on me: rather than run the risk that the festivity of the rural weekend be delayed even one minute beyond the drudgery of the working week, some gracious soul had decided to proclaim the party from the top of the firehouse — the 4:55 siren was the drinking siren. Miller Time on Shelter Island.

Opsías dé genoménēs. Heaven is Miller Time. Heaven is the party in the streaming sunlight of the world's final afternoon. Heaven is when all the rednecks, and all the wood-butchers, and all the plumbers who never showed up — all the losers who never got anything right and all the winners who just gave up on winning — simply waltz up to the bar of judgment with full pay envelopes and get down to the serious drinking that makes the new creation go round. It is a bash that has happened, that insists upon happening, and that is happening now — and by the sweetness of its cassation, it drowns out all the party poopers in the world.

Heaven, in short, is fun. And if you don't like that, Buster *(hetaíre),* you can just go to . . . well, you'll have to use your imagination.

You'll need it: this is the only bar in town.

CHAPTER FIVE

Resurrection and Judgment

THE RAISING OF LAZARUS

Following the Aland chronology, we shift now to the Gospel of John — and to one of the most notable of all Jesus' acted parables, the Raising of Lazarus (John 11:1-44; Aland no. 259). As I mentioned earlier, there was a long period in the twentieth century when John was considered off-limits as a source for legitimate insights into the historical development of Jesus' thought. Things are better now; but since that prejudice still persists here and there, let me make just a few observations about it.

To adapt what Charles Williams once said of the Book of Job: no matter what the critics say about the Fourth Gospel, it is still possible to read it as an English book. I would add that it is not only possible to do so but essential: it is precisely the English version of John's Gospel *as it now stands* (or the Greek original, if you read Greek) that is your best clue to what the Holy Spirit wanted to tell you when he finally said (sometime early in the second century) "Okay, that's a take."

The nonhistorical character of John has been vastly overdone. This is not the place to go into the matter in detail, but for the record, note the following. First, despite certain transpositions (the Cleansing of the Temple in particular), John's chronology is more explicit, and sometimes more reliable, than the synoptics. Second, Jesus' dialogues in John are not just theological flights of fancy; they have about them a realism — or as Dorothy Sayers put it, a verisimilitude, a dramatic reproducibility — that the synoptics do not often achieve. And third, the passion narrative in John is both chronologically and geographically more verifiable than the accounts in the other three Gospels.

It is simply misleading, therefore, to act as if John is nothing but a theological rhapsody ungrounded by any connection with Jesus' actual ministry. Every one of the Gospels is a theological tract; none of them is the work of a mere chronicler. Their several theologies differ, of course, and John's is admittedly later and "churchier" than the rest. But that is hardly a fatal flaw: Matthew, Mark, and Luke are themselves later than Jesus and every one of them was produced in a context of inescapable churchiness. So say goodbye to the fantasized nonhistorical Jesus of an over-theologized Fourth Gospel. And welcome to the real world of the assorted but unremittingly theological documents by which the New Testament hands us the only Jesus anyone knows beans about.

Accordingly, I make no apology for threading in the Johannine account of the raising of Lazarus here. If its place in the overall Gospel sequence cannot neatly be squared with the differing chronologies of the synoptics, it nonetheless occurs in John at approximately the same point to which Matthew, Mark, and Luke have now brought us, namely, the time just before Palm Sunday. Far more important, though, is the fact that John's account squares perfectly with — no, that is too weak: it actually highlights and gives more convincing evidence for — the *tone,* the subtext, if you will, that the synoptic writers have established for Jesus' words and deeds at this juncture. Because if the other three Gospels show us a Jesus who is working up a head of judgmental steam in anticipation of his approaching death, John gives us a vivid picture of the fire under the boiler, namely, the hostility of the Judean authorities.

In the sections immediately preceding the Raising of Lazarus (John 10:22-42; Aland nos. 257-258), we see Jesus provoking the charge of blasphemy that was to be the basis of his trial and condemnation. The authorities gather around him and ask, "How long will you keep us in suspense? If you are the Christ, tell us plainly." Jesus answers them, "I told you, and you do not believe . . . because you do not belong to my sheep. My sheep hear my voice . . . and no one is able to snatch them out of my Father's hand. I and the Father are one." At those words, the authorities once again try to stone him for blasphemy; but Jesus, after a few more altercations and yet another attempt to arrest him, escapes from their hands, going away across the Jordan. And many came to him, John says, "and believed on him there."

The persistent effort on the part of the Judean authorities to arrest Jesus deserves some comment. It is by no means absent from the synoptics, of course: the plot to destroy *(apolésōsin)* him is noted in Mark 3:6 and Matt. 12:14, and (after Palm Sunday) in Mark 11:18 and Luke 19:47. But it is in John that the specific word *arrest (piázein,* to seize, to catch) is used again and again (John 7:30, 32, 44; 8:20; 10:39; and 11:57). John, accordingly, is the writer who most assiduously develops the subtext of the authorities' plan to proceed against Jesus by the legal device of a charge of blasphemy — and John is the only writer who gives it full play at this point (10:39 and 11:57).

One other note, by now a bit overdue. John's Gospel makes frequent use of the phrase *hoi Ioudaíoi* — which can be translated either as "the Jews" or as "the Judeans." As you may have noticed, I have a number of times taken the liberty of translating it as "the Judean authorities." Granted, translating it as "the Jews" is certainly appropriate at many points in the Fourth Gospel — points at which it is simply explanatory (John 7:2: "the Jews' feast of Tabernacles") or descriptive ("many of the Jews came to comfort Martha and Mary"). But when it takes on a negative connotation — especially when it is used to identify the plotters against Jesus — I find that translation inappropriate, if not downright misleading. I do not think that the author of the Fourth Gospel seriously intends to imply that the Jews, qua Jews, are the villains of his narrative. For one thing, he often uses *hoi Ioudaíoi* in a completely neutral way. He even, on occasion, uses it in a positive way ("Salvation is of the Jews," he has Jesus say in John 4:22; "Many of the Jews . . . believed in him," says the Gospel writer in John 11:45). Jesus was, after all, a Jew: he stood proudly on his own Jewishness; and while he associated scandalously with non-Jews (and even made a non-Jew the hero of his parable of the Good Samaritan), there is no way of turning him into an anti-Semite.

But second, I think that the so-called anti-Semitism of the Fourth Gospel needs a good knock in the head. True enough, there are pejorative uses of *hoi Ioudaíoi* in John; and true enough, vengeful Christians, in shamefully large numbers and for disgracefully long centuries, have gone along with the wickedness. But on any fair reading, John is no more an anti-Semite than Jesus. When he uses *hoi Ioudaíoi* as a pejorative, he is most commonly stigmatizing the Judean authorities, not all Jews; and it is precisely in their status as authorities, not in their status as Jews, that he faults them. If God had become incarnate above the Arctic Circle, the Eskimo authorities would just as readily have tried to do him in; if he had been born in Bethlehem, PA, the Governor of Pennsylvania would have been the one who fudged the law in order to get him. The Messiah we see in the New Testament would have had enemies in high places no matter where he landed. Unfortunately, though, on the principle that "Everybody's got to be somewhere, man," the Judean authorities were the ones whose neighborhood property values were ruined by the incarnate Lord's moving in. Which makes them, as far as I am concerned, more to be pitied than censured. They did God's dirty work for him. It was not nice of God to arrange things that way, but it was at least expectable. The God who tried to murder Moses in an inn (Exod. 4:24) — the God who kept the children of Israel in the wilderness for forty years (Exodus, interminably), the God who blasted Uzzah (2 Sam. 6:7) just for trying to keep the Ark of the Covenant from falling off an ox-cart — never advertised himself as the God of Good Manners.

With apologies all around, therefore (too late, too little, too bad), "the Judean authorities" it is. On to the Raising of Jesus' Dead Friend (John 11:1-44).

The story, which appears only in John, begins by identifying the principal character, Lazarus, as living in Bethany and as being the brother of Mary and Martha. These same two sisters appear in Luke 10:38-42 and again in John 12:1-8. Mary, as it is noted here (John 11:2), is the one who, just before Palm Sunday, anointed the Lord with ointment and wiped his feet with her hair. She is also — if you follow the dubious old practice of scrunching together as many biblical characters as possible — the "woman of the city" who was a sinner (Luke 7:36-50). She is even, if you carry the practice to its extreme, Mary Magdalene.

It is Lazarus, though, who is the most fascinating character. The oddest thing about him — and one of the few scripturally certain things — is that neither here nor elsewhere in the Gospels does he say a word. He appears at a dinner party in John 12:1-8; his name is used by Jesus in Luke 16:19-31 for the beggar in the parable of the Rich Man and Lazarus (an exceedingly odd turn on Jesus' part, because in no other spoken parable does he assign a proper name to one of the characters); and finally, after Lazarus has been raised from the dead, the high priests make plans to kill him all over again "because on account of him, many of the Jews were going off and believing in Jesus" (John 12:9-11). Nowhere, however — not even in the parable in Luke, where "Lazarus" is shown, strikingly, as risen from the dead and resting on the bosom of Abraham — does he have a single line.

But that is not the only oddity. Throughout John 11 the author goes out of his way to establish the uniqueness of the relationship between Lazarus and Jesus. In verse 5, he notes that "Jesus loved Martha and her sister and Lazarus"; in verse 33, he observes that Jesus was angrily upset *(enebrimésato)* by all the weeping of the mourners; in verse 35, he has Jesus himself weep when he sees the tomb in which Lazarus is buried; in verse 36, the bystanders say "See how he loved him!"; and in verse 38, Jesus approaches the tomb angrily upset again *(embrimómenos)*. This is a remarkable amount of emotion for a Gospel writer to assign to Jesus. But if you add to it another of John's peculiarities, it becomes more remarkable still.

Only *after* this point in the Gospel does the author begin his strange series of references to an unnamed disciple who reclined on Jesus' breast at the Last Supper — a disciple whom he further identifies as an "other *(állos)* disciple" and also as "that *(ekeínos)* disciple" whom "Jesus loved" (see, for example, John 13:23-25; 18:15-16; 20:2-8; 21:7, 20-23). Indeed, so notable are these references that some commentators have suggested the possibility that this "Beloved Disciple" may actually be Lazarus himself. If that is so, the next to the last verse of the Gospel (John 21:24) takes on a fascinatingly different meaning. The words,

"This is the disciple who bore testimony to these things and wrote them down . . . ," become thus a reference to Lazarus who, himself brought back to life by Jesus, becomes the Gospel's principal theological witness to Jesus' own victory as the Resurrection and the Life; and by contrast, the rest of the sentence, namely, ". . . and we know *(oídamen)* that his testimony is true," becomes the voice of the author of the Fourth Gospel.

There is, however, one more singularity about this whole business that I want to note. In some contemporary circles, the suggestion is often made that Jesus and the Beloved Disciple/Lazarus were homosexual lovers; by many contemporary squares, however, that suggestion is met with howls of "Blasphemy!" Let me pour oil on both their waters.

I think the right analogy here is Renaissance art. When the painters of that period depicted, say, the Annunciation, they showed the angel wearing the Sunday-go-to-meeting clothes of their own day: Gabriel looked exactly like some Venetian yuppie. They did not, presumably, think that such a getup was a faithful reproduction of the angel's actual clothing as Mary first saw it: lacking any hard information about first-century styles, they simply imposed their own fashions on the scene and got on with their proper artists' business of trying to show what it meant.

So too with the artistic license involved in making Jesus and the Beloved Disciple lovers. For my money, the inner circles that like that sort of thing are quite within their rights to indulge in it, provided they are doing what the Renaissance painters did: using deliberate anachronism — employing contemporary material to make vivid the historical manifestation of the love of God in Christ Jesus. But I feel they are quite off the mark if they think they can assert with a straight face that a first-century Jewish Messiah candidate, however nonconforming, would actually have been gay. (I feel the same way about the often-dropped heterosexual innuendo that Jesus and Mary Magdalene had something going: as anachronism, run with it; as fact, forget it.) Likewise, the squares are just as right and just as wrong. Jesus was no doubt as straight as any die they want to imagine. Still, they should watch their step: if people who have been beaten up on for lack of straightness want, by a flight of fancy, to make the point that Jesus loves them, too, it ill behooves the rest of us to beat up on them some more.

But enough digression. With peace to everybody's house, back to the story.

When it starts (John 11:1-6), Jesus is not in Bethany but in some other (unidentified) place with his disciples. Mary and Martha send him a message: "Lord, he whom you love is sick." Jesus, however, downplays the news. He tells his disciples that "This sickness is not unto death; it is for the glory of God, so that the Son of God may be glorified by means of it." And he stays right where he is for two days longer. But then he says to the disciples, "Let's go to Judea again." Predictably, they find that foolish: the authorities, they remind him, are still out to get him. But he tells them he'll take his chances: "Lazarus, our friend, has fallen asleep," he says; "but I am going to awake him out of sleep." At first, they misunderstand, thinking that he means Lazarus is enjoying the rest that leads to recovery; but Jesus corrects them, saying plainly that Lazarus is dead (John 11:14). So off they all go.

When Jesus arrives at Bethany, Martha comes out to meet him, but Mary stays in the house. Martha says to him, "Lord, if you had been here, my brother would not have died." (The reader knows, of course, what Martha doesn't, namely, that Jesus has deliberately stayed away — that he has staged his absence to set up the situation: the author of the Gospel is obviously using every device he knows to stamp this episode as an acted parable.) Martha does indeed go on to add that she knows that whatever Jesus asks from God, God will give him. But Jesus is not interested in what she thinks she knows; he is concerned with what she is willing to believe — concerned, that is, not with her theology but with her faith. So he simply says to her, "Your brother will rise again" (John 11:23).

Time for a halt here. In all likelihood, Mary, Martha, and Lazarus were reared either as Pharisees or under the influence of Pharisaic teaching — as was Jesus himself perhaps. In any case, when Martha responds to Jesus in the very next verse (John 11:24), she sounds exactly as if she is repeating a lesson learned in Pharisee Sunday School: "Oh yes," she says. "I know that. I know he will rise again at the last day."

(The notion of a general resurrection at some future date was standard Pharisaic teaching. Not all Jews of the time ascribed to it: the Sadducees, notably, denied the idea outright — see, for example, Mark 12:18-28. At any rate, it is clear from Martha's reply that she for one has bought the idea lock, stock, and barrel.)

What Jesus next says to her, though, goes far beyond anything she or the Pharisees had in mind. "No!" he says to her in effect; "your brother will not rise at the last day, he will rise *now*, because I am the resurrection and the life; he who believes in me, though he die, yet shall he live, and whoever lives and believes in me shall never die." But then he asks her, "Do you believe this?" As I said, he is challenging her to trust in him rather than to rely on her own credence of theological propositions. And Martha comes through: "Yes, Lord," she says, "I believe that you are the Christ, the Son of God, he who is coming into the world."

F. D. Maurice once said that this exchange between Jesus and Martha depressed him. How sad it is, he observed, that after two thousand years, the church has gotten most Christians only to the point to which the Pharisees got Martha: resurrection in the future, resurrection a week from some Tuesday. Only a handful have ever gotten past that point and made the leap of faith that Jesus got Martha to make: the leap to resurrection *now* — to resurrection as the fundamental mystery of creation finally manifest in his own flesh. And yet that mystery is all over the pages of the New Testament. Not only is it in such epistles as Ephesians and Colossians (see Eph. 2:5-6, for example, or Col. 3:1-4). It is also perfectly plain in the Gospels: *Jesus never meets a corpse that doesn't sit up right on the spot.* Consider. There is the widow of Nain's son (Luke 7:11-17); there is Jairus's daughter (Luke 8:41-56); and there is Lazarus himself. They all rise not because Jesus does a number on them, not because he puts some magical resurrection machinery into gear, but simply because *he has that effect on the dead.* They rise because he is the Resurrection even before he himself rises — because, in other words, he is the grand sacrament, the real presence, of the mystery of a kingdom in which everybody rises.

Back to the text. Martha goes to tell her sister, "The Teacher is here and is calling for you," and Mary comes out quickly to meet him. She too says, "Lord, if you had been here, my brother would not have died." But Jesus is upset *(enebrimēsato)* and does not reply. (The verb *embrimásthai* is used only a few times in the New Testament; but when it is applied to Jesus, it is used in situations where he is seemingly out of control — where, if I may say so, the power of the mystery that he *is* practically overwhelms the plausible structure of what he is doing. See, for example, Matt. 9:30 and Mark 1:43: the healings that he performs are more extorted from him than done by him. See especially the healing of the woman with the hemorrhage in Luke 8:43-48: the verb *embrimásthai* is not used, but Jesus is so snappish he gives the woman the shakes. In all these instances, Jesus seems less than his own master. He feels [to reach for an analogy] more like a cafeteria counter of power from which people take what they want than like a restaurateur who can give them what he chooses to serve. And it makes him . . . well, churlish: the Gospels — and John's Gospel in particular, with its eye for telling detail — show the emotional price he paid for being the sacrament of the mystery.)

Nevertheless, Jesus plows on: he orders the stone at the door of the cave-tomb to be taken away. Practical Martha observes (another convincing Johannine detail) that Lazarus has been dead four days and that by now, in the words of the KJV, "he stinketh." But Jesus simply reminds her of her promise to trust, lifts up his eyes, thanks his Father for hearing him, and then says, with a loud voice, "Lazarus, come out!" "And," the Gospel says, "the dead man came out, his hands and feet bound with bandages and his face wrapped in a cloth." Jesus says, "unbind him, and let him go" (John 11:44). And that, said John, was that.

For one thing, it was the beginning of the end. In the immediately following passage (John 11:45-53), the chief priests and the Pharisees gather together in council and Caiaphas the high priest gives it to them straight. They are a bunch of know-nothings, he tells them. It's time to stop all the generalized handwringing about what a threat Jesus is and make some concrete plans to have him killed. He says this, John adds, not of his own accord but in his official capacity as high priest and prophet of the people: his lethal dictum, in other words, is to be taken as nothing less than divinely inspired. The God of Bad Manners rides again: one more semi-innocent bystander — this time a prudent ecclesiastical politician just trying to do his job — is suckered into doing the dirty work of salvation. And so the plot goes into action: "From that day on," the Gospel says (John 11:53), "they took counsel how to put him to death."

It is all downhill from there. In John 11:54–12:11, Jesus briefly goes into hiding in a town called Ephraim; he moves on to Bethany and shows up at a dinner where Mary, Martha, and Lazarus are present; during the meal, Mary anoints his feet with some high-priced ointment and Judas Iscariot objects that if she had sold the whole jar instead, it would have fetched $1200 for the poor (yet another sensible type lights up one of God's exploding cigars); Jesus tells him to get off her back and let her keep it for the day of his burial; a crowd comes — not only to see Jesus but to gawk at Lazarus so recently dead — and as a result of the hubbub, the chief priests decide that Lazarus, too, has to be killed (bystander number three finds himself looking down the divine drain). And then comes Palm Sunday (John 12:12).

But the Raising of Lazarus is more than just the beginning of Jesus' end: I find it to be one of the seminal passages on the meaning of resurrection. Accordingly, I am going to use it as the occasion of a theological interlude I have been waiting for some time now to make. I want you to think about Jesus' insistence to Martha that resurrection is something that happens *now* rather than in the future — that it is a *present* reality rather than just a coming one.

There are two ways of looking at the work of Jesus, two ways of coming at both his incarnation in general and at the several particular manifestations of it in his birth, teaching, miracles, death, resurrection, ascension, and second coming. The first is to go with T. S. Eliot and conceive of it all as the "intersection of the timeless with time." If you do that, you propose to yourself two very different realms — the timeless as opposed to the time-bound, the eternal as opposed to the temporal, or even, if I may stretch the matter a bit, God's "time" as opposed to our "times" — and you thus make the incarnate Lord "the still point of the turning world," the point at which these two realms coincide. Indeed, if you want to put it vividly, as Eliot does, you say that they cross at the Cross — that on Good Friday, God's eternal way of doing business overrides and reconciles our temporal botching of the job. As far as it goes, that is a good enough way of talking about the two — and it is certainly one of the principal ways in which Scripture talks about them. But it is not the only way, and it is not the best way.

It has drawbacks. For if you say only that the incarnation is *an* action at *a* point in history, you find yourself at odds with some important parts of Scripture. In a number of places, the New Testament insists that the mysterious powers made manifest in the Word's becoming flesh — the absolving grace of Jesus' death, for example, or the reconciling grace of his resurrection, or the vindicating grace of his judgment — cannot be confined to back-then-sometime or back-there-somewhere. Rather, they are right-here-now — and not just in your "now" and mine but in every now that ever was or will be. The mystery does not simply coincide with the world at one point; it coinheres in the world at all points. It is present to all times, not just to the time when Jesus appeared in history; and it is present to all places, not just to the spots where he happened to show up.

Watch the way the New Testament's case for that builds. In Rom. 7:4, Paul says that even while we are alive, we are already "dead to the law by the body of Christ." Jesus' death, you see, is a present reality: besides being a fact of past history, it is a cosmic fact that underlies all history. In Col. 3:3, that fact is buttressed: "You died," Paul says to the historically quite alive Colossians, "and your life is hid with Christ in God." Even before we literally die, therefore, we are already dead in Jesus' death and alive in Jesus' resurrection. But the case is made most clearly in Eph. 2:5-6: since we are thus dead in the mystery of his death, all of us have also, right now, been "made alive together with him" and "raised up together with him" and "seated together with him in the heavenly places." In other words, Scripture shows God in Christ not simply as intersecting history at one moment of time but as being the *eternal contemporary of every moment of time.* What he did in Jesus was neither more nor less than what he had been doing all along.

That makes a considerable difference. If Jesus is only a sacrament of intersection, then the events of the incarnation become saving moments that we have somehow to reach back into history for — that we appropriate chiefly by memory and credence. But if he is the sacrament of concurrence — if what we are invited to believe is that his death and resurrection are the underlying realities of our present existence, if we are called to see those events as manifestations, in a specific time and place, of the mystery that infuses all times and places — then instead of having to *get back to him* by credence, we have only to *reach down to him* in trust and lay hold of the Resurrection and the Life who has been with us all along.

But it is when we come to the subject of what we call his second coming that the theology of concurrence makes the biggest difference of all. For if we think of Jesus simply as coming back for one final intersection of the timeless with time, one last, judgmental stab at tidying up the mess of history, we inevitably conceive of ourselves as pretty much on our own in the meantime. But if we see his judgment, his *krísis* of history, as yet another concurrence with our lives, as one more presence *in every moment of our history,* we are not on our own: his sovereign vindication of all time is with us at every time.

In a fascinating way, Scripture supports this concurrence theology more easily than you might think. The phrase "second coming," despite its popularity, is not the way the New Testament talks about Jesus' appearance in history as judge. The normal term it uses is *parousía* — a word that means simply *presence.* (To be sure, it is easy to read *parousía* as "presence at the end"; but in the light of the "now" passages quoted above, it is just as important to see it as "presence all along.") Indeed, it is precisely in order to stress this present concurrence of judgment with our lives that modern theologians have taken to using another (nonscriptural) Greek word to talk about the *parousía:* its reality, they say, is "proleptic." And what is a *prólepsis?* It is an anticipation in one time of something that will not occur historically until another time. Appropriately enough, they go on to add that this *prólepsis* of judgment is not just a mental anticipation but somehow a real one — an actual, if advance, participation in the final fact. I find that cumbersome, though. Why do mental gymnastics like that when the simpler (and more biblical) notion of concurrence covers the same ground better? Watch.

409

The mystery manifested in Jesus' death forgives us now because it is as present now as it was on the cross; the mystery manifested in his resurrection restores us now because it is as present now as it was when he left the tomb; and the mystery manifested in his judgment vindicates us now because it is as present now as it will be when he appears in glory. Those events — the specific "mighty acts of salvation" — were indeed (or indeed will be) sacramental events, real presences of the mystery under historical signs; but like true sacraments, they are not the only instances of its presence. Above all, they are by no means presences of something that wasn't there before. Just as, in communion, Jesus is really present in the bread and wine but cannot be said to have shown up in a gathering from which he was absent (the church that consecrates the eucharistic sign of the body of Christ), so too in the saving acts of his ministry, past or future: the sacramental appearance of Jesus as judge at the last day is indeed a real presence in the courtroom of history, but it is not his arrival in that courtroom for the first time. It is (if you will allow me an extravagance) his popping up from behind the bench and saying, "Surprise! I've been down here on the floor all along, hunting for your indictments; but since I don't seem to find any, go home and have a nice day."

One last theological point while we're on the subject of resurrection and judgment. Perhaps the biggest obstacle to our seeing the judgment of Jesus as the grand sacrament of vindication is our unfortunate preoccupation with the notion of the immortality of the soul. The doctrine is a piece of non-Hebraic philosophical baggage with which we have been stuck ever since the church got out into the wide world of Greek thought. Along with the concomitant idea of "life after death," it has given us almost nothing but trouble: both concepts militate against a serious acceptance of the resurrection of the dead that is the sole basis of judgment.

Consider their effects. If you take the view that there is some imperishable part of you that will go on willy-nilly after you die, you come up with two pieces of bad news. On the one hand, if you think that your immortal soul is all covered with dirty deeds from its trip through life, you are forced to conclude that it will come before Jesus at the last day in very unforgivable shape indeed: the resurrection will give you back your body, but you will still be as guilty as ever in your soul. (Hence the invention of purgatory, that pre-heavenly carwash for souls muddied by traffic on earth.) On the other hand, if you think your immortal soul is squeaky clean and needs only fitting out with a new body to do it justice, you make Jesus practically unnecessary. What do you need him for? All he becomes on that basis is some kind of celestial mechanic who bolts new bodies onto old souls. Worse yet, he becomes an idiotic mechanic who then proceeds to throw away most of his repair jobs because the souls were no good to begin with. His saving work becomes a waste of time *and* eternity.

But if you are willing at least momentarily to suspend your attachment to the idea of a soul that lives after death (I don't suppose you ever will — or even should, maybe — get rid of it altogether), you will finally be able to see the Good News, which is that Jesus came to raise the dead. Not just dead bodies, but dead souls as well. In the beginning, the Word brought creation into being not out of some preexistent glop, but out of nothing; in the end, the incarnate Lord will bring the new creation into being not out of a bunch of used souls but out of death: stone-cold, body-and-soul, nothing-at-all *death*. And therefore all the so-called unbelievers who horrify Christians by saying, "When you're dead, you're dead; there is no life after death," are actually closer to faith in the Gospel than they know: it's the dead who are Jesus' dish, not the living; *nothing* is all he needs — and all he will accept — for the making of anything, old creation or new.

And that, Virginia, is why we look forward with joy to his coming — why we are able to stand with confidence at his *parousía*. By the power of the Resurrection who works in our total death, none of our garbage goes with us into the new creation. Lose your immortal soul, then, and you'll get an everlasting life that's worth living.

CHAPTER SIX

The Onset of the Hurricane

THE FINAL PREDICTION OF THE PASSION
JAMES AND JOHN
BLIND BARTIMAEUS
ZACCHAEUS
THE PARABLE OF THE COINS

Back now to the synoptic Gospels for the first of the full-fledged parables of judgment: the parable (Aland no. 266) of the Coins (Luke 19:11-27), or of the Talents (Matt. 25:14-30). However, since Aland's *Synopsis* lists four transitional episodes between the point at which we just left John's Gospel (Aland no. 261) and the point at which Jesus tells this parable, let me devote a few paragraphs to each of them in order to set the stage.

In Aland no. 262 (Matt. 20:17-19; Mark 10:32-34; Luke 18:31-34), Jesus makes the final prediction of his approaching passion and death. Mark's version is the most vivid: Jesus and his followers are on the road to Jerusalem and Jesus is walking on ahead of them all by himself. They are "amazed" *(ethamboúnto)*, Mark says; and they are "afraid" *(ephoboúnto)*. Clearly, everyone in Jesus' company senses that something dire is just down the road; and sure enough, taking the twelve aside, he repeats for the third time his prophecy of the death and resurrection of the "Son of man." (I know, Virginia: some people say he wasn't talking about himself in any of these predictions — that it is only a later ecclesiastical tradition that says Jesus and the Son of man are one and the same. What do I think about that? I find it hard to square with Mark: if Jesus was just rattling on about some third party's demise, why was he giving off vibes that scared the living daylights out of his followers? And as far as "ecclesiastical tradition" is concerned, his followers were just as much the church as any group that came later. Their consternation suggests to me that this tradition, if that's what you want to call it, started rather early — right on the Gospel spot, in fact, and precisely because Jesus himself caused it to start there.)

In any case, what we have in all three Gospel accounts of this prediction is the same thing we just had in John: the synoptic writers are cranking up the heat of passion and death before launching into the events of Holy Week, and they are doing so to give the proper introduction to Jesus' "hot" parables of judgment. As I said, Jesus is not on a stroll here through the groves of academe. He is on his way to the dreadful *éxodos* spoken of by Moses and Elijah at the transfiguration and he is not cool about it: in addition to foreseeing the pain, he knows full well that practically nobody — hardly any of his disciples and certainly none of his fellow countrymen — will be able to make head or tail of it.

His prescience is amply vindicated by what happens next in Matt. 20:20-28 and Mark 10:35-45 (Aland no. 263). James and John, if you follow Mark (or their mother speaking for them, if you follow Matthew), come to Jesus and ask that they be granted the privilege of sitting on his right hand and on his left in glory. These lines are so bizarre that any scriptwriter who tried to get away with them would be told to go back and write something that didn't completely ignore the scene before. It simply strains credulity to think that Jesus' disciples, having just heard him predict his death, could so completely gloss over what he said and go blathering on about heavenly seating arrangements.

But if you understand the disciples as Jesus did — if you see them in the hot light of his certainty that they do not understand a thing about what he is really doing — the bizarreness of their request makes perfectly good dramatic sense. They are amazed and they are afraid. They are out of their depth completely. So, just as Peter at the transfiguration burst out with the first plausible, let's-get-hold-of-ourselves idea

413

that came into his head ("Let's make three tents . . ."), James and John put as much distance as they can between themselves and the awful Main Subject. "Let's talk about something more cheerful," they say, hoping perhaps to cheer up Jesus as well in the process; "let's talk about what it will be like when this is all over." Jesus, however, will not be jollied. He asks them if they are able to drink the cup that he drinks, or to be baptized with the baptism with which he is baptized. And when, predictably, they say, "Sure," he lets out a long, resigned breath and says "O . . . kay; because that will be exactly what you'll get. I'm into death and resurrection here, and that's all I'm into. The business of who gets what seats is not my job."

The other ten, of course, are no better than James and John: hearing Jesus' words only as a rebuke to a cheeky request, they become indignant at the two brothers. But Jesus ignores their dim-wittedness too and presses on with the Main Subject. "Forget all this nonsense about precedence," he tells them; "that's not what I called you for. If any of you wants to be great, he's going to have to be servant of all; and if any of you wants to be first, he's going to have to be slave of all. *For the Son of man came not to be served but to serve, and to give his life as a ransom for many.*" Nothing, you see — not even rampant incomprehension from his disciples — can get Jesus off his preoccupation with death.

The passage that follows next (Matt. 20:29-34 and parallels; Aland no. 264) may seem to be a digression, but it is not. Since all three of the synoptics agree in placing a healing of the blind at this very point, the presumption is either that Jesus did one here, or that the writers thought it fit here, or both. At any rate, whether it was the restoring of sight to just one man (Mark and Luke) or to two (Matthew), it is an acted parable of the blindness of everyone to Jesus' real work. Consider. The crowd around him rebukes the blind beggar: the important Rabbi, they seem to think, must not be exposed to this loser, especially when they are trying so resolutely to soft-pedal the Rabbi's own preoccupation with losing. But Jesus heals blind Bartimaeus anyway (the name occurs in Mark), and at the end he says, "Go your way; your faith has saved you." And, as all three synoptic writers report, "immediately he received his sight" and followed Jesus. In other words, the accounts are making the same point Jesus made with Martha: he is not interested in what those around him think they know, only in what they can be led to believe. They will be saved not by following their own dim ideas about how the kingdom ought to work but by coming to him blindly in the mystery of his death and following him through it into the healing of his resurrection.

The last episode before the parable of the Coins occurs as Jesus nears Jerusalem and is passing through Jericho: in Luke 19:1-10 (Aland no. 265), he meets a man named Zacchaeus who is "a chief tax collector, and rich." The story is not only charming; it is a fascinating excursus on judgment as well. Zacchaeus, for all his wealth, has two problems. Not only does everyone hate him for being a publican, a tax farmer in the employ of the Romans; they also give him bad marks for being ridiculously short: five-foot-two, maybe, or four-foot-eleven. So as Jesus passes by, Zacchaeus is out of luck twice. The crowd won't let him up front because he is a traitor to his people, and his height makes it impossible for him to see anything from down in back. Zacchaeus, however, is not fazed: he runs on ahead and climbs up into a sycamore tree for a better view of the parade. But when the entourage reaches his tree, he gets a surprise: Jesus looks at him and says, "Zacchaeus, hurry up and get down out of there; I'm having dinner with you today."

Zacchaeus is thrilled, of course, but the crowd is appalled: Jesus, they mutter, is going to be the guest of a man who is a sinner! Nevertheless, Jesus goes right on in. But just as he settles down for a nice, relaxed meal, Zacchaeus stands up and launches into a during-dinner speech. "Look, Lord," he says, trying to dispel his universally bad press; "I give half of what I have to the poor, and if I have given anyone a raw deal, I make it up to him four times over."

Time out. When I expounded the parable of the Pharisee and the Publican in *The Parables of Grace*, I said that everybody has a problem with it. Sure, we rejoice that the smarmily good Pharisee is condemned and that the publican — who does nothing more than admit he is worthless — "goes down to his house justified rather than the other." But I also noted that if we are honest, we don't like that very much. I maintained that if we were to imagine a sequel to the parable in which we sent the publican back to the temple one week later, we would almost certainly feel obliged to send him back with some improvement in his life to lay before God — that we would, in short, be tempted to send him back with what amounts to the Pharisee's speech in his pocket.

Do you see now what the acted parable of Zacchaeus is all about? It is precisely a publican making the Pharisee's speech — a loser who thinks that, thank God and his better instincts, he has gotten over his losing behavior and become a twenty-four-karat winner. And what does Jesus say to him? He says something straight off the wall: with no intervening explanation, Jesus announces, "Today salvation has come to this house, since he also is a son of Abraham. For the Son of man came to seek and to save the lost." In other words, Jesus brings Zacchaeus back down to the only ground on which he can possibly stand and receive a favorable judgment: the ground of the last, the lost, the least, the little, and the dead.

As to why that odd bit about "a son of Abraham" is in there, I frankly have no good idea. Maybe it means that it is not Zacchaeus's list of good deeds that saves him but simply his status as one more loser in the long history of God's preference for losers — for types like over-the-hill Abraham, under-the-gun Moses, down-the-drain Jeremiah, or for that matter the entire out-of-luck nation he clutched to his bosom as his chosen people. Then again, maybe it doesn't. But the bit about "seeking and saving the lost" is crystal clear: Jesus is uttering a judgment here, and he is uttering it on the only basis he will allow. He will not judge the cluttered business of our lives, because on that basis none of us will be anything but condemned. He will judge us only as he raises us, reconciled and restored, out of the uncluttered nothingness of our death.

And so you come to the final twist in this acted-out version of the Pharisee and the Publican. In the spoken parable, both characters go down from the temple to their houses, the one condemned for taking his stand on a life that cannot bear judgment, the other justified for taking his stand on a death that can. In this acted parable, however, *the Temple himself* — the Lord who dies and rises, the One who in John 2:19

said, "Destroy this Temple [his body] and I will raise it up in three days" — *comes to Zacchaeus's house and brings salvation.* Just because Jesus is the Resurrection and the Life — just because he has *that effect* on the dead — and just because Zacchaeus is standing there as a solid brass dead duck, Jesus raises him up uncondemned. "Look, Zacchaeus," he says in effect, "just bag it, will you? I have no use for all this chin music about your life. I'm on my way to make the death you're avoiding safe — to make it the only ticket anyone will ever need. Sit down and eat up. Let's just have a quiet dinner before I go down into the silence and solve your problem."

With all of that by way of preface, we turn now to the parable of the Coins/Talents. In Luke's Gospel, this story occurs right after the episode with Zacchaeus (Luke 19:1-10) and right before Palm Sunday (19:28-44). In Matthew, however, the material appears in a somewhat different form and in another place: he presents it as the parable of the Talents and he puts it in at Matt. 25:14-30, just before the beginning of the passion narrative. I am tempted, of course, to go with the Lukan version at this point not only because it is in strict sequence with what we have just been reading but also because it has a number of fascinating convolutions. Nevertheless, since Matthew, too, makes unique contributions to the story, I think it best to expound the parable by reading back and forth between the two versions, especially in view of the possibility that their differences may not be due to the authors, but to Jesus himself: he may perfectly well have told this story twice and, like an entertainer who ad-libs on his own material, put in just these variations.

Let us begin with Luke. "As they heard these things," the Gospel says (19:11), "Jesus proceeded to tell a parable. . . ." Initial questions: Where is Jesus when he tells this parable; who are "they"; and what "things" is Luke talking about? Answers: Jesus is still in Zacchaeus's house, or else he is continuing on the road to Jerusalem; "they" are at least a portion of the same group that heard him in Zacchaeus's house; and the "things" are either what he said to Zacchaeus or even, possibly, all the things he said from Luke 18:31 on. But then Luke continues his introduction to the parable by giving two reasons why Jesus tells it. The first is, "because he was near to Jerusalem," and the second, "because they supposed that

417

the kingdom of God was to appear immediately." The next question, therefore: What is Luke trying to indicate by this unusually explanatory preface? Answer (I think): he is suggesting that the behavior of Jesus just prior to this point — his foreboding manner and especially his repeated use of the phrase "the Son of man" — has made everyone around him think of things like the coming of the kingdom and the judgment of the world. They have all, Luke implies, leapt straight to one of the human race's favorite subjects: eschatology. But he also wants to indicate that Jesus is unhappy with such a facile leap. For one thing, Jesus knows that *for now* the manifestation of the mystery will not be anything like what they expect: the kingdom will be revealed by way of his death and resurrection, not by way of some direct, razzle-dazzle intervention in the affairs of the world. It will, in short, be paradoxical rather than plausible. For another thing though, Jesus feels a need to correct their equally erroneous notion of what the coming of the kingdom means *for then* — for the future. He wants to challenge their customary thinking about the subject of judgment, because even the judgment, he is convinced, will be nothing like what they have in mind.

For what they expect on that count is something equally plausible: a coming of the Son of man to knock heads and settle scores, to reward the good and punish the wicked by simple, right-handed justice. Note here, incidentally, that this is precisely what the phrase "Son of man," in its then current meaning, would have led them to think. Even though I have said that I think Jesus did indeed identify himself with "the Christ" (the Messiah) and "the Son of man" (reinterpreting both concepts mightily in the process), I nevertheless think it important to remember that his followers would not necessarily have equated those two figures either with Jesus or with each other. On the one hand, "the Christ," as far as they were concerned, was to be God's chosen agent for the bringing in of the kingdom; on the other hand, "the Son of man" was to be an eschatological figure who would preside over the last judgment. In any case, since Jesus has, by his words and behavior, put both the kingdom and the judgment on the table, as it were, Luke clearly wants us to bear both subjects in mind as we read the parable that now unfolds in all its left-handed, implausible detail.

"A nobleman went into a far country," Jesus begins, "to receive kingly power and then return." Let me interrupt myself right at the start and alert you to a procedural device I have decided to use. Even though I think it is generally a poor idea to make point-for-point theological identifications of the details of Jesus' parables, I am going to make an exception here: after certain words or phrases in Luke's text, I shall use square brackets [ ] to flag what I consider to be the likely theological referents of the several elements in this parable. I shall make these insertions without comment as I go along; but by the end of my exposition, I think you will find that they have become quite understandable. Accordingly, let me repeat the parable's opening line quoted above, this time putting in the theological flags I want to wave at you.

"A nobleman (*eugenés*, well-born) [this nobleman is the Christ-figure of the parable, corresponding to Jesus, the *monogenés*, the only begotten of God] went into a far country [death] to receive kingly power [to rise from the dead] and then return [to appear to his disciples after the resurrection, and also to sit in universal judgment at the *parousía*]. Calling ten of his servants, he gave them ten *mnas*, ten coins [since each servant received one coin, this stands for every human being's equal reception of the sovereign grace of resurrection from the dead]. And he said to them, 'Trade *(pragmateúsasthe)* with these till I come.'"

Matthew, who begins the parable only at this point — and without anything corresponding to Luke's preface — says there were just three servants; furthermore, instead of having them receive equal shares, he assigns to the first, five talents *(tálanta),* to the second, two, and to the third, one. Luke, however, having established the number of servants as ten, seemingly distracts our attention from them by inserting a strange paragraph about the nobleman's other subjects. He tells us, in Luke 19:14: "But his citizens hated him [the paradox of going away into death is profoundly repugnant to everyone: to the disciples, to the authorities, to the crowds, to us], and they sent representatives after him with the message, 'We do not want this man to reign over us' [the paradox is also radically unacceptable]."

But there are still more differences at this point between the two versions of the parable. At Matt. 25:16, on the one hand, we find a brief, anticipatory summary of what the servants did with their several talents — the information that will be repeated later in the "judgment" section of the story. Luke, on the other hand, omits this duplication and goes straight to the day of reckoning (Luke 19:15): "When the nobleman returned, having received kingly power [when, that is, Jesus returns in both the resurrection and the *parousía*], he commanded that these servants to whom he had given the money be called to him in order that he might know what they had gained by trading [that is, by accepting — or in the case of the 'wicked,' not accepting — the freely given acceptance by grace]." The subtle difference between the Matthean and the Lukan accounts, therefore, now begins to be manifest. Luke's version just quoted leaves open the possibility of interpreting the nobleman's return as either the resurrection or the *parousía* — even, perhaps, of interpreting the *parousía* as a present as well as a future fact. Matthew, however, tilts very much toward a last-day, last-judgment interpretation: he has Jesus say, "Now *after a long time* the master of those servants came and settled accounts with them."

Nevertheless, the two versions of the parable proceed in substantial agreement from here on. Matthew's first servant comes and reports that his five talents have earned him five more; Luke's, that his one coin has made him ten. Incidentally, the *mna,* or mina, was a coin worth about 1/60th of a *tálanton* — or, to put it in terms of smaller denominations, worth about 100 *denarii,* a *denarius* being the equivalent of a day's pay. You may work out the modern equivalents of the various sums if you like; I find something else far more interesting. In Matthew, the original grants to the servants are all different, but the increments earned are the same as the grants: five on top of five; two on top of two. In Luke, however, the grants are the same (one coin for each), but the increments are all different. Luke, it seems, is taking a page from Mark's version of the parable of the Sower (where the seed sown is Grace himself; the Word incarnate in Jesus). In that account, an equal sowing results, even on uniformly good ground, in an unequal harvest: some thirty-, some sixty-, some a hundredfold. Even though Luke omits this note of diversity of yield from his own account of the Sower, he apparently feels obliged to put it in here (because, perhaps, he finds it congruent with the *sovereignty of grace over judgment* that is the unique feature of his version of the parable).

At any rate, both Luke and Matthew next bring on the second servant and have him report: Luke's man has made five coins with his one; Matthew's, two talents with his two. And in the case of both the master in Matthew and the nobleman in Luke, the response is a judgment of approval. "Well done, good and faithful *(pistós)* servant," says the master (Matt. 25:21); "you have been faithful over a little *(epí olíga)*, I will set you over much; enter into the joy of your master." The same note is struck in Luke 19:17: "Well done, good servant! Because you have been faithful *(pistós)* over a very little *(en elachístō, in the least)*, you shall have authority over ten cities [Jesus works in leastness, littleness, lastness, lostness, and death: those, plus *faith in him*, are the only things his resurrecting grace passes judgment on; the good works and good results in this parable are praised only as sacraments, effective signs of the fidelity-in-littleness that the story is really about]."

But then comes the crucial point of the parable: the judgment issued against the servant who acts not out of faith but out of prudence (just as we do when we fearfully try to deal with God on the basis of what we *think he is like* rather than on the basis of what we *trust him to be* in Jesus). Up comes the weasel himself: "Oh Sir," he says (I conflate the accounts), "here is your coin, which I have kept bright and shiny in a handkerchief in my bureau drawer. Because, you see, I was afraid. I *know* you. You are a hard (Matthew: *sklērós;* Luke: *austerós*) man. I know you grab everything, even if it doesn't belong to you. So I thought to myself, 'Watch your step, Arthur; if he keeps track of every penny everywhere like that, even when it's not his, just think how mad he could get if you should happen to lose something that *was* his.' And so, Sir, here I am and here's your money, in full and on time. Tell me I'm a good boy."

"No!" roars the nobleman, twice as angry as anything Arthur ever imagined. "I will judge *(krínō)* you out of your own mouth. You are not a good boy. You are not even a good weasel. If you knew *(ḗdeis)* I was such a tough customer, why didn't you at least put my money into a savings account? What? You thought I'd be mad at a measly 4 1/2 percent? You think I'm not madder at zero percent? But you know something? That's not really what I'm mad about. Look, Arthur. I invited you into a fiduciary relationship with me. That's *fiduciary*, f-i-d: as in *fides* in Latin — and as in *pístis* in Greek, which is the language this story will end up in — and as in *faith*, in plain English. I didn't ask you to make money, I asked you to do business — that's *pragmateúsasthai*, remember? — to exercise a little pragmatic trust that I meant you well and that I wouldn't mind if you took some risks with my gift of a lifetime. But what did you do? You decided you had to be more afraid of me than of the risks. *You* decided. You played it safe because of some imaginary fear. And so now, instead of having gotten yourself a nice new life as mayor of at least a small city, you have only the crummy little excuse for a life you started with. As a matter of fact, Arthur, you haven't even got that, because you know what I'm going to do? I'm going to take what I gave you and just for fun [to show the outrageousness of grace, as in the Laborers in the Vineyard] I'm going to give it to that guy over there who already has more than he knows what to do with. And you know why I'm going to do that? First of all, to remind everybody that when I give you a gift [grace, forgiveness], I expect you to do business with it, to keep it moving [to forgive others as you are forgiven — see the Lord's Prayer], not just to keep it to yourself in some damned napkin [some low-risk spiritual life in which you neither sin much nor love much — see Luke 7:36-50]. But second, I'm going to give him your gift to show everybody that I never really cared about results anyway [the Laborers in the Vineyard again — the gift of grace is not a reward for hard work or good behavior, it is a lark, a joke, a hilariously inequitable largesse: it is, in a word, a *gift*]. Don't you see, Arthur? It's all a game. All that matters is that you play at all, not that you play well or badly. You could have earned a million with the money I gave you, or you could have earned two cents. You could even have blown it on the horses for all I care: at least that way you would have been a gambler after my own heart. But when you crawl in here and insult me — *me*, Mr. Risk Himself [Jesus the vindicating judge] — by telling me you decided that I couldn't be trusted enough for you to gamble on a two-bit loss, that I was some legalistic type who went only by the books [judgment by law instead of grace], well. . . ."

422

The two accounts of this tirade diverge here; so let me, in the style of John Fowles, give you two endings to it. Matthew 25:30 first:

". . . you just listen, you little creep," the master roars on. "If you can't live with my kind of acceptance — which is that I can accept absolutely everything except distrust in my acceptance — you can get the hell out of here. Boys! Show Arthur the door. I know it's dark out there, but what does he care? He's got a weasely little concept of me in his weasely little mind and he thinks that if he chews on it long enough, it will turn into a bright idea. But it never will, so get rid of him. Let him wear out his weasely little teeth gnawing on it forever."

If, however, you find that a bit strong for your stomach — if you are hoping that blessed Luke, the patron saint of healing grace, will come through with something softer — don't hold your breath. The outrage of law violated is nothing compared to the white-hot fury of grace spurned. Watch the Lukan ending (Luke 19:27):

". . . Hey!" says the nobleman [the dead and risen Jesus], "I've got an idea. Instead of just kicking Arthur the hell out of here, why don't we make a real hell of this and give him some company in his misery? You remember all those other types, Boys? All the ones who were so mad at me for going into the far country [Jesus' death] and for receiving kingly power [Jesus' resurrection]? The ones who wouldn't trust me and even tried to overthrow my government [Jesus' easy yoke and light burden, his gracious rule of grace beyond the rules] . . . well, drag them in here and kill them all in front of me. Not only will it do the universe a favor to get rid of such a bunch of wet blankets; it will do them a favor too. They're dead already and don't know it: the second death shouldn't bother them at all. Why, they'll hardly even. . . ."

See? I told you it would be worse. So just to cheer you up, I will write my own ending to the Lukan ending. Maybe you won't be happy with this one either (some people are hard to please, even with good news); but at least you won't be able to say I didn't try. So here goes nothing, taking it from "the second death" just before we left off:

". . . the second death shouldn't bother them at all. Why, they'll hardly even . . ." But suddenly the nobleman brightens. "Come to think of it," he says, "that gives me an idea. If death and faith are all I need to make everybody a mayor, what difference does it make whether it's first death or second death? Maybe if I could figure out some way of getting them to trust me even in *that . . .*" But then, just as suddenly, he frowns: "I don't know, though. It'd be a tough nut to crack [the theologians would never sit still for a God who wants to be a barefaced universalist]. . . still, it's an idea; so . . . [and thus in the end, God formulates plan Z, the ultimate eschatological cure-all: he doesn't ask the theologians' permission; he goes ahead and does it anyway, offering *them* the second death just in case they need a fallback position to guarantee the eternity of hell]."

I thank you for your patience with me through this long exercise in doing three or four things at once. Let me now, with plain words and as straight a face as I can manage, sum up the parable of the Coins/Talents.

It is about the "one thing necessary" (see Luke 10:42): the response of trust, of faith in Jesus' free acceptance of us by the grace of his death and resurrection. It is, in other words, about a faithful, Mary-like waiting upon Jesus himself as the embodiment of the mystery — and about the danger of substituting some prudent, fretful, Martha-like business of our own for that waiting. It is not at all about the rewarding of good works or the punishment of evil ones. The servants who gained varying amounts by their faithful trading gained them by the luck of the draw, not by (at least in Luke) the proportionate effectiveness of the original grant (it was the same in all cases), and probably not even by any proportionate exertions of their own (at any rate, we are told of none). And the servant who was cast out was not guilty of doing any substantive evil thing (the money he was given was returned in full). The parable, therefore, declares that the only thing that is to be examined at the judgment is faith, not good deeds; and it declares that the only thing that can deprive us of the favorable judgment already passed upon us by Jesus is our unfaith in his gracious passing of it (see, once again, John 3:16ff.; chapter 2, above).

One last point. The precise form that the condemned servant's unfaith took was the hiding of the coin "in a napkin." What that says to me is that if we keep Jesus only as a memento — or better said, if we keep the sacramentalities by which he disclosed the mystery only as events to be remembered or as ideas and doctrines to be kept intact — we put ourselves out of the reach of his reconciliation. Because just as the nobleman was present to his servants in and through the coins even in his apparent absence from them, so Jesus is present to us *now* and he calls us to faith in him *now*. Jesus our Death is with us now; Jesus our Resurrection is with us now; and Jesus our Vindicating Judge is with us now — if only now we will *believe*. Not *think*, because all we will ever think of on our own is the godawful God we have made in the image of our worst fears. Not *ratiocinate*, because drawing logical conclusions from our habitual, dreadful premises will only make us more fearful still. And not *reason* and not *speculate* and not *theologize*; just *trust*. Just, "Yes, Jesus. Thank you."

After that, of course, we can intellectualize ourselves silly. After the good servants had been faithful, they were free to write MBA theses on sound management techniques if that sort of thing appealed to them. But not before. Which is why — to end on a suitably theological note, having made my prior act of faith — the "quest for the historical Jesus" is a crashing mistake. We are not in the business of going back in time to look for some intellectually creditable character whom we can then decide to trust. All that ever accomplishes is to fob off on Jesus the trendy qualities we have decided will pass muster: he becomes a good example, or a wise guru, or an ethical authority — none of which could ever even save you a seat on the subway, let alone redeem a sinful world. We are in the business not of going back to him in time but of going down to him in faith — of taking the whole weird Jesus we now find in the Scriptures, and the whole, even weirder Jesus we now have to put up with in the church, and the whole, quintessentially weird Jesus now present to us in everything, nice or not nice — and of laying hold, in him, of the salvation we already have, *now*.

For if we do that, we will have done the only business that we, or the servants in the parable, ever had to do in the first place: trust the Lord in his grace and let the results be whatever we can manage to make them. Good, bad, or indifferent, we are home free, just for the believing.

CHAPTER SEVEN

God's Action in History

PALM SUNDAY
THE WEEPING OVER JERUSALEM
THE CLEANSING OF THE TEMPLE
THE CURSING OF THE FIG TREE

We come now at last to Palm Sunday, and to the succeeding days of Jesus' final ministry in Jerusalem. At the beginning of this book, I gave you some statistics to show how disproportionate a space the canonical Gospels give to the passion narrative strictly so called, that is, to the events from the Last Supper on Thursday to Jesus' Death on Friday. But if you work out the percentages of space they give to the extended passion narrative — to the events from Palm Sunday to the Ascension (a period of a month and a half at the most) — the disproportion is even more evident. Here are the figures: in Matthew, this climactic sequence occupies 29 percent of the book; in Mark, 38 percent; in Luke, 21 percent; and in John, 43 percent.

Startling as those figures are, though, I find another fact even more remarkable at this point: Jesus begins the week of his passion and death with a sustained series — no, that is not strong enough — with a catena, a chain of *acted parables*. Palm Sunday (Aland no. 269) is followed immediately by his Weeping over Jerusalem, his Cleansing of the Temple, and his Cursing of the Fig Tree (Aland nos. 270-275). I want, therefore, to make a pause here and spend a little time on the theological significance of the concept of the acted parable.

As I have used the phrase so far, its meaning is clear enough: an acted parable is an episode in Jesus' ministry in which his deeds rather than his words carry the freight of what he is trying to communicate. His spoken parables are fictions; our response to them in faith is based solely on *his having made them up,* not on there having been, say, an actual good Samaritan, or a real nobleman who gave money to his servants. But his acted parables are historical deeds; in their case, our faith-response depends on *his personally having done them* — so much so, that if we take the view that they are simply stories about him concocted by others, they lose the taproot of their authority. To put it differently, Jesus is the star of the drama of salvation; if these bits of stage business that we respond to as communications without words are only creative fictions from the fertile minds of his reviewers, they hardly deserve the kind of attention the Gospels invite us to give them. Accordingly, their historicity — their authenticity as part of the original performance — becomes a consideration of central importance, not just a frill that can be dismissed as a matter of indifference. That historical significance is just what I propose to enlarge upon in this theological excursus. I am going to suggest that Jesus' acted parables are a key to understanding the fundamental nature of the entire play. I shall try to help you see that it is not only the Triumphal Entry or the Cleansing of the Temple that are parabolic deeds; all of the weightier actions of the Savior are acted parables, too: the Crucifixion, the Resurrection, the Ascension, the Second Coming — even, if you will, all of his anticipatory, "antityping" acts in the Old Testament (more on the notion of antitypes in a little while).

My reason for taking this tack is simple. For most of the past century, biblical criticism has been caught over the barrel of whether Jesus' mighty acts were historical events or just subsequent mythologizings designed to make vivid the "faith-experience" of the early church — over the question, in plain English, of whether they were fact or fiction. It seems to me that the concept of the acted parable offers a way of converting this devitalizing "either/or" into a robust "both/and" that allows us to posit not only the historicity of, say, the Resurrection or the Ascension but the theological significance as well. It enables us to say that Jesus did indeed do the things the Scriptures say he did; but it also makes it possible to see those historical actions as parables, as acted-out stories — even, if you will, as *mythic* (not, please note, mythical) events. It makes them, in short, not *mere* anything: neither mere history stuck back there in time somewhere, nor mere fabrications of faith floating unmoored in a nonhistorical sea of significance. They are all, *then* and *now*, history and myth at once.

But since this both/and approach can itself be formulated in two ways — since you can see divine revelation by means of authentic historical occurrences in two different, even contradictory, lights — I propose to illustrate the problem for you by resorting to the classroom teacher's device of going to the blackboard. Watch closely, therefore. The first line I shall draw will represent the entire history of the world (or even the universe, if you like) from start to finish, from the moment of creation to the end of time, from *a* to *z*:

a ————————————————————————————————— z

History

Now then. The question arises: how, on this analogy, shall we depict the mighty acts of salvation? The first (and less than adequate) answer is easy. Since God, the Alpha and the Omega, the A and Ω, is up there above history, I shall draw a series of descending lines to represent his several comings down — his interventions in history, his intersections with history. These will be (to select a small but significant sample) the Creation, the Call of Abraham, the Ministry of Moses, the Birth of Jesus, the Crucifixion, the Resurrection, the Ascension, and the Second Coming. My illustration will now look like that on the top of page 429.

Things are going swimmingly. Not only is God really acting in history; we ourselves are doing justice to the language of the Nicene Creed: "*he came down from heaven,* and became incarnate, etc."

But things are also starting to sink. The picture we have drawn looks like nothing so much as a divine sewing machine, with the needle

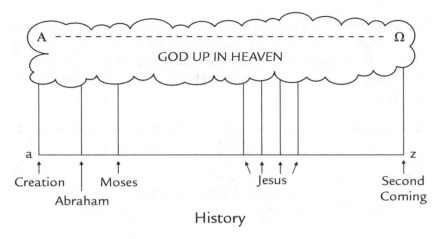

History

coming down at various points (though not at others) and tacking history to God. It is salvation as the divine basting stitch. Even if the thread holds, there is more of creation unsewn to its Maker and Redeemer than there is sewn. God's mighty acts have become just so many discrete *transactions,* just so many *jobs done* — and done, in fact, only at specific points. Our drawing, in short, is good as far as historicity is concerned (the points at which the needle enters the cloth of the world are indeed real times and places, real events); but it is not so good as far as the mystery of God's presence to all of history is concerned (the spaces between the needle thrusts still constitute most of the world's actual days and years).

Let me show you, therefore, another way of drawing the picture. This time, I shall represent the whole of history, from *a* to *z,* as a body of water:

History

But now, let me posit God not as a divine tailor in heaven sending down an interventionist needle from time to time but as a divine iceberg present under all of time. On that analogy, one-tenth of his presence to history will be visible above the surface of its waters and nine-tenths will

429

be invisible below the surface, *but his presence out of sight will be just as much a part of history as his presence in broad daylight.* Or to put it the other way around, all of history will thus be intimately and immediately present to the mystery of his entire work and being. Let me draw the mystery part first:

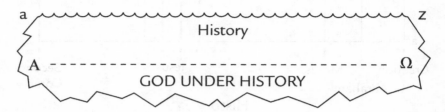

Do you see? If we now proceed to sketch in the mighty acts of God in history, we will not show him as coming down from somewhere else and intervening in a process from which he was absent; we will instead represent his appearances above the surface of history — his revelations of the mystery — as outcroppings, as emergences into plain sight of the tips of the one, continuous iceberg under all of history. Thus, when we draw in our same previous series of mighty acts, they become not *forays into history* of an alien presence from above but *outcroppings within history* of an abiding presence from below.

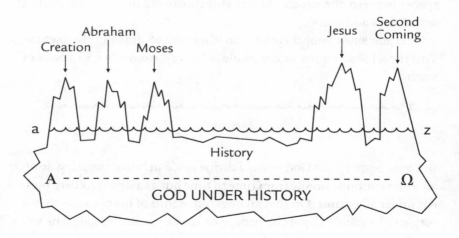

That's better. Although it started out sinkingly — with God down there in the drink out of sight — it ends up going more swimmingly than the first illustration: it does justice to the principle of sacramentality I have been stressing all along in this book. The divine acts in history are not just occasional interventions of a reality that wasn't present before; they are precisely acted parables — sacraments, if you will, real presences — of a reality that was there all along. Like Jesus' presence in the Holy Communion on a Sunday morning, they are real events in real times and places. But like that same presence, they are not simply arrivals upon a scene from which he was absent; they are manifestations, at a specific point, of a mystery that was never absent at any point.

Better yet, the *whole* of the mystery that thus underlies creation is present every time one of those sacramental outcroppings of the mystery occurs. It is not, for example, that the mystery of the Creation occurs only at the beginning, to be superseded later on by the mystery of the Passover and then by the mystery of the Cross, the mystery of the Resurrection from the dead, and the mystery of the Judgment at the End. It is that those several manifestations are outcroppings of a single, age-long mystery of Creation-Call-Passover-Redemption-Resurrection-Judgment that is fully present in every one of them. Just as each upthrusting of the iceberg is one and the same iceberg in a visible aspect, so each upthrusting of the mystery is a visible aspect of one and the same mystery. The Word who becomes incarnate in Jesus is the same Word who spoke the world into being from the start. The Lamb slain on Calvary is the same Paschal Lamb whose blood kept the angel of death from the Jews in Egypt. And the Judge who comes at the end is none other than the gracious, vindicating Savior who rose from the dead — and who, in fact, is present to the whole of history, whether at the raising up of Adam from the dust, or of Isaac from the altar of sacrifice, or of the Jews from the Babylonian captivity, or of Lazarus from the tomb.

As you may be aware, this unifying, Jesus-is-everywhere-in-the-Bible method of interpreting the history of salvation has been around for a long time. If you have ever looked at the running page headings printed in some editions of the King James Bible, you will recall that the compilers of that version felt quite free to read Christ into the Old Testament. It was not just that they found *prophecies* of him in the text (see, for example, the heading over Isa. 28: "Christ, the sure foundation, promised"); they also found *presences* of him (see the heading over Isa. 49: "Christ sent to the Gentiles with promises," or over Isa. 52: "Christ's free redemption"). Nor was this sort of interpretation simply a patristic or Reformation device. It is found in Scripture itself: see 1 Cor. 10:4, where Paul, in speaking of the wilderness experience of the Jews after the Exodus, says that "they drank from the spiritual Rock that followed them, and the Rock was Christ."

The word normally used to describe this "finding of Christ in the Old Testament" is *typology*, or *antityping* — a *type*, or *antitype*, being a prefiguring of a later event. But such a way of defining the concept has a drawback: people take it as positing a merely *mental* connection between, say, Jesus and the Paschal Lamb. Accordingly, what I have been trying to do here (with my analogy to the iceberg and my playing of variations on the theme of sacramentality) is provide a theological basis for seeing this antityping as a *real anticipation*, an *actual pre-presence*, a *prolepsis in fact* of the mystery finally manifested in Jesus. For if we do not posit some such basis, the whole tissue of the Christian view of Scripture as one grand revelation of God in history falls apart. It either degenerates into a series of discrete, incremental bits of weaving, or it unravels into a tangle of arbitrary, imported allegorizations. But with the theological undergirding I have suggested, Scripture's own single-revelation view of itself — not to mention such audacious Christian insistences as the notion that the God of the Old Testament is none other than the Holy and Undivided Trinity — is amply vindicated.

I commend this approach to you, therefore. It saves, quite literally, everything. It leaves all the historical events fully historical, yet it does not limit their sacramentalizing of the mystery to their contemporary significance alone. It allows you to postulate a revelation as progressive as you like, but nonetheless to see its sequential details (even the most primitive of them) as the actions of the one God in the fullness of his mysterious presence. It juxtaposes time and eternity in a way that neither keeps them unsavingly separated nor confounds them in a mish-mash that violates both. Principally, though, it does justice to the immediate presence of the entire, eternal mystery to every moment of time and every scrap of space. It lets God be the creating and redeeming God of *all* the particulars of history. It does not confine his action simply to the more notable moments of Scripture, or even to the moments of Scripture alone. It lets you say not only that Jesus died in the Paschal Lamb and in the death of Lazarus, but also that he died in the deaths of six million Jews during the Holocaust — and for that matter in all deaths, everywhere and always. Above all, it allows you to proclaim your faith that in the power of his resurrection, he is present to the whole of creation, not just to those who happen to be Christians. In short, it finally makes solid, earthly sense of Jesus' words, "I, if I be lifted up from the earth, will draw *all* to myself" (John 12:32).

Accordingly, with no apologies for having dragged you through a bit of theological heavy sledding, I go straight to the catena of acted parables — to the remarkable series of tips of the iceberg — that the Gospels present to us at the beginning of Holy Week.

Palm Sunday first (Aland no. 269). The mystery that Jesus is sacramentalizing by riding triumphally into Jerusalem on the back of a donkey is his *parousía,* his coming as a king in peace and as a judge in vindication. Had he been coming as a king to make war, or as a judge to settle scores, he would presumably have come on horseback to signify such aggressive intentions. But even though he made his peaceable disposition clear — even though (as Matthew points out) his choice of a donkey was a fulfillment of the irenic prophecy, "Tell the daughter of Zion: Behold, your king is coming to you, humble, and mounted on an ass" (Matt. 21:5; cf. Zech. 9:9) — the sacramental significance of his action was lost on the crowd that acclaimed him. Expecting only an interventionist, plausible Messiah, they hailed him only as such — only as one who would, then and there and by right-handed power, bring in "the kingdom of our father David that is coming" (Mark 11:10). Nevertheless, as Jesus rides into the city, there is one thing and one thing only uppermost in his mind; namely, his left-handed, implausible death. And he knows in his bones, even if he does not yet realize it in his mind, that this same crowd will paradoxically provide him with the messianic death they refuse even to think about now: on Good Friday, precisely because he will have given them no sustained evidence of right-handed intervention on his part, they will be the very ones who cry, "Crucify him!"

The Triumphal Entry, therefore, is a parable of both grace and judgment. It is a parable of the judgment that descends only on the refusal of grace; and it is a parable of the grace that remains forever sovereign over judgment. For if the peaceable manner of his entry into a city at war with his methods is a judgment on their unwillingness to accept a dying/rising Messiah, so it is also (by being a voluntary going to his death) a proclamation of the grace that will absolve even their non-acceptance of him on the cross: "Father, forgive them" will be his last word on the subject. The iceberg, if you will, will thrust up above the surface of history on Good Friday as well as on Palm Sunday and proclaim for all time the way God perennially works.

The next two tips of the iceberg, however — the next two acted parables in the Holy Week sequence — proclaim grace and judgment not only simultaneously but also in tandem. First comes Jesus' Weeping over Jerusalem (Luke 19:41-44; Aland no. 270), and immediately afterward comes his Cleansing of the Temple (Aland no. 271: the episode is reported at this point by all three synoptics, but much earlier in the Fourth Gospel). In the abstract, it would seem that the Weeping might represent grace, and the Cleansing, judgment; but when the passages are actually examined, that turns out not to be the case. Each event is charged with both; and remarkably, the accounts of the Cleansing of the Temple actually contain more examples of what I have called the vocabulary of grace — more emphasis on littleness, lostness, leastness, etc. as the vehicles of salvation — than does the report of the Weeping over the City. This will become clear as I proceed, so let me begin by dealing with the Weeping first.

As the story opens, Jesus is drawing near to the city (presumably, this episode takes place on Palm Sunday, just prior to his arrival at the gates). Only moments before, Luke reports (Luke 19:39-40), some Pharisees in the crowd say to him, "Master, rebuke your disciples"; and Jesus answers, "I tell you, if these were silent, the very stones would cry out." It would seem, therefore, that even though Jesus has been aware all along that he is riding straight into the teeth of nonacceptance, the fact now hits him emotionally in a peculiarly powerful way. Everything he has predicted is now coming home to roost, and the sad enormity of it overwhelms him with both pity and anger: pity that the city cannot accept him; anger that it will not.

But in the speech that follows, it is anger that gains the upper hand. "If only you could know," he begins graciously enough, "even you, on this day, the things that make for peace. . . ." (I think that the Greek of that half-sentence can actually be read two ways: graciously, as implying "but sadly, you can't"; or judgmentally, as implying "but you damned well won't, as far as I'm concerned" — compare the Greek of Ps. 95:11, quoted in Heb. 3:11.) In any case, the rest of the sentence says, neutrally, that the city just doesn't know these things: "but now they are hid from your eyes." And the remainder of the passage goes on to spell out prophetically the condemning judgment that will be imposed: the city's enemies will surround it, and raze it to the ground together with all its inhabitants, and they will not leave in it one stone upon another *because it did not know the time of its visitation (episkopés).*

The Greek word here for "visitation" is a variant of the word for "bishop" *(epískopos,* overseer) and it provides a springboard for the application of this passage to the whole world as well as to Jerusalem. God's "visitation" of the world — both his mysterious, intimate presence to it below the surface of history and his *parousía* above that surface in the mighty acts of salvation — is the visitation of an overseer, not an avenger. It is the presence of the Good Shepherd, not the wolf (see 1 Pet. 2:25 for the identification of "shepherd" with *epískopos,* and of both with Jesus). But it is the presence of a Shepherd and Bishop who, given the way the world is, can be seen by that world only as an angry judge. For the world, by its own stubborn choice and its own irreversible pride, is going to hell in a handbasket. That is why its messianic overseer weeps: angry tears, judgmental tears, to be sure; but tears nonetheless. Tears from the same Messiah who earlier said, "Jerusalem, Jerusalem . . . , how often have I wanted to gather your children as a hen gathers her chicks under her wings, and you were not willing" (Luke 13:34).

His divine oversight, of course — his all-reconciling *episkopé* — will triumph in the end: to say it again, grace remains forever sovereign over judgment. The new Jerusalem, the new heavens, and the new earth — the whole redeemed order of the new world — will come down from heaven out of God, adorned as a bride for her husband (Rev. 21:1-2). Every tear will be wiped away. But in the meantime, for as long as the world insists on its own oversight — for as long as we will not abandon our domestic madness and our public folly — judgment will inevitably seem sovereign over grace. Guilt will estrange our faces from forgiveness; we will never, by our own devices, find the things that belong to our peace.

And so Jesus proceeds to the next of his acted parables. Going into the temple (still on Palm Sunday, at least in Matthew and Luke), he drives out all who sold and bought in the temple, overturns the tables of the money changers and the seats of those who sold pigeons, and says to them, "My house shall be called a house of prayer, but you make it a den of robbers." His *episkopé* — his visitation, his gracious shepherding and bishoping of creation — once again asserts itself. Of all the places in the world that should have stood witness to grace and truth, the temple was that place; but the world has infected even it, and there is nothing to be done with such a ship of fools but to pronounce upon it the judgment it deserves. Nevertheless, even after he parabolically acts out that judgment, his visitation remains one of grace: "and the blind and the lame [losers all] came to him in the temple, *and he healed them*" (Matt. 21:14).

"But when the chief priests and the scribes saw the wonderful things he did [I am following Matt. 21:15-17 here], and the children [more losers and little ones] crying out in the temple, 'Hosanna to the Son of David,' they were indignant; and they said to him, 'Do you hear what these are saying?' And Jesus said to them, 'Yes; have you never read: *Out of the mouths of babes and nursing children* [yet more of the last and the least] *you have perfected praise*'? And leaving them, he went out of the city to Bethany and lodged there."

436

Mark and Luke do not report this rhapsody on losing, but John goes it one better: he links the Cleansing of the Temple with the ultimate saving loss, the death and resurrection of Jesus himself. This is not the place to go into John's possible reasons for placing this episode at the beginning of Jesus' ministry — at John 2:13, after the "sign" of changing water into wine at the wedding at Cana. Suffice it to say that this early placement of the Cleansing not only makes good Johannine sense; John's version of the event also makes the same point that Matthew's does. Watch. The Judean authorities, having witnessed the Cleansing, respond to Jesus by asking (John 2:18), "What sign are you showing us by doing these things?" Jesus answers them, "Destroy this temple and I will raise it up in three days." At first, the authorities mock him, thinking he is referring to the temple he has just wrought havoc in: "This temple took forty-six years to build," they say, "and you're going to raise it up in three days?" But Jesus, John notes, was speaking of "the temple of his body" — and he goes on to note that when Jesus was raised from the dead, "his disciples remembered that he said this, and they believed the Scripture and the word that Jesus had said."

It is the sovereignty of grace over judgment all over again. It is the exaltation of losers who are willing to believe in grace over winners who think they can make it on their own. Judgment indeed falls on the world; but since the world is populated entirely by losers (in the end, none of us ever wins here) there is hope for everybody. Grace perennially waits for us to accept our destruction and, in that acceptance, to discover the power of the Resurrection and the Life.

Finally, though, in Matt. 21:18-19 and Mark 11:12-14 (Aland no. 272), there follows the bizarre episode of the Cursing of the Fig Tree (Luke omits it at this point, but includes it earlier — transformed, significantly, into a parable of grace — at Luke 13:6-9). Jesus comes back to Jerusalem the following day, and, seeing a fig tree by the side of the road, he goes to it and finds nothing but leaves (Mark adds the comment, "because it was not the season for figs"). Then Jesus says to the tree, "May no one ever eat fruit from you forever" (*eis tón aiôna*, to the age). According to Matthew, "the fig tree withered at once"; Mark, who puts the Cursing of the Fig Tree likewise on Monday, but before the

Cleansing of the Temple, delays the discovery of its having withered until Tuesday. In either case, the upshot is similar: Jesus, after an exceptionally harsh, if not unintelligible, act of judgment on the fig tree's unreadiness for him (and by extension, on both Jerusalem's and the world's unreadiness), goes back to grace again. But because Mark strikes the note of grace even more clearly, let me conclude by following him.

As Jesus and his disciples pass by the next morning, they see that the fig tree has "withered away to its roots" (Mark 11:20-26 and parallels; Aland no. 275). Peter remembers what happened the day before and says, "Master, look! The fig tree you cursed has withered." And Jesus answers him, "Have faith *(pístin)* in God. Truly I say to you, whoever says to this mountain [Jerusalem: Mt. Zion], 'Be taken up and be cast into the sea,' and does not doubt in his heart, but believes *(pisteúē)* that what he says will come to pass, it will be done for him."

It is tempting, of course, to take this as a general exhortation to prayer; but I think that is the wrong tack in this context. Jesus has been speaking of the judgment of destruction that will fall on Jerusalem (and the world) because it will not forsake what it thinks it knows in favor of what he wants it to believe. Therefore it is the believing, the faith, that should be emphasized in this passage, not the bizarre results — either of praying that a fig tree be cursed or of praying that Jerusalem go flying into the Mediterranean. Jesus is saying that even in the apparently harsh judgments of destruction that he has just issued, faith — trust in him — will still be able to turn death into resurrection. Grace that saves through faith can prevail anywhere.

I realize that such an interpretation is unusual to the point of being idiosyncratic, but stay with me for a moment. Because what Jesus says next (Mark 11:24-25) makes better sense under the aegis of a faith-reading than under the "pray-hard" banner. "For this reason, I tell you," he continues, (I translate literally here) "all things whatsoever you pray for and ask, believe *(pisteúete)* that you have received, and it will be to (or for) you." I don't want to lean too hard on an admittedly contestable point, but it is at least worth noting that the words *it* or *them* (referring to the things asked for) are not actually in the Greek text. It may even be worth suggesting that the "it" in "it will be to you" need not necessarily refer to those things either: "it" just might be something further back and deeper down in Jesus' mind. With great tentativeness, therefore, I am going to suggest that maybe — only maybe — it is possible to interpret the "things" we are supposed to believe we have received as the mystery of grace working in death and destruction, and to interpret the "it" that will be to us or for us as the mystery of resurrection.

Be that as shaky as it may, the rest of the passage bears it out remarkably well. "And whenever you stand praying," Jesus says, "forgive, if you have anything against anyone, so that your Father also who is in heaven may forgive you your trespasses." If this whole monologue of Jesus' is just a lecture on how to damage strangers' fruit trees on a spiritual whim, or take Jerusalem off the map by prayer, what's the point of dragging in forgiveness of all things? That only drops the discourse back into the out-of-context, grunt-and-groan-when-you-pray mode. Forgiveness becomes just one more impossible thing — one more tough and threatening job — that you have to break your spiritual back over. But if Jesus is indeed talking about the forgiving grace that works through the worst, then forgiveness begins to make more sense here.

For how is it that we so frequently run afoul of the worst in our lives? Oh, admittedly some of it comes from the changes and chances of this mortal life, from the malice of the devil or of man — from *the outside,* in short: from things we never wanted and certainly never invited. But a great deal of it comes from *the inside,* from our actually getting a "yes" to a prayer for something we once wanted so badly we could taste it, but which, when we finally got it, turned out to be mostly a millstone around our necks. The friends we now hate, the husbands or wives we are now estranged from, the children who have put both themselves and us on the psychiatrist's couch — all the dire burdens that now fall on us like judgments — all of them were once earnestly invited. Might it not just be that what Jesus is saying here is that *forgiveness* is the only way life's burdens, invited or not, can be lifted? Might he not be telling us, by these two illustrations of the frankly disastrous consequences of prayer (the fig tree withered, Mt. Zion sunk), that even the self-willed calamities of our lives are not hopeless as long as we believe in the gra-

439

cious One who forgives — and are willing to pass his forgiveness along to others? Might it not mean simply that the world, despite the catastrophes it has brought on itself by its stupid wish-lists, and despite the judgment that must necessarily be pronounced on such follies, is always — even at its willful worst — just one breath away from total reconciliation, *if only it will forgive?*

I, for one, would like to think this passage means that. But whether it does or not, there is no question in my mind that that is what all these acted parables, all these surfacings of the iceberg, have been about — and that *that* is what Jesus calls us to believe. So thank you and goodnight. Whatever else we may be sure or unsure of, at least we know the one thing that belongs to our peace.

CHAPTER EIGHT

The Eye of the Hurricane

THE QUESTION OF JESUS' AUTHORITY
THE TWO SONS
THE WICKED TENANTS

All the rest of Jesus' spoken parables of judgment occupy a space of not more than four days, if you follow Matthew and Luke — or even as few as three, if you follow Mark. His acted parables of messianic authority (Palm Sunday, the Cleansing of the Temple) have now been accomplished: from here on — in the relatively quiet time before the beginning of the passion on Maundy Thursday evening — there is nothing but talk recorded in the Gospels. Jesus, for his part, tells one judgmental story after another and speaks in apocalyptic discourses; the Judean authorities, for theirs, respond with baited questions, trying their best to catch him in a chargeable offense. This is the eye of the hurricane, the ominous calm that is everyone's last chance to speak before the second onslaught of the redemptive storm.

The first two parables he tells in this interlude are those of the Two Sons and the Wicked Tenants (Aland nos. 277, 278); but since these are both presented in the light of the official hostility to him, I shall preface them by dealing first with Aland no. 276: the Questioning of Jesus' Authority by the establishment figures who are out to destroy him (the Gospel passages are Matt. 21:23-27; Mark 11:27-33; and Luke 20:1-8).

"They came again to Jerusalem," Mark says, placing the episode on Tuesday. "And as he was walking in the temple, the chief priests and the

441

scribes and the elders came to him and they said to him, 'By what authority *(exousía)* are you doing these things, or who gave you authority to do them?'" The recurrence at this point of the word *exousía* is one of the notable symmetries in the synoptic Gospels. At the beginning of Jesus' ministry, it was precisely his teaching "as one who had *exousía,* and not as the scribes" (Mark 1:22) that attracted the crowds to him and led the establishment, even at that early date, to "take counsel against him to kill him" (Mark 3:6). Now, at the end, it is that same *exousía* of his, that same sui generis authority — that underivative, even arrogant style of operating by no one's leave but his own — that returns as the *leitmotiv* of the drama. The seemingly interventionist manifestations of it are the cause of the people's enthusiasm at the Triumphal Entry and in the Temple (Jesus has nerve!); and the ultimately noninterventionist mystery of it is the cause of their forsaking him on Good Friday ("Some nerve! We like our Messiahs unique, but not so unique as to die"). But above all, Jesus' *exousía* is the cause of the urgency with which the ruling class now moves to do him in. Between the fear that Jesus will upset their political balancing act with Rome and the resentment they feel at his attacks upon themselves, they decide that his (to them) pretense of *exousía* has to be stopped forthwith. Hence their question, "By what authority. . . ?"

But Jesus' *exousía* — his unique claim to an authority based on *who he is,* not on *what he can prove himself to be* — is not something he can justify to their satisfaction. He is asking them to believe in him; they, at best, are trying to decide whether they can find room for him in their minds. And because Jesus knows there is no way of ending such a standoff, he simply contents himself with parrying their thrusts. In the face of their questions, he continually frustrates them by being what he always was, a fox, a rebel, a bad boy who refuses to answer except with questions of his own. "Tell me," he says. "The baptism of John — was it from heaven or from men?" In an instant, he has put them in a bind. If they say, "From heaven," they know he will ask them, "Why then didn't you believe *(episteúsate)* him?" and if they say, "From men," they will have to answer to the people, "because all held that John was really a prophet" (Mark 11:29-32). Accordingly, they run for the first shabby intellectual cover they can find: "We do not know," they answer him. And Jesus, diving nervily into the same cover, replies, "Neither will I tell you by what *exousía* I do these things."

In its form, this exchange is simply an example of Jesus' facility with the tricks of rabbinical argument; but in its substance, it is far more than that. As far as he is concerned, there are only two central considerations in his ministry, now or ever: his own authority — his *exousía* as who he is — and their trust *(pístis)* or distrust in him personally. He is not in the business of giving them arguments that will prove he has some derivative right to their attention; he is only inviting them to believe. This is the hard stone in the gracious peach of his Good News: salvation is not by works, be they physical, intellectual, moral, or spiritual; it is strictly by faith in him. And therefore it is not just these present, official questioners whom he refuses to answer: Jesus never answers any such questions. He frustrates James and John when they ask for seats on his right and his left (Mark 10:35-45); he replies in riddles to the Judean authorities when they demand to know what sign he is showing by cleansing the temple (John 2:18-22); and even at the end, he refuses to give an answer to the apostles when they inquire whether he will "at this time restore the kingdom to Israel" (Acts 1:6). Furthermore, these frustrating refusals go on and on, not only after the ascension but right up to the present day: Jesus obviously does not answer many questions from you or me. Which is why apologetics — the branch of theology that seeks to argue for the justifiability of God's words and deeds — is always such a questionable enterprise. Jesus just doesn't argue. Even when he involves himself in disputations, the most obvious thing about him is that he is refusing to cooperate with his disputers. He does not reach out to convince us; he simply stands there in all the attracting/repelling fullness of his *exousía* and dares us to believe.

I have spent some time on these notes of authority and faith because they are crucial points in the interpretation of the two parables we are about to take up. They are, in fact, the very nub of the message of the Two Sons and the Wicked Tenants; I intend, therefore, to resist the temptation to let other interpretations put them in the shade. Take the

Two Sons first. As it appears in the Gospel (only at Matt. 21:28-32; Aland no. 277), it is presented as the uninterrupted continuation of the wrangle over Jesus' *exousía* we have just dealt with. Moreover, its clinching, final lines are precisely a reference to the ministry of John the Baptist that Jesus has just alluded to. Accordingly, even on the face of the Gospel account, Jesus is holding steadfastly to the same subject he has been pursuing all along.

"What do you think?" he asks the rulers. "A man had two sons; and he went to the first and said, 'Son, go and work in the vineyard today' [flag up: this parable will carry within it not only the force of the immediately previous discussion but that of the Laborers in the Vineyard as well (Matt. 20:1-16)]. And the first son answered, 'I will not'; but afterward he repented and went. And he went to the second and said the same; and he answered, 'I go, Sir,' but did not go. Which of the two," Jesus then asks, "did the will of his father?"

Time for a break, in order to note two false leads in the interpretation of this parable: it is not primarily about the Gentile/Jew controversy in the early church, and it is not at all about works mattering more than words. The Gentile/Jew reading is a wrong start because, while the influx of Gentile Christians on the basis of faith alone is a possible minor point of exposition, it cannot be the main point unless you take this passage as an ecclesiastical gloss rather than as the words of Jesus himself. But to me, that is both cumbersome and unlikely. Jesus is, after all, talking to Jews here. Accordingly, the most likely reading is that the two sons represent two different responses (faith and unfaith), each of which is a response that Jews have made to both John the Baptist and Jesus. Similarly, the works-versus-words reading is a mistake. Jesus is on the subject of faith in his own *exousía,* not on the subject of legalistic fine slicing by which a no that turns into a yes can be construed as a more meritorious work than a yes that turns out to be a no.

In any case, Jesus continues the parable (Matt. 21:31-32) by speaking only of Jews. "Amen, I say to you, the tax collectors and the harlots go into the kingdom before you. For John came to you in the way of righteousness and you did not believe *(episteúsate)* him, but the tax collectors and the harlots believed him; and even when you saw it, you did not afterward repent and believe him."

This is, of course, a parable of judgment. But I want you to note how it is that Jesus shows the imposition of the judgment here. Let me rephrase his question ("Which of the two did the will of his father?") in the form of a series of questions and answers that may help clarify not only his own reasoning but the reasoning of Scripture as a whole:

Q: On which of these two sons will judgment fall?
A: On the second.

Q: Why?
A: Because he did not do the will of his father.

Q: And what then is the father's will?
A: [I quote from Jesus himself, in John 6:40]: "This is the will of my Father, that every one who sees the Son [Jesus — just standing there, and speaking there, and hanging there on the cross] and believes *(pisteúōn)* in him may have everlasting life, and I will raise him up at the last day."

Do you see? The incidental devices by which the two sons arrived at believing or nonbelieving behavior — at faith or unfaith, at a yes-out-of-a-no or at a no-out-of-a-yes — are not the main point. That point is simply that judgment falls adversely on unfaith alone. And it is underscored by Jesus' insistence that the tax collectors and the harlots will go into the kingdom before the rulers. It is not that those disreputable types will be saved because they straightened up and flew right; it is that they will be saved just because they believed. And it is not that the rulers will run a poor second because they took a nosedive into evil works after a previously respectable flight pattern. Like the Pharisee in the Pharisee and the Publican, they are condemned for not repenting of their unfaith — for their faithless nonacceptance of the grace that works by raising the dead. Therefore even the failure to repent of which Jesus finally accuses the rulers is not a moral matter. As a matter of fact, they had no more moral turpitude to repent of than the Pharisee did. They were good people. And as far as the tax collectors and the harlots were concerned, they, like the publican in the parable, had more strikes against them than any mere reform could cancel: they were bad people — losers, outcasts, social dead ducks.

All of this is convincingly present in the parable of the Two Sons, if you scratch beneath its surface. The "repentance" of the one son cannot possibly have removed the factual outrage of his refusal to work; and the shirking of the other cannot have obliterated the prior goodness of his prompt compliance. The first son's initial no to his father remains the insult it always was, and the second son's yes stands as an irrevocable joy. It is not that either the evils of the first are reformed away or that the goodnesses of the second go into the discard; it is just that the one finally, and in living fact, takes his stand on trust in his father's *exousía* while the other in fact repudiates it.

Accordingly, this parable is indeed charged with all the judgment-on-the-refusal-of-grace overtones that are present in the Laborers in the Vineyard. Just as in that parable the last laborers hired get full pay simply as a result of their trusting the word of the lord of the vineyard, and living out that trust for a single, less-than-meritorious hour, so with the first son here. And just as the laborers who worked all day labored only in hope of reward for their works — and refused to trust the lord when he proclaimed grace, not reward, as his only real interest — so with the second son. As a matter of fact, if you wanted to press the parable, you might even postulate that the second son was fully aware of his father's acceptance of his brother's too-easy repentance after insubordination, and that he decided to teach the freewheeling pair of them (especially his father) a lesson. *He* would puncture the tires of all this freedom in faith by just not showing up to do any of the works he was famous for. They thought they could count on *him*, did they? Well, they'd be sorry.

And if you then expand upon the parable, you get an instant application of it to the life of the church in all ages. For no matter how much we give lip service to the notion of free grace and dying love, *we do not like it*. It is just too . . . indiscriminate. It lets rotten sons and crooked tax farmers and common tarts into the kingdom, and it thumbs its nose at really good people. And it does that, gallingly, for no more reason than the Gospel's shabby exaltation of dumb trust over worthy works. Such nonsense, we mutter in our hearts; such heartless, immoral folly. We'll teach God, we say. We will continue to sing "Amazing Grace" in church; but we will jolly well be judicious when it comes to explaining to the riffraff what it actually means. We will assure them, of course, that God loves them and forgives them, but we will make it clear that *we* expect them to clean up their act before we clasp them seriously to our bosom. We do not want whores and chiselers and practicing gays (even if they *are* suffering with AIDS) thinking they can just barge in here and fraternize. Above all, we do not want drunk priests, or ministers who cheat on their wives with church organists, standing up there in the pulpit telling us that God forgives such effrontery. *We* never did such things. Why, we can hardly even bear to think. . . .

Do you see now? We are second sons, elder brothers, respectable Pharisees, twelve-hour, all-day laborers whose moral efforts have been trampled on by the Feet Beautiful upon the Mountains. We are resentful at being the butts of the divine joke of grace that says nothing matters except plain, old, de facto, yes-Jesus faith. And when we institutionalize that resentment by giving the impression that the church is not for sinners and gainsayers, we are a disgrace to the Gospel — a bushel of works hiding the Light of the world. We are under judgment. Oh, yes; we say we believe. But what we believe is largely an ethico-theological construct of our own devising, a system in our heads that will make the world safe for democracy, and for thrifty, brave, clean, and reverent ex-sinners like ourselves. Like the second son, our only real trust is in our own devices. Just trusting Jesus — the friend of tax collectors and sinners, the one who, while we are still sinners, dies for the ungodly — is not our idea of how to run a lifeline.

"Diffidam mihi, fidam in te," said Augustine to God; "I will distrust myself, I will trust in you." The first son had the grace to distrust his own first formulation of what was actually going on between him and his father and to eat crow, turning his self-regarding no of works into an other-regarding yes of faith. And for that faith, he is commended as having done the will of his father — the whole will, not just some preliminary velleity on his father's part but *all he ever wanted.* And that will

is one thing and one only: believing. It is trust in him — anytime, anywhere, anyhow. But the second son turned Augustine's prayer around: *"Fidam in meipsum, diffidam tibi"*: "I will trust myself, I will distrust you." He kept scores where his father kept none, books where his father had stopped making entries; and for that reliance on works (nasty, negative, I'll-teach-them works), he is condemned.

So it is with me, if I am honest. And so it is with you. The Father's will for you — his whole will, his entire plan of salvation — is that you believe in Jesus, nothing more. He has already forgiven you, he has already reconciled you, he has already raised you up together with Jesus and made you sit together in heavenly places with him. And better yet, Jesus himself has already pronounced upon you the approving judgment of having done his Father's will. But if you do not believe him — if you insist on walking up to the bar of judgment on your own faithless feet and arguing a case he has already dismissed — well, you will never hear the blessed silence of his uncondemnation over the infernal racket of your own voice. "He who argues his own case has a fool for a lawyer" is true in any court. But in this court you will be more than a fool if you try that trick. You will be an idiot. There is no case. There is no evidence against you. And there is no courtroom to display your talents in. It is all quashed, all over but the fun of having an eternal drink with the Judge who makes Harry Stone look serious. This is the Gospel as *Night Court.* All you have to do is hoist your glass and say, "Yes, Judge. Cheers! *Skal! Salute! Ein Prosit!* Bottoms up!" The whole thing, you see, stands forever on its head: the last shall be first — just for believing.

The parable that immediately follows the Two Sons takes up the same topics of faith and *exousía* from an opposite point of view. The story of the Wicked Tenants looks at the picture of rejection-by-unbelief from God's side rather than from ours. It occurs in all three synoptics (at Matt. 21:33-46; Mark 12:1-12; and Luke 20:9-19; Aland no. 278); but I shall continue to follow Matthew's account for two reasons. First, because it forms a logical sequel to the parable of the Two Sons, which only Matthew records. But second, because it is the fuller version. Indeed, if you will permit me an aside on the subject of biblical criticism, its very fullness serves as an argument in favor of the ancient view of the relationships among the synoptic Gospels. The modern view, of course, is that Mark was written first and that his Gospel was thus available to both Matthew and Luke; it also holds that, along with their own peculiar sources, designated as M and L, they had had material from a source common to them both but missing from Mark — a source designated as Q. In earlier times, however, it was generally assumed that Matthew came first, that Mark subsequently revised and abridged Matthew, and that Luke then used both of them, adding his own material where he thought appropriate. For well over a hundred years now, the modern view has reigned unquestioned and the ancient one has been treated as having no respectable claims at all. But if you look carefully at the parable of the Wicked Tenants in all three Gospels, you will see that the matter is not quite so clear-cut.

For one thing, Matthew and Mark agree at certain points and Luke is the odd man out (compare the first verse of the parable in all three accounts). Score one for the old, "updated abridgment" theory of Mark. The ancients were not just blindly caving in to the tradition that put Matthew first in the canon of Scripture; there are a number of instances in the synoptic Gospels where Luke inexplicably omits certain Markan passages which, on the modern view, he supposedly had right in front of him. See, for example, the parable of the Mustard Seed (Aland no. 209; Mark 4:30-32 and parallels), the passage on Divorce and Celibacy (Aland no. 252; Mark 10:2-12 and parallels), or the passage on the Sons of Zebedee and their request to sit on Jesus' right and left in glory (Aland no. 263; Mark 10:35-45 and parallels). But for another thing, Mark and Luke sometimes agree against Matthew (compare, in this parable, Mark 12:4-5 and parallels), suggesting that when Luke did use Mark, he did so because he felt it was a better account than Matthew's — provided, of course, he had access to the Matthean version.

My purpose in mentioning all this is not to advocate the abandonment of the modern view (on balance, it does seem to explain the complexities of the synoptic interrelationships a bit better). I only want to note that those interrelationships are indeed complex, and that it may well be true that no hypothesis about them will ever cover the ground with complete satisfaction. In any case, back to the text in Matthew.

"Hear another parable," Jesus says, picking up right after the story of the Two Sons. "There was a householder who planted a vineyard, and set a hedge around it, and dug a winepress in it, and built a tower, and let it out to tenants, and went into another country." Once again, Jesus recurs to the image of the vineyard, echoing not only his own parables, but also such passages as Isa. 5:7, "The vineyard of the Lord of hosts is the house of Israel, and the people of Judah are his pleasant planting." As in the parable of the Two Sons, I am once again going to resist the temptation to leap to a Jew/Gentile interpretation here. Jesus is still talking to Jews at this point: while such an interpretation is fair enough for certain expository purposes (and is even supported by the uniquely Matthean passage in verse 43), the main thrust of the parable goes to the more general matter of rejection of Jesus' *exousía* by unfaith. (Verse 43's consequent giving of the kingdom to another "nation [*éthnei*] producing the fruits" of faith is simply a forceful, prophetic instance of the perils of that rejection.)

Israel, the parable is saying, has been chosen by God as his vineyard and God has let that vineyard out to the tenants now in charge, namely, the Judean authorities whose hostility and defective stewardship Jesus is now addressing. Look at the text: "When the season (*kairós*, high time, due season) of fruit drew near, he [the householder] sent his servants to get his fruit." Plainly, in adducing this first group of servants, Jesus is referring to the prophets who, as he sees it, have prepared the way for his own coming — and who, in their own time, were no more acceptable to the authorities than Jesus is now. As he puts it, the tenants took those servants and "beat one, killed another, and stoned another." But then, after having the householder send still more servants to the same fate, Jesus has him decide to send his son to them, saying, "They will respect my son." Just as plainly, this is a setup for the condemnation of the authorities of Jesus' day.

In strict logic, the parable becomes tortured, if not fantastic at this point: Jesus is clearly trying to show their rejection as folly. There is no good reason, for example, why the tenants should alter their unfaithful stewardship now (the son is just one more interference with their plans); correspondingly, there is also no good reason, in real life, for Jesus to hope that the authorities he is dealing with will alter their unbelief (to them, he is simply a dangerous nuisance). Furthermore, the reason the tenants give for their plan to kill the householder's son is equally absurd: there is no real chance that murdering the heir of the vineyard will result in their inheriting it, especially since the householder is still alive, well, and breathing down their necks at the end of the parable (see Matt. 21:40). The only way their reasoning could make sense is if they assumed that the householder was so far away (or, in the case of the Judean authorities, that the day of reckoning was so far off) that they could live out the time of their stewardship before the judgment descended upon them.

That, of course, is a possible interpretation: and if you like it, it enables you to open up the parable considerably. Watch. The precise assumption of the authorities facing Jesus is that the judgment is a long way in the future. Their further assumption is that when it does come, it will not only be recognizable as a right-handed, score-evening operation that will make Israel the top dog of the world; it will also feature a Messiah (or a Son of man) who will himself be recognizable as a nose-punching interventionist. They are not at all prepared for the appearance of some ineffective messianic pretender whose idea of saving action is aggravating God's representatives into exterminating him — which, of course, is exactly what Jesus' paradoxical arrival on their scene looks like to them. And because they will not trust him in such a mild arrival, because they can conceive only of their own, vindictive version of the coming in judgment, for that very reason, the real, vindicating judgment — the judgment that will inquire only if they have trusted, not how well or badly they managed — will fall on them anyway, condemning their unfaith.

Therefore, having postulated the fantastic, pointless killing of the householder's son, Jesus asks the clinching, rhetorical question: "When the owner (*kýrios*, lord) of the vineyard comes, what will he do to those tenants?" And they answer him ("they," presumably, being the authorities Jesus is aiming this parable at): "He will put those wretches to a miserable death and let out the vineyard to other tenants who will give him the fruits in their seasons *(kairoís)*." The setup, you see, has worked perfectly. Jesus has gotten them to say exactly what he would have said himself: the stewardship of the mystery of salvation will be taken away from the present authorities who have exercised it in unfaith and it will be given to others who will exercise it in faith. Moreover, those others will be able to stand at the judgment that looks only at faith because they will have done the "one thing necessary": they will have accepted, rather than rejected, the Son in his paradoxically mild coming. They will have recognized his all-reconciling, left-handed *exousía* and they will stand approved because of their trust. But the authorities — even though they, too, are in fact just as much *within* the power of his reconciliation — will have cut themselves off from that power.

Jesus then goes on to tie up the parable (Matt. 21:42-46). He says to them, "Have you never read the Scriptures [he is continuing to drive home the point that the Old Testament — to which he has referred by his allusions to the vineyard and to the prophets — promises *his* kind of Messiah, not theirs]: 'The stone that the builders rejected has become the very cornerstone; this was the Lord's doing, and it is marvelous (*thaumasté*, astonishing, even shocking) in our eyes'? [he is quoting from Ps. 118:22-23]." Jesus is saying quite clearly, in other words, that not only is his own mild *exousía* unacceptable to their unfaith; it is also and nevertheless — *in its very unacceptability* — the cornerstone of their salvation, even though they will not trust it. The world is saved only by his passion, death, and resurrection, not by any of the devices that, in its unbelief, it thinks it can take refuge in. Furthermore, that same unacceptability will be the cornerstone of their judgment and of the world's — a truth that Matthew will set forth as Jesus' final word before the passion in the parable of the Last Judgment (Matt. 25:31-46). In that great scene, where the sheep are finally separated from the goats, the criterion for the rewarding of the sheep is nothing other than their blind acceptance by faith of a king who has appeared to the world only under the guise of the last, the lost, the least, and the little. Even the righteous, you see, will know of no *reason* for their vindication; they will only have *experienced* it through the King's paradoxical presence on the underside of creation. They will simply have trusted; and that trust will have already brought them home justified. And as for the goats . . . well, the wicked, too, will have experienced the same presence (the authorities of Jesus' day, for example, were as *involved* in his redeeming death as anybody — Caiaphas, the Sanhedrin, even Judas, were all intimate with his saving *exousía*); but they will not have trusted. They will have been justified and they will have been brought home; but because of the blindness of their unbelief, they will have cut themselves off from the salvation they already had — from the favorable judgment that, but for the noise of their own works, they would otherwise have heard.

Finally, though, Jesus prophetically spells out the end result of the authorities' faithless stewardship of the mystery. "Therefore I tell you, the kingdom of God will be taken away from you and given to a nation producing the fruits of it." Then, referring back to himself as the cornerstone, he says, "And he who falls on this stone will be broken to pieces; but when it falls on anyone it will crush him to dust." This last verse, while less well supported by the textual evidence, still makes perfectly good sense as the concluding line of the parable. It is the generalizing of the judgment that Jesus made specific in the verse before. His paradoxical messiahship is a great stone in the whole world's way: Christ Jesus, as Paul said later in 1 Cor. 1:23, is a stumbling block *(skándalon)* to the Jews, and foolishness *(mōrían)* to the Greeks. The world perennially trips over him in unbelief; and when he comes in judgment to its unfaith, his vindication of it by grace through faith simply grinds to powder the irrelevant, lost life on which it chose to rely.

The authorities, predictably, respond to this statement by trying once again to arrest Jesus. But fearing the multitudes — prudently apprehensive that a popular uproar might bring down the political house of cards that has been their life's work — they put off their plans till they can con the populace into being ground to a powder along with them. Mark and Luke add the detail here that "they perceived that he had told this parable against them" — a perception that any five-year-old could have come up with, but that still deserves a final word. For Jesus *was* against them. And he is against the world, too. He stands in judgment against everyone who will not accept his acceptance of the world by faith alone; but he brings down his gavel only on the folly that will not see that *he judges nothing else* — not goodness, not badness, not anything. And that is such a strange kind of againstness, such a blessed resistance of the world's insistence on judgment by works, that you'd think it would make us all laugh out loud. But the self-justifying world (including an alarmingly large number of Christians who think that being well behaved is more important to God than just trusting his forgiveness) can see it — and him — only as a threat. As any preacher who seriously preaches the Gospel of grace can tell you, the troops are not amused by the prospect of absolutely free salvation. The first instinct of most Christians, after they have smiled indulgently at the preacher's charmingly easygoing concept of salvation, is to nail him to the wall for knocking the props out from under divine retribution for nasty deeds. They do not want grace, they want law. Like the stupid tenants in the parable, they try to stop the coming of the paradoxical Power that alone can keep them in business, and they take their refuge in a lot of prudential nonsense that only insures their going out of it.

They don't stop the Power, of course. Jesus died for the sins of those who killed him — even for the sins of unbelief by which *we* kill him all over again. In the end, though, it is just sad. How unhappy to put ourselves on the losing end of a deal that even our messing up can't really sour! How melancholy not to believe that all he ever wanted was for us to believe!

How just plain dumb!

CHAPTER NINE

The Deluge of Judgment by Mercy

THE KING'S SON'S WEDDING

The parable of the King's Son's Wedding (Matt. 22:1-14; Aland no. 279) is quite plainly a variation on the parable of the Great Banquet in Luke 14:15-24. But when the two versions are compared, their differences of tone, content, and context are so marked as to make you wonder whether they even deserve the name parallel passages. You pay your money and take your choice, of course, as to how they got that different. For example, some critics like to assign responsibility for the Matthean version to some first- or second-century ecclesiastical source. But my dollar goes down on a more economical explanation, namely, that the parable appears twice because Jesus told it twice. Like a good preacher, however, he did not simply reach into the barrel and use previous sermons unchanged; he varied his material, giving even an old parable a new form for a new occasion.

Take the present parable as an instance. Jesus told it in its first form (in Luke) at a meal in the house of one of the chief Pharisees: in that context, it was predominantly a parable of grace, with a short judgmental kicker at the end. On second telling, however (in Matthew, during Holy Week), he transformed it into a full-fledged parable of judgment, with grace tucked down below as the subtext. I leave it to you to compare the two in detail; for myself — since I have already treated Luke's version in the previous volume, *The Parables of Grace* — I proceed directly to the Matthean rendering, reminding you only of my insistence that, even when he speaks in judgment, Jesus is careful to make grace sovereign over all.

The story occurs in Matthew with the simplest of introductions: "And again Jesus spoke to them in parables, saying. . . ." The logical antecedent of the "them" is of course the chief priests and Pharisees (Matt. 21:45-46) against whom Jesus has just spoken (and acted out) his immediately preceding parables of judgment — and who, in fact, are trying to arrest him and kill him. We should expect, therefore, that this version will be far "hotter," far more filled with severity and even death, than his previous telling of the story over dessert and coffee at a dinner party; and so it is. But before we dwell on its uniqueness, I want you to put in the back of your mind two striking details that Jesus carries over from the earlier version. First, he uses the imagery of a wedding *(gámos)* in both presentations of the parable: in Matthew, the word occurs in the opening words of the parable itself; in Luke, it occurs in the immediately preceding parable (14:7-8) shortly before he relates the parable of the Great Banquet. Accordingly, since I have been insisting all through this book on a full-court, whole-New-Testament press in my interpretation of the parables, I want you to set this parable not only in the context of the Gospels but also in the light of the wedding that is the climactic image of Scripture, the final wrap-up of the entire Bible, namely, the Marriage Supper *(deípnon)* of the Lamb (Rev. 19:9ff.).

The second detail follows logically from that: in both versions, Jesus makes extensive use of the imagery of a festive meal. In Luke, he not only tells the parable while he is "eating bread on the sabbath" in the Pharisee's house; he also uses the word *doché* (banquet, reception, Luke 14:13) just before he tells the story and the word *deípnon* (supper, banquet, Luke 14:16, 17, 24) in the parable itself. And in Matthew, he uses the word *áriston* (breakfast, noonday dinner, feast, Matt. 22:4) to specify the nature of the party the king gives to celebrate his son's wedding. Add therefore to your computer memory bank as many dinner parties, suppers, and wedding receptions as you can gather up out of Scripture: not only the final Supper of the Lamb (Rev. 19), but the marriage feast at Cana of Galilee (John 2), the Last Supper (Matt. 26; Mark 14; Luke 22), the evening meal at Emmaus on the night of Easter Day (Luke 24), the breakfast of broiled fish by the lakeside at one of Jesus' resurrection appearances (John 21) — and for good measure, the Passover meal in Exod. 12, all sabbath meals everywhere, the feast for the prodigal son (Luke 15), and the Lord's Supper throughout Christian history. In other words, this parable must be read in the context of all the gracious invitations to "sit together in Christ Jesus" (Eph. 2:6), be they Old Testament antitypes, Gospel events, present realities, or eschatological promises. The world has been summoned precisely to a party — to a reconciled and reconciling dinner *chez* the Lamb of God; judgment is pronounced only in the light of the acceptance or declination of that invitation.

For that reason, I simply note the immediate context of the parable and move on: Jesus is speaking for openers here about the rejection by the authorities of his invitation to believe in him. But only for openers. The reach of this parable goes far beyond the Jews of Jesus' own time, and even beyond the Jew/Gentile conflict in the early church: it ultimately defines the nature both of the salvation he offers to the whole world and of the judgment he pronounces on the rejection of that offer. It is, in a word, catholic; I will not sell it short by dwelling on parochial interpretations.

"The kingdom of heaven," Jesus begins (tying the story back to all the parables of a mysterious, actual, catholic kingdom he told earlier in his ministry), "may be compared to a king who gave a marriage feast (*gámous*) for his son." Score a happy point for the all-reconciling party and its preeminence as a biblical image. God, the King, is not mad at anybody: because of his Son — because his Son, by death and resurrection, has drawn all creation to himself as the bride of the Lamb — God wills above all to celebrate. And because when God is happy, everybody should be happy, he extends a gracious invitation to join him in his joy: "And he sent his servants to call those who were invited to the marriage feast." Sadly, though, the situation is not that simple: those who were invited, Jesus says, "would not come." Score a sad point, therefore, for the unhappy truth that the world is full of fools who won't believe a good thing when they hear it. Free grace, dying love, and unqualified acceptance might as well be a fifteen-foot crocodile, the way we respond to it: all our protestations to the contrary, we will sooner accept a God we will be fed to than one we will be fed by.

But since Jesus, in telling the parable, now goes on a roll, let us roll with him in the interpretation. The king, undaunted, sends yet more servants: "Tell those who are invited," he commands them, "Behold, I have made ready my feast *(áriston)*, my oxen and my fat calves are killed, and everything is ready; come to the marriage feast." The invited guests, however, make light of it (the Greek is *amelésantes:* disregard, reject, care nothing for, not give a damn about), and they go off, one to his farm and another to his business interests — while the rest make crystal clear to the king what they really think of his monomaniacal insistence on having a party: they seize his servants; they treat them disgracefully; and last but not least, they kill them.

It seems an odd way to run a social life. Most of us are content with just thinking such thoughts: "Another one of those ghastly slow leaks the Hopkinsons try to pass off as a blowout? Why don't we tell them the mailman stepped on a land mine in the lawn and we never got the invitation?" But Jesus is out to stigmatize the incongruous enormity of the rejection, so he insists on nothing less than heaps of murdered mailmen. And he follows it with an absolute festival of death presided over by the king himself. Carrying the note of deadly seriousness to its logical extreme — driving home the nail of an unappeasable determination to celebrate, and not caring that he leaves brutal hammer marks all over the woodwork of his story — he has the king respond in kind to the depredations of the first-invited guests: "The king was angry," Jesus says, "and he sent his soldiers and destroyed those murderers and burned their city." The scene is straight out of the *A-Team:* bazookas firing, napalm enveloping ladies in summer frocks, Rolls Royces being blown up by TOW missiles, hundred-room mansions being burned to the ground. But unlike TV, it features real blood and genuine corpses. This is not just the old Newport-Southampton social snub; this is crossing people off your list for good.

Please note, though, the real reason for such ferocity. Who in fact were all these corpses lying around like so much cordwood? They were the people who had a right to be at a royal wedding. They were the nobility, the jet set, the stars of stage, screen, and TV. They were, in short, the beautiful and the good. They did not lack for socially acceptable good works: they had the Mercedes Benzes, the Dior gowns, and the sixty-five-foot yachts; above all, they had the *style* to make even a royal wedding look better. But for all that, they were totally lacking in the trust, the faith, that is the only divinely acceptable quality. And so they take their place in Jesus' cavalcade of winners who lose: they are the Pharisee in the temple reading off his list of good deeds; they are Zacchaeus with his speech about what an honest crook he is; and they are you, and they are me. They are all of us who live in the twin certainties that our good works will earn us the right to attend the Supper of the Lamb, and that God's good nature will absolve us from having to sit through it if we happen to have other plans. Why the ferocity, then? Simply this: since neither they nor we could possibly be wronger about either of those two certainties, Jesus insists on displaying both of them as dead wrong. Salvation is not by works, and the heavenly banquet is not an option. We are saved only by our acceptance of a party already in progress, and God has paid for that party at the price of his own death. And since he counts only those two things — only faith and grace — nothing else counts. Outside of the party, there is no life at all.

Which is why Jesus now has the king proceed to what for him is plan B, but what for God has been plan A all along: "Then he said to his servants, 'The wedding is ready, but those invited were not worthy' [in their reliance on their own worth, they lost completely the sole worthiness of faith]; go therefore into the streets of the city and invite to the marriage feast as many as you find.' And those servants went out into the streets and gathered all whom they found, *both bad and good.*"

Stop right there. This last detail is not just a peculiarity of this parable; it is practically the hallmark of Jesus' major parables of the kingdom and of grace. In the Sower, a catholic sowing has both good and evil results, all of which are within the kingdom. In the Wheat and the Weeds, good and evil are allowed to grow together until the harvest. In the Net, the kingdom gathers of every kind. And in the Good Samaritan, the Prodigal Son, and the Pharisee and the Publican, Jesus goes out of his way to make heroes of life's losers. Evil, in short, is not a problem for the kingdom: it has already been aced out by the power of Jesus' death and resurrection. The only thing that can possibly be a problem for the kingdom is a faithless nonacceptance of God's having solved the problem of evil all by himself, and without ever once having mentioned the subject of reform. He does not invite the good and snub the bad. He invites us all, while we are yet sinners; and he simply asks us to trust that invitation. And therefore because the remaining inhabitants of his kingdom, good and bad, did just that — because the working poor and the walking wounded, the bag ladies, the prostitutes, and the derelicts drinking Muscatel in doorways just said yes and came to the wedding — they are all home free at the party: "the wedding hall," Jesus says, "was filled with guests."

It is necessary here, I think, to supply a detail in the parable — a detail made reasonable by the events that are shortly to unfold. Since the types who have now been dragooned into the festivities right off the streets could not possibly have had tuxedos and ball gowns in their shopping carts and brown paper bags, I am going to postulate that the king, in order to give the royal wedding a properly royal ambience, supplied his last-minute guests with suitable clothes on the way in. He opened the royal wardrobe and had his gentlemen and ladies in waiting carry its entire contents down to the front door of the palace. Then, as each one approached, he or she was given something splendid to wear: a Bill Blass original, a Balenciaga creation, whatever.

Now then. The king, satisfied that he has done everything needed to make this the party to end all parties, comes in to survey the splendor of the scene. And what does he see? He sees a perfect spectacular gathering, inexplicably marred by one character totally out of character. Make this man's clothes any style you like: shabby genteel, seedy tweedy, skidrow disreputable or punk-rock garish — all they have to be is inappropriate enough to make him a sore thumb in the royal eye. So the king goes over to him and addresses him with a word that is by now familiar to you as a less-than-friendly greeting: "Buster *(hetaíre),*" he says, "how did you get in here without a wedding garment?" And the gentleman in question, Jesus tells us, "was speechless."

I want you to strike a trial balance on the entries in the parable so far. Entry one: the first-invited guests were all recipients of the king's favor. By his gracious invitation to the wedding, he had said to every last one of them, "You're okay in my book; I want you at my party." The *invitation,* you see, is the principal judgment in this parable — the sentence of vindication from which all the incidental judgments in the story subsequently proceed. It is a judgment filled with grace, and it never once, through the whole parable, loses its status as such. But when it is refused in distrust — when the first guests on the list contradict the king's "You're okay" with their own overwrought refusal to believe him — it simply descends on them. But it does not lose its vindicating character: he still wills nothing but the party. If they will not accept his vindication, that is no skin off his nose: he will rub them, still vindicated, off his list of fun people and go hunt for others who can recognize a good deal when they hear it.

Entry two: the guests invited as replacements are likewise recipients of the king's favor. He doesn't care a fig that they look like pigs and smell worse. He doesn't care that they don't know *hors d'oeuvres* from Havana cigars. He doesn't care that they eat with their hands and blow their noses without handkerchiefs. In other words, he does not make any stipulations about them at all. They do not have to get their act together in order to be worthy of the party, any more than the prodigal son had to guarantee amendment of life before getting the fatted calf. They have only, like the prodigal, to accept the acceptance and go with the flow. The king and the father, you see, are party people. They will take only yes for an answer; anybody who wants to say no has gone to hell already.

Entry three: all of the above is as true of the man without the wedding garment as it was of all the rest. Nobody in the parable is outside the king's favor; everybody starts out by being, as far as the king himself is concerned, irrevocably *in.* The invitation that is the judgment stands forever, reaching out to all.

Trial balance, therefore: *Nobody is kicked out who wasn't already in.* Hell may be an option; but if it is, it is one that is given us only after we have already received the entirely nonoptional gift of sitting together in the heavenly places in Christ Jesus. And even for those in hell, God

461

never withdraws that gift because, as Paul says in Rom. 11:29: "The gifts and the calling of God are without repentance *(ametaméléta)*." Please note the Greek in that quotation, because it proves the sum we have just arrived at for all these entries. The root *mel* (meaning "care") in *ametaméléta* is the same root that appears in the word *amelésantes*, used to describe the disdain of the first-invited guests at Matt. 22:5. *(Amelésantes* is formed from *a*, "not," plus *mel*, "care"; *ametaméléta* is formed from *a*, "not," plus *metá*, "change," plus *mel*, "care.") Put that all together and you get the picture: we, like the guests, may cease to care about our acceptance, but God never has a change of heart about having offered us acceptance in the first place. Accordingly, while this parable certainly says that God, like the king, will tell those who refuse to trust him to go to hell, hell nevertheless remains radically unnecessary: there will never be any *reasons,* from God's point of view, for anyone to end up there, precisely because God in Jesus has made his grace, and not our track record, the sole basis of salvation. There is therefore now no condemnation to the world as it is held in Christ Jesus, because there is nothing in the world, neither height, nor depth, nor any other thing — and especially not our long-since-cancelled sins — that can separate us from the love of God that is in Christ Jesus our Lord. The entire world is home free at the eternal party. The only ones who will not enjoy the Marriage Supper of the Lamb are those who, in the very thick of its festivities, refuse to believe they are at it.

On then with the rest of the parable. The man without the wedding garment is speechless precisely because there are no good reasons that unfaith can give for not trusting such a sweet deal. But bad reasons? Alas, there are plenty. Try a few on him for size:

1. (assuming he was one of the first-invited guests and that he just happened to be out of town when the king's SWAT team paid their call): "If he thinks I'm going to put on an unfitted tuxedo and hobnob with all those deadbeats. . . ."
2. (assuming he was dragged to the party with group two): "Hey! I want to be recognized for myself, not just accepted because somebody put a monkey suit on me."

462

3. (assuming he was a gate-crasher): "Maybe if I say nothing and just look dumb, he won't notice how poorly I'm dressed."

Do you see? If he had said anything, anything at all — if he had, even for the worst and most stupid of reasons, *put himself in relationship with the king* — he would have been alright. There is nothing to which a king who operates for no reasons whatsoever cannot give an absolving reply:

to #1   "Oh, just shut up, will you, and have a drink on the house."
to #2   "Dummy! The monkey suits are just for fun; it's the people in them I went to the bother of dragging here. Try the caviar; it's real Beluga."
to #3   "Turkey! You actually think I invited all these losers because they passed some kind of test? Relax; this whole party is *free*."

But because the man said nothing — because he would not bring himself to relate to the king in any way — all the reassurances the king might have given him remain unheard. And so Jesus brings down on him the sentence of condemnation that he has already invoked upon himself by not trusting: "Bind him hand and foot," he has the king say to the servants, "and throw him into the outer darkness — out there where there is only weeping and gnashing of teeth. For many are called (*klētoí*) but few are chosen (*eklektoí*)."

Jesus is not always this harsh. In the parable of the Prodigal Son, where he is at pains to portray unqualified grace and acceptance, he has the father go out and plead with the elder brother, reassuring him of their unbreakable relationship. But then that may be because the elder brother was willing to bellyache openly about the indiscriminateness of grace. He made a godawful speech, but at least he wasn't speechless: grace still looks to triumph in the end. In this parable, though (as in the parable of the Coins), it is judgment that finally has the last word — judgment that falls like a thunderclap on the refusal of grace, and that, in the process, defines the true nature of hell. For hell, ultimately, is not the place of punishment for sinners; sinners are not punished at all;

they go straight to heaven just for saying yes to grace. Hell is simply the nowhere that is the only thing left for those who will not accept their acceptance by grace — who will not believe that at three o'clock on a Friday afternoon, free for nothing, the Lamb slain from the foundation of the world actually declared he never intended to count sins in the first place.

What then do I make of, "Many are called but few are chosen"? Just this. The sad truth of our fallen condition is that we don't want anything to do with a system of salvation that works by grace through faith. We want our merits, sleazy though they may be, rewarded — and we want everybody else's obviously raunchy behavior punished. We are like pitiful little bargain-hunters going to a used-car lot with $265 worth of hard-earned cash in our pockets and looking for the ultimate transport of delight. But just as we are about to give up and go away, the salesman comes up to us with a smile on his face. "You really want a car?" he whispers in our ear. "Come around to the back of the lot. Have I got a deal for you!" And back there, gleaming in the sun, is a brand-new Porsche. "It's yours for free," he says. "The boss just likes you; here are the keys."

Many are called: there is no one in the whole world, good, bad, or indifferent, who isn't walked around to the back of the lot by the divine Salesman and offered heaven for nothing. But few are chosen: because you know what most of us do? First thing — before we so much as let ourselves sink into the leather upholstery or listen to the engine purr — we get suspicious. We walk around the car and kick the tires. We slam the doors. We jump up and down on the bumpers to test the shocks. And then, even if we do decide to take it, we start right in worrying about the warranty, fussing about the cost of insuring a sports car, and even — God help us — fuming about whether, if our no-good neighbor came in here, *he* might be offered a Rolls Royce Silver Cloud. But God doesn't help us — at least not with all that tough-customer routine. He just sits up there in the front office and remains Mr. Giveaway, the Mad Dog Tyson of Parousia Motors, the Crazy Eddy of Eternity whose prices are *insane*. He gives heaven to absolutely everybody: nothing down, no interest, no payments. And he makes hell absolutely unnecessary for anybody. The only catch is, you have to be as crazy as God to take the deal, because your every instinct will be to distrust such a cockamamy arrangement. You have to be willing to believe in an operation that would put any respectable God out of the deity business.

Which, nicely enough, lands us right back at the parable: a king who throws parties any other king would be ashamed of, representing a God who refuses to act like one; and a hell only for idiots who insist on being serious.

CHAPTER TEN

The Waters of Judgment Rise

THE AUTHORITIES CHALLENGE JESUS
THE SYNOPTIC APOCALYPSE

The next parables to appear in the Gospels — the Fig Tree, the Flood, and the Faithful Servant/Bad Servant (Aland nos. 293, 296, and 297) — all occur at the end of Matt. 24. But since they function there as the finale of a long section of nonparabolic material (Aland nos. 280-292; Matt. 22:15–24:31 and parallels), and since the synoptic writers report this section as Jesus' words during Holy Week, I am going to devote an entire chapter to it before turning to the parables themselves. I think it important to do this because the section constitutes essential stage-setting not only for the parables in question but also for the passion narrative itself. Bear with me, then. My aim will not be to comment in detail on the several passages but rather to give just so much of their gist as will enable you to follow the thread of Jesus' thinking through them all.

The material at hand falls into two parts. The first (Aland nos. 280-286) contains a series of exchanges between Jesus and various Jerusalem authorities, culminating in Jesus' Lament over Jerusalem and his observations about the Widow's Mite. In it, we see him constantly fencing with the scribes, Pharisees, Herodians, and Sadducees, all the while building up a judgmental head of steam that will explode in the immediately following passages. The second part is the explosion itself (Aland nos. 287-297) — a discourse commonly referred to as the synop-

466

tic apocalypse because of its style and eschatological content. In this section, Jesus speaks prophetically and warningly of the end *(télos)*, and he proclaims the signs of his *parousía* (presence, coming) that will mark that end.

First section first. Immediately after the parable of the King's Son's Wedding, Matthew reports (Matt. 22:15; Aland no. 280), the Pharisees go and take counsel how to ensnare Jesus with questions. As a result, they send their disciples and some of Herod's party to him with a prepared script: after a bit of unctuous flattery about his reputation for truth telling and his independence of mind, these flunkies are supposed to get him to answer a catch question. The object of the game is to set him up so that if he answers one way the Roman authorities will see him as seditious, and if he answers in another, the Jewish authorities will brand him a blasphemer. And so they do. "Tell us," they challenge him, "is it lawful [for Jews, that is] to pay taxes to Caesar, or not?" But Jesus, aware of their subterfuge (Matthew calls it "malice," Mark, "hypocrisy," and Luke, "craftiness"), falls back once again on the rabbinical trick of answering a question with a question. "Why are you trying to entrap me?" he asks them. "Show me the coin you pay the tax with." When they do, he simply points out that the coin already belongs to Caesar since it has his face and name stamped on it, and he gives them one of the great nonanswers of all time: "Well then, pay Caesar what belongs to him, and pay God what belongs to God." It is the first of a series of skillful parries to his enemies' thrusts, all of which are designed by Jesus to deny the authorities any solid grounds for proceeding against him. Like Thomas More, he is walking a legal tightrope, trying to insure that the case they ultimately bring against him will have to be a trumped-up one. Accordingly, no interpreter should try to prove anything by this passage other than that Jesus was a consummate fox. In particular, no preacher in his or her right mind should ever think of trying to squeeze a sermon on church and state out of it. This is a masterful piece of waffling, not a treatise on the sacred versus the secular; it is not cool theology but the crafty avoidance of hot pursuit. The wise expositor, therefore, will stress its relevance to judgment in general and to the passion in particular — and let it go at that.

467

The Pharisees' disciples then retire in amazement at Jesus' debating skill, and a fresh team of tempters — the Sadducees (Matt. 22:23-33; Aland no. 281) — come on the field to have a crack at him with a parable of their own. Since, unlike the Pharisees, they deny the notion of a resurrection at the last day — and since Jesus has already made resurrection from the dead the hallmark of his messianic claim — they try to kill two birds (Jesus *and* the Pharisees) with one stone. They tell a story about seven brothers, each of whom successively marries the same woman in order to perpetuate the family line of the brother who predeceased him; then they ask, "To which of the seven will she be married in the resurrection?" Once again, though, Jesus outfoxes the opposition. He simply asserts that the resurrection is a whole new ballgame to which the present rules of marriage do not apply; but then he goes on to prove, by what to modern ears sounds like narrow reasoning indeed, that even the Torah proves there is a resurrection. Since God is the God of Abraham, Isaac, and Jacob, he argues — and since those three patriarchs were not all alive at the same time on earth — therefore, in order for God to be their God, they must all be alive together in some other-than-earthly state, namely, the resurrection. Q.E.D. Once again, I enter a plea for no irrelevant commentaries. Jesus is not talking about the theology of Holy Matrimony here; he is not even talking about what he means by resurrection. Resurrection, for him, is a hot subject, inseparable from his own impending death. It is simply wrongheaded to try to make serious resurrection theology out of what is, at bottom, just a fencing match with cold-blooded doctrine-choppers. The real purpose of the passage, like the purpose of Jesus' argument, is to build up tension in anticipation of his passion, not to answer theological posers.

Next, after yet more astonishment at his cleverness on the part of the people, the Pharisees come back for another round of efforts at entrapment (Matt. 22:34-40; Aland no. 282). They are delighted, of course, at Jesus' silencing of the Sadducees; but their real hope is presumably to get him to continue playing too-clever-by-half games with the Torah. If he was willing to do that kind of fine slicing with Abraham, Isaac, and Jacob, they reason, maybe they can corner him into shaving a few points off a really important part of the Law. So they ask him: "Teacher, which is the great commandment in the Torah?" It is not entirely clear what they expected him to answer. Perhaps they were hoping for one of those sermon-on-the-mountish reinterpretations of his ("You have heard it said by them of old . . . but *I* tell you") that would lead him out onto the thin ice of his own *exousía*. Perhaps not. In any case, Jesus outfoxes them yet again, this time simply by quoting Deut. 6:5 and Lev. 19:18 (about loving God and neighbor) and adding what the Pharisees presumably believe anyway, namely, "On these two commandments hang all the Law and the Prophets." Once more, he is just too fast for them.

Mark notes at this point (Matthew and Luke do so a bit later on) that, "after that, no one dared to ask him any more questions." Jesus, however, now executes a remarkable turn: as if to exasperate his now silent adversaries, he abruptly stops diving for intellectual cover and asks a trick question himself. It is almost as if the fox has found the hunt a disappointment and now comes out, waves at the hounds, and shouts, "Over here!" With the Pharisees still gathered in front of him (Matt. 22:41-46; Aland no. 283), he says to them, "What do you think about the Messiah? Whose son is he?" They answer, predictably enough, "The son of David" — echoing the traditional belief that the Messiah would be, among other things, an earthly monarch in the Davidic line. But Jesus has yet another rabbinical-style gambit up his sleeve. Cleverly raising the subject of messianic *exousía,* but giving them no grounds for accusing him of actually making a personal claim to it, he asks them, "How is it then that David, inspired by the Spirit, calls the Messiah his Lord?" For good measure, he even quotes them a proof text, Ps. 110:1: "The Lord said to my lord, sit on my right hand, till I put your enemies under your feet." (A bit of background here: in the Hebrew, the first "Lord" is *YHWH,* the tetragrammaton, the sacred Name of God; the second "lord" is the word *adonai,* which can apply to others as well as God. But since both words were pronounced as *adonai* by custom [the tetragrammaton was never spoken], Jesus is relying here not only on the obvious fact that a king's descendant cannot properly be called his lord [small *l*], but also on the aural coincidence by which the sacred name "Lord" seems to be uttered twice.) Jesus does not, of course, press the latter point. He just leaves the poser as a poser and says nothing more. And so the question-and-answer phase of this first section comes to an end as a shutout: the score is Jesus, four, authorities, zero.

Finally though, with all his pursuers effectively thrown off, Jesus apparently decides that the time for foxiness is over and the time for passion is at hand. The head of steam now starts to blow off. What follows (Matt. 23:1-36; Aland no. 284) is a diatribe against the hypocrisy of the scribes and Pharisees. He has had enough of their insidious pussy-footing: he goes on the attack against them openly. The passage is long, and I do not choose to comment on it in detail. Instead, let me make just two general observations. First, I want you to note that it is strongly, if not viciously, *ad hominem*. Jesus goes after these authorities personally, finding fault after specific fault with their stewardship of the mystery of God. Once again, this is white-hot, human anger on Jesus' part, not calm analysis. But second — precisely because the vehemence of his attack invites not only his immediate hearers but his later expositors to take every word seriously — I want to issue a caveat to preachers. We should be on our guard against the temptation to make abstract ethics out of this passage. Jesus is not doing moral theology here—not giving a lecture on assorted topics such as oaths or the relationship between ritual and righteousness. Rather, he is castigating blind guides and blind fools — compulsive winners who live only by their wisdom and who cannot trust the losing, dying grace, the divine foolishness by which alone God offers salvation to the world. He is a furious Messiah whose messiahship has been rejected by the very people who, in any proper scheme of things, ought to have been the ones to acknowledge it. So he deliberately gives them no quarter. He simply roars on until he runs out of anger and turns, suddenly but with utter realism, to pity. It is another case of sovereign grace speaking in the thick of judgment. Watch how he juxtaposes the two in the last few verses of the passage (Matt. 23:34-39).

He begins his peroration with a wrathful judgment: "Therefore I send you prophets and wise men and scribes, some of whom you will kill and crucify . . . that upon you may come all the righteous blood shed on earth, from the blood of innocent Abel to the blood of Zecha-

470

riah the son of Barachiah, whom you murdered between the sanctuary and the altar. Truly, I say to you, all this will come upon this genera-tion." But then he goes on without a break into the gracious lament over the city and its inhabitants: "O Jerusalem, Jerusalem, killing the prophets and stoning those who are sent to you! How often would I have gathered your children together as a hen gathers her chicks under her wings, and you would not! Behold, your home is cut off from you. For I tell you, you will not see me again, until you say, 'Blessed is he who comes in the name of the Lord.'"

It is a stunning ending. For the thirty-three verses of his diatribe just prior to the words quoted in the preceding paragraph, he left him-self out of the picture: the word *I (egō)* was not mentioned once. But from verse 34 on, he returns forcefully to the solemn exercise of his own unique authority — of the *exousía* that will manifest itself finally in his dying and rising. The whole series of utterly personal proclamations cited above now burst forth: "*I* send"; "Amen, *I* say to you"; "How often would *I* have gathered"; "*I* tell you"; "You will not see *me*." He has, in short, brought them, and us, back to the center he never left — to the death and resurrection he has been foretelling ever since the feeding of the five thousand. It is the sovereignty of the passion all over again — the triumph of the grace that works only in the last, the lost, the least, the little, and the dead.

And as if to underscore that fact, Mark and Luke include at this point, as a kind of dying fall, the quiet passage about the Widow's Mite (Mark 12:41-44; Luke 21:1-4; Aland no. 286). Jesus, apparently ex-hausted by his own vehemence, sits down opposite the treasury and looks at the scene over which he has just pronounced judgment by grace. He sees many rich people putting in large sums, but his eye fas-tens only on a poor widow who puts in two copper coins. Calling his disciples, he says to them, "Amen, I say to you [one further, mild exer-cise of his *exousía*], this poor widow has put in more than all those who are contributing to the treasury. For they all contributed out of their abundance, but she out of her lack has put in everything she had, her whole life *(bíon)*." The Widow's Mite, therefore, is another acted para-ble (in this case, an action by someone else) that Jesus chooses to hold

471

up as an authentic manifestation of the mystery of salvation-through-loss of which he himself is the ultimate sacrament. There is no balm in this Gilead of winners, he says in effect; there is no physician in this whole city, even though it is hell-bent on saving its life. There is at this moment before judgment only the divine Physician himself — the wounded Surgeon who will shortly die for the city and the world — and one little old lady who, in her lack, is the sign of the only healing there is.

So much for the first of the two stage-setting sections with which I promised to deal. Let me take a slightly different tack on the second (the so-called synoptic apocalypse) and give you a table of contents for the whole before touching on the parts. Its several pericopes are as follows: the Prediction of the Destruction of the Temple (Aland no. 287); the Signs of the Parousia and of the Consummation of the Age (Aland no. 288); the Coming Persecutions (Aland no. 289); the Desolating Sacrilege (Aland no. 290); False Christs and False Prophets (Aland no. 291); and the Coming of the Son of Man (Aland no. 292).

The thread I choose to follow through all of these is the same one I have been following all along, namely, judgment by grace — the cross and the empty tomb as God's ultimate, vindicating sentence on the whole world. However much Jesus may be using conventional, end-of-the-age imagery here, he is proclaiming that his own end in his death and resurrection is the key to it all. I am not about to maintain, of course, that Jesus can be interpreted as literally saying what some commentators have tried to say, namely, that his passion and death are all there is to his *parousía,* or second coming. He was too clearly speaking of an end beyond the next few days for such an interpretation to hold water. But he does, I think, radically refigure that ultimate end by making himself, dead and risen, the cornerstone of it. Watch.

As Jesus leaves the temple, his disciples come to him (Matt. 24:1-2 and parallels) pointing out, like a group of sightseers, the splendor of the buildings of the temple. But he answers them, "Amen, I say to you [once again, a solemn expression of his own *exousía*], there will not be left here one stone upon another. . . ." As they often do, the disciples are simply covering their confusion with small talk. They sense something darkly mysterious about him, and rather than face it, they try their best to get off the subject. Jesus, though, refuses to be deflected by them. He has just mourned over both the city and the temple. He has seen, in the light of his own approaching end, the end of the entire present dispensation. And he has seen the unfaith that will preclude any saving participation in that end on the part of those who reject him. But he is not about to stop placing himself, in his death and resurrection, in the center of the picture. (This passage, incidentally, needs to be read in connection with the rending of the curtain of the temple at Jesus' death — Matt. 27:51 and parallels — recorded by all three synoptics. Strange as that phenomenon may be, the Gospel writers obviously report it as a corroboration not only of Jesus' predictions of the end of the city and the temple, but also of all of his eschatological pronouncements.)

The subject of the end having been raised, however, and the centrality to it of Jesus himself having been adumbrated, the disciples at last work up the nerve to bring up both subjects — but only in terms of their own, unreconstructedly interventionist eschatological thinking. Coming to Jesus as he sits quietly by himself on the Mount of Olives, they ask him the one question that seems to them important. "Tell us," they say (Matt. 24:3), "when will this be, and what will be the sign (*sēmeíon*, sign, the most common Gospel word for 'miracle') of your coming (*parousías*, presence) and of the consummation of the age (*synteleías toú aiónos*)?" Jesus' answer to this question needs close scrutiny. He does indeed go on to list many signs of the end; but not before he warns the disciples against those who will lead them astray by claiming to be merely plausible messiahs — to be, in other words, right-handed, problem-solving saviors rather than left-handed, problem-sharing ones.

The text, I think, bears this out. The rest of this apocalyptic discourse, taken in its proper Holy Week context, is not the interventionist scenario it first seems. Rather, it is a proclamation of tribulations and death as the true signs of the end — a declaration that the real sacrament of the consummation is *the world's passion as it is taken up in Jesus' passion*. What follows here is not simply an apocalyptic catalogue of woes to be visited on the recalcitrant; it is a picture of the dying/rising Savior reigning in the midst of universal shipwreck. Jesus tells his disciples that they will hear of wars and rumors of wars. But they are not to be alarmed: these things, he says in effect, are simply the way he does business. He saves the world *in* its death, not out of it; therefore the very things that look like a judgmental end to be dreaded will in fact be sacramental signs of the gracious end God has always had in mind. For the real end, the genuine consummation *(syntéleia)*, will not be something that supervenes from elsewhere on a disaster from which history must be rescued; it will be something that rises out of the very disaster of history by the power of Jesus' resurrection. He tells them, therefore, that even when they see all these signs of the end, the end itself is not yet. Redemption, he insists, involves neither the rejection of the world in its folly nor the remedying of that folly by right-handed intervention. It consists in letting the folly go all the way into death and then bringing resurrection out of that death.

There is a lesson here for the church as well as the world. Too often, the church preaches resurrection but effectively denies the death out of which alone the grace of resurrection proceeds. Its cure of choice, for its own ills or for the world's, is not death but simply more doomed living. The church, for example, will keep sinners (the morally dead) in its midst only as long as they do not presume to look dead — only as long as they can manage to make themselves seem morally alive. Moreover, ecclesiastical institutions are no more capable of accepting death for themselves than they are of tolerating it in their members. Like all other institutions, they cannot even conceive of going out of business for the sake of grace: given a choice of laying down their corporate lives for a friend or cutting off the friend at the knees, they almost invariably spare themselves the axe. Worst of all, when the church speaks to the world, it perpetuates the same false system of salvation. It is clearly heard as saying that the world can be saved only by getting its act together. But besides being false, that is an utterly unrealistic apologetic. For everyone knows perfectly well that the world never has gotten its act together and never will — that disaster has been the hallmark of its history — and that if there is no one who can save it *in* its disasters, there is no one who can save it. And therefore when the church comes to the world mouthing the hot air that the future is amenable to reform

— that the kingdom can be built here by plausible devices, by something other than the mystery of the passion — the church convinces no one. Murphy's Law *vincit omnia:* late or soon, the world is going down the drain; only a Savior who is willing to work at the bottom of the drain can redeem it. The world does indeed have a future and the church alone has that future to proclaim. But that future is neither pie on earth nor pie in the sky. It is resurrection from the dead — and without death, there can be no resurrection.

In the rest of the synoptic apocalypse, Jesus drums on with the same insistent beat. He tells the disciples (Matt. 24:9-14 and parallels; Aland no. 289) that they, as well as the world, will be caught up in his passion and death. Nothing will go right or come out right. The authentic sign of his *parousía* — the one, effective sacrament to the mystery of his redemption — will be their enduring to the end in the unrightness of it all: Jerusalem will fall, the temple will be profaned, the Jewish nation will be scattered (Matt. 24:15-22 and parallels; Aland no. 290), and "there will be great tribulation, such as has not been seen from the beginning of the world until now, no, nor ever will be." But then he adds what I think is a pregnant verse: "And if those days had not been cut short, no human being would be saved; but for the sake of the elect, whom he chose [Mark 13:20 adds this last phrase], he has cut short the days."

Think about that. I have no doubt that in the minds of Jesus' disciples at the time — and very likely in Jesus' mind too — those words constituted a reference to the duration of the specific passion of Israel he was talking about: to the cutting short, the ending of that passion by the merciful action of God. But I think it also has a wider meaning — one that is borne out not only in the Gospels themselves but in the wider context of the Bible as a whole: the "cutting short of the days" is ultimately a reference to death itself. First of all, Jesus' passion in the Gospels is cut short only by death. It leads not to some ameliorative action — not to a coming down from the cross — but to nothing. It is only after that nothing that the saving resurrection occurs. Second, though, Christians (beginning with Paul) have commonly interpreted Adam and Eve's expulsion from Eden (and the concomitant sequestering of the Tree of Life) as meaning that death came into the world not simply as a punishment for sin but as a *preparatio evangelica,* a merciful provision. For not only does death cut short sin in our present, fallen lives; it also becomes, in the Good News of Jesus' death, the sole condition of our being raised to newness of life by the power of his resurrection. All our days have been cut short, therefore: the world's, Jerusalem's, yours, and mine. For the sake of saving whom he will, he has removed the threat of no salvation from every human being (*pása sárx,* all flesh) by making death the universal safe harbor.

And so Jesus returns to the theme with which he began the synoptic apocalypse. "Then if anyone says to you," he tells the disciples (Matt. 24:23-28 and parallels; Aland no. 291), "'Lo, here is the Christ!' or 'There he is!' do not believe it. For false Christs and false prophets will arise and show great signs and wonders [marvelous, and no doubt ameliorative, programs], so as to lead astray, if possible, even the elect." The warning is as necessary now as it was then, because "the elect" have been, and still are, regularly led astray. I am not about to get into a discussion of the mischief wrought throughout the history of Christian theology by efforts to identify the elect on some moral or spiritual basis. I want only to point out that in many of the New Testament uses of the word (the Greek is *eklektoi*), it is simply an alternative way of referring to the church (see, for example, 2 Tim. 2:10; 1 Pet. 1:1; 2 John 1, 13). Accordingly, I am disposed to think that Jesus' warning in this passage has a singular relevance to the church. For what is the church? It is not, in any sound theology, an exclusive club of the saved. It is rather the elect sign, the chosen sacrament of the salvation wrought by Jesus for the whole world. It is, in short, catholic. And yet what has this elect sign, this sacrament of catholicity, so often done? It has acted as if *it* were the salvation of the world and as if its members were the sum total of the saved. It has risen up like a false Christ and stipulated the spiritual signs and wonders by which it thinks the kingdom can be brought in. It has said that Jesus is only in the correct, or the good, or the spiritual. It has even implied that he is the sole property of the ecclesiastical institution itself.

But against all that, Jesus says, "Don't believe it" (Matt. 24:26). "For as the lightning comes from the east and shines as far as the west, so will the coming *(parousía)* of the Son of man be: wherever the body is, there the eagles will be gathered together" (verse 27). Once again, the imagery is pregnant. Not only does Jesus' reference to the simultaneous and universal presence of lightning throughout the whole sky clearly underscore the "presence" aspect of his *parousía* (Jesus does not *arrive somewhere* to announce the end of the world, he is already *present everywhere* in the very fact of that end); his use of the imagery of the body and the eagles even more clearly underscores the centrality of his death to consummation of the world. For what are eagles? They are, of course, birds of prey, accipiters. But since Jesus is presumably referring to them here as birds of carrion (like vultures), they appear in this imagery as accepters of death, as feeders upon death. They are, in other words, an image of faith — of faith in the death of Jesus that is the only touchstone of salvation. What the verse means to me, therefore, is that since the dead Jesus is present in all deaths, all those who trust — who by faith accept him in that *parousía* — will be saved. Accordingly, the only test of the church's own fidelity is whether it is being true or false to the Good News of his death and resurrection. That was its first and only apostolic proclamation, and that proclamation remains its only real claim to catholicity. If the church preaches faith in anything other than the resurrection — if it gives so much as the impression that anything else, be it political action, moral achievement, or spiritual proficiency, can save the world — it becomes just one more false, parochial prophet leading the world away from the catholic *parousía* of Christ in the universal death of history.

Fittingly enough, it is in the very darkness of that proclamation that Jesus begins the finale of the synoptic apocalypse (Matt. 24:29-31 and parallels; Aland no. 292). Let me set it forth in full for you, giving my interpretation as I go. *"Immediately after the tribulation of those days,"* he says, *"the sun will be darkened and the moon will not give its light and the stars will fall from heaven and the powers of the heavens will be unsettled."* This is the hour of grace, the moment before the general resurrection when a whole dead world lies still — when all the successes that could never save it and all the failures it could never undo have gone down into the silence of Jesus' death. *"And then the sign of the Son of man will appear in heaven and all the tribes of the earth will mourn."* This is the hour of judgment, the moment of the resurrection when the whole world receives its new life out of death. And it is also the moment of hell, when all those who find they can no longer return to their old lives of estrangement foolishly mourn their loss of nothing and refuse to accept the only reality there is. *"And they will see the Son of man coming on the clouds of heaven with power and great glory; and he will send out his angels with a loud trumpet and they will gather his elect from the four winds, from one end of heaven to the other."*

This, at last, is the end: the triumph of the acceptance that is heaven and the catastrophe of the rejection that is hell. And the only difference between the two is faith. No evil deeds are judged, because the whole world was dead to the law by the body of Christ (Rom. 7:4). And no good deeds are required, for Christ is the end of the law so that everyone who believes may be justified (Rom. 10:4). Judgment falls only on those who refuse to believe there is no judgment — who choose to stand before a Judge who no longer has any records and take their stand on a life that no longer exists.

And heaven? Heaven is the gift everyone always had by the death of the Lamb slain from the foundation of the world (Rev. 13:8, NIV, KJV). All it ever took to enjoy it was trust.

CHAPTER ELEVEN

The Flood of Judgment by Mercy

THE FIG TREE

THE FLOOD

THE FAITHFUL SERVANT AND THE BAD SERVANT

All three synoptic Gospels agree in placing the parable of the Fig Tree (Matt. 24:32-36 and parallels; Aland no. 293) right after the eschatological discourses we have just dealt with, thus making it a kind of coda to the synoptic apocalypse. But beyond that point, they differ considerably as to how they tie things up before starting the passion narrative (at Matt. 26; Mark 14; Luke 22). Luke's conclusion is brief: he ends (Luke 21:34-36; Aland no. 295) with Jesus' warning not to be weighed down with dissipation and the cares of this life, but rather to "watch at all times." Mark's ending is even briefer (Mark 13:33), but he follows it up with a pruned-down version (in Aland, no. 294) of the parable of the Talents/Coins with which I have already dealt. Matthew, however, is in no such rush to get off the subject of eschatology: not only does he include the Fig Tree, the Flood, and the Two Servants in chapter 24; he devotes the whole of chapter 25 to three more parables of judgment: the Ten Virgins, the Talents, and the Great Judgment. Accordingly, since all of these remaining parables will now appear sequentially in Matthew, I choose to follow that Gospel from here on.

First, then, the parable of the Fig Tree. "Learn the lesson (*parabolén*, parable) of the fig tree," Jesus says, wrapping up everything he has been saying about the end and the signs of the *parousía* of the Son of man:

479

"when its branches become green and tender, and it puts forth leaves, you know that summer is near. So also, when you see all these things, you know that he is at the very door *(engýs estin epí thýrais)*. As I read these words, they corroborate the notion I put forth in the previous chapter, namely, that the apocalyptic end-events (wars, persecutions, earthquakes, etc.) are not just warm-up acts for a coming of Christ that will supersede them, but *that very coming itself,* under the form of death. For just as the leaves of springtime are not mere advertisements for summer, but the very engines that will enable the plant to do summer's work, so with the tribulation and death at the consummation. Those things do not merely represent the passion and death of Christ; they *are* his passion and death already knocking at the world's door for acceptance by faith. They are, as I have said, not mere signs but genuine sacraments, real presences of the mystery of redemption.

I am aware you may think that forced, but it is not. If it bothers you, it does so chiefly because of the unfortunate habit of referring to the *parousía* of Jesus as his "second coming." Let me say again, therefore, that our usual notion of Jesus' coming to the world — or even of the coming of the kingdom — is not only theologically suspect but biblically unsound. For "coming" inevitably carries with it the implication of "not here yet" — which, of course, simply will not wash in the case of the Word who became incarnate in Jesus. The Word did not "show up" in a world from which he was previously absent; he was here all along. In particular, though, the notion of "showing up" will not wash in the case of the *parousía*. For the incarnate Lord who will manifest himself at the end of history is none other than the Lamb slain from the foundation of the world. The mystery of his reconciliation of the world has been present in it from the start; no manifestation of that mystery — not even his *parousía* at the end — is a merely future event. The resurrection of the dead is not stuck out there in traffic on the thruway trying to get to our house. The judgment is not in a phone booth somewhere struggling to make a connection. And the ultimate re-creation of all things in heaven and earth is not in the mail, waiting for the celestial post office to get its act together. All those things are present, now and always, because the incarnate Word is present, now and always, *in the world's mortality.* We are baptized into those things by being baptized in Jesus' death. We feast upon those things by partaking of the power of Jesus' resurrection in a eucharistic meal that presents him as dead — in his body broken and blood shed. And we — and the whole world, Christian or not — live every second of our lives in the very presence of the judgment by resurrection from the dead that vindicates us all.

As we normally conceive of "coming," therefore, Jesus is not coming at all; he is here. And Scripture bears that out. When Jesus announces the kingdom (for example, Mark 1:15), he says it "has drawn near" *(éngiken,* a verb in the perfect tense, signifying an already accomplished action standing as a present reality). Moreover, in this parable of the Fig Tree, he says, "when you see all these things, you know he is near, at the door" *(engýs estin epí thýrais)* — meaning, of course, that he is *here at the house,* not across town or down the block. And when Jesus uses the word *thýrais,* "doors," he reinforces that note of presence mightily. In Rev. 3:20 he says, "Behold, I stand at the door *(thýran)* and knock" — which means that he is present to us at every moment, waiting only for us to acknowledge his presence and let him in by faith. But above all, Jesus himself *is* the door. In John 10, where he sets himself forth as the Good Shepherd who lays down his life for the sheep, he says, "I am the door *(thýra);* if anyone enters by me, he will be saved and will go in and out and find pasture" (John 10:9). In this ultimate image, therefore, Jesus stunningly reverses all our preconceptions about coming: he does not come to us — does not enter our lives — by some kind of divine locomotion; instead, *he* stands still — in his own death on the cross and in his constant presence in all deaths — and *we* come to him. Or, to put it in T. S. Eliot's words, Jesus' death is the "still point of the turning world": whenever we come in faith to our own death, we find it to be that same "still point," the abiding Door to resurrection and life.

All of which is borne out by the words that follow in the parable of the Fig Tree: "Amen, I say to you, this generation shall not pass away till all these things take place. Heaven and earth will pass away, but my words will not pass away" (Matt. 24:34-35). If you grapple with that text on the basis of a mere second-coming interpretation, you only indulge yourself in silly speculations about whether Jesus thought he was coming back in fifty days, fourteen months, six years, or two millennia — speculations, please note, that no one has any way of confirming or denying, and that Jesus himself specifically discourages in the immediately following verse. But if you grapple with it in terms of the *parousía* as his *having already come* — as the sacramental manifestation of a kingdom already here, already fully operative in *all* the acts of his ministry, past, present, or future — it lights up brilliantly. Because then you can take the text, "this generation shall not pass away *till all these things be fulfilled*," as referring either to his death-resurrection or to his second coming — on the ground that his *parousía* is just as fully manifested by the former as by the latter. Which, fascinatingly enough, simply lands you right back at what sound Christian doctrine has always insisted on, namely, that the death and resurrection of Jesus are nothing less than *the whole story* — the full, perfect, and sufficient sacrifice, oblation, and satisfaction for the sins of the whole world. What "this generation" saw fulfilled a mere two days later, therefore, was indeed the fulfillment of all things. They couldn't possibly have seen more, even if they could have lasted a million years. Even at the clap of doom, the job they would see done then would be nothing more and nothing less than the job they were about to see done now: some different special effects, perhaps, but the same age-long business of grace raising the dead.

And with that, the concluding verse of the parable lights up as well. All through the illustration of the Fig Tree so far, Jesus has been talking of present, knowable manifestations of his *parousía* — of signs that, like the tender leaves of the fig tree, are sacramental manifestations of the eternal summer, not just extrinsic advertisements for it. Now though, in Matt. 24:36, he allows himself one reference to the *parousía* as a future event — to his "coming" at the end of history as the final sacrament of his presence all along: "But of that day and hour no one knows, not even the angels of heaven, nor the Son, but the Father only." Do you see? He contrasts *this generation,* which will shortly see all there is to see in his death and resurrection, with *that day,* on which the whole world will finally see it all as well. He contrasts faith in the mystery hidden in his dying and rising with the open vision of that mystery at the end of time. And as I said, he has only one thing to say on the subject:

since no one, not even he, knows beans about the timing of that day, nothing counts now but our trust that, in him, everything is already fulfilled. The summer is at hand *(engýs);* we don't have to do anything but believe it. We will all get a gorgeous tan in the due season; all we have to do now is be sure we can find the bikini of faith — the light, free-and-easy, postage-stamp-size garment of acceptance of his acceptance — that will expose us to as much of the Sun as possible.

It is just this notion of faith, as I see it, that is picked up in the next parable, Jesus' eschatological recapitulation of the tale of Noah and the Flood (Matt. 24:37-44; Aland no. 296). The true scriptural function of the story of Noah is more often than not obscured by interpretations that pay attention only to its judgmental aspects. It is not an account of the wrath of God at the disaster of human history; it is the proclamation of God's mercy as God's ultimate way of dealing with sin. The principal symbolic element that gives it a preeminent place in the Scriptures is not the flood at its beginning but the rainbow at the end. God, after forty days' murderous exercise of his anger over sin, hangs up his judgmental artillery as a sign of his solemn determination to exercise mercy instead. He "sets his bow in the clouds" — sets, that is, a perennial, natural sign of remission and peace — as a witness to the covenant of grace that constitutes his ultimate relationship to the world. Even as early as Gen. 6–9, therefore, the sovereignty of grace over judgment is clearly intimated in Scripture.

More than that, though, Noah himself becomes one of the first great signs of faith — even before Abraham, the father of faith, appears on the scene. In Heb. 11:7, the author makes faith the touchstone of the flood: "By faith *(pístei)* Noah, being warned by God concerning the events as yet unseen, took heed and constructed an ark for the saving *(sōtērían,* salvation) of his household; by this he condemned the world and became an heir of the righteousness that comes by faith *(katá pístin).*" Moreover, Noah's faith is precisely a trust in the operation of God in disaster — the very thing Jesus has been talking about all through the synoptic apocalypse. All of which Jesus picks up when he chooses the Flood as a parable of the *parousía,* of the *presence in disaster* of the Son of man. "As were the days of Noah," Jesus begins, "so will be

483

the coming *(parousía)* of the Son of man. For as in those days before the flood they were eating and drinking, marrying and giving in marriage, until the day when Noah entered into the ark, and they did not know until the flood came and swept them away, so will be the coming (*parousía* again) of the Son of man."

Yet once more, the theme I have been trying to develop fairly leaps from the text. On the one hand, the eating, drinking, and marrying that Jesus adduces are stand-ins for all the plausible, winning, life-saving activities by which the human race loses its life; on the other hand, the faithful obedience of Noah is a stand-in for the losing and death by which alone our life is saved. It is not that Noah is excused from the flood; it is that he rides it out by faith (losing everything but his own skin and his immediate family) and finds, in the disaster itself, the grace of God. Indeed, in 1 Pet. 3:18-22, the author of that epistle not only stresses this note of salvation by disaster (the very waters that killed the disobedient were the ones that bore up the ark, saving the eight souls in it); he also goes on to tie the imagery of the flood to the waters of baptism in which we both die with Christ and rise with Christ. (Yes, Virginia, that *is* a long reach; but since I didn't think it up, I feel no compunction about putting it before you. At the very least, it will tell you why baptistries in medieval churches had *eight* sides.)

But above all, what leaps most clearly from Jesus' parable of the Flood is the centrality of faith to the mystery of the *parousía*. Again and again, he insists that his coming is not a matter of knowledge (Matt. 24:39, 42, 43: "they" did not know; "you" do not know; "the householder" does not know). The way God runs the world, no one will ever *know* anything but that things are a mess. Some may be taken and some left, but none of us, any more than Noah, is excused from the passion that is history. The incidentals of our involvement in the disaster may vary, but the disaster remains the chosen place of his *parousía*. "Watch, therefore," Jesus says (Matt. 24:42); and "be ready" (verse 44). Whatever it may be that we know or think we know — whatever it is that we can contrive to do or to avoid — none of it does anything but drive us closer to the rocks year by year. But what we are invited to watch for and be ready for — what we are invited *now* to wait for in faith — is the Savior who reigns in the midst of the rocks, who is himself the Stone of Stumbling and the Rock of Offense, and who, if we will only believe, is the Cornerstone of the new creation.

And that brings us at last to Matthew's ending of the synoptic apocalypse: the parable of the Faithful Servant and the Bad Servant (Matt. 24:45-51 and parallels; Aland no. 297). I know I have tried your patience with all my harping on faith as the key to both the *parousía* and the judgment, but this is no time to stop. We are all of us so enthralled by a moralistic approach to the Gospel that no effort to break its hold on us can ever be too much; and this parable, on its very face, is an example of the antimoralism of Scripture too perfect to miss. For in spite of the tens of thousands of sermons that have expounded it as proclaiming reward for the good and punishment for the bad, it never once identifies the rewarded servant as good, only as faithful *(pistós)* and wise *(phrónimos)*.

It cannot be said too often that in the New Testament, the opposite of sin is not virtue, it is faith. Not only does Paul say as much in Rom. 14:23: "All that is not of faith is sin"; his endless insistence that salvation is not by the works of the law but by grace through faith (not to mention Jesus' constant habit of making prodigals, unjust stewards, tax collectors, and sinners into heroes) bears witness to the fact that our morals have nothing to do with either our salvation or our damnation. We are saved only because God, immorally, has accepted us while we are yet sinners; and we are damned only if we stupidly (that is, as neither faithful nor wise) insist on rejecting that acceptance by unbelief. Nothing else whatsoever enters into the case.

Yes, Virginia? No, Virginia, that is not overstated. I know you are dying to get me to qualify it, but I am not going to. What's that? You don't want me to qualify it? You only want me to add that for those who truly believe, good behavior will inevitably spring forth out of gratitude for grace? Well, Virginia, it may come as a surprise to you, but I refuse to do that either. Because I suspect you of being a closet moralist. You protest that you are not? I shall prove that you are.

Take Harry. Make him an adulterer who believes. Is he saved? Yes. Is he saved because he stopped shacking up? No. He is saved by trusting the free grace of Jesus' death and resurrection, no questions asked. If there were no Jesus, Harry could stop shacking up till the cows came home and still not be saved. It's Jesus, therefore, who makes all the difference, not Harry's avoidance of shacks.

But to come to your pet point, take Harry again. Make him a believing adulterer who has for three years last past not cheated on his wife. But then slip him back between the motel sheets for another fling. What are you going to say now? That he never really believed? Why? He was saved just saying yes to Jesus, not by the amount of teeth clenching he put into it, or by the integrity of the reforms he tacked onto it. Or do you want to say that he has undone his previous acceptance by subsequent rejection and so has blown his chances by kicking God in the head? Why? The Word became incarnate for the express purpose of being kicked in the head. In fact, Jesus got kicked so hard he ended up with a dead brain — which is about as close as you can get to a God who doesn't even think about sin, let alone have problems with it. What are you trying to do? Turn the God who cancelled the handwriting against us into a welsher who keeps a black list in his pocket for sinners whose timing was no good — who sinned after faith instead of only before it? Turn faith into some kind of work-in-progress which, if interrupted, gets a rejection slip? I will tell you what you are trying to do, Virginia. You are trying to send the publican back to the temple with the Pharisee's speech on his lips. You are trying to turn the Good News of grace into the bad news of law. *You are trying to make an honest man out of God.* And it is driving you straight up the wall, because God is not an honest man. God is a crook (I knew I should have picked up on the word thief, *kléptēs,* in the parable of the Flood). He comes like a thief (Rev. 3:3); he cheats on the accounts and then congratulates himself for being unjust (Luke 16:1-8); and he is such a dishonest judge that he pronounces favorable judgment on the world just because it is a pain in the neck (Luke 18:1-8). And you know why you are trying to turn him into an honest man like that? Because you are disgusted at the ungodly indiscriminateness of accepting every last sinner in the world without checking out even a single one beforehand. Because you are scared witless at your entirely correct suspicion that the situation is even worse than you thought — that God is so sure of his acceptance of us in Jesus that he doesn't even put our *faith* to the test. Oh, I know. You say you believe that. You pray, "Lead us not into temptation (*peirasmós*, test, trial)." But when push comes to shove, you want a nasty-nice little judge who will keep crimes against faith off the streets. But God won't even do that, Virginia. Unfaith is its own punishment. All God ever does is confirm the stupid sentence of alienation it pronounces on itself; all he ever condemns are people who want to be more respectable than he is.

But enough. The best part of it all is that even your insistence on being a moralistic turkey (or even mine on flying off the handle) doesn't matter. Nothing ever matters — nothing ever will matter — but faith. Back to the parable.

"Blessed (*makários*, happy) is that servant," Jesus says, praising the wisdom of waiting in faith, "whom his master (*kýrios*, lord) when he comes will find so doing. Amen, I say to you, he will set him over all his possessions" (Matt. 24:46-47). Salvation is not a matter of getting a reward that will make up for a rotten deal; it is a matter of entering by faith into the happiness — the hilarity beyond all liking and happening — that has been pounding on our door all along. Oh, admittedly, the deal of life in this world is rotten enough: God in his crooked wisdom has not taken the disasters out of life, he has become our Life in the midst of the disasters. But if we believe that! If we live through the irremovable disasters trusting that every last, bitter twist of fate is nothing but Jesus, Jesus, Jesus — well, that is rather more happiness than anyone could possibly have bargained for here. It is being in a snug harbor all through a stormy voyage. It is being home free all the while we were lost.

And when the Lord comes at the end — when Jesus makes the last, grand sacramentalization of his perennial presence to all of history, when he sets his faithful servants over all his possessions — well, I suppose *then* it will indeed be pie in the sky. But not a new pie, or a pie after a meal of nothing but watery soup and no meat. It will be seconds — and thirds, and thousandths, and billionths — from a pie that was always under the table and from which, by faith, we constantly filched unjust deserts. Mother earth, that dreadful old cook, may have given us no better than we deserved; but our Father in heaven, through our faith in the death and resurrection of Jesus, has been slipping us the ultimate dessert all along.

Which, if you will permit me now to go back to the opening verse of this parable (Matt. 24:45), gives me a way of expanding upon the image of food (*trophé*, nourishment) that Jesus throws out at the start. It is not just that we are happy because we ourselves have, by faith, been feasting all our lives (in the eucharist, in our own passion) on the Bread of Heaven — tasting that the Lord is indeed good; it is that we are happy because we are a church (if we have been faithful to our stewardship) that has been slipping the world the same goodies. The mission of the church is not to be humanity's bad cook, pushing at it the lumpy mashed potatoes of morality or the thin gruel of spiritual uplift; the mission of the church is to be the Lord's own conspirator, sneaking to the world the delectability of grace, the solid chocolate Good News that God, in the end, has a sweet tooth. Our joy as the stewards of the mystery is to have been in on the joke that God is just a big, bad boy. He doesn't really care a fig for teaching the world lessons about what's good for it; he only wants to make it smile.

But what of the unfaithful servant, the bad church? What of the church that wickedly says, "My Lord *chronízei*" — my Lord is making a big mistake here, taking his own sweet time about the serious business of salvation? What of the church that begins to beat its fellow servants' knuckles with the carving knife of ethical requirements and to get drunk on the cheap wine of successful living or the rotgut booze of spiritual achievement? Well, Jesus tells us what: "The Lord of that servant will punish him, and put him with the hypocrites; there men will weep and gnash their teeth" (Matt. 24:48-51). There is indeed a judgment on such a church. But it is precisely a condemnation for its having made a serious business — a tissue of works — out of the divine lark of grace. The wickedness of the church can be one thing and one only: *turning the Good News of Jesus into the bad news of religion.* Christianity is not a religion; it is the announcement, in the death and resurrection of Jesus, of the end of religion — of the end of any and all requirements for the salvation of the world. And therefore, when the church preaches anything but faith alone in Jesus, it is an unfaithful church and deserves only to be put with the rest of the world's hypocrites who think they can be saved by passing tests. It is a church that has stopped being funny and happy in the freedom of faith, and has gone dead in its own earnestness.

Is that another long reach, Virginia? I don't think it is; but since I owe you one, call it whatever you like. You and I have had our last run-in; time now to head for the barn.

CHAPTER TWELVE

The End of the Storm (I)

THE WISE AND FOOLISH VIRGINS

It is a commonplace of literary criticism that authors give themselves away in their last chapters. However much they may have allowed themselves a certain latitude of expression during the earlier parts of their work, they do at last tighten their focus and give their readers the crispest possible picture of what they have been trying to say all along. It is with that in mind that I come now to Matt. 25 (Aland nos. 298-300), the final chapter of Jesus' entire corpus of parables. For the three parables that it comprises — the Ten Virgins, the Talents, and the Great Judgment — are indeed the capstone of his teaching. Not only are all of the notes he has previously struck present in them; in addition, those notes are at last harmonized and given their ultimate expression.

Before proceeding to the parables themselves, however, I want to alert you to two of the notes that Jesus singles out for special emphasis. The first is the absence of the main character from the part of the parable that corresponds to our life now. This note of the missing or hidden Lord — of the *Deus absconditus* — has of course been sounded before: the king in the King's Son's Wedding, for example, does not appear at the party until all the guests have made their several responses to his invitation; the lord in the Faithful Servant and the Bad Servant is not only away, but takes his time *(chronízei)* about finally showing up in person. But in these last three parables, the note of absence becomes practically the fulcrum of the judgment *(krísis)* that takes place when the main character finally appears. In the Ten Virgins, the bridegroom delays his coming (the word, again, is the verb *chronízein*); in the Talents, the lord of the servants returns "after a long time"; and in the Great Judgment, the King judges both the sheep and the goats on the basis of what they did to him when he was completely hidden from them "in the least of his brethren."

Accordingly, these parables are about a judgment pronounced on a world from which God, through all its history, was effectively *absent* — or to put it more carefully, was present in a way so mysterious as to constitute, for all practical purposes, an absence. And therefore, insofar as they address themselves to humanity's response to that hidden God — and to that God's judgment of the response — they are not about practical good works. They do not make moral behavior or spiritual achievement the matter of judgment; rather, they base the judgment solely on faith or unfaith in the mystery of the age-long presence-in-absence — the abiding *parousía* under history — of the divine redemption. Obviously, this note of faith in the mystery of grace has been a constant emphasis in all of Jesus' parables so far, and it has certainly been the note I myself have chosen to stress above all others. But in these last parables, it is, quite simply, everything.

The second note I want to alert you to has the same characteristics. It is none other than what I called, at the very beginning of this book, the master principle of interpretation for all the parables of judgment, namely, the principle of inclusion before exclusion — the rule that any characters who are made outsiders at the end of the story must always be shown as insiders at the beginning. It too has been demonstrated many times before. The man without the wedding garment in the King's Son's Wedding was just as much an accepted guest as all the others, bad or good. The servant who hid the coin in a napkin was no less a recipient of his lord's trust, and thus no less a beneficiary of his lord's presence-in-absence, than the other nine. But now Jesus reinforces the principle by three illustrations in a row. All of the ten virgins, wise or foolish, are equally members of the wedding from the start. All three servants who received the talents are fully accepted by their lord. Both the sheep and the goats have lived their entire lives in the full, if hidden, presence of the King in the least of his brethren. Once again, therefore, faith is set forth as the only criterion of judgment. Those who are congratulated at the end are those who believed in the mysterious, vindicating *parousía* of the main character and who lived their lives on the basis of that trust. Those who are condemned are those who did not. It is not the good works of the blessed that saves them, any more than it is the evil deeds of the cursed that damns them. It is only faith or unfaith that matters.

But there is also something else here. In these last parables, the primacy of faith is finally set forth in a way that meets a lurking objection you have probably felt every time I brought it up. That objection, to give it its proper name, was about the danger of quietism. Almost always, when salvation by faith alone is seriously preached, we feel that somehow it has all been made too easy. Assuming, falsely, that faith is simply a kind of intellectual assent to a proposition, we then go on to conclude that the general reaction of the human race to salvation by faith will be an equally intellectual reaction of indifference. We are afraid they will say, "Well, if all the real work of salvation has already been done, and the only thing we have to do is believe it, why should we bother trying to be good, kind, or loving? If the world is saved in spite of its sins, what's to stop us from going right on doing rotten things?"

Since those are two separate questions, let me deal with them in order. The fallacy in the first is precisely the assumption already noted that faith is assent to a proposition. It is not. It is the living out of a trust-relationship with a person. If it were only something in our heads, then we might well conclude that it had no implications for what we might do with our hands or our feet or with any of our other members or faculties. But since nothing is simply in our heads — since we will always, as long as we live, be *doing something* — that is a false conclusion. Therefore a better form of this first question would be, "If he has already done it all for me already, why shouldn't I live as if I trusted him?" If he has made me a member of the Wedding of the Lamb why shouldn't I act as if I am at the party? If he has already reconciled both my wayward self and my equally difficult brother-in-law, or children, or wife, why shouldn't I at least try to act as if I trust him to have done just that and to let his reconciliation govern my actions in those relationships?

Quietism, you see — do-nothingism — is not a viable option. And it is not viable for one simple reason: Jesus' reconciled version of all relationships is the only version that really counts — the only one that in the end will be real at all. When we die, we lose whatever grip we had on our unreconciled version of our lives. And when we rise at the last day, the only grip in which our lives will be held will be the reconciling grip of Jesus' resurrection. He will hold our lives mended, cleaned, and pressed in his hand, and he will show them to his Father. And his Father, seeing the only real you or me there is to see, will say, "Wonderful! Just what I had in mind." He will say over the Word's new creation of us at the last day exactly what he said over the Word's first creation of us on the sixth day: "Very good!"

That is the final answer to quietism. And therefore the best of all possible forms of the first question is, "Since he has already made me new — since there really isn't any of the old me around to get in my way any more — why should I be so stupid as to try to go on living in terms of something that isn't even there?" Faith, you see, is simply taking his word about what really is and trying our best to get all the unreal nonsense out of our lives. Strictly speaking, faith does not save us; *he* does; but because faith, once given, inexorably leads us to try to stop contradicting what he has done, it becomes the only instrument of salvation that we need to lay a hand to.

The second question is likewise based on a fallacy. To ask, "If the world is already saved in spite of its sins, what's to stop people from sinning?" is to misunderstand the nature of sin. Sin is not something the human race has any choice about. The occasional sin (small *s*), we might manage to stop: some of us might possibly avoid this lie or that adultery. But none of us will ever avoid that trust in ourselves — and that distrust of anyone else — that lies at the root of the world's problems. Those twin falsities of faith in self and unfaith in others are as irremovable by human effort as they are unpardonable by human good will. And therefore if they are ever to be removed or pardoned, it will only be by God's gift. But that gift, please note, stands in no *causal* relationship whatsoever to our responses. It will neither force us to be better nor enable us to go on being worse. It is simply a fact, to be trusted or not as we choose. That it is the only real fact, happens to be true; but that it will strong-arm an unreality-loving world into reversing gears and loving reality is just not in the cards. It is a free gift, and it aims to elicit only a free response of faith. Without constraining anyone or condoning anything, it just hands us a new creation and invites us to live as if we trusted it.

One last note on all three of these parables. Their insistence that the judgment upon faith will be a judgment on faith-in-action, not on faith-with-folded-hands, goes to the heart of the biblical view of history. In the Bible, the course of the world and the course of God's action in it are like an arrow shot toward a target, not like a planet endlessly pursuing an unchanging, circular course. And nowhere is this "linear as opposed to circular" view more manifest than in the biblical notion of judgment. In a "circular" system, there is no possibility of judgment, of history-altering and history-fulfilling *krísis*, happening *from within the system*. The only controlling *parousía* (presence) in the orbit, say, of Mars around the sun is the constant presence of gravitation producing an equally constant repetition of course: Mars is not going anywhere but *around*. If there is a *krísis*, it will have to come from outside the system — from, for example, a collision with an alien body. But in a "linear" system, judgment is built in; *krísis* is the whole point of the system. The target is where the arrow is *going*, and every action in the whole of the arrow's course — the drawing of it from the quiver, the setting of it on the bowstring, the releasing of the bow, and the flight of the arrow through the air — everything, quite literally, is governed by the history-fulfilling judgment of the bull's-eye at the end: it partakes of the nature of that *krísis* at every point.

So it is with the biblical view of history in general, and so it is with Jesus' parables of judgment in particular. Both it and they are about an action going somewhere to happen. They are not about a system of static recurrences in which time goes on forever — where there is always, by the rules of the system, time for a second chance at everything. They do not allow you the luxury of a historical perspective in which a step taken too soon or a move made too late can always be remedied the next time around. Rather, they are about a world in which too early or too late can be crashing, fatal mistakes — in which there is only one chance for anything: one moment to aim the arrow, one brief, high time to make allowances for the crosswind, one critical instant to shoot, and one final judgment, hit or miss, on the entire proceeding. In the Ten Virgins, for example, the bridegroom comes late, the oil of the foolish has run out, the storekeepers' shops are closed, and the door to the marriage feast is shut. In the Talents, the time for doing business is finally over for good. And in the Great Judgment, the day of ministry to the King who lives in the least is gone forever. Just as history is a series of unrepeatable, even unrehearsable performances, so the history of salvation is just one *krísis* after another, with no going back.

These final parables, therefore, give the ultimate lie to the view of faith as intellectual assent to static truths. What God saves by grace through faith is precisely the *dynamic* of history, the once-and-never-again quality of a world he was pleased to make that way. He saves history by history; and at the end, it is history that he brings home smack in the center of the target. Even faith, therefore, is something that must somehow, somewhere be *done*. And if it is left undone . . . , well, there will be a price for that. Though you may not have expected me to say it, I am too much of an orthodox Christian, and too much of a historical realist, to think there is any way of getting hell out of the scriptural account of the final reconciliation. We should not, of course, be too eager to set up our rules for what constitutes the limit, temporal or eternal, of God's patience with unfaith. But these parables say plainly enough that there is a limit and there will one day be a *kairós,* a high time of *krísis,* beyond which the unreal will be allowed no further truck with reality. He wills the eternal picnic to begin. The party poopers do not have forever to go on praying for rain.

On then with the parables themselves. Jesus begins the Ten Virgins (Matt. 25:1-13; Aland no. 298) by harking back to the style of introduction that characterized his earliest parables: "Then the kingdom of heaven shall be likened to ten maidens." The word *then* refers clearly enough to the end, the climactic manifestation of the *parousía* of the

Son of man that Jesus has been speaking of just prior to this point. But in joining it to the words "the kingdom of heaven shall be likened to . . . ," he brings his whole parabolic opus to completion. At the beginning of his ministry, in the parables of the kingdom, he proclaimed the mystery of a kingdom already present in this world. In the parables of grace that followed, he proclaimed the device by which that mystery operates, namely, grace working through death and resurrection. Now though, he comes full circle and gives, in the concluding parables of judgment, a series of pictures of how it ultimately triumphs, separating those who accept the mystery in faith from those who, by unfaith, reject his freely given acceptance of them in the resurrection of the dead.

The ten maidens, he says, "took their lamps and went to meet the bridegroom." The image is as charming as it is earnest. Here are ten girls (permit me to make them fourteen-year-olds) on their way, every last one of them, to a party. They are, presumably, tickled to the point of teenage giggliness at their happy prospects. The *krísis* of their possible nonmembership in the wedding — the danger of their receiving a snub rather than an invitation to be bridesmaids — is past and they see nothing but tea and cakes from here on out. "But five of them were foolish *(mōraí)* and five were wise *(phrónimoi.)*" *Phrónimoi*, of course, is the word used to describe the faithful and wise servant in the immediately preceding parable, so I am disposed to run with it in my interpretation. The foolish maidens represent the wisdom of this world — the live-by-what-you-see wisdom *(sophía)* that "God has made foolish *(emōranen:* 1 Cor. 1:20)." But the wise represent the wisdom of faith — the wisdom of trusting the foolishness of God in Christ crucified (1 Cor. 1:21-25) — the wisdom of living by the all-governing reality of the party to which the Bridegroom has invited all of creation. In actual fact, of course, both sets of girls have all they need for now, just as both the faithful and the unfaithful have identical shares of the world's goods or ills. But only the wise have the faith that will get them through their lives in solid contact with the presently unseeable and unknowable Bridegroom.

"For when the foolish took their lamps, they took no oil with them." The image is that of life lived on the ordinary, prudential basis of what is likely to happen. It is a picture of happy little winners assuming that their luck will always hold and that they need make no efforts to deal with the implausible. "But the wise took flasks of oil with their lamps." Notice how Jesus deliberately stands things on their heads. The five supposedly foolish girls, knowing that they have been invited to a daytime wedding that will last only into the early evening, reasonably assess their needs and content themselves with taking filled lanterns with them. Nothing could be more sensible. But the other five insist on dragging along bleach bottles full of kerosene, just in case. Nothing could be more idiotic: they have complicated their lives by preparing for an utterly unlikely contingency. Why does Jesus thus make the first group seem wiser than the second? He does it, I think, to preclude our interpreting the oil in the lamps as good works. The foolish girls are quite wise enough — quite sufficiently possessed of all the good works they will reasonably need for any wedding festivities the world may send their way. And the wise girls are not wise in any normal sense of the word; their possession of good works is portrayed as nothing less than neurotic: they are a bunch of belt-and-suspenders fussbudgets preoccupied with what might possibly go wrong.

But the point of the story — the point that ultimately makes wisdom of their apparent folly — is that, in this world, something always does go wrong. And so in this parable, Jesus introduces just such a critical (from *krísis*) contretemps. "When the bridegroom took his time arriving *(chronízontos dé toú nymphíou),*" he says, "they all slumbered and slept." The giggles go on through the day and into the evening. The lamps are lit and the ten maidens talk on into the night about which of their friends is pregnant by whom and how they would just die before they could ever confront their parents with a problem like that. Finally, though, the wedding feast turns into a slumber party: all ten are sacked out on couches and across the floor.

"But at midnight there was a cry, 'Behold, the bridegroom! Come out to meet him!'" There are, I think, three things to note about this particular verse. First, it is a parable of the course of the world as it really is. The unexpected does happen — regularly. As God brings the arrow of history to the bull's-eye, he does it very much in the style of the

497

old joke about Jesus and Moses playing golf: by having it blown off course into the trees, bounced out into the rough, picked up by a passing hawk, and finally dropped on the target (conveniently knocked over by the divine Fox himself) because the hawk just got tired of wasting his hunting time on arrows. The bridegroom's delayed arrival is a silly, gratuitous detail that can be justified only by one fact: it fits perfectly in a silly, gratuitous world.

Second — and more darkly — this verse bears witness to the complicity of God not only in the slapstick way the world is run, but in the failures of those who counted on its being run in a more respectable fashion. For whose fault is it, ultimately, that the prudentially correct amount of oil in the foolish girls' lamps ran out? The bridegroom's, that's whose. And whose fault is it, finally, that Peter denied Jesus or that Judas betrayed him? It is God's. If God had left Peter in the fishing business, Peter would never have gotten into waters he couldn't navigate. If God had left Judas to be just the smartest CPA in the county, Judas would never have been tempted to run Jesus' career for him. I said before that God is not an honest man. Well, he is not an innocent man either. He is just the only God we've got, and we're stuck with him. That he is also stuck with us — and stuck by us — may take the curse off it all; but it does not do a thing about his complicity in our failures. Why he couldn't have figured out a way of getting rid of sin without creating more sinners in the process is a big question. And the big answer is that there is no answer. No answer except Job's, "Though he slay me, yet will I trust him." No answer except Jesus', "Take this cup from me; nevertheless, not my will but yours be done."

There is, however, a third point to be made. "Behold, the bridegroom!" has become the church's watchword as it begins every Christian year with the season of Advent. That gives us a hint as to how we are to reconcile ourselves to both the slapstick of history and the complicity of God in evil. It is only as we wait in faith that all of the above ceases to matter and we are able to lay hold of the reconciliation that lies below the mess of history. Because if he finally does deliver on his promise to draw all to himself, if the reconciliation really is all ours no matter what our sins — if even Peter, even Judas, is within the drawing of his love and subject to the voice of his calling — then all we need is the faith to accept the reconciliation, no questions asked, from the hand of the one who brings it, no questions answered. Advent, therefore, is the church's annual celebration of the silliness (from *selig*, which is German for "blessed") of salvation. The whole thing really is a divine lark. God has fudged everything in our favor: without shame or fear we rejoice to behold his appearing. Yes, there is dirt under the divine Deliverer's fingernails. But no, it isn't any different from all the other dirt of history. The main thing is, he's got the package and we've got the trust: Lo, he comes with clouds descending. Alleluia, and three cheers.

But now Jesus brings on the *krísis* of unfaith, the judgment pronounced on those who thought that history could be brought home by something neater and more plausible than the mystery. "Then all those maidens rose and trimmed their lamps." They all take the ordinary, prudential steps that life in this world dictates as necessary. But then they discover something. All the wick trimming in the world — all the brilliant steps that might be taken to make a properly designed operation run right — are irrelevant. The operation is not properly designed. The bridegroom is late for his own party: God has taken so long to do anything that the world has dug its own grave in the meantime. Unless there is something other than the wisdom of the world to help it, there is nothing for the world to do but to lie down and die.

It is that something, therefore, that becomes the only matter of judgment in the parable. Now that all of the girls, wise or foolish, have found out there is no way of going on from here simply by going on from here, faith comes to the fore as the sole criterion for distinguishing between them. "And the foolish said to the wise, 'Give us some of your oil, for our lamps are going out.' But the wise replied, 'Perhaps there will not be enough for us and for you; go rather to the dealers and buy for yourselves.'" Time has at last run out, as it always does in real life. And since faith is at bottom something we do in real life, the time for faith has run out too. As I said, we should be slow to extrapolate from the parable and specify the historical or theological circumstances that might constitute such a dreadful expiration in our own or others' lives. But the parable does seem to say that since faith is a relationship with God, there will inevitably be a point at which he will say that the relationship does or does not exist. He will tell us whether we said yes or no. No one will get away with saying maybe forever.

I am aware that it is easy to object to the behavior Jesus assigns to the wise maidens. They are simply snotty. "There won't be enough for us if we give you some" is hardly an example of Christian sharing; furthermore, they know perfectly well that oil dealers go home at six, if not at four, in the afternoon. But if I have just gotten through urging you to accept a parcel from a Deliverer with grubby fingernails, I am not about to balk at bad manners from a Watchman trying to warn us there will be a time when our time will have run out. For that is the whole point of the parable: some day, late or soon, it will be too late even to believe. We become what we do. If we trust, we become trusters, and we enter into the sure possession of him whom we trust. If we distrust, we become distrusters and close out the only relationship with reality ever offered to us.

That closure is the note on which the parable ends. "While they went to buy, the bridegroom came, and those who were ready went in with him to the marriage feast; and the door was shut. Afterward the other maidens came also, saying, 'Lord, lord, open to us.' But he replied, 'Amen, I say to you, I do not know you.'" The shut door is God's final answer to the foolish wisdom of the world. In the death of Jesus, he closes forever the way of winning — the right-handed, prudential road to the kingdom, the path of living as the path of life. All the silly little girls with their Clorox bottles — all the neurotics of faith, all the wise fools who were willing to trust him in their lastness, lostness, leastness, and death — have gone into the party. And all the bright, savvy types who thought they had it figured are outside in the dark — with no oil and even less fun. The dreadful sentence, "Amen, I say to you, I never knew you," is simply the truth of their condition. He does not say, "I never called you." He does not say, "I never loved you." He does not say, "I never drew you to myself." He only says, "I never knew you — because you never bothered to know me."

Someone once said, "The world God loves is the world he sees in his only begotten Son." That fits here. For the world God sees in his only begotten Son consists of all those who have accepted their visibility in Jesus by faith. But those who have not accepted it, those who have pretended to make themselves invisible by their rejection of his acceptance of them, have the sentence of their self-chosen invisibility ratified by God. There was no relationship on their part; therefore God just says as much on his and gets on with the feast.

"Watch therefore," Jesus says at the end of the parable, "for you know neither the day nor the hour." When all is said and done — when we have scared ourselves silly with the now-or-never urgency of faith and the once-and-always finality of judgment — we need to take a deep breath and let it out with a laugh. Because what we are watching for is a party. And that party is not just down the street making up its mind when to come to us. It is already hiding in our basement, banging on our steam pipes, and laughing its way up our cellar stairs. The unknown day and hour of its finally bursting into the kitchen and roistering its way through the whole house is not dreadful; it is all part of the divine lark of grace. God is not our mother-in-law, coming to see whether her wedding-present china has been chipped. He is a funny Old Uncle with a salami under one arm and a bottle of wine under the other. We do indeed need to watch for him; but only because it would be such a pity to miss all the fun.

CHAPTER THIRTEEN

The End of the Storm (II)

THE TALENTS
THE SHEEP AND THE GOATS

The parable of the Talents (Aland no. 299; Matt. 25:14-30 — the Matthean version of the parable of the Coins in Luke) has already been dealt with in chapter six of this book. I want to note here only how it picks up and enlarges upon some of the themes I have expounded in the parable of the Ten Virgins.

First, it is about a judgment rendered on faith-in-action, not on the results of that faith. Not only does the lord of the servants who doubled their talents praise them precisely as faithful ("well done, good and faithful [*pistós*] servant"); the doubling seems to be due more to the talents themselves than to the efforts the servants put into doing business with them. The servant who was given five makes five more; the one who received two makes two more. To me that says that the grace of acceptance does its own work; all we have to do is trust it. It emphatically does not say that God is a bookkeeper looking for productive results. The only bookkeeper in the parable is the servant who decided he had to fear a nonexistent audit and who therefore hid his one talent in the ground. And as if to underscore the indifference of God to bookkeeping, Jesus gives two twists to the parable. He has the lord say (to the useless servant) that he would have accepted anything — even rock-bottom savings-account interest — that the one talent might have produced as a result of faith-in-action. And he has the lord take the talent

502

away from that servant and give it to the one who has ten. Were Jesus at pains to show that God was interested in bottom lines, why would he not have had the lord give it to the fellow with four? Why this bizarre enriching of the already rich, if not to show God's aversion to any counting at all? The goodness of his grace does all that needs doing. Here, therefore, as in the Laborers in the Vineyard, it is only the book-keeping of unfaith that is condemned; the rest of the story is about the unaccountable, even irresponsible joy of the Lord who just wants every-body to be joyful with him.

That brings us to the second theme. As the parable of the Ten Vir-gins was about the happiness of the bridegroom at his wedding, so this one is about the ebullience of the lord's joy at throwing his money around. It is the theme of the divine party again, the party that lurks be-neath the surface of history and calls only for a recognition by faith. It is the fatted calf served up for a prodigal who did nothing but come home in faith. It is the free champagne and caviar for wedding guests who did nothing but trust the king's insistence on providing fancy cos-tumes and party hats. It is the full pay for next-to-no-work-at-all given to grape pickers who just said yes to a last-minute promise. The only reason that judgment comes into it at all is the sad fact that there will always be dummies who refuse to trust a good thing when it's handed to them on a platter. That is indeed a grim prospect. And it is grim be-cause, if we have any knowledge of our own intractable stupidity, we know that those dummies could just as well be ourselves. But for all that, it is still about joy rather than fear. The final balance it strikes is the balance of Advent once again: without shame or fear we rejoice to behold his appearing because we have decided to believe him when he says he wills us nothing but the best.

And there is the third and last theme I want to underline: the sheer needlessness of fear, the utter nonnecessity of our ever having to dread God. The servant with his little shovel and his mousy apprehension that God is as small as himself is such a nerd! He is just one more of the pitiful turkeys that Jesus parades through his parables to shock us, if possible, into recognizing the stupidity of unfaith. The elder brother, the man without the wedding garment, the laborers who worked all day, the Pharisee who tried to wheedle God into thinking he was a good egg — all of these are cardboard figures, cartoon characters designed to elicit only a smile at the preposterousness of their behavior. It is also true, of course, that they are the figures we most easily identify with. But then that is because we are just as preposterous. We spend our lives invoking upon ourselves imagined necessities, creating God in the image of our own fears — and all the while, he is beating us over the head with the balloon of grace and the styrofoam baseball bat of a vindicating judgment. The history of salvation is slapstick all the way, right up to and including the end. It's the Three Stooges working only for laughs. God isn't trying to hurt anyone; he's not even mad at anyone. There are no lengths to which he won't go to prove there are no restrictions on the joy he wants to share with us. If you were never afraid of Curly, Larry, and Moe, you don't need to be afraid of the Trinity either.

Which makes a good enough introduction, I think, to the last of Jesus' parables, the story of the Great Judgment (Matt. 25:31-46; Aland no. 300). Because if it is in one way the heaviest, most fear-inspiring parable of all, it is also the lightest, the last laugh of the mighty act of salvation: it is the bestowal of the inheritance of the kingdom on a bunch of sheep who not only didn't know they were doing good works for God, but also never even knew they were faithful to him. And since no one who has heard this parable even once ever forgets it (I can still remember the Sunday afternoon in a Brooklyn church where I first heard it as a boy), I am not going to take you through it step by step. Instead, I shall try to set it in the context of Jesus' whole parabolic *oeuvre* (of which it is the grand finale) and to relate it to the general context of Scripture itself.

In the Great Judgment, all of the themes of Jesus' earlier parables come full circle. In the parables of the kingdom at the beginning of his ministry, he set forth a saving action of God that had five unique characteristics. He proclaimed a kingdom that was *catholic*, not parochial; that was *mysterious*, not recognizable; that was *actual*, not merely virtual or on the way; that was met with *hostility* as well as welcome; and that called for a *response of faith* rather than one of works. Now at the end we see those characteristics brought to fruition in a variety of ways.

The *catholicity* of the kingdom is *vindicated*. In this parable, it is precisely "*all* the nations" that are gathered together before the Son of man on his throne of glory. I am aware that the word "nations" (*éthnē,* the Gentiles) might tempt some to see this as an implicit exaltation of Gentiles over Jews, or even as bespeaking a rejection of the Jews. But since that requires attributing it more to the early church than to Jesus — and since I have pretty much stayed clear of Jew/Gentile interpretations in my treatment of the parables — I am not about to go in that direction at this late date. For one thing, Jesus was speaking to Jews: even though he clearly stigmatized the rejection of himself by the Jewish authorities, I do not think that any fair case can be made out for his excluding Jews as such from the operation of the kingdom — particularly since he first announced the catholicity of that operation to an exclusively Jewish audience. For another, though, the entire argument of Paul in the theological part of the epistle to the Romans is a progress toward verses 25-26 of chapter 11, in which he says specifically that "all Israel will be saved." Accordingly, I take the phrase "all nations" as referring to the whole world: the kingdom, which was first proclaimed as a catholic mystery, is now revealed as a catholic *fait accompli*. Not one scrap of creation, Jew or Gentile, good, bad, or indifferent, is left out of it. Jesus has literally drawn all to himself.

More than that, though, the catholicity of the kingdom is vindicated even with regard to goodness and badness: in the end as in the beginning, evil is not simply excluded but provided for — given a place in the final scheme of things. True enough, Jesus' parables of judgment are rife with images of separation: the outer darkness is the final destination of the man without the wedding garment and of the useless servant; the wrong side of the door is the portion of the foolish virgins. But in the Great Judgment, Jesus goes out of his way to stipulate that the Son of man "will separate them one from another *as a shepherd separates the sheep from the goats.*" Do you see what that means? Jesus is the Good Shepherd, and the Good Shepherd lays down his life for the sheep. But he lays down his life for the goats as well, because on the cross he draws *all* to himself. It is not that the sheep are his but the goats are not; the sheep are his sheep and the goats are his goats. Any separation that occurs, therefore, must be read as occurring *within* his shepherding, not as constituting a divorce from it. (It was common in biblical times for a shepherd to keep both sheep and goats: see Gen. 30:32, for example; but see especially Exod. 12:5, where it is specified that even a goat can serve as the Paschal Lamb — "you shall take it from the sheep or from the goats.") Accordingly, Jesus' *drawing of all to himself* remains the ultimate gravitational force in the universe; nothing, not even evil, is ever exempted from it. Hell has no choice but to be within the power of the final party, even though it refuses to act as if it is at the party. It lies not so much outside the festivities as it is sequestered within them. It is hidden, if you will, in the spear wound in Christ's side to keep it from being a wet blanket on the heavenly proceedings; but it is not, for all that, any less a part of Jesus' catholic shepherding of his flock.

The *mystery* of the kingdom, to take up the next characteristic, is *revealed* at this final juncture. The iceberg of the divine presence under all of history at last thrusts itself up in one grand, never-to-be-hidden-again *parousía*. The Son of man has come in glory and everything is out in the open. All the waiting upon the mystery in faith is over and everyone, faithful or not, knows it. Time has not just run out; it has, like the fig tree, run its full course from winter's death to spring's new life: summer is now at hand. Not one bit of the operation of the kingdom will ever be hidden again, and all the previous sacraments of its working in the last, the lost, and the least are finally understood. Jesus has made all things, even the bad old things, new.

As for the *actuality* of the kingdom — its real presence through the whole course of history — that note is *triumphant*. Since the kingdom cannot possibly become more present than it has been all along, this parable displays it as simply its own unchanged self, victorious. The kingdom prepared from the foundation of the world — the whole mysterious inheritance that has always been available to faith — now publicly dazzles its inheritors with a knowable, palpable beauty. Jesus has had a party going from the first day in Genesis; now, at the Marriage Supper of the Lamb, he drinks a toast to the fact that it will never end.

That leaves just two further characteristics of the kingdom — *hostil-*

ity and *response* — for this parable to fulfill; and since I am going to read it as relating both of them to faith, I shall deal with the two simultaneously. On the one hand, the hostility with which the kingdom was met throughout history was never portrayed by Jesus as anything other than *unfaith;* on the other, the response called for by the kingdom was never stipulated as anything but *faith.* This is particularly important because of the facility with which interpreters of this parable slip into moralistic expositions. It is so easy to make the cursed goats at the King's left hand into bad people loaded down with sins of omission; and it is even easier to make the blessed sheep at his right hand into do-gooders. But that simply will not bear the light of comparison with the rest of Jesus' teaching. We need to remind ourselves again that he habitually avoids depicting badness as an obstacle to the kingdom, just as he carefully steers clear of making goodness one of its entrance requirements. In the parables of grace, for example, he displays unreformed bad people (the prodigal, the publican) as acceptable by faith rather than by works; and in the parables of the kingdom, he goes out of his way to show both good and evil as existing side by side *within the kingdom:* in the Wheat and the Weeds, he lets both grow together until the harvest; in the Net, he says that the kingdom gathers every kind. True enough, he says that at the consummation there will be a separation of the good from the bad — and in this parable, admittedly, he says much the same thing. I have, however, two observations to make about all that.

The first is an extension of what I said above about Jesus being the Shepherd of both the sheep and the goats. The separation of the two is a disposition made by the Good Shepherd himself in the interests of his own goodness, not in regard to some supposed inability on his part to put up with evil. It is a provision by the King for the best possible government of all the subjects of his kingship. At least in some sense, therefore, the separation remains within the flock and within the kingdom. The Shepherd/King does not have a problem with evil: Jesus has taken all the evil of the world into himself. The final dispensation is not a destruction of evil; it is precisely a sequestration of evil in the Son of God. Accordingly, whatever else hell may be, it is not where God isn't: if it exists at all, it exists because he, in his creating Word, is intimately and immediately present to it. Jesus is the Life even of those who go down into the second death; he is the shepherd even of the goats whom he divides from his sheep. Accordingly, on this point I want simply to run up a flag: the separation imagery of the parables is a tricky piece of business; for my money, it should not be interpreted in a way that portrays Jesus as having taken off the velvet glove of grace and put on brass knuckles. Above all, it should not be read in this parable as turning the Good Shepherd into the wolf.

My other observation goes to the centrality of faith as the criterion of the separation. As I have said, throughout the whole body of his parables, Jesus spends a great deal of time denying that goodness or badness has anything to do with salvation. The gift of grace, as he portrays it, is a gift of acceptance already granted — a gift that it takes only a response of trust to enjoy. The prodigal is not portrayed as cleaning up his life, only as accepting his father's acceptance. The eleventh-hour laborers are not shown as having earned their pay by twelvefold exertions, only as having trusted the vineyard owner. And the publican is not sent home justified because he said he would lead a better life, only because he had the faith to confess his death and to trust in a God who could raise the dead. Accordingly, as far as this parable is concerned, I am not about to come to it prepared to hear Jesus say that he wasted his time establishing faith rather than goodness as the means of appropriating the gift of salvation. And therefore I am not about to interpret Jesus' attitude here as a new tack either on hostility against the kingdom or on response to it.

What do I say then about the note of hostility as it appears in this parable? The same thing I said about it when it appeared in the earlier parables: it was aced out in them; it is likewise aced out in this. Evil is not so much banished as provided for — and provided for in a way that draws its fangs. Its existence is not withdrawn but contained within the divine *áphesis,* the ultimately gracious dispensation of God's forgiveness. As the master of the house in the parable of the Wheat and the Weeds does the least damaging thing he can think of with the weeds ("Let [*áphete*] both grow together until the harvest"), so the King in this parable does the least damaging thing he can think of with the cursed ("You never did like my parties. Why don't you just go downstairs to do your sulking?"). To be sure, the language with which he issues that final invitation to get out is severe (everlasting fire prepared for the devil and his angels, eternal punishment); and since I am admittedly seeking a more graceful interpretation, my first temptation is to label it Oriental hyperbole and let it go at that. But on second thought, the language, hyperbolic or not, is not without a built-in reference to grace: it is of a piece, in fact, with the note of grace that Jesus often sounds when he broaches the theme of judgment in his parables. For while this parable is judgmental in the extreme, it cannot possibly come as a surprise since in a number of other parables the original catholic invitation to come into the party was itself a judgment, a *krísis* on the whole world that received it. In the parable of the King's Son's Wedding, for example, the *krísis* of the invitation falls upon the guests that reject it in the form of battle, murder, and sudden death. And why? Well, not because they had done unworthy things; as a matter of fact, the invitation itself had made them worthy from the start. No, the real reason it fell on them was that they did not trust the King's proclamation of their worthiness — because, in a word, they did not believe. And while such mayhem is indeed a dramatic way of showing how God chooses to throw a party, it is not one bit too dramatic for showing how terribly serious he is about his plans for the eternal season. For as the party in the Prodigal Son cost the fatted calf its life, so this party cost the King his life. He is not about to write it all off as a whim.

All of which tips my hand quite sufficiently as to what I have to say about the note of response to the kingdom. The response called for all through the parables is faith, not good works; therefore the response called for here at the end is the same. As the oil in the wise virgins' vessels should not be interpreted as quarts and quarts of ethical integrity, so the kindnesses of the blessed to the least of the King's brethren should not be taken as drumsful of industrial-strength good deeds. Indeed, the most notable feature of the parable of the Great Judgment is that the good works of the blessed are not presented as such. The King says not that the sheep have compiled a splendid moral record, but that they had a relationship with himself: "Amen, I say to you, inasmuch as you did it to one of the least of these my brethren, you did it to *me*." Or to put it even more precisely, they are praised at his final *parousía* for what they did in his *parousía* throughout their lives, namely, for trusting *him* to have had a relationship with them all along.

And what, finally, of the cursed whose response of unfaith — whose refusal to relate to him in the lost and the least — receives the King's condemnation? Well, I think we must be careful here. I have already issued two warnings against defining too narrowly the precise circumstances that will constitute grounds for such a sentence. I want now to issue a caveat against defining them at all. Jesus came to raise the dead, not to reform the reformable, and certainly not to specify the degree of nonreform that will nullify the sovereign grace of resurrection. He came to proclaim a kingdom that works only in the last, the lost, the least, and the little, not to set up a height-weight chart for the occupants of the heavenly Jerusalem. And while we may think we might do well to supply the ethico-theological requirements he has so carefully omitted — while we may be just itching to define what constitutes rejection of him at the hour of death or relationship with him in the underdogs of the world — we are wrong on both counts. In the first place, we don't know enough about anybody, not even ourselves, to say anything for sure. But in the second, Jesus shows us in this parable that even those who did relate to him didn't know what they were doing. "Come, you blessed of my Father," the King says to those on his right hand, "and inherit the kingdom . . . for I was hungry and you fed me, I was thirsty and you gave me drink, I was a stranger and you welcomed me. . . ." And the righteous answer and say to him, "Uhh . . . pardon us, Your Highness, but when was that?"

Do you finally see? Nobody *knows* anything. The righteous didn't know they were in relationship with the King when they ministered to the least of his brethren, any more than the cursed knew they were despising the King when they didn't so minister. Knowledge is not the basis of anybody's salvation or damnation. Action-in-dumb-trust is. And the reason for that is that salvation comes only by relationship with the Savior — by a relationship that, from his side, is already an accomplished eternal fact, and that therefore needs only to be *accepted by faith,* not known in any way. "No man," Luther said (if I may quote him one last time), "can know or feel he is saved; he can only believe it." At the final *parousía,* we will not be judged by anything except our response of faith or unfaith to the Savior whose presence was coterminous with our whole existence. And at that day he will simply say whether, from our side (by faith, that is — but with no other conditions specified as to knowledge or any other human achievement), we related to that presence. He will simply *do the truth* from his side — simply affirm his eternal, gracious relationship with all of creation — and honor what both the sheep and the goats did with that truth from their side.

It is John 3:16ff. all over again. The Gospel truth is, "God so loved the world that he gave his only begotten Son, that everyone who believes in him should not perish but have everlasting life." And that truth *as it vindicates us* is, "The one who believes in him is not judged: but the one who does not believe has been judged already because he has not believed in the name of the only begotten Son of God." But that truth *as we are to respond to it in our lives* is not at all a matter of our intellectual scrutiny. From our side, we can respond to it only by "doing the truth" ourselves, that is, by admitting our death and "coming to the light," that it may be made manifest that our deeds — all of them, good or bad — were done in the God who makes all things new.

What counts, therefore, is not what we know (most of that can only count against us) but what *he* knows. And what he knows is that "God did not send his Son into the world to judge the world, but that the world might be saved by him." His saving relationship with the world has already been established — and it will stay established forever. The only question at the end is whether we trusted the truth of it and made it a two-sided relationship, or whether we distrusted it and left it a relationship from his side only. And Jesus alone knows the answer to that question. In this last parable of all, he deliberately deprives us of any way of even thinking about it: the only ground the Great Judgment gives us for hope is *trust in his presence in the passion of the world.* But since no one will ever quite manage to be apart from that passion — since we do not need to stipulate anyone's participation in it — this parable also deprives us of the luxury of telling the world all the complicated things it has to do to get on the right side of his eschatological presence. The only thing we can possibly do is give the world the living witness of our trust in his presence in its passion. We need only to act as if we really believe he meets us in leastness and death. The rest is his business, not ours.

And therefore all the theological baggage about repentances that come too late or acts of faith that peak too soon, all the fine slicing about how maybe a suicide who has time to think between the bridge and the river is in better shape than one who blew his brains out — and all the doctrinal jury-rigging designed to give the unbaptized a break or to prove that unbelievers are invincibly ignorant — all of it is idle, mischievous, and dead wrong. We simply don't know, and we should all have the decency to shut up and just trust him in the passion we cannot avoid. And we don't even have to know if we have succeeded in doing that, because Jesus is there anyway and he is on everybody's side. He is the Love that will not let us go. If anybody can sort it all out, he can; if he can't, nobody else ever will. Trust him, therefore. And trust him now.

There is nothing more to do.

CHAPTER FOURTEEN

Epilogue

I t is all bizarre. At the end of his parables, Jesus goes ahead and acts out what he has been talking about from the beginning. In his passion, death, resurrection, and ascension he manifests in his own person the nontransactional mystery of a kingdom that has always disposed all things mightily and sweetly by grace. But even in those fulfilling, mighty acts, the mystery remains nontransactional. They are not discrete pieces of business that the world is expected to enter into a cooperative relationship with. They are rather sacraments, acted parables of a relationship established from the foundation of the world. They are invitations to trust the passion, the *inaction* of the Incarnate Word of God in whom all things are already made new.

And that is bizarre because just as in the spoken parables nothing much is tidied up in the temporal order of things — just as the lastness, lostness, leastness, and death of Jesus' parabolic characters are shown not as inconveniences they are saved from but as disasters they are saved in — so in these culminating, acted parables. Neither Jesus' death, nor his resurrection, nor his ascension makes the least practical difference in the way the world now runs. We still die, even though we believe sin has been overcome by grace; and we are still nobodies, even though we believe we are heirs of the kingdom.

It is not an easy Gospel to proclaim: it looks for all the world as if we are not only trying to sell a pig in a poke, but an invisible pig at that.

513

The temptation, of course, is by hook or by crook to produce a visible pig for the world's inspection — to prove that trust in Jesus heals the sick, spares the endangered, fattens the wallet, or finds the lost keys. But it does not. And it does not because the work of Jesus is not a transaction — not a repair job on the world as it now is, but an invitation of the world as it now is into the death out of which it rises only in him. The only honest way to advertise the Gospel, therefore, is to admit that it proclaims two orders at once, the old and the new — and to confine our promotional efforts to the insistence that faith is the human race's only dependable way of breaking through from the first to the second.

I realize you can quote me a dozen passages to prove otherwise — to prove that Jesus or Peter or Paul spoke on occasion as if we ourselves were somehow responsible for making the kingdom happen in this world, for building Jerusalem in England's green and pleasant land. But I am still not persuaded. "The kingdom of God does not come in such a way as to be seen" (Luke 17:20). The only sure evidence of the kingdom we have ever seen is Jesus, and he died just as dead as any of us. To be sure, he also rose; but then he left, leaving us only with his mysterious presence in the world's passion as the meeting point of the two orders. The pig or, better said, the Lamb in the poke disappears, leaving us holding only the bag, in faith.

That may sound depressing, but it is not. And it is not depressing precisely because the bag we hold — the crumpled and tattered sack of history — is the grandest of all the sacraments of his presence. It is the one place, both now and at the end, where we are invited to believe we will find him. We are not told that he expects us to iron the bag smooth before he will come and dwell in it; we are told, in his parables and on the cross, that he is in it already by the power of his death and resurrection. And therefore when the church tries to iron the bag — when it implies that its primary mission is to make history smooth here and now — it fails both its Lord and the world. It fails its Lord, because it is trying to do something Jesus in the end neither said nor did; and it fails the world, because it is offering it a false hope. Neither history nor revelation encourages the least expectation that plugging in anyone's iron — even God's — is going to turn the world back into Eden. What we are really invited to believe is that there is a New Jerusalem waiting to come down and marry the Lamb who was in the bag all along. If you reduce the promise of the Gospel to anything less bizarre than that, you simply turn the leap of faith into a mere standing on tiptoes to see something that isn't going to happen.

But if you aggravate the bizarreness of the promise — if you take your stand on salvation by grace, on salvation through faith, on salvation in the very shipwreck of history — all the lights go on. Not only do you have the only unassailable apologetic there is (you need never ask anyone to believe anything other than what is, only to trust Jesus in it all); you also have the joy of being in on the divine mirth. For the promise is wild beyond all imagining. It is the gift of life in the midst of death, of a Way out simply by remaining in, of everything for nothing. It is the promise that the God who has been with us all along in the old world will be with us forever in the new. "Behold, the tent of God is with men and he will dwell among them and they will be his people and God himself will be with them and be their God. And he will wipe away every tear from their eyes and death will be no more, neither will there be mourning nor crying nor pain any more, for the former things have passed away" (Rev. 21:3-4).

Trust him, therefore. There really is nothing more to do.

Index of Scripture References

517